7/06

PHP

IN A NUTSHELL

Other resources from O'Reilly

Related titles
Essential PHP Security
Learning PHP 5
MySQL in a Nutshell
PHP Cookbook
PHP Hacks

PHPUnit Pocket Guide
Programming PHP
Upgrading to PHP 5
Web Database Application
with PHP and MySQL

oreilly.com
oreilly.com is more than a complete catalog of O'Reilly books. You'll also find links to news, events, articles, weblogs, sample chapters, and code examples.

Conferences
O'Reilly brings diverse innovators together to nurture the ideas that spark revolutionary industries. We specialize in documenting the latest tools and systems, translating the innovator's knowledge into useful skills for those in the trenches. Visit *conferences.oreilly.com* for our upcoming events.

Safari Bookshelf (*safari.oreilly.com*) is the premier online reference library for programmers and IT professionals. Conduct searches across more than 1,000 books. Subscribers can zero in on answers to time-critical questions in a matter of seconds. Read the books on your Bookshelf from cover to cover or simply flip to the page you need. Try it today for free.

PHP

IN A NUTSHELL

Paul Hudson

O'REILLY®

Beijing · Cambridge · Farnham · Köln · Paris · Sebastopol · Taipei · Tokyo

PHP in a Nutshell
by Paul Hudson

Copyright © 2006 O'Reilly Media, Inc. All rights reserved.
Printed in the United States of America.

Published by O'Reilly Media, Inc., 1005 Gravenstein Highway North, Sebastopol, CA 95472.

O'Reilly books may be purchased for educational, business, or sales promotional use. Online editions are also available for most titles (*safari.oreilly.com*). For more information, contact our corporate/institutional sales department: (800) 998-9938 or *corporate@oreilly.com*.

Editors:	Allison Randal
	Tatiana Apandi
Production Editor:	Adam Witwer
Cover Designer:	Karen Montgomery
Interior Designer:	David Futato

Printing History:

October 2005:	First Edition.

 This book uses RepKover™, a durable and flexible lay-flat binding.

ISBN: 0-596-10067-1

[M]   [2/06]

Table of Contents

Preface

Now installed on more than 20 million Internet domains around the world, PHP is the undisputed king of web programming languages. Its users cite many reasons for deployment, such as database connectivity, powerful extensions, and rich object-orientation, but nearly everyone would agree that, above all, PHP is just plain easy to use. This is the feature that continues to drive the language forward, attracting new users and enabling existing programmers to do more with their skills.

The release of PHP 5 has introduced many new features to the language, making this an exciting time for the language. Many people who had not previously considered PHP are now finding it a good fit for their needs—the new object-orientation system is a big plus, for example. More importantly, many people who had a large investment in PHP 4 are trying to migrate their code to the new release with minimum breakage. Fortunately for all of us, it's not too hard to retain backward compatibility, and it's very easy to take advantage of the many new features.

So, welcome to PHP. I think you'll find it a fun, interesting, and flexible language that might finally disprove the old saying, "Cheap, good, on time: choose any two."

Audience

This book has been designed to be of maximum use for existing PHP developers looking for a complete, compact, and portable reference guide to the language. If this is your first time using PHP, but you have experience using similar languages such as Perl, Python, or C, then you should be able to treat the book as a learning guide.

As any PHP programmer will tell you, the online PHP manual is of a very high standard. The aim of this book is not to compete with or replace the online manual. Although this book is designed to stand alone, you will find the topic grouping, tips, and examples here complement the online guide.

Assumptions

This book assumes you are familiar with variables, loops, and other basic programming concepts. Although this material is explained to a degree, it is recommended that you at least have some experience using PHP or a similar programming language.

Contents of This Book

Chapter 1, *Introduction to PHP*, covers the general characteristics of the PHP language and its implementations, and discusses where to get help and information.

Chapter 2, *Installing PHP*, explains how to obtain and install PHP.

Chapter 3, *The PHP Interpreter*, covers the PHP interpreter and its use for running PHP programs on a web server or on the command line.

Chapter 4, *The PHP Language*, covers PHP syntax, variables, control structures, includes, and user-defined functions.

Chapter 5, *Variables and Constants*, examines the different variable types in PHP.

Chapter 6, *Operators*, outlines the basic operators in PHP.

Chapter 7, *Function Reference*, is a reference chapter for the most commonly used built-in functions of PHP.

Chapter 8, *Object-Oriented PHP*, explains object-oriented programming in PHP.

Chapter 9, *HTML Forms*, is an introduction to creating HTML forms and processing them in PHP.

Chapter 10, *Cookies and Sessions*, explains the tools for using cookies and sessions in PHP.

Chapter 11, *Output Buffering*, describes how to buffer your output, and when you would want to do so.

Chapter 12, *Security*, covers a few essential security considerations when running PHP websites.

Chapter 13, *Files*, is a reference to the functions for interacting with files.

Chapter 14, *Databases*, gives a brief introduction to accessing MySQL and SQLite databases in PHP, and to PEAR::DB, which provides a consistent interface to many different database packages.

Chapter 15, *Regular Expressions*, covers some powerful ways to process strings, including matching, extracting substrings, and replacing text.

Chapter 16, *Manipulating Images*, shows how to create and alter images with the GD library that ships with PHP.

Chapter 17, *Creating PDFs*, shows how to create PDFs in PHP using PDFlib.

Chapter 18, *Creating Flash*, shows how to generate Flash movies in PHP using the Ming library.

Chapter 19, *XML & XSLT*, covers modules for processing XML with PHP.

Chapter 20, *Network Programming*, explains socket programming, custom HTTP headers, HTTP authentication, sending email, and sending data over FTP and HTTP with Curl.

Chapter 21, *Distributing Your Code*, describes a few considerations when you prepare to distribute your code to other users.

Chapter 22, *Debugging*, is about the tools available to help you track down errors in your PHP code.

Chapter 23, *Performance*, offers a few tips on getting the most out of PHP.

Conventions Used in This Book

The following typographical conventions are used in this book:

Plain text
> Indicates menu titles, menu options, menu buttons, and keyboard accelerators (such as Alt and Ctrl).

Italic
> Indicates new terms, URLs, email addresses, filenames, file extensions, pathnames, directories, and Unix utilities.

Constant width
> Indicates commands, options, switches, variables, attributes, keys, functions, types, classes, namespaces, methods, modules, properties, parameters, values, objects, events, event handlers, XML tags, HTML tags, macros, the contents of files, or the output from commands.

Constant width bold
> Shows commands or other text that should be typed literally by the user.

Constant width italic
> Shows text that should be replaced with user-supplied values.

 This icon signifies a tip, suggestion, or general note.

 This icon indicates a warning or caution.

Using Code Examples

This book is here to help you get your job done. In general, you may use the code in this book in your programs and documentation. You do not need to contact us for permission unless you're reproducing a significant portion of the code. For example, writing a program that uses several chunks of code from this book does not require permission. Selling or distributing a CD-ROM of examples from O'Reilly books does require permission. Answering a question by citing this book and quoting example code does not require permission. Incorporating a significant amount of example code from this book into your product's documentation does require permission.

We appreciate, but do not require, attribution. An attribution usually includes the title, author, publisher, and ISBN. For example: "*PHP in a Nutshell* by Paul Hudson. Copyright 2006 O'Reilly Media, Inc., 0-596-10067-1."

If you feel your use of code examples falls outside fair use or the permission given above, feel free to contact us at *permissions@oreilly.com*.

Safari® Enabled

 When you see a Safari® enabled icon on the cover of your favorite technology book, that means the book is available online through the O'Reilly Network Safari Bookshelf.

Safari offers a solution that's better than e-books. It's a virtual library that lets you easily search thousands of top tech books, cut and paste code samples, download chapters, and find quick answers when you need the most accurate, current information. Try it for free at *http://safari.oreilly.com*.

How to Contact Us

Please address comments and questions concerning this book to the publisher:

> O'Reilly Media, Inc.
> 1005 Gravenstein Highway North
> Sebastopol, CA 95472
> (800) 998-9938 (in the U.S. or Canada)
> (707) 829-0515 (international or local)
> (707) 829-0104 (fax)

We have a web page for this book, where we list errata, examples, and any additional information. You can access this page at:

> *http://www.oreilly.com/catalog/phpnut*

To comment or ask technical questions about this book, send email to:

> *bookquestions@oreilly.com*

For more information about our books, conferences, Resource Centers, and the O'Reilly Network, see our web site at:

> *http://www.oreilly.com*

Acknowledgments

Like most authors, I have many people to thank for helping with the production of this book. First and foremost is Josette Garcia—someone who is a familiar face at UK Free Software events, but otherwise works tirelessly in the back rooms at O'Reilly to make the magic happen. Without her efforts, this book would still be on the drawing board—*je vous remercie de tout coeur*.

To Allison Randal, I owe an overwhelming debt of gratitude. She has devoted an immense amount of time and energy to the production of this book, and I feel blessed to have had the chance to work with someone so talented—and patient!

A number of people have contributed corrections, improvements, and comments to this book, and I want to thank them for taking the time to help. Six people stand out particularly: Peter MacIntyre, Tom McTighe, Ian Morse, Adam Tracht-enberg, and Zak Greant all added a lot of extra quality and value to the text, and Sean Burke was, well, Sean Burke. When Sean was assigned to work on this book, I thought, "That's nice, he seems like an interesting guy." Sean is more than an interesting guy: he's a harsh (but fair!) critic, a language pedant just the way I like, and a maddening perfectionist without whom this book ought to have been enti-tled *PHP in a Coconut Shell*. I'm lucky to have had Sean, for without him, this book would be only a shadow of what it is.

Finally, I want to thank my wife for her love and support during the times I was locked away with a computer, my parents for the love and support they gave me while I was learning the trade as a youngster, and God, for His love and support, period.

1

Introduction to PHP

PHP hasn't always been around, so what came before it? More importantly, why was PHP created in the first place? In this chapter, we'll look at the history behind PHP, where it has advantages over other programming languages, and where you can get help to further your PHP programming career.

PHP History

Contrary to what some might have you believe, there was a lot of activity on the web development front before PHP was invented. Prior to its invention, code for server-side scripting was usually written in C or Perl, both of which are general programming languages that were adapted to use on the Internet.

The original PHP release was created by Rasmus Lerdorf in June 1995, to make various common web programming tasks easier and less repetitive. The name originally stood for "Personal Home Page," but has since become a recursive acronym, standing for "PHP: Hypertext Preprocessor." The goal of that release was to minimize the amount of code required to achieve results, which led to PHP being HTML-centric—that is, PHP code was embedded inside HTML.

The second PHP release, known as PHP/FI 2.0, was the first to achieve widespread popularity, and despite the parsing inconsistencies, it managed to attract a few converts.

The release of PHP 3 was largely driven by Zeev Suraski and Andi Gutmans, who rewrote PHP from the ground up and removed the parsing problems. PHP 3 also made it much easier for others to extend the language—particularly keen developers could now easily write their own modules for the language, adding functionality at the core level.

With PHP 3, the language had also gained limited object-oriented support, and this added extra fuel to the fire of PHP's growth. By the time PHP 3 was replaced in the middle of 2000, it was installed on over 2.5 million web site domains, as compared to 250,000 just 18 months before. Its successor, PHP 4, contained numerous major changes, including the switch to what is called the Zend Engine.

Zend is a company founded by Zeev Suraski and Andi Gutmans to promote PHP in the corporate environment, and the engine they produced brought with it numerous advantages. By taking over the core of PHP, the Zend Engine introduced reference counting to ensure there were no memory leaks; introduced web server abstraction so that PHP ran on Apache 1.3.x, Apache 2, Microsoft's IIS, Zeus, AOLServer, and more; and also changed the way that PHP code was executed so that code was read once, converted to an internal format, then executed. This new execution paradigm allowed the use of external code caches, also known as PHP accelerators, that further boost performance.

Although not as vast as the jump from PHP 3 to PHP 4, the move from PHP 4 to PHP 5 is still a big one. Along with hugely improved object orientation, the addition of try/catch error handling, and exceptions, there are two major new extensions: SimpleXML, a fast and easy-to-learn way to interact with XML documents, and SQLite, a new flat-file database API that eases the burden of deploying simple database solutions.

Advantages of PHP

If you ask a group of PHP programmers why they use PHP, you will hear a range of answers—"it's fast," "it's easy to use," and more. This section briefly summarizes the main reasons for using PHP as opposed to a competing language.

The HTML Relationship

When used to output text, PHP is embedded inside the text in code islands, in contrast to languages like Perl, where text is embedded inside the Perl script. The most common way to open and close PHP code blocks is by <?php and ?>. Here is an example of a simple page, shown in Perl first and then in PHP—don't worry about what the code means for now:

```
#!/usr/bin/perl
print <<"EOHTML"
<html>
<body>
<p>Welcome, $Name</p>
</body>
</html>
EOHTML
```

And now in PHP:

```
<html>
<body>
<p>Welcome, <?php print $Name; ?></p>
</body>
</html>
```

The PHP version is only three lines shorter but easier to read, because it doesn't have the extra complexity around it. Some modules for Perl (particularly CGI.pm) help, but PHP continues to have a lead in terms of readability. If you wanted to, you could write your PHP script like the Perl script: switch to PHP mode and print everything out from there.

Apart from legibility, another advantage to having most of the page in HTML is that it makes it possible to use integrated development environments (IDEs), whereas products like Dreamweaver and FrontPage muddle up Perl's print statements.

Interpreting Versus Compiling

Behind the scenes, PHP compiles your script down to a series of instructions (called *opcodes*), and these instructions are then executed one by one until the script terminates. This is different from conventional compiled languages such as C++ (but unlike Java), which compile the code into an executable run time and then run that executable whenever the code is encountered again. This constant recompilation may seem a waste of processor time, but it helps because you no longer need worry about recompiling your scripts when you make any changes. On the flip side, many scripts take longer to compile than they do to execute; fortunately, that is nullified by the use of PHP code caches.

One major advantage to having interpreted code is that all memory used by the script is managed by PHP, and the Zend Engine automatically cleans up allocated memory after every script has finished. This means that you do not need to worry about closing database links, freeing memory assigned to images, and so on, because PHP will do it for you. That isn't to say you should be lazy and make PHP do all the work—there are functions available for you to specifically clean up your memory, and you should use them if you have very tight memory requirements.

Output Control

In general use, PHP is embedded inside HTML in code islands that start with <?php and end with ?>, but you can reverse this by writing your whole script as one big PHP code island and printing HTML as necessary. Going back to the example shown previously, PHP code can look almost identical to the Perl code by printing the HTML from inside our PHP code:

```
<?php
        print "<html>\n";
        print "<body>\n";
        print "<p>Welcome, $Name</p>\n";
        print "</body>\n";
        print "</html>\n";
?>
```

The print( ) function outputs the text enclosed in quotation marks to the client. "\n" means "start new line in the output" and it serves as a "pretty printer"— something that makes the output look more attractive.

PHP also has powerful output buffering that further increases your control over the output flow. An output buffer can be thought of as a place where you can queue up content for outputting. Once you start a buffer, any output is automatically put into that buffer and not seen unless the buffer is closed and flushed.

The advantage to this output buffering is twofold. First, it allows you to clean the buffer if you decide that the content it holds is no longer needed. When a buffer is cleaned, all its stored output is deleted as if it were never there, and the output for that buffer is started from scratch.

Second, output buffering allows you to break the traditional ordering of web pages—that of headers first and content later. Owing to the fact that you queue up all your output, you can send content first, then headers, then more content, then finally flush the buffer. PHP internally rearranges the buffer so that headers come before content.

Performance

PHP is one of the fastest scripting languages around, rivalling both Perl and ASP. However, the developers continue to target performance as a key area for improvement, and in PHP 5.1 (still under development at the time of this writing), many areas have seen significant optimization.

When combined with a code cache, PHP's performance usually at least doubles, although many scripts show much larger increases.

Getting Help

If you have tried debugging and failed, don't fret—there are still support options where you might find your solution.

The Documentation

The first place to check should always be the PHP documentation, available online from *http://www.php.net/manual*. The manual contains documentation on all PHP functions, as well as various usage examples, and also user comments. Very often it's the user comments that are most helpful, because people recount problems they've experienced in the past and how they got around them. The PHP manual is an excellent resource that should help you deepen your understanding of all aspects of the language.

Mailing Lists

There are several mailing lists that focus specifically on PHP, the most popular of which are hosted by the PHP web site itself. Visit *http://www.php.net/mailing-lists. php* to see a list of possibilities. You will most likely want the general mailing list, as it includes hundreds of questions and answers being sent each day.

Before you post:

- Read the list for a while to get a flavor of how to ask questions and to make sure the list covers the right area for your question.

- Make sure you have HTML mail disabled in your email client; only plain-text emails are accepted.

- Never attach files to your email.

- If you are having a problem, give a code example showing the problem in the simplest way. It helps people more if you say what you expected to get as output, what you did get, as well as other information such as what version of PHP you have, etc.

- Do not post to the Internals list unless you really know what you are doing. This list is not for questions about how to install PHP, how to use a certain function, or why a script does not work—it is for the actual developers of PHP to discuss code changes and new releases of PHP. You do not need to post to this list asking whether you can use or redistribute PHP—the answer is "yes."

IRC

One of the fastest ways to get answers about PHP is to use one of the two popular PHP IRC channels. They both regularly have 200–300 people on there who program in PHP, of which between 10 and 20 are chatting away about something. Peak activity times are evenings in U.S. EST (five hours behind GMT).

If you have an IRC client installed (such as the Firefox extension ChatZilla: *https://addons.mozilla.org/extensions/moreinfo.php?id=16*), connect to Efnet (see *http://efnet.org*) or FreeNode (see *http://freenode.net*) and go to channel #php. Note that both channels (EFNet #php and FreeNode #php) have very strict rules: do not ask to ask (that is, do not say, "Can I ask a question about XYZ?"—just ask), do not post more than two lines of code into the channel at one time, do not start evangelistic fights over Perl/Java/etc., and so on. Be sure to check the channel rules as you enter, or you may find yourself kicked out for breaking them.

A word of warning: don't believe everything you hear about PHP in IRC channels, particularly if the person talking isn't a channel operator. Many people come and go, and they aren't necessarily experienced enough to give authoritative answers.

Furthermore, be prepared to show people your code when on IRC. A popular site is *http://www.pastebin.com*, which lets you paste your PHP code online and pass the URL out to other people on IRC so that they can look at it and discuss potential fixes with you directly.

Conferences

Going along to one of the PHP events around the world is a great way to meet up with your peers and share ideas, solutions, and learn new things. These conferences are usually a mix of general discussion between attendees, a sponsor expo where you can see companies involved in the PHP arena, and tutorials where you can listen to lectures from luminaries in various fields about new developments in PHP.

If you're only going to go to one conference, I'd recommend you make it O'Reilly's Open Source Convention: it covers a variety of programming languages and platforms, but PHP always puts on a good show there. If not that, then consider either the International PHP Conference (*http://www.phpconference.com*)

or the Zend PHP Conference (*http://zend.kbconferences.com*), which cover more detailed topics due to their specific focus on PHP.

If you've never been to a big conference before, here are some hints: take a spiral-bound half-page (A5) notepad with you for writing, a selection of cheap pens (you'll lose most of them, but should get freebies to replace them while at the conference), some small snacks to keep you going between meals, business cards, a USB thumb drive (memory stick), and, of course, a WiFi-compatible laptop. Apple laptops are becoming increasingly prevalent, but anything that supports 802.11b/g is good.

User Groups

If you're not into the conference scene, user groups might be more your style. Most parts of the world already have Linux user groups (LUGs) where you can ask for help on everything from setting up your Apache server to debugging scripts—there are usually people there who are skilled in PHP, too. Some cities also have PHP user groups that are, obviously, more helpful for direct PHP-related questions.

The best place to look for PHP user group information is directly on the PHP site itself: the PHP events calendar (*http://www.php.net/cal.php*) is regularly updated and should provide you with all the information you need.

Submitting a Bug

If you are convinced you have found a problem with PHP, it is quite possible you are correct and should notify the developers. Note that many hundreds of "bogus bugs" have been reported in the past, which are usually the result of people not reading the manual correctly or otherwise missing a flaw in their code. If you think you have found a problem, follow these steps before you submit a bug:

1. Go to *http://snaps.php.net* and download the latest PHP snapshot for your machine. Take a backup of your existing installation, then install the snapshot—this essentially gives you the bleeding-edge version of PHP. If your problem still exists, go to step 2.

2. Go to IRC and ask people there to reproduce the problem. It is possible that the problem lies in your PHP configuration, DBMS, operating system, or any other of a dozen potential culprits. If the problem is reproduced by others on IRC, then go to step 3.

3. At this point you have almost certainly got a bug. However, before you send it off to the developers, you must reproduce your problem using the *shortest possible* chunk of code. While it is possible that your 3000-line masterpiece does show up a bug in PHP, it is also very hard for other developers to verify the problem. Take out every line that does not stop the bug from appearing—the shorter your script, the faster others can pick it up and reproduce the problem.

4. You should now clearly be able to see what sequence of events causes the bug to show itself. You now need to make sure the bug has not been reported before, so go to *http://bugs.php.net* and search for it.

5. If there is no record of a bug like yours existing, you can file a bug report from the same URL. Try to be as descriptive as possible, as your bug report will be mailed off to everyone on the PHP Internals mailing list for analysis.

6. Once your bug has been submitted, you will be notified as to its progress. All being well, it will be fixed immediately, but you may find that the developers need to ask you a few questions before they can get to work.

7. Finally, developers will fix your bug and a new version of PHP will be available on *http://snaps.php.net* for you to download and try out. If the bug has been fixed, write back and say it is working fine so that the bug can be signed off. The most common problem when fixing a bug is no feedback—a possible fix has been applied, but the original finder hasn't gotten back to say it's fixed. Don't let this be you!

Getting Certified

Zend and MySQL offer certification for PHP and MySQL respectively, which means that if you take a few tests and pass with sufficiently high grades you can add "Qualified PHP and MySQL developer" to your résumé. The exams themselves aren't too hard, and both have study guides to help you brush up on your skills, but you should have at least six months' experience using PHP/MySQL before you try them.

If you want to be sure of high grades, you could try taking a course in the topic of your choice—there are training partners around the world who can coach you toward Zend/MySQL certification, and this vastly increases your chances of success.

PHP Resources

If you're looking to learn more about PHP and related topics like databases, security, and XML, try starting with something from these lists.

Books

A Practical Guide to Curl by Kevin Hanegan (Charles River Media)
Quite a slow read, but you will learn a lot from it despite it being relatively short.

Advanced PHP Programming by George Schlossnagle (Sams)
Pitched at quite a high level, but it is the only book currently available that deals exclusively with making PHP work in highly scalable environments.

Beyond Fear by Bruce Schneier (Springer)
If you want a general introduction to the field of security, this is for you.

Disappearing Cryptography by Peter Wayner (Morgan Kaufmann)
Highly recommended as a general introduction to Crypto topics.

Database Systems by Thomas Connolly et al. (Addison-Wesley)
An excellent all-around reference to database theory and SQL.

Essential PHP Security by Chris Shiflett (O'Reilly)
Soon to be released, but my copy is already on pre-order.

HTML and XHTML by Chuck Musciano and Bill Kennedy (O'Reilly)
A long but worthwhile read that can take you quite far in the topic.

Learning PHP 5 by David Sklar (O'Reilly)
This is the easiest way to learn PHP 5 from scratch.

MySQL by Paul DuBois (Sams) and *PostgreSQL* by Korry Douglas (Sams)
These are exceptionally comprehensive books and should really be on the bookshelves of all serious MySQL/PostgreSQL database adminstrators.

PHP Cookbook by David Sklar et al. (O'Reilly)
A bit out of date, but it's still an excellent, task-based reference.

Practical Cryptography by Niels Ferguson and Bruce Schneier (Wiley)
This is highly technical, but fascinating, if you're looking to indoctrinate yourself in the security field.

Practical Unix and Internet Security by Simson Garfinkel et al. (O'Reilly)
Quite long and certainly not an exciting read in places, but fulfills its goal of being a comprehensive guide to security for Unix system administrators.

SVG Unleashed by Andrew Watt and Chris Lilley (Sams)
This book doesn't cover SVG. But if you want to know more about XML this is the first place to look.

The Art of Computer Programming by Donald Knuth (Addison-Wesley)
The second volume is particularly of interest for more insight into randomization.

The Art of Deception by Kevin Mitnick (Hungry Minds)
Kevin Mitnick is the ultimate bad guy turned good, and he approaches the topic of social engineering in an original and enlightening way.

The Mythical Man-Month by Frederick Brooks (Addison-Wesley)
Those looking to learn the fundamental principles of team management should look no further.

Unix Shell Programming by Stephen Kochan and Patrick Wood (Sams)
General Unix and C programming is very similar to PHP, so you can learn a lot about PHP by learning about the Unix shell.

Upgrading to PHP 5 by Adam Trachtenberg (O'Reilly)
The only book to buy if you want a stress-free guide to migrating from PHP 4 to 5.

Web Database Applications with PHP and MySQL by Hugh Williams and David Lane (O'Reilly)
A mixed bag of tricks for aspiring web developers.

XML Pocket Reference by Simon St. Laurent and Michael Fitzgerald (O'Reilly)
Short and to the point, this is the quick fix guide to most XML problems.

Magazines

International PHP Magazine
  http://www.phpmag.net

PHP Architect
  http://www.phparch.com

PHP Magazin Germany
  http://www.php-mag.de

PHP Solutions
  http://www.phpsolmag.org

Web Sites

- The PHP manual is available from *http://www.php.net/manual*, and it is a consistently high-quality read.

- Zend (*http://www.zend.com*) has a good set of PHP tutorials, and they also print various other popular editorials about the state of PHP.

- PHP Builder (*http://www.phpbuilder.com*) publishes a number of high-quality PHP tutorials each year, and also has very active forums full of people ready to help.

- DevShed (*http://www.devshed.com*) isn't as good as PHP Builder, but serves as a great backup resource if you have questions that aren't getting answered elsewhere.

- Several application vendors try to boost their marketing efforts by offering PHP content. Oracle is perhaps the most prevalent, as it had several top PHP hackers write the Hitchhiker's Guide to PHP, available online for free at *http://otn. oracle.com/pub/articles/php_experts*. Similarly, IBM developerWorks has published a number of PHP tutorials at *http://www-130.ibm.com/developerworks*, some of which are actually good.

- PEAR::DB has its own sets of documentation online, available at *http://pear. php.net/manual/en/package.database.php*. The database is thorough, if a little out of date now and then.

- The online documentation for the SQLite library is at *http://www.hwaci.com/ sw/sqlite*. I have found that it complements the PHP manual well.

- All the content at *http://www.cookiecentral.com*. is available for free, and there is also an active messageboard for you to ask questions or see what others are saying.

- There's a gentle (but quick) introduction to XPath at *http://www.w3schools. com/xpath/default.asp*.

- To learn more about HTTP and protocols relating to it, the best and most authoritative source is the World Wide Web Consortium (W3C). You can view their HTTP information store online at *http://www.w3.org/Protocols*.

- There are W3C specifications for XML, XPath, and XSLT online at *http:// www.w3.org/TR/2004/REC-xml-20040204*, *http://www.w3.org/TR/xpath*, and *http://www.w3.org/TR/xslt*. They are quite dull and hard to understand—you have been warned!

- Don't try to remember all the ASCII codes—you can find them online at *http://www.asciitable.com*.
- Finally, if all else fails and you're still hunting around, you can visit my personal website at *http://www.hudzilla.org*, where I keep my own brand of PHP help.

2

Installing PHP

Even if you intend to use a remote web server for your site, where PHP is already installed, it is still beneficial to be able to install PHP on your own machine so that you can test your pages more easily.

Installing PHP yourself opens up many possibilities: you get to choose exactly which extensions are available, which options are enabled, and the filesystem layout that you want. Of course, if you intend to upload your scripts to a different server at the end of the process, you should be careful to mimic the remote configuration on your local machine.

This chapter goes through a full install of PHP on Windows and Unix, installing extensions, and also configuring settings in the *php.ini* configuration file.

Installing on Windows

For installation on Windows, you need to download the Windows binary zip package from *http://www.php.net/downloads.php*. This contains the main PHP executables and DLLs, plus many extensions pre-compiled and ready to use.

When you extract the zip file, it should create a folder similar in name to *php-5.0.4-Win32*. I suggest you rename it to "php" and move it to the root of your hard drive, giving *c:\php*.

Browse to the new *c:\php* directory, and you'll see a number of files. Copy the *php5ts.dll* file into your *c:\windows\system32* directory (note: this may be *c:\winnt* on some versions of Windows), then copy the *php.ini-recommended* file into your *c:\windows* directory, renaming it to *php.ini*. This is the file where you will be setting all your PHP configuration options.

Your basic Windows PHP installation is now complete. If you want to set up PHP to use a web server, read the appropriate section below. You may also want to enable some extensions—that, too, is covered in subsequent pages.

Installing Apache

The first step to install Apache is to download the Windows installer from *http:// httpd.apache.org*. This is packaged using the Microsoft Installer system (MSI), so you may be prompted to install the MSI software if you have an older release of Windows.

As Apache is packaged into a friendly installer, you need only answer a few basic questions and click "Next" until you have completed the installation. The default installation is placed into *c:\program files\apache group\apache2*. Inside there is the *conf* directory, which contains Apache's configuration files.

Inside the *conf* directory, you'll find the *httpd.conf* file. This contains most of the configuration settings for Apache, and you need to edit this in order to enable PHP. Any line that starts with a # symbol is a comment, and may provide further documentation to guide you in your edits. First, search for the string "Load-Module." There should be a collection of these LoadModule lines in there already, so scroll to the bottom and add this new one:

```
LoadModule php5_module c:/php/php5apache2.dll
```

If your PHP installation is in a place other than *c:\php*, you will need to enter something different. Note, though, that all backslashes should be converted to forward slashes to avoid problems.

The next step is to search for the string AddType, and again you should see one or two lines of this type already in there. Underneath them, add this line:

```
AddType application/x-httpd-php .php
```

That associates scripts with the extension *.php* with our PHP module. If you want different script extensions, here is the place to set that up.

That completes the basic configuration. If you click Start, then Run, and run the command services.msc, you should see the Windows Services list appear. Look for Apache2, then click the button with the Stop and Play symbols on it to restart the service—this should enable PHP.

Once Apache has been restarted, open a web browser and go to *http://localhost*. You should see the "If you can see this, it means that the installation of the Apache web server software on this system was successful" default page on Apache. To test your PHP install, turn to the "Testing Your Configuration" section, later in this chapter, using *c:\program files\apache group\apache2\htdocs* as the HTML directory.

To change the directory from which Apache should serve web pages, search for the two instances of "C:/Program Files/Apache Group/Apache2/htdocs" in your *httpd.conf* and replace them with another directory on your system.

Installing Microsoft IIS

Although Apache is the preferred web server platform irrespective of the OS you choose, PHP can also be used with Microsoft Internet Information Services (IIS). This is available on Windows NT, Windows 2000, Windows XP, and Windows Server 2003; however, the client versions (e.g., XP) are limited in their abilities compared to the server versions. These instructions were written for Windows XP, but the instructions should be broadly similar for other versions of Windows and IIS.

To install IIS, go to the Add/Remove Programs dialog in the Control Panel, then select "Add/Remove Windows Components" from the sidebar. After a moment, a list of components will appear, and "Internet Information Service (IIS)" will be one of the options. Check the box next to it, then click Next. You may be asked for your Windows CD, so have it ready.

After installation has finished, open up Internet Explorer and point it at *http:// localhost*; all being well, you should see the "Your Web service is now running" page. Note that you should use Internet Explorer as opposed to other browsers—IIS doesn't play well with Firefox or others.

 It is highly recommended that you go to the Windows Update site immediately after installing IIS. The version installed from your CD will almost certainly be out of date, so you should download and install the latest patches before proceeding.

To configure IIS to use PHP, you need to bring up the Internet Information Services Management Console snap-in. This is available from Administrative Tools options, which may be in your Start menu or in your Control Panel, depending on your configuration.

The default view shows your computer in the left-hand tree; you need to double-click that to bring up the "Web Sites" branch, then double-click on "Web Sites" to reveal the "Default Web Site" branch. The default web site is configured to serve pages from *c:\inetpub\wwwroot*, and we're going to configure that to be able to serve PHP scripts too.

Right-click on the "Default Web Site" branch in the left-hand pane, and select Properties. From the dialog that appears, go to the Home Directory tab, and click the Configuration button at the bottom right. This is where you configure the programs that handle scripts on the server, and you'll see things such as ASP already configured.

Click the Add button in the Application Configuration dialog, then click Browse to search for the PHP script handle for IIS. By default, the Open File dialog box that appears is set to "Executable files (*.exe)," but you need to change that to "Dynamic Link libraries (*.dll)." Now browse to where you installed PHP (e.g., *c:\ php*), and select the file *php5isapi.dll,* and click OK.

Back in the "Add/Edit Application Extension Mapping" dialog, enter *.php* for the extension, and click OK. Click OK in the Application Configuration dialog, then OK again in the Default Web Site Properties dialog, and you'll be back at the IIS snap-in again.

To test out your configuration, turn to the "Testing Your Configuration" section, later in this chapter, using *c:\inetpub\wwwroot* as the HTML directory.

To change the directory from which IIS should serve web pages, go back to the Default Web Site Properties dialog, go to the Home Directory tab, and edit the Local Path field to something other than *c:\inetpub\wwwroot.*

Configuring Extensions

The PHP zip file for Windows comes with a number of extensions compiled for you. To enable them, you need only edit *php.ini* and remove the comment symbol (a semicolon) from the start of the line. Once you have finished your edits, restart your web server to have it reload the modules, and you'll be ready to go.

For example, to enable the Tidy extension, bring up *c:\windows\php.ini* in Notepad, search for "tidy", and you'll see a line like ";extension=php_tidy.dll." To enable the extension, remove the semicolon from the front (to make the line "extension=php_tidy.dll"), then restart your web server.

Installing on Unix

Installation on Unix can be done in one of two ways: you can use a package manager (such as YaST on SUSE Linux, Yum on Red Hat Linux, or URPMI on Mandriva Linux), or you can compile the programs from source code. If you are configuring a production web server, it is highly recommended that you use your package manager so that patching is kept easy. However, if you're installing PHP onto a local machine for test and programming purposes, you will probably want to compile it yourself to get you extra control.

One major advantage to installing from source code is that you can easily get the latest version of PHP. Many Linux distributions ship only older releases of PHP and Apache in order to ensure the system is stable enough for enterprise use. If you compile from source, you can choose to use an older, more mature release, or the very latest cutting-edge release.

Installing Using Packages

Installing PHP and Apache through your distributions package manager is fast, easy, and usually also provides some extra extensions. For the purpose of this guide, Mandriva Linux 2005 was used, but the process is similar for other distributions.

To get started, open up the Mandriva Control Center and select Add Software. Type **apache2** in the Search box, and click Search to list all packages that relate to Apache. In that list will be a package similar to apache2-2.0.53-9mdk. Select that, and you'll be prompted to include all the dependencies also (these are required). If you scroll down the list of search results, you should also see apache2-mod_php-2.0.53-4.3.10-7mdk, which is the package for PHP 4.3. Yes, that's quite out of date, but that's the result of installing through a package manager.

Once you have selected the Apache and PHP packages (and their dependencies), you might also want to run a search for "php" to look for any other software you want. For example, php-mysql-4.3.10-7mdk installs the PHP MySQL extension, and php-cli-4.3.10-7mdk installs the command-line interpreter (CLI) for PHP 4.3.

Having selected all the packages you want, insert your install media in your drive and click Install to continue. Once the installation has completed, open up a console (such as Konsole, if you're using KDE), run su, insert your password, then run /etc/init.d/httpd start to start Apache.

To test your configuration, turn to the "Testing Your Configuration" section, later in this chapter, using /var/www/html as the HTML directory.

Compiling from Source

Compiling PHP and Apache from source code gives you absolute control over the version numbers and configuration of the finished system. This gives you more control, but also more responsibility: it is harder to do, and harder to maintain.

Before you attempt to compile anything from source, please ensure that you have the following installed on your system: GCC (or another working GCC-compatible compiler), the standard C development libraries, libxml2-devel, flex, bison, Perl, and make. These should all be available through your package manager: make sure you have the "devel" versions of software installed along with the non-devel, as these are required for compiling your own software.

To get started, go to *http://www.php.net/downloads.php* and download the complete source code package in tar.bz2 format. Then go to *http://httpd.apache. org* and download the tar.bz2 source code for Apache 2.0, too.

Once the downloads have finished, open up a terminal window (such as Konsole, if you're using KDE), and browse to the location where you downloaded your files. For example, if they downloaded to */home/paul/desktop*, then type **cd /home/ paul/desktop**. Now execute these commands, changing the version numbers to suit the files you downloaded:

```
tar xvfj httpd-2.0.54.tar.bz2
tar xvfj php-5.0.4.tar.bz2
cd httpd-2.0.54
./configure --enable-so
make
su
<enter your password here>
make install
exit
cd ../php-5.0.4
./configure --with-apxs2=/usr/local/apache2/bin/apxs
make
su
<enter your password here>
make install
cp php.ini-recommended /usr/local/lib/php.ini
exit
```

Note: executing the configure and make commands may take some time. This is quite normal!

What those commands will give you is a working installation of Apache (installed into *usr/local/apache2*) and a working installation of PHP in *usr/local/lib/php*. The two are not joined as yet, though.

The next step is to configure Apache to use PHP. As root, open up *usr/local/apache2/conf/httpd.conf* in your favorite text editor. Search for "LoadModule"—you should hopefully see the line "LoadModule php5_module modules/libphp5.so," which the PHP installer might have added for you. If not, add the line beneath any existing LoadModule lines.

Now search for "AddType," and you should see some other lines already in there. Go to the bottom of the other AddType lines, and add this:

```
AddType application/x-httpd-php .php
```

That configures Apache to route the processing of all *.php* files through to PHP. Save the file, and close your text editor. Still as root, execute this command: /usr/local/apache2/bin/apachectl start. That will start your Apache web server.

To test your configuration, turn to the "Testing Your Configuration" section, later in this chapter, using *usr/local/apache2/htdocs* as your HTML directory.

Configuring Extensions

Compiling PHP from source gives you a number of extensions by default, such as CTYPE, SimpleXML, and SQLite. As long as you have the libraries installed, you can compile and install other PHP extensions by re-running the configure command from your PHP source code directory.

There are a great number of switches you can use when configuring PHP, but they follow a very general pattern. For extensions that require an external library to be installed, you use --with-xxx. For extensions that don't require an external library—potentially because PHP comes bundled with that library—you use --enable-xxx. There are a number of other options you can set that will affect core PHP functionality.

Table 2-1 shows a list of the most common options for PHP configuration, along with what they do. For ease of reference, it's sorted without the --with or --enable part.

Table 2-1. Configuration options for PHP

--with-apxs	Enables support for Apache 1.3
--with-apxs2	Enables support for Apache 2.0
--enable-bcmath	Enables support for bcmath arbitrary-precision mathematics
--with-curl	Enables support for the Curl library
--enable-debug	Compiles in debug information (PHP engine developers only)
--with-gd	Enables support for the GD image library
--with-imap	Enables support for the IMAP mail library
--with-ldap	Enables support for the LPAP directory library

Table 2-1. Configuration options for PHP (continued)

`--enable-mbstring`	Enables support for multibyte strings
`--with-mcrypt`	Enables support for the mcrypt encryption library
`--with-ming`	Enables support for the Ming Flash-generation library
`--with-mysql`	Enables the MySQL extension
`--with-mysqli`	Enables the MySQLi extension (for MySQL 4.1 and above)
`--with-ncurses`	Enables support for the Ncurses text-mode graphics library
`--with-pgsql`	Enables support for the PostgreSQL database library
`--enable-soap`	Enables support for SOAP protocol library
`--enable-sockets`	Enables support for Internet sockets
`--with-tidy`	Enables support for the Tidy HTML/XML library
`--with-zlib`	Enables support for zlib; needed for some graphics formats

For more information on these and other options, use `./configure --help` to see the full list.

Testing Your Configuration

To test your configuration, create the file *info.php* in your HTML directory. Enter this text in there, and save it:

```php
<?php
    phpinfo( );
?>
```

That calls the `phpinfo( )` function, which outputs basic configuration information about your PHP installation. To access this script, go to *http://localhost/info.php* in your web browser. All being well, you should see a lot of information printed out about your PHP configuration. This is actually a handy script to keep around for debugging purposes, as it tells you exactly what extensions you have installed and what their configuration options are. Of course, it also tells any hackers about your system configuration, so don't advertise its existence!

System Configuration

Now that you have PHP and your web server up and running, you will probably want to configure PHP to your liking. All of PHP's settings are available in its *php.ini* file, which, if you followed these installation instructions, is available either in */usr/local/lib/php* (Unix) or *c:\windows\php.ini* (Windows). Open this in your text editor of choice (you will need to be root on Unix).

A list of popular options, what they do, and their default values (if you use *php.ini-recommended* as the default) is given in Table 2-2. Note that lines starting with a semicolon (;) are comments, and are ignored by PHP.

Table 2-2. Configuration options for PHP

Option	Meaning	Default
assert.active	Enables the assert( ) function	On
display_errors	Sets whether PHP should output error messages to the screen	Off
error_reporting	Decides what types of errors PHP should notify you of	E_ALL
expose_php	Allows PHP to identify itself to clients through the web server	On
extension	Loads a PHP extension	N/A
extension_dir	Sets the directory where PHP should look for extensions	./
file_uploads	Decides whether PHP should accept users uploading files	On
log_errors	Determines whether PHP should store error messages in a log file	On
magic_quotes_gpc	Determines whether PHP should automatically run form data through addslashes( ) before you get it	Off
max_execution_time	Determines how long a script may run for before timing out	30 seconds
mbstring.func_overload	Converts non-multibyte string functions to their multibyte equivalents	0
memory_limit	Sets the maximum amount of RAM a PHP script may consume	8M
precision	Determines number of decimal places for floating-point numbers	14
register_globals	Decides whether all superglobal arrays should have their elements exported to the global scope	Off
safe_mode	Enables high security mode for shared server environments	Off
session.save_path	Selects the directory in which session data will be stored	/tmp
short_open_tags	Enables <? for opening PHP code blocks	On
SMTP	Sets the mail server address for the mail( ) function.	
variables_order	Determines the order in which variables are parsed: G is GET, P is POST, C is cookie, and S is session	GPCS

 If you intend to use sessions, make sure you set the sessiondir variable to a directory that a) exists, and b) Apache has read and write access to.

3

The PHP Interpreter

This chapter discusses how PHP runs, both through the command line and through a web server, how PHP can be extended through built-in and third-party modules, and what can cause your scripts to terminate unexpectedly.

Running PHP Scripts

You can execute your scripts in one of two ways: through a web server where the output is sent to a web browser, or through the command-line interface (CLI) where the output is sent to standard output. Of the two, the former is more popular, but the latter is steadily growing in popularity.

The primary difference between outputting text to the command line and to a web browser is the format of new lines—through the CLI, you need to use \n for a new line, whereas for web browsers, you need to use the HTML line break, <br />. If you want to take a script designed for CLI and make it work through the Web, swap \n for <br />, and vice versa for converting web scripts to command line scripts.

If everything is configured properly, running scripts through your web server is as simple as putting the PHP script into your web server's public directory, then navigating to the appropriate URL with your browser. Running scripts through the command line is done using the CLI interpreter, which, if you are using Windows, is *php.exe* in the directory of your PHP installation. That is, if you have installed PHP into *c:\php*, the CLI program will be *c:\php\php.exe*. If you are using Unix, the availability of CLI PHP is down to how you installed PHP—make sure and issue the command **make install-cli** after the rest of the configure and **make install** process in order to install it.

The technical term for the command-line interpreter version of PHP is the CLI *SAPI*. SAPI stands for Server Application Programming Interface, and this standard interface allows PHP to work on multiple web servers, or, in the CLI SAPI's case, the command line.

If you are unsure whether PHP is set up correctly, run the following script:

```
<?php
        phpinfo( );
?>
```

That calls the function phpinfo( ), which outputs information on your PHP configuration—how it was configured, what server it is running on, what modules are available, and more. It is handy to keep around when you are developing, as it will answer most questions you have about configuration.

Once you have PHP working, you can try running some more complex scripts. For example:

```
<?php
        $name = "Bob";
        $age = 27;
        $double_age = $age + $age;
        echo "Hello, $name!\n";
        echo "You are $age\n";
        echo "In $age years time you will be $double_age\n";
?>
```

To run that through your local web server, save the file as *first.php* and place it in your public HTML folder. For Windows this is usually *c:\inetpub\wwwroot*, and for Unix this is usually */var/www/html*, but the location of the Unix public HTML folder does vary greatly. Once the file is there, load it through your web browser using the URL *http://localhost/first.php*.

If you are running your scripts through the command line, you need to find the location of your PHP executable. On Unix, you can usually just run php and it will work, e.g., **php first.php**. On Windows, go to Start, Run, then enter **cmd** and press Return. Then type **cd \php** followed by Return, then **php c:\location\of\your\ script\first.php**.

Extending PHP

The base of the PHP language is simple, having just enough to set and retrieve variables, work with loops, and check whether a statement is true or not. The real power behind PHP comes with its extensions—add-ons to the base language that give it more flexibility. PHP has hundreds of extensions, which can be broken down into five types: core, bundled, PECL, third party, and DIY.

- Core extensions are extensions bundled with PHP itself and enabled by default. For all intents and purposes they are part of the base language, because, unless you explicitly disable them (few people do, and sometimes you cannot), they are available inside PHP. For example, the mechanism to handle reading and saving files in PHP is handled by an extension automatically compiled into PHP.

- Bundled extensions are extensions included with PHP but not enabled by default. They are commonly used, which is why they are included, but they are not available unless you specifically enable them. For example, the mechanism to handle graphics creation and editing is handled by an extension that is bundled with PHP but not enabled by default in *php.ini*.

- PECL (pronounced "pickle") stands for "PHP Extension Code Library" and was created as a place where rarely used or dormant extensions could be moved if they were no longer considered relevant to the core PHP distribution. PECL has grown since its founding, and is now the home of many interesting and experimental extensions that are not yet important enough for the mainstream.

- Third-party extensions are written by programmers who wanted to solve a particular problem that was unsolvable without a new extension. A variety of third-party extensions are available, with the sole difference between a third-party extension and a PECL extension being that there are various rules about submitting code to PECL. Third-party extensions can sometimes be unstable.

- Finally, Do-It-Yourself (DIY) extensions are simply extensions you create yourself. PHP has a rich extension creation system that makes it simple to add your own code, as long as you are proficient in C. Note that creating your own extension requires that you have the ability to compile PHP.

PEAR

The PHP Extension and Application Repository, or PEAR for short, contains reusable code written by others that enables you to create powerful scripts using just a few simple commands.

PEAR contains two types of pre-written code: PECL code and PHP code. PECL code, as mentioned already, are full extensions written in C that interact with external libraries. Extensions reside in PECL when they are considered useful, but not popular or much used. However, most of PEAR is PHP code, which means you can use it on any PHP server without enabling any extensions or recompiling PHP.

The most famous package in PEAR is called PEAR::DB, and provides an object-oriented, database-independent framework for reading from and writing to your database. PEAR::DB is covered in depth in Chapter 14.

PHP comes with "go-pear," an easy way to configure PEAR for use on your computer. To use it, simply run **go-pear** from the command line and follow the on-screen instructions. Windows users will need to change to the directory where PHP is, e.g., *c:\php*.

The output of go-pear is shown in Figure 3-1.

Once you have PEAR installed on your system, you will see the pear command—this allows you to search for and download new PEAR modules for your PHP installation.

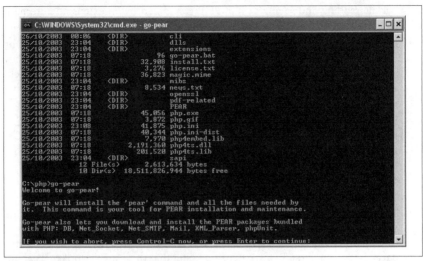

Figure 3-1. Running go-pear will set up PEAR on your computer

Abnormal Script Termination

Most scripts will execute from start to finish, but sometimes they might end prematurely. There is a variety of reasons why this will happen:

1. You've screwed up somewhere, and PHP cannot execute your code.
2. PHP has screwed up somewhere due to a bug and cannot continue.
3. Your script has taken too long to execute and gets killed by PHP.
4. Your script has requested more memory than PHP can allocate and gets killed by PHP.

To be brutally honest, the first situation is unequivocally the most common. This will change a little as your skill with PHP improves, but the first situation is still the most common, even among the most veteran programmers.

Common errors include missing semicolons and parentheses, for example:

```php
<?php
    $i = 10
    $j = 5;
    if (($i + 2) - ($j + 5) == 10 {
        print "Success!";
    }
?>
```

The first line is missing a semicolon, which will cause PHP to flag an error on the second line. Also, the second line is missing a parenthesis after "== 10", causing another error.

4

The PHP Language

This chapter forms a complete introduction to the basics of PHP programming, covering variables, comments, conditional statements, loops, and more. If you have little experience with PHP, this is the best place to start. Otherwise, you may only need to dip into parts of this chapter to refresh your memory.

The Basics of PHP

By default, PHP operates with PHP mode turned off, which means that PHP will consider the content to be plain text (i.e., not PHP code) unless PHP mode has been enabled. This method of parsing means that the PHP elements of a script are "code islands"—standalone chunks of code that can work independently of the HTML "sea" around them.

PHP scripts are generally saved with the file extension *.php* to signify their type. Whenever your web server is asked to send a file ending with *.php*, it first passes it to the PHP interpreter, which executes any PHP code in the script before returning a generated file to the end user. The basic unit of PHP code is called a statement, and ends with a semicolon to signify it is a complete statement. For clarity, one line of code usually contains just one statement, but you can have as many statements on one line as you want. These two examples do the same thing:

```
<?php
        // option 1
        print "Hello, ";
        print "world!";

        // option 2
        print "Hello, "; print "world!";
?>
```

PHP purists like to point out that print is technically not a function and, techni-cally, they are correct. This is why print doesn't require brackets around the data you pass to it. Other language constructs that masquerade as functions (and are herein referred to as such for the sake of sanity) include array, echo, include, require, return, and exit.

You can use parentheses with these constructs, and doing so is harmless:

```php
<?php
        print("Hello!");
?>
```

Although on the surface, print and echo appear the same, they are not. The print construct behaves more like a function than echo because it returns a value (1). However, echo is more useful because you can pass it several parameters, like this:

```php
<?php
        echo "This ", "is ", "a ", "test.";
?>
```

To do the same using print, you would need to use the concatenation operation (.) to join the strings together, rather than a comma. If you have several things to print out, as in that example, then echo is preferred for the sake of clarity.

Variables

Variables in PHP—that is, things that store data—begin with $ followed by a letter or an underscore, then any combination of letters, numbers, and the underscore character. This means you may not start a variable with a number. One notable exception to the general naming scheme for variables are "variable variables," which are covered in the next chapter. A list of valid and invalid variable names is shown in Table 4-1.

Table 4-1. Valid and invalid variable names

$myvar	Correct
$Name	Correct
$_Age	Correct
$___AGE___	Correct
$91	Incorrect ; starts with a number
$1Name	Incorrect ; starts with a number
$Name91	Correct; numbers are fine at the end and after the first character
$_Name91	Correct
$Name's	Incorrect; no symbols other than "_" are allowed, so apostrophes are bad

Variables are case-sensitive, which means that $Foo is not the same variable as $foo, $FOO, or $fOO.

Assigning variables is as simple as using the assignment operator (=) on a variable, followed by the value you want to assign. Here is a basic script showing assigning and outputting data—note the semicolons used to end each statement:

```php
<?php
        $name = "Paul";
```

```
        print "Your name is $name\n";
        $name2 = $name;
        $age = 20;
        print "Your name is $name2, and your age is $age\n";
        print 'Goodbye, $name!\n';
    ?>
```

There we set the $name variable to be the string Paul, and PHP lets us print out that variable after Your name is. Therefore, the output of the first print statement is Your name is Paul, because PHP will substitute $name for its value whenever it finds it by itself, or inside a double-quoted string (that is, one starting and ending with").

We then set $name2 to be $name, which effectively copies $name's value into $name2. $name2 is now set to Paul. We also set up the $age variable to be the number 20. Our second print statement outputs both variables at once, as again, PHP will substitute them inside the string.

However, the last print statement will not replace $name with Paul. Instead, it will print:

```
Goodbye, $name!\n
```

The reason for this is that PHP will not perform variable substitution inside single-quoted strings, and won't even replace most escape characters (the exception being \'). In double-quoted strings, PHP will replace $name with its value; in a single-quoted string, PHP will consider $name to mean that you actually want it to output the text $name just like that.

When you want to append something to your variable while inside a string, PHP may consider the characters to be part of the variable. For example:

```
<?php
        $food = "grapefruit";
        print "These $foods aren't ripe yet.";
    ?>
```

While the desired output was These grapefruits aren't ripe yet, the actual output is different: because we have added the "s" to the end of the variable name, we have changed it from trying to read $food to trying to read $foods. The variable $foods does not exist, so PHP will leave the space blank and may generate an error. There are two ways to solve this:

```
<?php
        $food = "grapefruit";
        print "These ${food}s aren't ripe yet.";
        print "These {$food}s aren't ripe yet.";
    ?>
```

The braces, { and }, technically signal a variable variable when used inside a string, but in the example above, they are used to tell PHP where the variable ends. You don't need to use braces where characters being appended to a variable would make the variable name illegal, like this:

```
<?php
        $food = "grapefruit";
        print "This $food's flavour is bad.";
    ?>
```

That will work because you are not allowed to use apostrophes as part of your variable names.

Whitespace

Spaces, tabs, and blank lines in between statements have no effect on how the code is executed. To PHP, this next script is treated like any other, regardless of the fact that some statements are on the same line, and others are separated by several line breaks:

```php
<?php
        $name = "Paul"; print "Your name is $name\n";
        $name2 = $name; $age = 20;



        print "Your name is $name2, and your age is $age\n";


        print 'Goodbye, $name!\n';
?>
```

You should use whitespace to separate your code into clear blocks, so that its meaning can be understood by visually inspecting the layout.

Heredoc

If you have a long string, you ought to consider using heredoc syntax. Put simply, heredoc allows you to define your own string delimiter so that you can make it something other than a double or single quote. So, for example, we could use the string EOT (end of text) for our delimiter, meaning that we can use double quotes and single quotes freely within the body of the text—the string only ends when we type EOT.

It is a little more complicated than that in practice, but not much—the string delimiter needs to be by itself on a line, in the very first column. That is, you cannot add spacing or tabs around it. Here is a working example:

```php
<?php
$mystring = <<<EOT
        This is some PHP text.
        It is completely free
        I can use "double quotes"
        and 'single quotes',
        plus $variables too, which will
        be properly converted to their values,
        you can even type EOT, as long as it
        is not alone on a line, like this:
EOT;

?>
```

There are several things to note about heredoc and the example above:

- You can use anything you like; EOT is just an example.
- You need to use <<< before the delimiter to tell PHP you want to enter heredoc mode.
- Variable substitution is enabled, which means you need to escape dollar symbols if you don't want PHP to replace variables with their values.
- You can use your delimiter anywhere in the text, but not in the first column of a new line.
- At the end of the string, type the delimiter with no whitespace around it, followed by a semicolon.

Without heredoc syntax, complicated string assignments can become very messy.

Brief Introduction to Variable Types

Variables in PHP can be of type integer (a whole number), floating-point (usually called "float"; a fractional number), string (a set of characters), array (a group of data), object (a complex mix of data and functionality), or a resource (any external information, such as an image). We will be looking at data types in more depth later on; for now, you only need to know what variables are and how they work.

Code Blocks

PHP makes extensive use of code blocks—chunks of PHP code that are separate from the rest of the script. As you read the following sections in this chapter, you will notice that PHP uses braces, { and }, to open and close code blocks.

Opening and Closing Code Islands

There are many ways to open a PHP code island (to enter PHP parsing mode), and you are welcome to choose which you prefer. The recommended manner is to use <?php to enter PHP mode, and ?> to leave PHP mode, but you can also use the short tags version, <? and ?>.

The short version has one big advantage and two big disadvantages: you can output information from your script by using a special short tags hack, <?=, like this:

```
<?="Hello, world!" ?>
```

Here is the equivalent, written using the standard open and closing tags:

```
<?php
        print "Hello, world!";
?>
```

As you can see, the short tags version is more compact, if a little harder to read. However, the first downside to the short version is that it clashes with XML (and therefore XHTML), which also uses <? to open code blocks. This means that if

you try to use XML and short-tagged PHP together, you will encounter problems—this is the primary reason people recommend using the normal open and close tags. Short tags are always dangerous because they can be disabled in the PHP configuration file, *php.ini*, which means your scripts may not be portable.

Two other, lesser-used variants exist: <% %>, which opens and closes code blocks in the same way as Microsoft's ASP, and also <script language="php"></script>. These two often work better with visual editor programs such as Dreamweaver and FrontPage, but they are not recommended for general use because they need to be enabled to work.

You can switch into and out of PHP mode by using <?php and ?> whenever and as often as you want to.

Comments

While in PHP mode, you can mark certain parts of your code as a comment that should not be executed. There are three ways of doing this: //, /* */, and #. // and # mean "Ignore the rest of this line," whereas /* means "Ignore everything until you see */." Some complications exist with /* and */ that make them less desirable to use.

```
<?php
        print "This is printed\n";
        // print "This is not printed\n";
        # print "This is not printed\n";
        print "This is printed\n";
        /* print "This is not printed\n";
        print "This is not printed\n"; */
?>
```

That chunk of code shows all three types of comments in action, but does not demonstrate the problem with the /* */ form of commenting. If you were to start a /* comment on line one, and end it on the line near the bottom where the other /* comment is started, you would find that the script would fail to work. The reason for this is that you cannot stack up, or "nest," /* */ comments, and attempting to do so will fail spectacularly.

It is generally best to stick to // for your commenting purposes, simply because it is easy to spot, easy to read, and easy to control.

Conditional Statements

PHP allows you to choose what action to take based on the result of a condition. This condition can be anything you choose, and you can combine conditions to make actions that are more complicated. Here is a working example:

```
<?php
        $Age = 20;
        if ($Age < 18) {
                print "You're young - enjoy it!\n";
        } else {
```

```
        print "You're not under 18\n";
    }

    if ($Age >= 18 && $Age < 50) {
        print "You're in the prime of your life\n";
    } else {
        print "You're not in the prime of your life\n";
    }

    if ($Age >= 50) {
        print "You can retire soon - hurrah!\n";
    } else {
        print "You cannot retire soon :( ";
    }
?>
```

At the most basic level, PHP evaluates if statements left to right, meaning that it first checks whether $Age is greater or equal to 18, then checks whether $Age is less than 50. The double ampersand, &&, means that both statements must be true if the print "You're in the prime of your life\n" code is to be executed—if either one of the statements is not true for some reason, "You're not in the prime of your life" is printed out instead. The order in which conditions are checked varies when operator precedence matters; this is covered in the next chapter.

As well as &&, there is also || (the pipe symbol printed twice) which means OR. In this situation, the entire statement is evaluated as true if any of the conditions being checked is true.

There are several ways to compare two numbers. We have just looked at < (less than), <= (less than or equal to), and >= (greater than or equal to). We will be looking at the complete list later, but first I want to mention one important check: ==, or two equals signs put together. That means "is equal to." Therefore 1 == 1 is true, and 1 == 2 is false.

The code to be executed if the statement is true is in its own block (remember, a block starts with { and finishes with }), and the code to be executed otherwise is in an else block. This stops PHP from trying to execute both the true and false actions.

One key thing to note is that PHP practices "if statement short-circuiting"—this is where PHP will try to do as little conditional work as possible, so it basically stops checking conditional statements as long as it is sure it can stop. For example:

```
    if ($Age > 10 && $Age < 20)
```

If $Age evaluates to 8, the first check ($Age > 10) will fail, so PHP will not bother checking it against 20. This means you can, for example, check whether a variable is set and whether it is set to a certain value—if the variable is not set, PHP will short-circuit the if statement and not check its value. This is good because if you check the value of an unset variable, PHP will flag an error.

A helpful addition to if statements is the elseif statement, which allows you to chain conditions together in a more intelligent way:

```php
<?php
        if ($Age < 10) {
                print "You're under 10";
        } elseif ($Age < 20) {
                print "You're under 20";
        } elseif ($Age < 30) {
                print "You're under 30";
        } elseif ($Age < 40) {
                print "You're under 40";
        } else {
                print "You're over 40";
        }
?>
```

 Perl users should note that it is spelled elseif and not elsif.

You could achieve the same effect with if statements, but using elseif is easier to read. The downside of this system is that the $Age variable needs to be checked repeatedly.

If you only have one statement of code to execute, you can do without the braces entirely. It's a readability issue.

So, these two code chunks are the same:

```php
if ($banned) {
        print "You are banned!";
}

if ($banned) print "You are banned!";
```

Case Switching

Your if...elseif blocks can become unwieldy when you have a series of conditions that all test against the same variable, as here:

```php
<?php
        $Name = "Bob";
        if ($Name == "Jim") {
                print "Your name is Jim\n";
        } elseif ($Name == "Linda") {
                print "Your name is Linda\n";
        } elseif ($Name == "Bob") {
                print "Your name is Bob\n";
        } elseif ($Name == "Sally") {
                print "Your name is Sally\n";
        } else {
                print "I don't know your name!\n";
        }
?>
```

PHP has a solution to this: switch/case. In a switch/case block, you specify what you are checking against, then give a list of possible values you want to handle. Using switch/case statements, we can rewrite the previous script like this:

```php
<?php
    $Name = 'Bob';
    switch($Name) {
    case "Jim":
            print "Your name is Jim\n";
            break;
    case "Linda":
            print "Your name is Linda\n";
            break;
    case "Bob":
            print "Your name is Bob\n";
            break;
    case "Sally":
            print "Your name is Sally\n";
            break;
    default:
            print "I don't know your name!\n";
    }
?>
```

Switch/case statements are frequently used to check all sorts of data, and they take up much less room than equivalent if statements.

There are two important things to note in the PHP switch/case statement code. First, there is no word "case" before "default"—that is just how the language works. Second, each of our case actions above end with "break;". This is because once PHP finds a match in its case list, it will execute the action of that match as well as the actions of all matches beneath it (further down on your screen). This way of working is taken directly from C, and is generally counterintuitive to how we think—it is rare that you will want to exclude a break from the end of your cases.

The default case is executed if PHP doesn't find a match in one of the other cases, or if the case before it was executed and didn't end with a break statement.

The keyword "break" means "Get out of the switch/case statement," and has the effect of stopping PHP from executing the actions of all subsequent cases after its match. Without the break, our test script would print out this:

```
Your name is Bob
Your name is Sally
I don't know your name
```

Loops

PHP has the following loop keywords: foreach, while, for, and do...while.

The foreach loop is designed to work with arrays, and works by iterating through each element in the array. You can also use it for objects, in which case it iterates over each public variable of that object.

The most basic use of foreach extracts only the values from each array element, like this:

```php
foreach($array as $val) {
        print $val;
}
```

Here the array $array is looped through, and its values are extracted into $val. In this situation, the array keys are ignored completely, which usually makes most sense when they have been autogenerated (i.e., 0, 1, 2, 3, etc.).

You can also use foreach to extract keys, like this:

```php
foreach ($array as $key => $val) {
        print "$key = $val\n";
}
```

When working with objects, the syntax is identical:

```php
<?php
        class monitor {
                private $Brand;
                public $Size;
                public $Resolution;
                public $IsFlat;

                public function __construct($Brand, $Size, $Resolution,
$IsFlat) {
                        $this->Brand = $Brand;
                        $this->Size = $Size;
                        $this->Resolution = $Resolution;
                        $this->IsFlat = $IsFlat;
                }
        }

        $AppleCinema = new monitor("Apple", "30", "2560x1600", true);

        foreach($AppleCinema as $var => $val) {
                print "$var = $val\n";
        }
?>
```

PHP while loops are used for executing a block of code only so long as a given condition is true. For example, this code will loop from 1 to 10, printing out values as it goes:

```php
<?php
        $i = 1;
        while($i <= 10) {
                print "Number $i\n";
                $i = $i + 1;
        }
?>
```

Notice that, again, PHP uses code blocks to represent the extent of our loop—while loops start with an opening brace ({) and finish with a closing brace (}) to tell PHP clearly which lines of code should be looped through.

Like if statements, you can put whatever conditions you choose into while loops, but it is crucial that you change the value of the condition with each loop; otherwise, the loop will execute forever.

While loops are most often used to increment a list where there is no known limit to the number of iterations of the loop. For example:

```
while(there are still rows to read from a database) {
        read in a row;
        move to the next row;
}
```

A more common form of loop is the for loop, which is slightly more complicated. A for loop is made up of a declaration, a condition, and an action: the declaration is where a loop-counter variable is declared and set to a starting value; the condition is where the loop-counter variable is checked against a value; and the action is what should happen at the end of each iteration to change the loop counter.

Here is how a for loop looks in PHP:

```
<?php
    for ($i = 1; $i < 10; $i++) {
            print "Number $i\n";
    }
?>
```

As you can see, the for loop has the three parts separated by semicolons. In the declaration, we set the variable $i to 1. For the condition, we have the loop execute if $i is less than 10. Finally, for the action, we add 1 to the value of $i for every loop iteration—that is, every time the loop code is executed.

When run, this script will count from 1 to 10, outputting text along the way. Note that it will not actually output Number 10 because we specify that $i must be *less* than 10, not less than or equal to it. Here is the output:

```
Number 1
Number 2
Number 3
Number 4
Number 5
Number 6
Number 7
Number 8
Number 9
```

The PHP do...while construct is similar to a while loop. The difference is that the do...while loop is executed at least once. Consider the following piece of code:

```
<?php
    $i = 11;
    do {
            print "Number $i\n";
    } while ($i < 10);
?>
```

Using that code, "Number 11" will be printed before $i is compared against 10. If $i is less than 10 when checked, the loop executes again. In comparison, that same code could be written using a while loop:

```php
<?php
    $i = 11;
    while ($i < 10) {
        print "Number $i\n";
    }
?>
```

The difference is that the while loop would output nothing, because it checks the value of $i before entering the loop. Therefore, do...while loops are always executed a minimum of once.

Infinite Loops

Perhaps surprisingly, infinite loops can often be helpful in your scripts. If you are writing a program to accept people typing in data for as long as they want, it just would not work to have the script loop 30,000 times or even 30,000,000 times. Instead, the code should loop forever, constantly accepting user input until the user ends the program by pressing Ctrl-C.

Here are the two most common types of infinite loops:

```php
<?php
    while(1) {
        print "In loop!\n";
    }
?>
```

As "1" also evaluates to true, that loop will continue on forever.

```php
<?php
    for (;;) {
        print "In loop!\n";
    }
?>
```

In that example, the for loop is missing the declaration, condition, and action parts, meaning that it will always loop.

Special Loop Keywords

PHP gives you the break and continue keywords to control loop operation. We already used break previously when we looked at case switching—it was used there to exit a switch/case block, and it has the same effect with loops. When used inside loops to manipulate the loop behavior, break causes PHP to exit the loop and carry on immediately after it, and continue causes PHP to skip the rest of the current loop iteration and go on to the next.

Perl users should note that break and continue are equivalent to Perl's last and next statements.

For example:

```php
<?php
    for ($i = 1; $i < 10; $i = $i + 1) {
        if ($i == 3) continue;
        if ($i == 7) break;
        print "Number $i\n";
    }
?>
```

That is a modified version of our original for loop script. This time, the output looks like this:

```
Number 1
Number 2
Number 4
Number 5
Number 6
```

Note that Number 3 is missing, and the script exits after Number 6. When the current number is 3, continue is used to skip the rest of that iteration and go on to Number 4. Also, if the number is 7, break is used to exit the loop altogether.

Loops Within Loops

You can nest loops as you see fit, like this:

```php
for ($i = 1; $i < 3; $i = $i + 1) {
    for ($j = 1; $j < 3; $j = $j + 1) {
        for ($k = 1; $k < 3; $k = $k + 1) {
            print "I: $i, J: $j, K: $k\n";
        }
    }
}
```

Here's the output:

```
I: 1, J: 1, K: 1
I: 1, J: 1, K: 2
I: 1, J: 2, K: 1
I: 1, J: 2, K: 2
I: 2, J: 1, K: 1
I: 2, J: 1, K: 2
I: 2, J: 2, K: 1
I: 2, J: 2, K: 2
```

In this situation, using break is a little more complicated, as it only exits the containing loop. For example:

```php
for ($i = 1; $i < 3; $i = $i + 1) {
    for ($j = 1; $j < 3; $j = $j + 1) {
```

```
        for ($k = 1; $k < 3; $k = $k + 1) {
            print "I: $i, J: $j, K: $k\n";
            break;
        }
    }
}
```

This time the script will print out the following:

```
I: 1, J: 1, K: 1
I: 1, J: 2, K: 1
I: 2, J: 1, K: 1
I: 2, J: 2, K: 1
```

As you can see, the $k loop only loops once because of the break call. However, the other loops execute several times. You can exercise even more control by specifying a number after break, such as break 2, to break out of two loops or switch/case statements. For example:

```
for ($i = 1; $i < 3; $i = $i + 1) {
    for ($j = 1; $j < 3; $j = $j + 1) {
        for ($k = 1; $k < 3; $k = $k + 1) {
            print "I: $i, J: $j, K: $k\n";
            break 2;
        }
    }
}
```

That outputs the following:

```
I: 1, J: 1, K: 1
I: 2, J: 1, K: 1
```

This time the loop only executes twice, because the $k loop calls break 2, which breaks out of the $k loop and out of the $j loop, so only the $i loop will go around again. This could even be break 3, meaning break out of all three loops and continue normally.

The break command applies to both loops and switch/case statements. For example:

```
for ($i = 1; $i < 3; $i = $i + 1) {
    for ($j = 1; $j < 3; $j = $j + 1) {
        for ($k = 1; $k < 3; $k = $k + 1) {
            switch($k) {
                case 1:
                    print "I: $i, J: $j, K: $k\n";
                    break 2;
                case 2:
                    print "I: $i, J: $j, K: $k\n";
                    break 3;
            }
        }
    }
}
```

The break 2 line will break out of the switch/case block and also out of the $k loop, whereas the break 3 line will break out of those two and also the $j loop. To break out of the loops entirely from within the switch/case statement, break 4 is required.

Mixed-Mode Processing

A key concept in PHP is that you can toggle PHP parsing mode whenever and as often as you want, even inside a code block. Here is a basic PHP script:

```php
<?php
    if ($logged_in == true) {
            print "Lots of stuff here";
            print "Lots of stuff here";
            print "Lots of stuff here";
            print "Lots of stuff here";
            print "Lots of stuff here";
    }
?>
```

As you can see, there are a lot of print statements that will only be executed if the variable $logged_in is true. All the output is encapsulated into print statements, but PHP allows you to exit the PHP code island while still keeping the if statement code block open—here's how that looks:

```php
<?php
    if ($logged_in == true) {
?>
    Lots of stuff here
    Lots of stuff here
    Lots of stuff here
    Lots of stuff here
    Lots of stuff here
<?php
    }
?>
```

The Lots of stuff here lines are still only sent to output if $logged_in is true, but we exit PHP mode to print it out. We then reenter PHP mode to close the if statement and continue—it makes the whole script easier to read.

Including Other Files

One of the most basic operations in PHP is including one script in another, thereby sharing functionality. This is done by using the include keyword, specifying the filename you want to include.

For example, consider the following file, *foo.php*:

```php
<?php
    print "Starting foo\n";
    include 'bar.php';
    print "Finishing foo\n";
?>
```

And also the file *bar.php*:

```php
<?php
        print "In bar\n";
?>
```

PHP would load the file *bar.php*, read in its contents, then put it into *foo.php* in place of the `include 'bar.php'` line. Therefore, *foo.php* would look like this:

```php
<?php
        print "Starting foo\n";
        print "In bar\n";
        print "Finishing foo\n";
?>
```

If you were wondering why it only writes in the `In bar` line and not the opening and closing tags, it is because PHP drops out of PHP mode whenever it includes another file, then reenters PHP mode as soon as it comes back from the file. Therefore, *foo.php*, once merged with *bar.php*, will actually look like this:

```php
<?php
        print "Starting foo\n";
?>
<?php
        print "In bar\n";
?>
<?php
        print "Finishing foo\n";
?>
```

PHP includes a file only if the include line is actually executed. Therefore, the following code would never include *bar.php*:

```php
<?php
        if (53 > 99) {
                include 'bar.php';
        }
?>
```

If you attempt to include a file that does not exist, PHP will generate a warning message. If your script absolutely needs a particular file, PHP also has the `require` keyword, which, if called on a file that does not exist, will halt script execution with a fatal error. Any file you include in your script will most likely be essential, so it is usually best to use `require`.

 In older versions of PHP, require was the equivalent of an unconditional include. If require was placed inside a conditional statement, the file would be included even if the conditional statement evaluated to false. This is no longer the case in PHP 5: files are included only when the conditional statement they are in (if any) evaluates to true.

The most common way to use include files is as storage for common functions, object definitions, and layout code. For example, if your site uses the same header HTML on every page, you can start each of your pages with this:

```php
include 'header.php';
```

That way, whenever you want to change the header of your site, you just need to edit *header.php*. Two more keywords that are likely to be of use are include_once and require_once, which operate in the same way as include and require, respectively, with the difference that they will only include a file once, even if you try to include it several times. Include_once and require_once share the same list of "already included" files, but it is important to note that operating systems that are case-sensitive, such as Unix, are able to include_once/require_once a file more than once if the programmer uses varying cases for their filenames. For example:

```php
<?php
        include_once 'bar.php';
        include_once 'BAR.php';
        include_once 'Bar.php';
?>
```

On Unix, that will attempt to include three entirely different files, because Unix is case-sensitive. The solution is simple: use lowercase filenames for everything. On Windows, filenames for inclusion are case-insensitive in PHP 5, meaning that including *BAR.php* and *bar.php* will include the same file.

When you try to include or require a file, PHP first checks the directory in which the script is running, and if it doesn't find it there, it looks in its include path. The include path is defined in your *php.ini* file using the include_path directive.

Each time you include a file using include or require, PHP needs to compile it. If you're using a code cache, this problem is avoided; if not, PHP really does compile the same file several times. That is, if you have various includes for the same file, it will need to be compiled and processed each time, so it's best to use include_once(). Failing that, the get_included_files() and get_required_files() functions tell you the names of the files you have already included—they are actually the same function internally, so you can use either one.

Functions

Despite the fact that PHP comes with such a large selection of functions to perform all sorts of tasks, you will want to create your own functions when the need arises. If you find yourself doing the same thing repeatedly, or you want to share code across projects, user functions are for you.

Writing monolithic programs—code that starts at the beginning and runs straight through to the end—is considered very bad for program maintainability, as you are not able to reuse code. By writing functions, you make your code shorter, easier to control and maintain, and less prone to bugs.

A Simple User Function

You can give your functions whatever name you like; they follow the same guidelines (without the $) as PHP's variables. You may not redefine PHP's built-in functions, and care should be taken to ensure that your function names do not collide with existing PHP functions—just because you don't have the imagepng( ) function available, it doesn't mean others also won't.

The simplest user function in PHP looks something like this:

```
function foo( ) {
        return 1;
}

print foo( );
```

You define your functions with the function keyword, followed by the name of the function and two parentheses. The actual code your function will execute lies between braces—in our example function $foo, our sole line of code is return 1; we will get to that in a moment.

After the function definition, we can treat foo( ) like any other function, as seen in line four where we print out the value it returns (known as its *return value*).

Return Values

You're allowed to return one (and only one) value back from functions, and you do this by using the return statement. In our example, we could have used "return 'foo';" or "return 10 + 10;" to pass other values back, but return 1; is easiest and usually the most common, as it is the same as return true;.

You can return any variable you want, as long as it is just one variable—it can be an integer, a string, a database connection, etc. The return keyword sets up the function return value to be whatever variable you use with it, then exits the function immediately. You can also just use return;, which means "exit without sending a value back." If you try to assign to a variable the return value of a function that has no return value (e.g., it uses return; rather than return $someval;), your variable will be set to NULL.

Consider this script:

```
function foo( ) {
        print "In function";
        return 1;
        print "Leaving function...";
}

        print foo( );
?>
```

That will output In function, followed by 1, and then the script will terminate. The reason we never see Leaving function... is because the line return 1 passes one back then immediately exits—the second print statement in foo( ) is never reached.

If you want to pass more than one value back, you need to use an array—this is covered in Chapter 5.

A popular thing to do is to return the value of a conditional statement, for example:

```
return $i > 10;
```

If $i is indeed greater than 10, the > operator will return 1, so it is the same as having return 1, but if $i is less than or equal to 10, it is the same as being return 0.

Parameters

You can design your functions to accept parameters by modifying the definition to include as many as you want. You need to give each parameter the name you will be using to refer to it inside the function—when you later call that function, PHP will copy the values it receives into these parameters, like this:

```
function multiply($num1, $num2) {
        $total = $num1 * $num2;
        return $total;
}

        $mynum = multiply(5, 10);
?>
```

After running that script, $mynum will be set to 50. The multiply( ) function could have been rewritten so that it was just one line: return $num1 * $num2, but it is good to show that you can make your functions as long as you want.

Passing By Reference

When it comes to references, things get more complicated because you need to be able to accept parameters by reference and also return values by reference. This is done with the reference operator, &.

Marking a parameter as "passed by reference" is done in the function definition, not in the function call. That is:

```
function multiply(&$num1, &$num2) {
```

is correct, whereas

```
$mynum = multiply(&5, &10);
```

is wrong. This means that if you have a function being used multiple times across your project, you only need edit the function definition to make it take variables by reference. Passing by reference is often a good way to make your script shorter and easier to read—the choice is rarely driven by performance considerations. Consider this code:

```
function square1($number) {
        return $number * $number;
}

$val = square1($val);

function square2(&$number) {
        $number = $number * $number;
}

square2($val);
```

The first example passes a copy of $val in, multiplies the copy, then returns the result, which is then copied back into $val. The second example passes $val in by reference, and it is modified directly inside the function—hence square2($val) is all that is required, instead of the first example's copying.

A reference is a *reference to a variable*. If you define a function as accepting a reference to a variable, you cannot pass a constant into it. That is, given our definition of square2(), you cannot call the function using square2(10); 10 is not a variable, so it cannot be treated as a reference.

Returning by Reference

Unlike passing values by reference, where you specify the referenced nature of the parameter in the function definition, to return references you need to specify such in the definition *and* at call time. To specify that a function should return a reference, you place the ampersand reference operator before the function name, and to specify that you wish to reference the result of the function as opposed to copying it, you use the normal reference assign that you learned earlier.

Here's how that looks:

```
function &return_fish( ) {
        $fish = "Wanda";
        return $fish;
}

$fish_ref =& return_fish( );
```

Default Parameters

When designing your functions, it is often helpful to assign default values for parameters that aren't passed. PHP does this for most of its functions, and it saves you having to pass in parameters most of the time, if they are usually the same.

To define your own default parameters for a function, add the constant value you would like them to be set to after the variables, like this:

```
function doHello($Name = "Paul") {
        return "Hello $Name!\n";
}

doHello( );
doHello("Paul");
doHello("Andrew");
```

That script will output the following:

```
Hello Paul!
Hello Paul!
Hello Andrew!
```

Now, consider this function:

```
function doHello($FirstName, $LastName = "Smith") { }
```

That does not mean that both $FirstName and $LastName should be set to Smith. Instead, only $LastName gets that value—PHP treats the two variables as functionally independent of each other, which means you can use code like this:

```
function doHello($FirstName = "John", $LastName = "Smith") {
        return "Hello, $FirstName $LastName!\n";
}
```

So, to greet three people named John Smith, Tom Davies, and Tom Smith, you would use this code:

```
doHello();
doHello("Tom", "Davies");
doHello("Tom");
```

If you wanted to greet someone named John Wilson, ideally you would let PHP fill in the first parameter for you, as John is the default for the function, and you would provide the Wilson part. But if you try code like this, you will see it does not work:

```
doHello("Wilson");
```

Instead of John Wilson, you will get Wilson Smith—PHP will assume the parameter you provided was for the first name, as it fills its parameters from left to right. The same logic dictates that you cannot put a default value before a non-default value, like this:

```
function doHello($FirstName = "Joe", $LastName) { }
```

If someone used doHello("Peter"), would they be trying to provide a value for $FirstName to use instead of the default, or do they want the default value in there and Peter for $LastName? Hopefully you can see why PHP will flag up an error if you attempt this!

Variable Parameter Counts

The printf() function (see Chapter 7) is able to take an arbitrary number of parameters—it could take just one parameter, or five, or fifty, or five hundred. It can take as many as are passed into it by the user. This is known as a variable-length parameter list, and it is automatically implemented in user functions. For example:

```
function some_func($a, $b) {
        $j = 1;
}


some_func(1,2,3,4,5,6,7,8);
```

Here the function some_func() is defined to take only two parameters, $a and $b, but we call it with eight parameters and the script should run without a problem. This is one aspect in which PHP varies greatly from C: in C, your functions must be used precisely as declared in their prototypes. In the example above, 1 will be placed into $a, and 2 will be placed into $b, but what happens to the other parameters?

Coming to your rescue are three functions: func_num_args( ), func_get_arg( ), and func_get_args( ), of which the first and last take no parameters. To get the number of arguments that were passed into your function, call func_num_args( ) and read its return value. To get the value of an individual parameter, use func_get_arg( ) and pass in the parameter number you want to retrieve to have its value returned back to you. Finally, func_get_args( ) returns an array of the parameters that were passed in. Here's an example:

```php
function some_func($a, $b) {
        for ($i = 0; $i < func_num_args( ); ++$i) {
                $param = func_get_arg($i);
                echo "Received parameter $param.\n";
        }
}

function some_other_func($a, $b) {
        $param = func_get_args( );
        $param = join(", ", $param);
        echo "Received parameters: $param.\n";
}

some_func(1,2,3,4,5,6,7,8);
some_other_func(1,2,3,4,5,6,7,8);
```

Using func_num_args( ), you can easily implement function error checking. You can, for example, start off each of your functions by checking to make sure func_num_args( ) is what you are expecting, and, if not, exit. Once you add func_get_arg( ) into the mix, however, you should be able to easily create your own functions that work with any number of parameters.

Variable Scope in Functions

Variables declared outside of functions and classes are considered *global*, which means they are generally available elsewhere in the script. However, as functions are independent blocks, their variables are self-contained and do not affect variables in the main script. In the same way, variables from the main script are not implicitly made available inside functions. Take a look at this example:

```php
function foo( ) {
        $bar = "wombat";
}

$bar = "baz";
foo( );
print $bar;
```

Execution of the script starts at the $bar = "baz" line, and then calls the foo( ) function. Now, as you can see, foo( ) sets $bar to wombat, then returns control to the main script where $bar is printed out. Function foo( ) is called, and, having no knowledge that a $bar variable exists in the global scope, creates a $bar variable in its local scope. Once the function ends, all local scopes are tossed away, leaving the original $bar variable intact.

Overriding Scope with the GLOBALS Array

The $GLOBALS superglobal array allows you to access global variables even from within functions. All variables declared in the global scope are in the $GLOBALS array, which you can access anywhere in the script. Here is a demonstration:

```
function foo( ) {
        $GLOBALS['bar'] = "wombat";
}

$bar = "baz";
foo( );
print $bar;
```

That would print wombat to the screen because the foo( ) function literally alters a variable outside of its scope. Even after it returns control back to the main script, its effect is still felt. You can read variables in the same way:

```
$localbar = $GLOBALS['bar'];
```

However, that is quite hard on the eyes. PHP allows you to use a special keyword, GLOBAL, to allow a variable to be accessed locally:

```
function myfunc( ) {
        GLOBAL $foo, $bar, $baz;
        ++$baz;
}
```

That would allow a function to read the global variables $foo, $bar, and $baz. The ++$baz line will increment $baz by 1, and this will be reflected in the global scope also.

Recursive Functions

Sometimes the easiest way to model a problem is to make a function call itself—a technique known as *recursive function calling*. Calculating factorials is a commonly cited example. The factorial of 6 is 6 * 5 * 4 * 3 * 2 * 1, or 720, and is usually represented as "6!". So, given that factorial 6 (6!) is 720, and "7!" is "7 * 6!", you need only calculate "6!" then multiply the result by 7 to get "7!".

This equation can be represented like this: "n! = n * ((n—1)!)". That is, the factorial for any given number is equal to that number multiplied by the factorial of the number one lower—clearly a case for recursive functions. What we need is a function that will accept an integer and, if that integer is not 0, call the function again—this time passing in the same number it accepted, minus 1—then multiply that result by itself. Here is a working script to calculate factorials:

```
function factorial($number) {
        if ($number == 0) return 1;
        return $number * factorial($number-1);
}

print factorial(6);
```

That will output 720, although you can easily edit the factorial( ) function call to pass in 20 rather than 6, for example. Factorials increase in value very quickly

("7!" is 5040, "8!" is 40320, etc.), so you will eventually hit a processing limit—not time, but merely recursive complexity; PHP will only allow you to have a certain level of recursion ("18!" is about the max you are likely to be able to calculate using the above code).

As you can see, recursive functions make programming certain tasks particularly easy, and it is not all math, either—consider how easy it is to write a function showchildren( ) for a forum, which automatically shows all replies to a message, and all replies to those replies, and all replies to the replies to the replies, and so on.

5

Variables and Constants

In this chapter, we examine the different variable types used in PHP, which to use and when, and also how to convert between them. This includes constants, which can—for the most part—be considered as variables that may be set only once.

You needn't understand some of the more complicated parts of this chapter, such as references or variable variables, unless you want full comprehension of the language. Most people will gain this knowledge through time and experience.

Types of Data

PHP has seven data types, and all but one hold a specific kind of information. The seven types are: string, integer, float, boolean, array, object, and resource. You'll be using them all at different times throughout this book, so it is worth remembering what they are.

Strings hold characters (literally: a string of characters) such as "a," "abc," "Jack and Jill went up the hill to fetch a pail of water," etc. Strings can be as short or as long as you want—there's no limit to size. PHP considers strings to be case-sensitive (i.e., Foo and FOO are different), which means that some string functions have case-insensitive equivalents.

Integers hold whole numbers, either positive or negative, such as 1, -20, 55028932, etc. There is a maximum limit to the size of integers—any numbers lower than -2147483647 and any numbers higher than 2147483647 are automatically converted to floats, which can hold a much larger range of values.

Floats hold fractional numbers as well as very large integer numbers, such as 4.2, 1.00000001, and 2147483647000.

Booleans hold either true or false. Behind the scenes, booleans are, in fact, just integers—PHP considers the number 0 to be false, and everything else to be true.

Arrays are a special variable type in that they hold multiple values like a container, and can even hold arrays of arrays (known as *multidimensional arrays*).

Like arrays, objects are complex variables that have multiple values, but they can also have their own functions (often called methods) associated with them. We cover this in Chapter 8.

Resources are anything that is not PHP data—this might be picture data you have loaded from a file, the result of an SQL query, and so on. Internally, a resource variable holds a handle to the actual data, because it is created outside of PHP. This means you should free up your resources when you are finished with them.

True or False

PHP considers some values to be equivalent to true, and others equivalent to false. Most numbers are true (e.g., 1, 59, 1,203,391,462), but 0, 0.0, 0.00000 are all false.

Nearly any string with a value in it is considered to be true, so "a," "193" (an integer inside a string), and "This is a test" are all true. However, an empty string ""and "0" are both false. Confusingly, though, "0.0" is true, as is "0.0000."

Strings

You can use {*x*} notation with strings to read or write individual characters. For example:

```
$mystr = "Jello, world?";
$mystr{0} = "H";
$mystr{12} = "!";
print $mystr;
```

Starting off with a string that doesn't make much sense, we change the first character (position 0) to H, then the twelfth character to an exclamation mark, forming "Hello, world!". As you can see, the first character in a string is numbered 0. That is, a string of length 13, as above, will have its last character at position 12.

Escape Sequences

Escape sequences, the combination of the escape character \ and a letter, are used to signify that the character after the escape character has a special meaning. If you wanted to have the string "And then he said, "That is amazing!", which was true," you would need escape characters because you have double quotes inside double quotes. The valid escape sequences in PHP are shown in Table 5-1.

Table 5-1. Escape sequences and their meanings

\"	Print the next character as a double quote rather than treating it as a string terminator
\'	Print the next character as a single quote rather than treating it as a string terminator
\n	Print a new line character

Table 5-1. Escape sequences and their meanings (continued)

\t	Print a tab character
\r	Print a carriage return (used primarily on Windows)
\$	Print the next character as a dollar rather than treating it as part of a variable name
\\	Print the next character as a backslash rather than treating it as an escape character

Here is a code example of these escape sequences in action:

```php
<?php
        $MyString = "This is an \"escaped\" string";
        $MySingleString = 'This \'will\' work';
        $MyNonVariable = "I have \$zilch in my pocket";
        $MyNewline = "This ends with a line return\n";
        $MyFile = "c:\\windows\\system32\\myfile.txt";
?>
```

Many people forget to escape Windows-style filesystem paths properly, but as you can see, it is simply a matter of adding the appropriate backslashes. If you were to print $MyFile, you would get this:

```
c:\windows\system32\myfile.txt
```

This is because the escape characters are there to ensure PHP reads the string correctly—PHP reads the \\, understands it to be an escape sequence, so just stores \.

Along the same lines, most escape sequences only work in double-quoted strings—if you type Hello!\n\n\n, PHP will actually print out the characters \n\n\n rather than converting them to new lines. The only escape sequence that works within a single-quoted string is \', which tells PHP that the single quote is not the termination of a string but a literal single quote. It is important to note that escape characters are considered just one character by PHP. They are represented as two in PHP because they cannot physically be typed using your keyboard.

Since the only escape sequence that works in single quotes is \', it is safe to use non-escaped Windows-style filenames in your single-quoted strings, like this:

```php
<?php
        $filename = 'c:\windows\me.txt';
        echo $filename;
?>
```

Integers

Most people specify their numbers using base 10, meaning that the digits 0 to 9 are used. However, you may also specify them in hexadecimal (base 16) or octal (base 8). The octal number system only uses the digits 0 to 7. For example, the decimal number 3291 represented in octal is 6333. Represented in hexadecimal, which uses 0 to 9, then A, B, C, D, E, and F, the same number is CDB.

Decimal, octal, and hexadecimal all share the digits 0 to 7, which means that a number like 6333 would look the same in any of the bases. Unless you are specific about which base you want, PHP assumes decimal. For example:

```
$octalnum = 6333;
```

PHP interprets that as 6333 in decimal, which would evaluate to 14,275 in octal. To specify that a number is written in octal and not decimal, you must precede it with a 0 (zero). So, to say that you mean $octalnum to be set to octal 6333 (decimal 3291), you would use this code:

```
$octalnum = 06333;
print $octalnum;
```

That script outputs 3291, as PHP always works with decimal internally, and converts octal 06333 to decimal 3291 when $octalnum is set. Because a leading zero causes numbers to be interpreted in octal, you should not try to align numbers on different lines by using leading zeroes unless you specifically want them in octal!

To specify a number in hexadecimal, precede it with 0x. To assign the number 68, you would use this:

```
$hexnum = 0x44;
print $hexnum;
```

Again, the value is printed out in standard decimal. Octal notation is very rarely used in PHP—if you are on Unix, you may have to use it to specify file access permissions, but that's generally the only use. Hexadecimal notation ("hex") is more common, mostly because many hashing algorithms return text using hexadecimal characters, and also because HTML's color codes are written in hex.

Floats

Integers are good for whole numbers, but for everything else you will need floating-point numbers, often called real numbers or just floats. These are numbers like 1.1, 1.1111112, -12345678.9123, and even 1.0. You may also specify an exponent with your float, i.e., 3.14159e4 is equal to 31415.9.

You may not specify your floats using anything but decimal, so -0x4.AF will generate an error. Unlike Perl, there is no thousands separator in PHP, so values such as 1_221_279 will not work.

Here are some examples of floating-point arithmetic:

```
$a = 1.132324;
$b = $a + 1;
$b = $a + 1.0;
$c = 1.1e15;
$d = (0.1+0.7) * 10;
```

Mixing a float with an integer, as in line two, results in another float so that PHP doesn't lose any accuracy. Line four specifies a very large exponent; if you print out the resulting number, you will actually get 1.1E+015 back because the number is so large.

The last example appears to assign the value 8 to $d, but owing to inherent inconsistencies in floating-point numbers, the value will actually be 7.9999999999999991. Usually this is not a problem, because rounding that value even to 10 decimal places gives you 8, but it does mean that you should avoid comparing floating-point numbers if possible.

Automatic Type Conversion

As PHP is loosely typed (which means that a given variable can change its type as needed), it will automatically convert one type of variable to another whenever possible. Most data types are freely convertible to most other data types; this code illustrates that point:

```
$mystring = "12";
$myinteger = 20;
print $mystring + $myinteger;
```

That script will output 32, despite the fact that one of the variables is a string and the other is an integer. PHP will convert the non-integer operand, $mystring, into an integer, and will find that it is, in fact, an integer inside a string. If PHP converts a string such as "wombat" to an integer, it becomes 0.

Problems with automatic conversion occur when either no meaningful conversion is possible, or when conversion yields unexpected results. For example, calling print on an array makes PHP print out Array; it doesn't automatically convert the array to a string of all its elements. An exception to this is treating an object like a string, and this is covered more deeply in Chapter 8.

Unexpected results occur when PHP converts values and produces unhelpful results. For example, converting from a boolean to a string will produce a 1 if the boolean is set to true, or an empty string if false. Consider this script:

```
$bool = true;
print "Bool is set to $bool\n";
$bool = false;
print "Bool is set to $bool\n";
```

That will output the following:

```
Bool is set to 1
Bool is set to
```

As you can see, it didn't print a 0 for false. To solve this problem, and others like it, tell PHP how you want the value converted by *typecasting*—forcing the result to be a specific type.

The above script should be rewritten to typecast the boolean to an integer, as this will force boolean true to be 1 and boolean false to be 0. To do this, we place the name of the type we're converting to in parentheses before our variable name, like this:

```
$bool = true;
print "Bool is set to $bool\n";
$bool = false;
print "Bool is set to ";
print (int)$bool;
```

This time the script outputs 1 and 0 as we wanted.

PHP will automatically convert data types as necessary—you need not worry about it happening. However, you can typecast any type of variable into any other type, like this:

```
$mystring = "wombat";
$myinteger = (integer)$mystring
```

At first, $mystring contains a string. However, we typecast it to be an integer, so PHP will convert it to an integer and place the result into $myinteger. You can typecast as boolean using (bool), string using (string), and floating-point using (float).

Typecasting is most often used to specifically enforce a type to provide extra security or to ensure a set type of data is being used. For example, if your script absolutely requires an integer number, it's a smart move to typecast your variable with (integer) so that PHP will convert any other type to integer or do nothing if the type is already integer. Converting a float to an integer will round the number down to the nearest whole number, and is actually faster than using the equivalent rounding function.

Checking Whether a Variable Is Set: isset( )

Although most functions are covered in Chapter 7, you need to know the isset( ) function (literally, "is a variable set?") to make the most of this chapter. To use the function, send it a variable as the only parameter, and it will return true or false depending on whether the variable has a value assigned to it. For example:

```
$foo = 1;
if (isset($foo)) {
        echo "Foo is set\n";
} else {
        echo "Foo is not set\n";
}

if (isset($bar)) {
        echo "Bar is set\n";
} else {
        echo "Bar is not set\n";
}
```

That will output "Foo is set" and "Bar is not set". Usually if you try to access a variable that isn't set, like $bar above, PHP will issue a warning that you are trying to use an unknown variable. This does not happen with isset( ), which makes it a safe function to use.

Variable Scope

Each variable has a life span in which it exists, known as its *scope*. It is technically possible for a PHP script to have several variables called $a in existence at one point in time; however, there can only be one *active* $a at any one time.

Any variables not set inside a function or an object are considered global—that is, they are accessible from anywhere else in the script, except inside another function or an object. We'll be looking at function and object scope later on, but for now, it is necessary only to understand that it is possible to have multiple variables of the same name.

Variable Variables

Variable variables are somewhat complicated to use, and even more complicated to explain, so you might need to reread this section a few times before it makes sense! Variable variables allow you to access the contents of a variable without knowing its name directly—it is like indirectly referring to a variable. Here is an example:

```
$bar = 10;
$foo = "bar"
```

From that point, there are two ways we can output the value of $bar: we can either use print $bar, which is quite straightforward, or we can take advantage of the concept of variable variables and use print $$foo;.

By using $$foo, PHP will look up the contents of $foo, convert it to a string, then look up the variable of the same name and return *its* value. In the example above, $foo contains the string "bar", so PHP will look up the variable named $bar and output its value—in this case, 10. It is possible to use as much indirection as you want, giving variables like $$$foo and $$$$$$$bar. That said, anything beyond one level of indirection can lead to very subtle bugs, and so is best avoided.

Variable variables are often used to choose between two values dynamically, so that the output part of a script references $var but another part of the script actually sets what $var points to. For example, if you have calculated the temperature in Fahrenheit and Celsius and want to choose only one to print out, you might use this code:

```
$temperature_f = 59;
$temperature_c = 15;
$units = "temperature_f";
$t = $$units;
```

That assigns the value of $temperature_f to $t.

Variable variables can be helpful from time to time, but are clumsy to use. Furthermore, they only get *more* clumsy the more indirection you use. For example, the next script outputs "Variable!" four times, but I hope you agree it is not very easy to read:

```
$foo = "Variable!\n";
$bar = "foo";
$wom = "bar";
$bat = "wom";
print $foo;
print $$bar;
print $$$wom;
print $$$$bat;
```

Superglobals

Variables that come into PHP arrive inside one of several special arrays known collectively as the *superglobals*, so named because they are available throughout your script, even inside objects and other arrays. Superglobals include form data sent from your visitor, cookie data, session information, local server information, and more, making them good to keep around. Superglobals were not available in PHP prior to v4.1, but there were older alternatives that provided much of the functionality. Superglobals are superior, though, so it is recommended that all new scripts use them.

There are nine superglobal arrays available for use, categorized by type of variable. These are shown in Table 5-2.

Table 5-2. The superglobal arrays

Name	Functionality
$_GET	Contains all variables sent via a HTTP GET request. For example, a URL of *myfile.php?name=Paul* would load *myfile.php* and give you $_GET["name"] with the value "Paul". Users of older PHP versions will have used $HTTP_GET_VARS array, which, although deprecated, is still available for use.
$_POST	Contains all variables sent via a HTTP POST request. This is similar to the old $HTTP_POST_VARS array, which, although deprecated, is still available for use.
$_FILES	Contains all variables sent via a HTTP POST file upload. This is similar to the old $HTTP_POST_FILES array, which is also deprecated.
$_COOKIE	Contains all variables sent via HTTP cookies. This is similar to the old $HTTP_COOKIE_VARS array, which is deprecated like the rest. See Chapter 10 for more information on cookies.
$_REQUEST	Contains all variables sent via HTTP GET, HTTP POST, and HTTP cookies. This is basically the equivalent of combining $_GET, $_POST, and $_COOKIE, and is less dangerous than using $GLOBALS. However, as it does contain all variables from untrusted sources (that is, your visitors), it is best avoided. There's no equivalent to $_REQUEST in versions of PHP before v4.1.
$_SESSION	Contains all variables stored in a user's session (server-side data store). This is similar to the old $HTTP_SESSION_VARS array, which is deprecated. See Chapter 10 for more information on sessions.
$_SERVER	Contains all variables set by the web server you are using, or other sources that directly relate to the execution of your script (see examples in the next section). This is similar to the old $HTTP_SERVER_VARS array, which is deprecated.
$_ENV	Contains all environment variables set by your system or shell for the script (see examples in the next section). This is similar to the old $HTTP_ENV_VARS array, which is deprecated.
$GLOBALS	An array containing all global variables in your script, including other superglobals. $GLOBALS has been available since PHP 3, and its operation has not changed.

Many programmers still use the old syntax for these variables ($HTTP_SERVER_VARS, etc.), so you may wonder why they are deprecated. There are two differences between the old versions and the new versions:

1. The new versions are much shorter to type. Most people would rather type $_GET than $HTTP_GET_VARS each time they want to access a variable.

2. The new versions are automatically global everywhere in your script, even inside functions. The older variables were not available inside functions unless you specifically requested for them to be available.

There are two superglobal arrays that you should avoid unless you particularly need them, namely, $GLOBALS and $_REQUEST. Both of these arrays are combinations of the other arrays and may include untrusted user data. When you use $_COOKIE['somevar'], you know that the value has come from a cookie on the user's machine, and not from someone editing your site's URL. When using $_REQUEST['somevar'], you no longer have that guarantee, and you are left wholly trusting the user. Of course, it is also possible that a user has edited the cookie on her machine, so place no more trust in $_COOKIE data than you have to.

Scripts written before superglobals were available need to be converted to use them. If you would rather not convert the script—either because you need the backward compatibility with very old PHP versions, or you simply don't have the time—then you have two options:

1. Enable register_globals in your *php.ini* file. This will revert PHP back to its insecure, pre-4.1 functionality—the superglobals will still be there, but all input will be automatically converted into variables.

2. Use the function import_request_variables() to extract a given superglobal's contents into normal variables.

One important thing to note is that $GLOBALS always contains itself too, which means that if you try to cycle through each variable in $GLOBALS in some older versions of PHP, you will enter into a recursive loop. Modern PHP releases detect array recursion and print the message "*RECURSION*" when $GLOBALS tries to print itself.

Using $_ENV and $_SERVER

Before you get control in your script, PHP sets several variables for you containing information about the server, the environment, and your visitor's request. These are stored in the superglobal arrays $_ENV and $_SERVER, but their availability depends on whether the script is being run through a web server or on the command line.

The most commonly used $_SERVER variables are shown in Table 5-3. Note: of these, only PHP_SELF is available on the command line.

Table 5-3. Useful preset variables in the $_SERVER superglobal

Name	Value
HTTP_REFERER	If the user clicked a link to get the current page, this will contain the URL of the previous page, or it will be empty if the user entered the URL directly.
HTTP_USER_AGENT	The name reported by the visitor's web browser.
PATH_INFO	Any data passed in the URL after the script name.
PHP_SELF	The name of the current script.
REQUEST_METHOD	Either GET or POST.
QUERY_STRING	Includes everything after the question mark in a GET request. Not available on the command line.

You need to use HTTP_REFERER and not HTTP_REFERRER. This is one of the few misspellings ever to make it into a web standard, but it's now in widespread use and too late to change.

Of those, HTTP_REFERER and HTTP_USER_AGENT are the most important, as you can use these two to find out a lot about your visitor and then take the appropriate action. For example:

```php
<?php
        if (isset($_SERVER['HTTP_REFERER'])) {
                print "The page you were on previously was {$_SERVER['HTTP_
REFERER']}<br />";
        } else {
                print "You didn't click any links to get here<br />";
        }
?>

<a href="refer.php">Click me!</a>
```

If you load that page in your browser by typing the URL in by hand, the "You didn't click any links to get here" text is shown because HTTP_REFERER has not been set. However, if once the page is loaded you follow the "Click me!" link, the page will reload itself; this time, HTTP_REFERER will be set and the other message should appear. Although it can be easily spoofed, HTTP_REFERER is generally a good way to make sure a visitor came from a certain page—whether you want to use that to say, "You can't download my files because you came from another site" or "Welcome, Google users!" is up to you.

The PATH_INFO element in $_SERVER is particularly interesting, because it allows you to grab directory information specified after the script. Consider this script:

```php
if (isset($_SERVER['PATH_INFO'])) {
        print "The page you requested was {$_SERVER['PATH_INFO']}<br />";
} else {
        print "You didn't request a page<br />";
}
```

Save that code as *pathinfo.php*, then load it in your web browser. You will see You didn't request a page. Edit the URL, adding a filename onto the end of *pathinfo.php*. For example: *www.yoursite.com/pathinfo.php/path/to/some/file.txt*. Now when you load the page, you should see that extra path information printed out. This is commonly used in online filesystems, as it means that the URL required to get to a file is just the name of the script followed by the filename wanted.

The referrer value is set by the web browser, which means it can be faked. One common example of this is to edit the "hosts" file of the computer (*/etc/hosts* in Unix; *c:\windows\system32\drivers\etc* hosts in Windows) so that the current computer is used as *www.example.com*. Then, J. Evil Hacker loads a simple page on his computer with a link to your "secure" script, and his browser will report that he came from *example.com*. As a result, you should never rely on HTTP_REFERER to be set, valid, or truthful, but it is a good start.

The $_ENV variable contains environment variables in your system. On Windows, this usually includes variables like "OS" (probably set to "Windows_NT"), "WINDIR" (probably set to "C:\WINDOWS"), and so on. If you are using PHP on the command line, the $_SERVER superglobal will include all the variables from $_ENV.

References

When you use the = (assignment) operator, PHP performs a "copy assignment"— it takes the value from operand two and copies it into operand one. While this is fine for most purposes, it doesn't work when you want to be able to change operand two later on and have operand one also change.

In this situation, references are helpful; they allow you to have two variables pointing to the same data. Once two variables are pointing to the same data, you can change either variable and the other one will also update. To assign by reference, you need to use the reference operator (&) after the equals operator (=), giving =&.

 Perl programmers should not confuse the PHP references with Perl references. Instead, the equivalent in Perl and some other languages is called *aliasing*.

Here's how it looks in PHP:

```
$a = 10;
$b =& $a;
print $a;
print $b;
++$a;
print $a;
print $b;
++$b;
print $a;
print $b;
```

Here we're using the reference operator to make $b point to the same value as $a, as can be seen in the first two print statements. After incrementing $a, both variables are printed out again, and both are 11, as expected. Finally, to prove that the relationship is two-way, $b is incremented, and again both $a and $b have been updated with the one call.

As of PHP 5, objects are passed and assigned by reference by default. Technically, each object has a "handle," which uniquely identifies that object. When you copy an object, you are actually copying its object handle, which means the copy will reference the same object as the original. This was different before PHP 5—objects were treated like other types of variables and copied entirely when assigned. This led to many programmers inadvertently copying lots of information in their scripts without realizing it, which was wasteful. Therefore, from PHP 5 onward, objects are always assigned by reference and passed into functions by reference, avoiding the speed hit. See Chapter 8 for more information.

References are also used to allow a function to work directly on a variable rather than on a copy.

Constants

If you find yourself setting a variable for convenience and never changing it during a script, chances are you should be using a constant. Constants are like variables except that once they are defined, they cannot be undefined or changed—they are constant, as the name suggests. Unlike many other languages, constants are not faster than variables in PHP. The primary advantage to using constants is the fact that they do not have a dollar sign at the front and, therefore, are visibly different from variables. Furthermore, constants are automatically global across your entire script, unlike variables.

To set a constant, use the define( ) function. It takes two parameters: the first being the name of the constant to set, and the second being the value to set. For example, the following line of code sets the constant SecondsPerDay, then prints it out:

```
define("SecondsPerDay", 86400);
print SecondsPerDay;
```

Note that it is not $SecondsPerDay or SECONDSPERDAY—the names of constants, like the names of variables, are case-sensitive—but unlike variables, they do not start with a dollar sign. You can change this behavior by passing true as a third parameter to define( ), which makes the constant case-insensitive:

```
define("SecondsPerDay", 86400, true);
print SecondsPerDay;
print SECONDSperDAY;
```

There are two helpful functions available for working with constants, and these are defined( ) and constant( ). The defined( ) function is basically the constant equivalent of isset( ), as it returns true if the constant string you pass to it has been defined. For example:

```
define("SecondsPerDay", 86400, true);
if (defined("Secondsperday")) {
        // etc
}
```

Note that you should pass the constant name into defined( ) inside quotes.

Finally, constant( ) is a function that at first seems redundant, but is important nonetheless: it returns the value of a constant. While you can get the value of a constant just by using it—e.g., "print MY_CONSTANT;"—how would you accomplish that if you didn't know the constant's name? If you were using a variable, you could use a variable variable, but this is not possible with constants—hence the constant( ) function.

```
define("SecondsPerDay", 86400, true);
$somevar = "Secondsperday";
print constant($somevar);
```

Preset Constants

There are a number of constants automatically set by PHP in order to save you having to recalculate complicated values each time in your script, but PHP also provides other helpful information. For example, PHP always sets the __FILE__, __LINE__, __FUNCTION__, __CLASS__, and __METHOD__ constants for you—note that there are double underscores on either side to make it unlikely you will use these names for your own constants.

These five preset constants are shown in Table 5-4.

Table 5-4. Helpful constants preset for you by PHP

Constant	Function
__FILE__	The name of the script that's running. Note that this reports the file that contains the current line of code, so this will report the name of an include file if applicable.
__LINE__	The line number PHP is executing. Like __FILE__, this holds the line number of the current line of code, which may be in an include file if applicable.
__FUNCTION__	The name of the function PHP is currently inside
__CLASS__	The name of the class of the object being used
__METHOD__	The name of the class function PHP is currently inside

Using these special constants, it is very easy to output complex error reports or other debugging information.

PHP defines numerous constants for use in its functions and extensions—a great many of these are outlined elsewhere in this book, and they help you remember values. For example, if you want to know the value of the mathematical figure pi, use M_PI, which is much easier than remembering 3.141592653. To extract (or "export") variables from an array using extract( ) and always using a prefix, use EXTR_PREFIX_ALL. Again, that's much easier to remember than a numerical value such as 3, but does the same thing.

There are some generic coding constants that you might find useful, such as PHP_EOL to grab the newline character for the current OS, PHP_OS to grab the name of the OS, PHP_VERSION to get the version number of the engine, and DEFAULT_INCLUDE_PATH to see where PHP will include files from, if it can't find them in the local directory.

There are predefined constants to do all sorts of things inside your code, and there is not room to cover them all here. For a comprehensive and up-to-date list, check the PHP manual at *http://www.php.net/manual/en/reserved.constants.php.*

Mathematical Constants

There are several values in mathematics that are used in math-related scripts but take some time to calculate, so, to save time, PHP defines them as constants available to you in every script. For example, if you want to use the value of pi, you can use the preset constant value M_PI.

So, to calculate the area a of a circle based upon its radius r, the formula is a = pi * r². Using PHP, we can write this as:

```
$area = M_PI * ($radius * $radius);
// or...
$area = M_PI * pow($radius, 2);
```

The most popular mathematical constants are listed in Table 5-5.

Table 5-5. Mathematical constants

Constant	Value	Meaning
M_PI	3.14159265358979323846	pi
M_PI_2	1.57079632679489661923	pi/2
M_PI_4	0.78539816339744830962	pi/4
M_1_PI	0.31830988618379067154	1/pi
M_2_PI	0.63661977236758134308	2/pi
M_SQRTPI	1.77245385090551602729	sqrt(M_PI)
M_2_SQRTPI	1.12837916709551257390	2/sqrt(M_PI)
M_SQRT2	1.41421356237309504880	sqrt(2)
M_SQRT3	1.73205080756887729352	sqrt(3)
M_SQRT1_2	0.70710678118654752440	1/sqrt(2)

Arrays

To model our surroundings accurately in a programming environment, we need to recognize that some types of data naturally group together. Colors, for example, naturally clump together into one group. Rather than having hundreds of separate variables—one for each color—it makes more sense to have one variable that holds a list, or array, of colors.

First Steps

PHP has built-in support for arrays of data, and you can create them using the array( ) function or using a special operator, [ ].

There are two things you need to understand before continuing:

- An array is a normal PHP variable, but it works like a container—you can put other variables inside it.

- Each variable inside an array is called an *element*. Each element has a *key* and a *value*, which can be any other variable.

Here is a basic example:

```php
$myarray = array("Apples", "Oranges", "Pears");
$size = count($myarray);
print_r($myarray);
```

On the first line, we see the most basic way to create an array, the array( ) function. This takes a series of variables or values as its parameters (you can pass no parameters to get an empty array, or as many as you want), and returns an array containing those variables. In that example, $myarray contains three elements. Line two contains a new function, count( ), that returns the number of elements existing in the array passed to it.

Line three contains another new function, print_r( ). This takes just one parameter, but it outputs detailed information about a variable, such as its type, length, and contents. In the case of arrays, print_r( ) iteratively outputs all elements inside the array—it's a good way to see how arrays work.

Here is the output of print_r( ) from the above code:

```
Array
(
[0] => Apples
[1] => Oranges
[2] => Pears
)
```

There are our three values—Apples is at index 0 in the array (signified by [0]=>), Oranges is at index 1 in the array, and Pears is at index 2 in the array. If you are running your scripts through a web browser as opposed to from the command line, you may find it helpful to put a HTML <pre> tag before your print_r( ) calls, as this will format them for easier reading.

Using the proper array terminology defined earlier, the 0, 1, and 2 indices are the keys of each element, the Apples, Oranges, and Pears are the values of each element. The key and the value together are the elements themselves.

Note that you can provide a second parameter to print_r( ), which, if set to true, will make print_r( ) pass its output back as its return value, and not print anything out. To achieve the same output using this method, we would need to alter the script to this:

```php
$myarray = array("Apples", "Oranges", "Pears");
$size = count($myarray);
$output = print_r($myarray, true);
print $output;
```

You can store whatever you like as values in an array, and you can also mix values. For example: array("Foo", 1, 9.995, "bar", $somevar). You can also put arrays inside arrays, but we will be getting to that later.

Variables and Constants

There is a similar function to print_r( ), which is var_dump( ). It does largely the same thing, but a) prints out sizes of variables, b) does not print out nonpublic data in objects, and c) does not have the option to pass a second parameter to return its output. For example, altering the first script to use var_dump( ) rather than print_r( ) would give the following output:

```
array(3) {
        [0]=>
        string(6) "Apples"
        [1]=>
        string(7) "Oranges"
        [2]=>
        string(5) "Pears"
}
```

In there, you can see var_dump( ) has told us that the array has three values, and also prints out the lengths of each of the strings. For teaching purposes, var_dump( ) is better, as it shows the variable sizes; however, you will probably want to use print_r( ) in your own work.

Finally, there is the function var_export( ), which is similar to both var_dump( ) and print_r( ). The difference with var_export( ) is that it prints out variable information in a style that can be used as PHP code. For example, if we had used var_export( ) instead of print_r( ) in the test script, it would have output the following:

```
array (
        0 => 'Apples',
        1 => 'Oranges',
        2 => 'Pears',
)
```

You can copy and paste that information directly into your own scripts, like this:

```
$foo = array (
0 => 'Apples',
1 => 'Oranges',
2 => 'Pears',
);
```

Associative Arrays

As well as choosing individual values, you can also choose your keys. In the fruits code above, we just specify values, and so we get an integer-indexed array; but we could have specified keys along with them, like this:

```
$myarray = array("a"=>"Apples", "b"=>"Oranges", "c"=>"Pears");
var_dump($myarray);
```

This time, var_dump( ) will output the following:

```
array(3) {
        ["a"]=>
        string(6) "Apples"
        ["b"]=>
        string(7) "Oranges"
        ["c"]=>
```

```
        string(5) "Pears"
}
```

As expected, our 0, 1, and 2 element keys have been replaced with a, b, and c, but we could equally have used Foo, Bar, and Baz, or even variables or other arrays to act as the keys. Specifying your own keys produces what is called an *associative array* (also known as a *hash*)—you associate a specific key with a specific value.

The one exception here is floating-point numbers, which make poor choices for array indexes. The problem lies in the fact that PHP converts them to integers before they are used, which essentially rounds them down. So, the following code will create an array with just one element:

```
$myarr = array(1.5=>"foo", 1.6=>"bar");
```

That will round both 1.5 and 1.6 down to 1, first storing "foo" index 1, then overwriting it with bar. If you really want to use floating-point numbers as your keys, pass them in as strings, like this:

```
$myarr = array("1.5"=>"foo", "1.6"=>"bar");
var_dump($array);
```

That should output the following:

```
array(2) {
        ["1.5"]=>
        string(3) "foo"
        ["1.6"]=>
        string(3) "bar"
}
```

This time the floating-point numbers have not been rounded down or converted at all, because PHP is using them as strings. The same solution applies to reading values out from an associative array with floating-point keys—you must always specify the key as a string.

The Array Operator

You can also create and manage arrays using square brackets [ ], which means "add to array" (earning it the name "the array operator"). Using this, you can both create arrays and add to the end of existing arrays, so this method is generally more popular—you will generally only find the array( ) function being used when several values are being put inside the array, as it will fit on one line. Here are some examples of the array operator in action:

```
$array[ ] = "Foo";
$array[ ] = "Bar";
$array[ ] = "Baz";
var_dump($array);
```

That should work in the same way as using the array( ) function, except it is more flexible because we can add to the array whenever we want to. When it comes to working with non-default indices, we can just place our key inside the square brackets, like this:

```
$array["a"] = "Foo";
$array["b"] = "Bar";
```

```
$array["c"] = "Baz";
var_dump($array);
```

Returning Arrays from Functions

You can return one and only one value from your user functions, but you are able to make that single value an array, thereby allowing you to return many values as one:

```
function dofoo( ) {
        $array["a"] = "Foo";
        $array["b"] = "Bar";
        $array["c"] = "Baz";
        return $array;
}

$foo = dofoo( );
```

Without returning an array, the most common way to pass data back to the calling script is by accepting parameters by reference and changing them inside the function. Passing arrays by reference like this is generally preferred, as it is less of a hack and also frees up your return value for a boolean to check whether the function was successful. For example:

```
function load_member_data($ID, &$member) {
        // this would connect to a database and load the data,
        // but for space reasons this is done by hand!
        $member["Name"] = "Bob";
        return true;
}

$ID = 22901221079;

$result = load_member_data($ID, $member);
// pass $member in for data storage, but get a return value too

if ($result) {
        print "Member {$member["Name"]} loaded successfully.\n";
} else {
        print "Failed to load member #$ID.\n";
}
```

One additional way to write the same thing is just to rely on the fact that an empty array, if typed as a boolean, is considered to be false, whereas an array with values is considered to be true. While that works, it is poor technique.

Array-Specific Functions

There are quite a few array functions, and you need not learn them all—your best bet is to give them all a try so that you at least know how they work. Then when you need them, you can look up their workings here or online.

array_diff( )

```
array array_diff ( array arr1, array arr2 [, array ...] )
```

The array_diff( ) function returns a new array containing all the values of array $arr1 that do not exist in array $arr2.

```
$toppings1 = array("Pepperoni", "Cheese", "Anchovies", "Tomatoes");
$toppings2 = array("Ham", "Cheese", "Peppers");
$diff_toppings = array_diff($toppings1, $toppings2);

var_dump($diff_toppings);
// prints: array(3) { [0]=> string(9) "Pepperoni" [2]=>
// string(9) "Anchovies" [3]=> string(8) "Tomatoes" }
```

You can diff several arrays simultaneously by providing more parameters to the function. In this situation, the function will return an array of values in the first array that do not appear in the second and subsequent arrays. For example:

```
$arr1_unique = array_merge($arr1, $arr2, $arr3, $arr4);
```

array_filter( )

```
array array_filter ( array arr [, function callback] )
```

The array_filter( ) allows you to filter elements through a function you specify. If the function returns true, the item makes it into the array that is returned; otherwise, it does not. For example:

```
function endswithy($value) {
        return (substr($value, -1) == 'y');
}

$people = array("Johnny", "Timmy", "Bobby", "Sam", "Tammy", "Joe");
$withy = array_filter($people, "endswithy");
var_dump($withy);
// contains "Johnny", "Timmy", "Bobby", and "Tammy"
```

In this script, we have an array of people, most of whom have a name ending with "y". However, several do not, and we want to have a list of people whose names ends in "y", so array_filter( ) is used. The function endswithy( ) will return true if the last letter of each array value is a "y"; otherwise, it will return false. By passing that as the second parameter to array_filter( ), it will be called once for every array element, passing in the value of the element as the parameter to endswithy( ), where it is checked for a "y" at the end.

array_flip( )

```
array array_flip ( array arr )
```

The array_flip( ) function takes an array as its parameter, and exchanges all the keys in that array with their matching values, returning the new, flipped array. You can see how it works in this script:

```
$capitalcities['England'] = 'London';
$capitalcities['Scotland'] = 'Edinburgh';
$capitalcities['Wales'] = 'Cardiff';
$flippedcities = array_flip($capitalcities);
var_dump($flippedcities);
```

The output is this:

```
array(3) {
        ["London"]=>
        string(7) "England"
        ["Edinburgh"]=>
        string(8) "Scotland"
        ["Cardiff"]=>
        string(5) "Wales"
}
```

As you can see, London, Edinburgh, and Cardiff are the keys in the array now, with England, Scotland, and Wales as the values.

array_intersect( )

```
array array_intersect ( array arr1, array arr2 [, array ...] )
```

The array_intersect( ) function returns a new array containing all the values of array $arr1 that exist in array $arr2.

```
$toppings1 = array("Pepperoni", "Cheese", "Anchovies", "Tomatoes");
$toppings2 = array("Ham", "Cheese", "Peppers");
$int_toppings = array_intersect($toppings1, $toppings2);

var_dump($int_toppings);
// prints: array(1) { [1]=> string(6) "Cheese" }
```

The array_intersect( ) function will try to retain array keys when possible. For example, if you are intersecting two arrays that have no duplicate keys, all the keys will be retained. However, if there are key clashes, array_intersect( ) will use the first array to contain it. For example:

```
$arr1 = array("Paul"=>25, "Ildiko"=>38, "Nick"=>27);
$arr2 = array("Ildiko"=>27, "Paul"=>38);

print "\nIntersect:\n";
var_dump(array_intersect($arr1, $arr2));
// Values 27 and 38 clashes, so their keys from $arr1 are used.
// So, output is Ildiko (38), and Nick (27)
```

You can intersect several arrays simultaneously by providing more parameters to the function. For example:

```
$arr1_shared = array_intersect($arr1, $arr2, $arr3, $arr4);
```

array_keys( )

```
array array_keys ( array arr [, mixed search [, bool strict]] )
```

The array_keys( ) function takes an array as its only parameter, and returns an array of all the keys in that array. For example, if you have an array with user IDs as keys and usernames as values, you could use array_keys( ) to generate an array where the values were the user IDs. For example:

```
$users[923] = 'TelRev';
$users[100] = 'Skellington';
$users[1202] = 'CapnBlack';
$userids = array_keys($users);
```

```
// $userids contains the values 923, 100, and 1202
```

There are two other parameters that can be passed to array_keys( ): the value to match and a flag indicating whether to perform strict matching. These two allow you to filter your array keys—if you specify TelRev, then the only keys that array_keys( ) will return are the ones that have the value TelRev. By default, this is done by checking each key's value with the == operator (is equal to); however, if you specify 1 as the third parameter, the check will be done with === (is identical to).

```
$users[923] = 'TelRev';
$users[100] = 'Skellington';
$users[1202] = 'CapnBlack';
$userids = array_keys($users, "TelRev");
// userids contains only 923
```

array_merge( )

array array_merge (array *arr1* [, array *arr2* [, array ...]])

The array_merge( ) function combines two or more arrays by renumbering numerical indexes and overwriting string indexes, if there is a clash.

```
$toppings1 = array("Pepperoni", "Cheese", "Anchovies", "Tomatoes");
$toppings2 = array("Ham", "Cheese", "Peppers");
$both_toppings = array_merge($toppings1, $toppings2);

var_dump($both_toppings);
// prints: array(7) { [0]=> string(9) "Pepperoni" [1]=>
// string(6) "Cheese" [2]=> string(9) "Anchovies" [3]=>
// string(8) "Tomatoes" [4]=> string(3) "Ham" [5]=>
// string(6) "Cheese" [6]=> string(7) "Peppers" }
```

 The + operator in PHP is overloaded so that you can use it to merge arrays, e.g., $array3 = $array1 + $array2. But if it finds any keys in the second array that clash with the keys in the first array, they will be skipped.

The array_merge( ) will try to retain array keys when possible. For example, if you are merging two arrays that have no duplicate keys, all the keys will be retained. However, if there are key clashes, array_merge( ) will use the clashing key from the last array that contains it. For example:

```
$arr1 = array("Paul"=>25, "Ildiko"=>38, "Nick"=>27);
$arr2 = array("Ildiko"=>27, "Paul"=>38);

print "Merge:\n";
var_dump(array_merge($arr1, $arr2));
// Values 27 and 38 clash, so their keys from $arr2 are used.
// So, output is Paul (38), Ildiko (27), and Nick (27).
```

You can merge several arrays simultaneously by providing more parameters to the function. For example:

```
$sports_teams = array_merge($soccer, $baseball, $basketball, $hockey);
```

array_pop( )

```
mixed array_pop ( array &arr )
```

The array_pop( ) function takes an array as its only parameter, and returns the value from the end of the array while also removing it from the array. For example:

```
$names = array("Timmy", "Bobby", "Sam", "Tammy", "Joe");
$firstname = array_pop($names);
// first is Timmy; last is Joe again
```

array_push( )

```
int array_push ( array &arr, mixed var [, mixed ...] )
```

The array_push( ) function takes an array and a new value as its only parameter, and pushes that value onto the end of the array, after all the other elements. This is the opposite of the array_pop( ) function:

```
$firstname = "Johnny";
$names = array("Timmy", "Bobby", "Sam", "Tammy", "Joe");
array_push($names, $firstname);
// first is Timmy; last is now Johnny
```

array_rand( )

```
mixed array_rand ( array arr [, int amount] )
```

The array_rand( ) function picks out one or more random values from an array. It takes an array to read from, then returns either one random key or an array of random keys from inside there. The advantage to array_rand( ) is that it leaves the original array intact, so you can just use that randomly chosen key to grab the related value from the array.

There is an optional second parameter to array_rand( ) that allows you to specify the number of elements you would like returned. These are each chosen randomly from the array, and are not necessarily returned in any particular order. The function also has these attributes:

- It returns the keys in your array. If these aren't specified, the default integer indexes are used. To get the value out of the array, look up the value at the key.
- If you ask for one random element, or do not specify parameter two, you will get a single randomly chosen variable back.
- If you ask for more than one random element, you will receive an array of variables back.
- If you ask for more random elements than there are in the array, you will get an error.
- If you request more than one random element, it will not return duplicate elements.
- If you want to read most or all of the elements from your array in a random order, use a mass randomizer like shuffle( ), as it is faster.

With that in mind, here's an example of array_rand( ) in action:

```
$natural_born_killers = array("lions", "tigers", "bears", "kittens");
$two_killers = array_rand($natural_born_killers, 2);
```

array_shift( )

```
mixed array_shift ( array &arr )
```

The array_shift( ) function takes an array as its only parameter, and returns the value from the front of the array while also removing it from the array. For example:

```
$names = array("Johnny", "Timmy", "Bobby", "Sam", "Tammy", "Joe");
$firstname = array_shift($names); // "Johnny"
var_dump($names);
// Timmy, Bobby, Sam, Tammy, Danny, and Joe
```

array_unique( )

```
array array_unique ( array arr )
```

The array_unique( ) filters an array so that a value can only appear once. It takes an array as its only parameter, and returns the same array with duplicate values removed. For example:

```
$toppings2 = array("Peppers", "Ham", "Cheese", "Peppers");
$toppings2 = array_unique($toppings2);
// now contains "Peppers", "Ham", and "Cheese"
```

array_unshift( )

```
int array_unshift ( array &arr, mixed var [, mixed ...] )
```

The array_unshift( ) function takes an array and a new value as its only parameter, and pushes that value onto the start of the array, before all the other elements. This is the opposite of the array_shift( ) function.

```
$firstname = "Johnny";
$names = array("Timmy", "Bobby", "Sam", "Tammy", "Joe");
array_unshift($names, $firstname);
// first is Johnny, last is Joe
```

array_values( )

```
array array_values ( array arr )
```

The array_values( ) takes an array as its only parameter, and returns an array of all the values in that array. This might seem pointless, but its usefulness lies in how numerical arrays are indexed. If you use the array operator [ ] to assign variables to an array, PHP will use 0, 1, 2, etc. as the keys. If you then sort the array using a function such as asort( ), which keeps the keys intact, the array's keys will be out of order because asort( ) sorts by value, not by key.

Using the array_values( ) function makes PHP create a new array where the indexes are recreated and the values are copied from the old array, essentially making it renumber the array elements. For example:

```
$words = array("Hello", "World", "Foo", "Bar", "Baz");

var_dump($words);
// prints the array out in its original ordering, so
// array(5) { [0]=> string(5) "Hello" [1]=> string(5)
```

```
// "World" [2]=> string(3) "Foo" [3]=> string(3) "Bar"
// [4]=> string(3) "Baz" }

asort($words);

var_dump($words);
// ordered by the values, but the keys will be jumbled up, so
// array(5) { [3]=> string(3) "Bar" [4]=> string(3) "Baz"
// [2]=> string(3) "Foo" [0]=> string(5) "Hello"
// [1]=> string(5) "World" }

var_dump(array_values($words));
// array_values() creates a new array, re-ordering the keys. So:
// array(5) { [0]=> string(3) "Bar" [1]=> string(3) "Baz"
// [2]=> string(3) "Foo" [3]=> string(5) "Hello"
// [4]=> string(5) "World" }
```

You will find array_values( ) useful to reorder an array's indexes either because they are jumbled up or because they have holes in them, but you can also use it to convert an associative array with strings as the indexes to a plain numerical array.

arsort( )

> bool arsort (array &*arr* [, int *options*])

The arsort( ) function takes an array as its only parameter, and reverse sorts it by its values while preserving the keys. This is the opposite of the asort( ). For example:

```
$capitalcities['England'] = 'London';
$capitalcities['Wales'] = 'Cardiff';
$capitalcities['Scotland'] = 'Edinburgh';
arsort($capitalcities);
// reverse-sorted by value, so London, Edinburgh, Cardiff
```

Note that arsort( ) works by reference, directly changing the value you pass in. The return value is either true or false, depending on whether the sorting was successful.

By default, the sort functions sort so that 2 comes before 10. You can change this using the second parameter—see the ksort( ) reference for how to do this.

asort( )

> bool asort (array &*arr* [, int *options*])

The asort( ) function takes an array as its only parameter, and sorts it by its values while preserving the keys. For example:

```
$capitalcities['England'] = 'London';
$capitalcities['Wales'] = 'Cardiff';
$capitalcities['Scotland'] = 'Edinburgh';
asort($capitalcities);
// sorted by value, so Cardiff, Edinburgh, London
```

Note that asort( ) works by reference, directly changing the value you pass in. The return value is either true or false, depending on whether the sorting was successful.

By default, the sort functions sort so that 2 comes before 10. You can change this using the second parameter—see the ksort( ) reference for how to do this.

explode( )

```
array explode ( string separator, string input [, int limit] )
```

The explode( ) function converts a string into an array using a separator value. For example, the string "head, shoulders, knees, toes" could be converted to an array with the values heads, shoulders, knees, toes by using the separator ",". Note that the separator is a comma followed by a space, otherwise the array values would be heads, shoulders, knees, and toes. For example:

```
$oz = "Lions and Tigers and Bears";
$oz_array = explode(" and ", $oz);
// array contains "Lions", "Tigers", "Bears"
```

To reverse this function, converting an array into a string by inserting a separator between elements, use the implode( ) function.

extract( )

```
int extract ( array arr [, int options [, string prefix]] )
```

The extract( ) function converts elements in an array into variables in their own right, an act commonly called "exporting" in other languages. Extract takes a minimum of one parameter, an array, and returns the number of elements extracted. This is best explained using code:

```
$Wales = "Swansea";
$capitalcities = array("England"=>"London",
  "Scotland"=>"Edinburgh", "Wales"=>"Cardiff");
extract($capitalcities);
print $Wales;
```

After calling extract, the England, Scotland, and Wales keys become variables in their own right ($England, $Scotland, and $Wales), with their values set to London, Edinburgh, and Cardiff, respectively. By default, extract( ) will overwrite any existing variables, meaning that $Wales's original value of Swansea will be overwritten with Cardiff. The new variables are copies of those in the array, and not references.

This behavior can be altered using the second parameter, and averted using the third parameter. Parameter two takes a special constant value that allows you to decide how values will be treated if there is an existing variable, and parameter three allows you to prefix each extract variable with a special string. The possible values of the second parameter are shown in Table 5-6.

Table 5-6. Possible values for the second parameter to extract( )

EXTR_OVERWRITE	On collision, overwrite the existing variable
EXTR_SKIP	On collision, do not overwrite the existing variable
EXTR_PREFIX_SAME	On collision, prefix the variable name with the prefix specified by parameter three
EXTR_PREFIX_ALL	Prefix all variables with the prefix specified by parameter three, whether or not there is a collision
EXTR_PREFIX_INVALID	Use the prefix specified by parameter three only when variable names would otherwise be illegal (e.g., "$9")
EXTR_IF_EXISTS	Set variables only if they already exist
EXTR_PREFIX_IF_EXISTS	Create prefixed variables only if non-prefixed version already exists
EXTR_REFS	Extract variables as references rather than copies

The last option, EXTR_REFS, can be used on its own or in combination with others using the bitwise OR operator, |.

Here are some examples based upon the $capitalcities array from the previous example:

```
$Wales = 'Swansea';
extract($capitalcities, EXTR_SKIP);
// leaves $Wales intact, as it exists already

print $Wales; // "Swansea"
print $Scotland; // "Edinburgh"

extract($capitalcities, EXTR_PREFIX_SAME, "country");
// creates variables $country_Wales, $country_Scotland, etc

print $Wales; // "Swansea"
print $country_England; // "London"
// Note that PHP places an underscore
// after the prefix for easier reading


extract($capitalcities, EXTR_PREFIX_ALL, "country");
// creates variables with prefixes, overwriting $country_England, etc

extract($capitalcities, EXTR_PREFIX_ALL | EXTR_REFS, "country");
// sets $country_ variables to be references to the array elements

$country_Scotland = "Stirling";
print($capitalcities["Scotland"]);
// prints "Stirling", because we changed it by reference
```

implode( )

string implode (string *separator*, array *pieces*)

The implode( ) function converts an array into a string by inserting a separator between each element. This is the reverse of the explode( ) function. For example:

```
$oz = "Lions and Tigers and Bears";
$oz_array = explode(" and ", $oz);
// array contains "Lions", "Tigers", "Bears"

$exclams = implode("! ", $oz_array);
// string contains "Lions! Tigers! Bears!"
```

in_array( )

bool in_array (mixed *needle*, array *haystack* [, bool *strict*])

The in_array( ) function will return true if an array contains a specific value; otherwise, it will return false:

```
$needle = "Sam";
$haystack = array("Johnny", "Timmy", "Bobby", "Sam", "Tammy", "Joe");
```

```
if (in_array($needle, $haystack)) {
        print "$needle is in the array!\n";
} else {
        print "$needle is not in the array\n";
}
```

There is an optional boolean third parameter for in_array( ) (set to false by default) that defines whether you want to use strict checking or not. If parameter three is set to true, PHP will return true only if the value is in the array and of the same type—that is, if they are identical in the same way as the === operator (three equals signs).

krsort( )

bool krsort (array &*arr* [, int *options*])

The krsort( ) function takes an array as its only parameter, and reverse sorts it by its keys while preserving the values. This is the opposite of the ksort( ). For example:

```
$capitalcities['England'] = 'London';
$capitalcities['Wales'] = 'Cardiff';
$capitalcities['Scotland'] = 'Edinburgh';
krsort($capitalcities);
// reverse-sorted by key, so Wales, Scotland, then England
```

Note that krsort( ) works by reference, directly changing the value you pass in. The return value is either true or false, depending on whether the sorting was successful.

By default, the sort functions sort so that 2 comes before 10. You can change this using the second parameter—see the ksort( ) reference for how to do this.

ksort( )

bool ksort (array &*arr* [, int *options*])

The ksort( ) function takes an array as its only parameter, and sorts it by its keys while preserving the values. For example:

```
$capitalcities['England'] = 'London';
$capitalcities['Wales'] = 'Cardiff';
$capitalcities['Scotland'] = 'Edinburgh';
ksort($capitalcities);
// sorted by key, so England, Scotland, then Wales
```

Note that ksort( ) works by reference, directly changing the value you pass in. The return value is either true or false, depending on whether the sorting was successful.

By default, the sort functions sort so that 2 comes before 10. While this might be obvious, consider how a string sort would compare 2 and 10—it would work character by character, which means it would compare 2 against 1 and, therefore, put 10 before 2. Sometimes this is the desired behavior, so you can pass a second parameter to the sort functions to specify how you want the values sorted, like this:

```
$array["1"] = "someval1";
$array["2"] = "someval2";
$array["3"] = "someval3";
$array["10"] = "someval4";
$array["100"] = "someval5";
$array["20"] = "someval6";
$array["200"] = "someval7";
```

```
$array["30"] = "someval8";
$array["300"] = "someval9";
var_dump($array);
ksort($array, SORT_STRING);
var_dump($array);
```

If you want to force a strictly numeric sort, you can pass SORT_NUMERIC as the second parameter.

range( )

```
array range ( mixed low, mixed high [, number step] )
```

The range( ) function creates an array of numbers between a low value (parameter one) and a high value (parameter two). So, to get an array of the sequential numbers between 1 and 40 (inclusive), you could use this:

```
$numbers = range(1,40);
```

The range( ) function has a third parameter that allows you specify a step amount in the range. This can either be an integer or a floating-point number. For example:

```
$questions = range(1, 10, 2);
// gives 1, 3, 5, 7, 9

$questions = range(1, 10, 3)
// gives 1, 4, 7, 10

$questions = range(10, 100, 10);
// gives 10, 20, 30, 40, 50, 60, 70, 80, 90, 100

$float = range(1, 10, 1.2);
// gives 1, 2.2, 3.4, 4.6, 5.8, 7, 8.2, 9.4
```

Although the step parameter should always be positive, if your low parameter (parameter one) is higher than your high parameter (parameter two), you get an array counting down, like this:

```
$questions = range(100, 0, 10);
// gives 100, 90, 80, 70, 60, 50, 40, 30, 20, 10, 0
```

Finally, you can also use range( ) to create arrays of characters, like this:

```
$questions = range("a", "z", 1);
// gives a, b, c, d, ..., x, y, z

$questions = range("z", "a", 2);
// gives z, x, v, t, ..., f, d, b
```

shuffle( )

```
bool shuffle ( array &arr )
```

The shuffle( ) function takes an array as its parameter, and randomizes the position of the elements in there. It takes its parameter by reference—the return value is either true or false, depending on whether it successfully randomized the array. For example:

```
$natural_born_killers = array("lions", "tigers", "bears", "kittens");
shuffle($natural_born_killers);
```

One major drawback to using shuffle( ) is that it mangles your array keys. This is unavoidable, sadly.

Multidimensional Arrays

Currently our arrays just hold standard, non-array variables, which makes them one-dimensional. In constrast, a two-dimensional array is where each element holds another array as its value, and each element in the child array holds a non-array variable. This allows us to store arrays within arrays (and arrays within arrays within arrays, etc.), and therefore lets us store much more information. Consider this script:

```
$capitalcities['England'] = array("Capital"=>"London", "Population"=>
40000000, "NationalSport"=>"Cricket");
$capitalcities['Wales'] = array("Capital"=>"Cardiff", "Population"=>5000000,
"NationalSport"=>"Rugby");
$capitalcities['Scotland'] = array("Capital"=>"Edinburgh", "Population"=>
8000000, "NationalSport"=>"Football");
var_dump($capitalcities);
```

That creates the $capitalcities array elements as before, but uses an array for each value. Each child array has three elements: Capital, Population, and NationalSport. At the end, there is a var_dump( ) call on the parent array, which gives this output:

```
array(3) {
        ["England"]=>
        array(3) {
                ["Capital"]=>
                string(6) "London"
                ["Population"]=>
                int(40000000)
                ["NationalSport"]=>
                string(7) "Cricket"
        }
        ["Wales"]=>
        array(3) {
                ["Capital"]=>
                string(7) "Cardiff"
                ["Population"]=>
                int(5000000)
                ["NationalSport"]=>
                string(5) "Rugby"
        }
        ["Scotland"]=>
        array(3) {
                ["Capital"]=>
                string(9) "Edinburgh"
                ["Population"]=>
```

```
        int(8000000)
        ["NationalSport"]=>
        string(8) "Football"
    }
}
```

Not only does var_dump( ) recurse into child arrays to output their contents too, but it indents all the output according to the array level.

 The count( ) function has a helpful second parameter that, when set to 1, makes count( ) perform a recursive count. The difference is that if you pass in a multidimensional array, count( ) will count all the elements in the first array, then go into the first array element and count all the elements in there, and go into any elements in there, etc. For example, the $capitalcities array above has three elements; if you do not use the second parameter to count( ), you will get 3 back. However, if you pass in 1 for the second parameter, you will get 12: three for the first-level elements (England, Wales, Scotland), and three each for the variables inside those elements (Capital, Population, NationalSport).

The Array Cursor

Each array has a "cursor," which you can think of as an arrow pointing to the next array element in line to be operated on. It is the array cursor that allows code like while (list($var, $val) = each($array)) to work—each( ) moves forward the array cursor of its parameter each time it is called, until it eventually finds itself at the end of the array, and so returns false, ending the loop.

The each( ) function does not move the array cursor back to the first element when you first call it; it just picks up from where the cursor was. It is in situations like this where you need to set the position of the array cursor forcibly, and the functions reset( ), end( ), next( ), and prev( ) do just that. They all take just one parameter—the array to work with—and return a value from that array.

You use the reset( ) function to rewind its parameter's cursor to the first element, then return the value of that element, whereas end( ) will set the array cursor to the last element and return that value. The next( ) and prev( ) functions both move the cursor pointer forward or backward one element respectively, returning the value of the element now pointed to. If any of the four functions cannot return a value (if there are no elements in the array, or if the array cursor has gone past the last element), they will return false. As such, you can use them all in loops if you want.

For example, this iterates over an array in reverse:

```
$array = array("Foo", "Bar", "Baz", "Wom", "Bat");
print end($array);

while($val = prev($array)) {
        print $val;
}
```

Note that we print the output of end( ), because it sets the array cursor to point at "Bat", and prev( ) will shift the array cursor back one to "Wom", meaning that "Bat" would otherwise not be printed out.

Holes in Arrays

Using prev( ) and next( ) is more difficult when using arrays that have holes. For example:

```
$array["a"] = "Foo";
$array["b"] = "";
$array["c"] = "Baz";
$array["d"] = "Wom";
print end($array);

while($val = prev($array)) {
        print $val;
}
```

You may think that will iterate over an array in reverse, printing out values as it goes; however, the value at key b is empty, which will cause both prev( ) and next( ) to think that the end of the array has been reached. So, when they hit b, they will return false, prematurely ending the while loop.

In this situation, it would have been better to reverse the array, then use each( ) to iterate over it. This will cope fine with empty variables and unknown keys.

Using Arrays in Strings

If you want to print array data inside a string, you need to use braces, { and }, around the variable to tell PHP that you are passing it an array to read from. This next code shows how:

```
$myarray['foo'] = "bar";
print "This is from an array: {$myarray['foo']}\n";
```

Saving Arrays

The serialize( ) function converts an array, given as its only parameter, into a normal string that you can save in a file, a session, and so on. The opposite of serialize( ) is unserialize( ), which takes a serialized string and converts it back to an array.

The two functions urlencode( ) and urldecode( ) also work in tandem, and convert their string parameter into a version that is safe to be passed across the web. All characters that aren't letters and numbers get converted into web-safe codes that can be converted back into the original text using urldecode( ).

Passing arrays across pages is best done using urlencode( ) and urldecode( ); however, you should consider using them both on any data you pass across the web, just to ensure there are no incompatible characters in there.

Take a look at this next script:

```
$array["a"] = "Foo";
$array["b"] = "Bar";
$array["c"] = "Baz";

$str = serialize($array);
$strenc = urlencode($str);
print $str . "\n";
print $strenc . "\n";
```

That will output two lines (the second of which I've forced to wrap so that it appears properly):

```
a:4:{s:1:"a";s:3:"Foo";s:1:"b";s:3:"Bar";s:1:"c";s:3:"Baz";s:1:"d";}
```

```
a%3A4%3A%7Bs%3A1%3A%22a%22%3Bs%3A3%3A%22Foo%22%3Bs%3A1%3A%22b%22
%3Bs%3A0%3A%22%22%3Bs%3A1%3A%22c%22%3Bs%3A3%3A%22Baz%22%3B%7D
```

The first is the direct, serialized output of our array, and you can see how it works by looking through the text inside there. The second line contains the urlencoded serialized array, and is harder to read (and web safe).

Once your array is in text form, you can do with it as you please. To return to the original array, it needs to be urldecode( )d, then unserialize( )d, like this:

```
$arr = unserialize(urldecode($strenc));
var_dump($arr);
```

6

Operators

In this chapter, we look at operators, which are the symbols such as + (adding), - (subtracting), and * (multiplying).

Operators are like functions in that they do something with values, but they use symbols rather than function names. In the equation 2 + 3, the 2 and the 3 are both operands, and the + is the operator. There are three types of operators: unary, binary, and ternary, which take one, two, and three operands respectively. As you can see, the + operator (used to add numerical values) is a binary operator, because it takes two variables as input.

Arithmetic Operators

The arithmetic operators handle basic numerical operations, such as addition and multiplication. The full list is shown in Table 6-1.

Table 6-1. The arithmetic operators

+	Addition	Returns the first value added to the second: $a + $b.
-	Subtraction	Returned the second value subtracted from the first: $a - $b.
*	Multiplication	Returns the first value multiplied by the second: $a * $b.
/	Division	Returns the first value divided by the second: $a / $b.
%	Modulus	Divides the first value into the second, then returns the remainder: $a % $b. This only works on integers, and the result will be negative if $a is negative.
+=	Shorthand addition	Adds the second value to the first: $a += $b. Equivalent to $a = $a + $b.
-=	Shorthand subtraction	Subtracts the second value from the first: $a -= $b. Equivalent to $a = $a - $b.
*=	Shorthand multiplication	Multiplies the first value by the second: $a *= $b. Equivalent to $a = $a * $b.
/=	Shorthand division	Divides the first value into the second: $a /= $b. Equivalent to $a = $a / $b.

If you're looking for an exponentiation operator—something that raises a number to the power of an exponent—then you should use the pow( ) function discussed in Chapter 7. Like C++ and Java, PHP has no operator equivalent to the ** operator found in Perl, so you should use pow( ).

To calculate $a % $b, you first perform $a / $b and then return the remainder. For example, if $a were 10 and $b were 3, $b would go into $a 3 whole times (making nine) with a remainder of 1. Therefore, 10 % 3 is 1. Here are some examples, with their answers in comments:

```
$a = 10;
$b = 4;
$c = 3.33;
$d = 3.99999999;
$e = -10;
$f = -4;

print $a % $b; // 2
print $a % $c; // 1
print $a % $d; // 1
print $a % $f; // 2
print $e % $b; // -2
print $e % $f; // -2
```

Line two returns 1 rather than 0.01 because the floating-point number 3.33 gets typecasted to an integer, giving 3. The float is *not* rounded, as can be seen on line three, where 3.99999999 still goes into 10 with 1 remainder, because everything after the decimal point is simply chopped off.

On line four ($a % $f), the result is 2 as in line one, because modulus only returns a negative number when the first value is negative. This is shown in line five with -10 and 4; this yields -2 because 4 goes into 10 twice with a remainder of 2, but the first value was negative, so the result is negative. The last line gets the same result as line five even though both numbers are negative; again, only the sign of the first value is considered.

Assignment Operators

The assignment operators set the values of variables either by copying the value or copying a reference to a value. They are shown in Table 6-2.

Table 6-2. The assignment operators

=	Assignment	Copies $b's value into $a, unless $b is an object, in which case the same object is in both places: $a = $b
=&	Reference	Set $a to reference $b: $a =& $b

String Operators

There are only two string operators in PHP: concatenation and shorthand concatenation. Both are shown in Table 6-3.

Table 6-3. The string operators

.	Concatenation	Returns the second value appended to the first: $a . $b
.=	Shorthand concatenation	Appends the second value to the first: $a .= $b

These operators are used to join strings together, like this:

```
$first = "Hello, ";
$second = "world!";

// join $first and $second; assign to $third
$third = $first . $second;
// $third is now "Hello, world!"

$first .= " officer!";
// $first is now "Hello, officer!"
```

Bitwise Operators

Bitwise operators aren't used very often, and even then only by more advanced PHP programmers. They manipulate the binary digits of numbers, which is more control than many programmers need. The bitwise operators are listed in Table 6-4.

Table 6-4. The bitwise operators

&	And	Bits set in $a and $b are set.
|	Or	Bits set in $a or $b are set.
^	Xor	Bits set in $a or $b, but not both, are set.
~	Not	Bits set in $a are not set, and vice versa.
<<	Shift left	Shifts the bits of $a to the left by $b steps. This is equivalent, but faster, to multiplication. Each step counts as "multiply by two." If you try this with a float, PHP ignores everything after the decimal point and treats it as an integer.
>>	Shift right	Shifts the bits of $a to the right by $b steps.

To give an example, the number eight is represented in eight-bit binary as 00001000. In a shift left, <<, all the bits literally get shifted one place to the left, giving 00010000, which is equal to sixteen. Eight shifted left by four gives 10000000, which is equal to 128—the same number you would have gotten by multiplying eight by two four times in a row.

The & (bitwise and) operator compares all the bits in operand one against all the bits on operand two, then returns a result with all the joint bits set. Here's an example: given 52 & 28, we have the eight-bit binary numbers 00110100 (52) and

00011100 (28). PHP creates a result of 00000000, then proceeds to compare each digit in both numbers—whenever it finds a 1 in both values, it puts a 1 into the result in the same place. Here is how that looks:

```
00110100 (52)
00011100 (28)
00010100 (20)
```

Therefore, 52 & 28 gives 20.

Perhaps the most common bitwise operator is |, which compares bits in operand one against those in operand two, and returns a result with all the bits set in either of them. For example:

```
00110100 (52)
11010001 (209)
11110101 (245)
```

The reason the | (bitwise or) operator is so useful is because it allows you to combine many options together. For example, the flock( ) function for locking files takes a constant as its second parameter that describes how you want to lock the file. If you pass LOCK_EX, you lock the file exclusively; if you pass LOCK_SH, you lock the file in shared mode; and if you pass LOCK_NB, you enable "non-blocking" mode, which stops PHP from waiting if no lock is available. However, what if you want an exclusive lock and to not have PHP wait if no lock is available? You pass LOCK_EX | LOCK_NB, and PHP combines the two into one parameter that does both.

Comparison Operators

Comparison operators return either true or false, and thus are suitable for use in conditions. PHP has several to choose from, and they are listed in Table 6-5.

Table 6-5. The comparison operators

==	Equals	True if $a is equal to $b
===	Identical	True if $a is equal to $b and of the same type
!=	Not equal	True if $a is not equal to $b
<>	Not equal	True if $a is not equal to $b
!==	Not identical	True if $a is not equal to $b or if they are not of the same type
<	Less than	True if $a is less than $b
>	Greater than	True if $a is greater than $b
<=	Less than or equal	True if $a is less than or equal to $b
>=	Greater than or equal	True if $a is greater than or equal to $b

Comparison operators such as <, >, and == return true or false depending on the result of the comparison, and it is this value that PHP uses to decide actions. For example:

```
if ($foo < 10) {
        // do stuff
}
```

The less-than operator, <, will compare $foo to 10, and if it is less than (but not equal to) 10, then < will return true. This will make the line read if (true) {. Naturally, true is always true, so the true block of the if statement will execute.

PHP programmers prefer != to <>, despite them doing the same thing. This bias is because PHP's syntax is based on C, which uses != exclusively, and it is worth holding on to. For example, 9 <> "walrus" is true, but not because 9 is either greater or less than "walrus" as the notation <> suggests. In this example, != just makes more sense.

The === (identical) operator is used very rarely compared to == (equality), but is useful nonetheless. Two variables are only identical if they hold the same value and if they are the same type, as demonstrated in this code example:

```
print 12 == 12;
print 12.0 == 12;
print (0 + 12.0) == 12;
print 12 + === 12;
print "12" == 12;
print "12" === 12;
```

When you run that script using the CLI SAPI, you will find PHP outputs a 1 for the first 5 lines, and nothing for the last line. As mentioned already, PHP outputs a 1 for true, which means that the statements 12 equals 12, 12.0 equals 12, 0 + 12.0 equals 12, 12 is identical to 12, and "12" equals 12 are all true. However, nothing is output for the sixth line, which means that PHP considers the statement to be false, which is expected. Although "12" and 12 are the same value, they are not the same type; the former is a string, and the latter is an integer.

The === operator becomes important when you want to ensure PHP's type conversion isn't getting in the way of what you are trying to do. For example, PHP considers an empty string (""), 0, and false to be equal when used with ==, but using === allows you to make the distinction. For example:

```
if (0 === false) {
        // this is true
}

if (0 === false) {
        // this is false
}
```

The strpos() function returns the index at which it found one string inside another. If it finds a match at character 0, it returns 0; if it finds no match at all, it returns false. As a result, you should be careful to use === when checking the return value of strpos(), so that you don't get confused between the two outcomes.

Incrementing and Decrementing Operators

The next two operators do different things, depending on where you place them. The difference is explained in Table 6-6.

Table 6-6. The incrementing and decrementing operators

++$a	Pre-increment	Increments $a by one, then returns $a
$a++	Post-increment	Returns $a, then increments $a by one
--$a	Pre-decrement	Decrements $a by one, then returns $a
$a--	Post-decrement	Returns $a, then decrements $a by one

The incrementing and decrementing operators can be placed either before or after a variable, and the effect is different depending on where the operator is placed. Here's a code example:

```
$foo = 5;
$bar = $foo++;
print "Foo is $foo\n";
print "Bar is $bar\n";
```

That will output the following:

```
Foo is 6
Bar is 5
```

The reason behind this is that ++, when placed after a variable, is the post-increment operator, which immediately returns the original value of the variable before incrementing it. In line 2 of our script, the value of $foo (5) is returned and stored in $bar, *then* $foo is incremented by one. If we had put the ++ before $foo rather than after it, $foo would have been incremented *then* returned, which would have made both $foo and $bar 6.

Logical Operators

When resolving equations using logic, you can choose from one of six operators, listed in Table 6-7.

Table 6-7. The logical operators

AND	Logical AND	True if both $a and $b are true
&&	Logical AND	True if both $a and $b are true
OR	Logical OR	True if either $a or $b is true
||	Logical OR	True if either $a or $b is true
XOR	Logical XOR	True if either $a or $b is true, but not both
!	Logical NOT	Inverts true to false and false to true: ! $a

There are two operators for logical AND and two for logical OR—this is to facilitate operator precedence in more complicated expressions. The && and || are more commonly used than their AND and OR counterparts because they are executed before the assignment operator, which is usually what you would expect. For example:

```
$a = $b && $c;
```

Most people would read that as "set $a to be true if both $b and $c are true," and that is correct. However, if you replace the && with AND, the assignment operator is executed first, which makes PHP read the expression like this:

```
($a = $b) AND $c;
```

This is sometimes the desired behavior. For example, one common use for the OR operator involves the die( ) function, which causes PHP to terminate execution immediately, like this:

```
do_some_func( ) OR die("do_some_func( ) returned false!");
```

In that situation, do_some_func( ) will be called, and, if it returns false, die( ) will be called to terminate the script. The reason that code works is because the OR operator tells PHP to execute the second function only if the first function returns false.

PHP uses conditional statement short-circuiting, which is a fancy way of saying, "If you write code that says A or B must be true, and PHP finds A to be true, it will not bother evaluating B because the condition is already satisfied." You can use OR very successfully with function calls so that PHP will attempt to run the first function, and, if that function returns false, PHP will run the second function.

Some Operator Examples

Here are some examples of most of these operators in action:

```
$somevar = 5 + 5; // 10
$somevar = 5 - 5; // 0
$somevar = 5 + 5 - (5 + 5); // 0
$somevar = 5 * 5; // 25
$somevar = 10 * 5 - 5; // 45
$somevar = $somevar . "appended to end";
$somevar = false;
$somevar = !$somevar; // $somevar is now set to true
$somevar = 5;
$somevar++; // $somevar is now 6
$somevar--; // $somevar is now 5 again
++$somevar; // $somevar is 6
```

The third line uses parentheses to control the order of operations. This is important, as the equation 5 + 5 - 5 + 5 can be taken in more than one way, such as 5 + (5 - 5) + 5, which is 10. There are some equations, such as the one on line five, where parentheses are not needed. There, 10 * 5 - 5 can only be taken to mean (10 * 5) - 5 because of the mathematical rules of precedence (rules of operations)— multiplication is considered higher in order (executed first) than subtraction.

Despite each operator having specific precedence, it is still best to use parentheses in order to make your meaning clear. Expressions inside parentheses are always evaluated first, and you can use any number of parentheses in order to get the expression correct.

The Ternary Operator

The ternary operator is so named because it is the only operator that takes three operands: a condition, a result for true, and a result for false. If that sounds like an if statement to you, you are right on the money—the ternary operator is a shorthand (albeit very hard to read) way of doing if statements. Here's an example:

```
$agestr = ($age < 16) ? 'child' : 'adult';
```

First there is a condition ($age < 16), then there is a question mark, and then a true result, a colon, and a false result. If $age is less than 16, $agestr will be set to 'child'; otherwise, it will be set to 'adult'. That one-liner ternary statement can be expressed in a normal if statement like this:

```
if ($age < 16) {
        $agestr = 'child';
} else {
        $agestr = 'adult';
}
```

So, in essence, using the ternary operator allows you to compact five lines of code into one, at the expense of some readability.

You can nest ternary operators by adding further conditions into either the true or the false operands. For example:

```
$population = 400000;

$city_size =
        $population < 30 ? "hamlet"
          : ($population < 1000 ? "village"
          : ($population < 10000 ? "town"
          : "city"))
        ;

    print $city_size;
```

In that example, PHP first checks whether $population is less than 30. If it is, then $city_size is set to hamlet; if not, then PHP checks whether $population is less than 1000. Note that an extra parenthesis is placed before the second check, so that PHP correctly groups the remainder of the statement as part of the "$population is not less than 30" block. Finally, if $population is not less than 10,000, $city_size is set to "city," with no further checks. At this point, you need to close the parentheses you have opened inside the stacked conditions.

The Execution Operator

PHP uses backticks (`) as its execution operator. Backticks are used very rarely in normal typing, so you might have trouble finding where yours is—it is usually to the left of the 1 key on your keyboard.

Backticks allow you to pass commands directly to the operating system for execution, then capture the results. PHP replaces the result of the execution with what you asked to be executed. For example:

```
print `ls`;
```

That will run the command ls and output its results to the screen. If you are using Windows, you will need to use dir instead, as ls is only available on Unix. You can perform any commands inside backticks that you would normally perform directly from the command line, including piping output to and from and/or redirecting output through other programs.

There are several functions that perform program execution like the execution operator—you can find a more comprehensive reference to them in Chapter 7. Either way, you should be very wary about executing external programs from PHP because of potential security problems.

Operator Precedence and Associativity

Like many languages, PHP has a set of rules (known as operator precedence and associativity) that decide how complicated expressions are processed. For example:

```
$foo = 5 * 10 - 1;
```

Should $foo be 49 or 45? If you cannot see why there are two possibilities, break them up using parentheses like this:

```
$foo = (5 * 10) - 1
$foo = 5 * (10 - 1);
```

In the first example, five is multiplied by ten, then one is subtracted from the result. But in the second example, ten has one subtracted from it, making nine, then that result is multiplied by five. If there is ambiguity in your expressions, PHP will resolve them according to its internal set of rules about operator precedence.

However, there's more to it than that—consider the following statement:

```
$foo = 5 - 5 - 5;
```

Like the previous statement, this can have two possible results, 5 and -5. Here is how those two possibilities would look if we made our intentions explicit with parentheses:

```
$foo = 5 - (5 - 5);
$foo = (5 - 5) - 5;
```

In this example, it is operator associativity that governs which answer is correct. PHP has been programmed to consider each operator left-associative, right-associative, or non-associative. For example, given the make-believe operator μ, it might be right-associative and therefore treated like this:

```
$foo = $a   $b   $c;
// would be treated as...
$foo = ($a   ($b   $c));
```

If PHP is programmed with μ as left-associative, it would start working from the left:

```
$foo = $a   $b   $c;
// would be treated as...
$foo = (($a   $b)   $c);
```

The equation 5 - 5 - 5 results in -5 because the subtraction operator is left-associative, giving (5 - 5) - 5.

These rules are only enforced if you fail to be explicit about your instructions. Unless you have very specific reason to do otherwise, you should always use parentheses in your expressions to make your actual meaning very clear—both to PHP and to others reading your code.

If you must rely on PHP's built-in rules for precedence and associativity, refer to Table 6-8 for the complete list of operators, precedence, and their associativity, ordered by the lowest-precedence operator to the highest-precedence operator:

Table 6-8. Operators, precedence, and their associativity

Operators	Associativity	
,	Left	"$x, $y, $z" is "($x, $y), $z"
or	Left	"$x OR $y OR $z" is "($x OR $y) OR $z"
xor	left	"x XOR y XOR z" is "($x XOR $y) XOR $z"
and	Left	"x AND y AND z" is "(x AND y) AND z"
= += -= *= /= .= %= &= |= ^= <<= >>=	Right	"$x /= $y /= $z" is "$x /= ($y /= $z)"
? :	Left	
||	Left	; "$x || $y || $z" is "($x || $y) || $z"
&&	Left	"$x && $y && $z" is "($x && $y) && $z"
|	Left	"$x | $y | $z" is "($x | $y) | $z"
^	Left	"$x ^ $y ^ $z" is "($x ^ $y) ^ $z"
&	Left	"$x & $y & $z" is "($x & $y) & $z"
== != === !==	Non-associative	
< <= > >=	Non-associative	
<< >>	Left	"$x >> $y >> $z" is "($x >> $y) >> $z"
+ - .	Left	"$x - $y - $z" is "($x - $y) - $z"
* / %	Left	"$x / $y / $z" is "($x / $y) / $z"
! ~ ++ -- (int) (float) (string) (array) (object) @	Right;	
[	Right	
new	Non-associative	

7

Function Reference

This chapter lists many of the most commonly used functions in PHP. Other functions are grouped together according to their topic, throughout this book.

Calling a function in PHP can be as simple as printing the name of a function with two parentheses, "()", after it. However, many functions require you to give them input to work on, called parameters, which you send inside the parentheses. On top of that, nearly all functions have a return value, which is the result that the function sends back to your script. These return values can often be ignored, but most of the time, you will want to store them in a variable for later use:

```
$string_length = strlen($mystring);
```

You can also use these return values as parameters to other functions, like this:

```
func1(func2(func3( ), func4( )));
```

Although most parameters are required, some are optional and don't need to be supplied. When optional parameters are omitted, PHP will assume a default value, which is usually good enough.

When you pass a parameter to a function, PHP copies it and uses that copy inside the function. This process is known as *pass by value*, because it is the value that is sent into the function rather than the variable. This means that when you pass variables to a function, it can change its copies of them however it likes, without affecting the original variables. To change this behavior, you can opt to pass by reference, which works in the same way as reference assigning for variables—PHP passes the actual variable into the function, and any changes you make will affect the original. This script demonstrates the difference:

```
somefunc($foo);
somefunc($foo, $bar);
somefunc($foo, &$bar);
somefunc(&$foo, &$bar);
```

The first line calls somefunc( ), passing in a copy of $foo; the second passes in copies of $foo and $bar; the third passes in a copy of $foo but the original $bar; and the last passes in both the original $foo and $bar. Passing by reference, as with $bar in line three and $foo and $bar in line four, means that these variables can be changed inside the function, which is often used as a way for functions to return information.

Variable variables were introduced in Chapter 5, and to complement them, PHP also has variable functions, allowing you to write code like this:

```
$func = "sqrt";
print $func(49);
```

PHP sees that you are calling a function using a variable, looks up the value of the variable, then calls the matching function. The code above will therefore return 7, the square root of 49.

Undocumented Functions

Despite the fact that the PHP documentation team works around the clock to document the language and all its functions, there are still quite a few functions you will not find in the PHP manual. That is not to say they are unimportant— just that either very few people know how to use them, or no one has had enough time to get around to them yet.

Although several of these functions are discussed in this book, there are probably dozens more still around. A list of all the undocumented functions is available at *http://zend.com/phpfunc/nodoku.php*. Sometimes the only way to be certain is to look up the source code yourself.

Handling Non-English Characters

ASCII only allows a set of 256 characters to be used to describe the alphanumeric characters available to print. That range, 0 to 255, is used because it is the size of a *byte*—8 ones and zeros, in computing terminology. Languages such as Chinese, Korean, and Japanese have special characters in them, which means you need more than 256 characters, and therefore need more than one byte of space—you need a *multibyte* character. The multibyte character implementation in PHP is capable of working with Unicode-based encodings, such as UTF-8; however, at this time, Unicode support in PHP is very weak. Full Unicode support is currently one of the key goals for future releases of PHP.

Dealing with these complex characters is slightly different from working with normal characters, because functions like substr( ) and strtoupper( ) expect precisely one byte per character and will corrupt a multibyte string. Instead, you should use the multibyte equivalents of these functions, such as mb_strtoupper( ) instead of strtoupper( ), mb_ereg_match( ) rather than ereg_match( ), and mb_strlen( ) rather than strlen( ). The parameters required for these functions are the same as their originals, except that most accept an optional extra parameter to force specific encoding.

If there is an existing script that you'd like to multibyte-enable, there's a special *php.ini* setting you can change: `mbstring.func_overload`. By default, this is set to 0, which means functions behave as you would expect them to. If you set it to 1, calling the `mail()` function gets silently rerouted to the `mb_send_mail()` function. If you set it to 2, all the functions starting with "str" get rerouted to their multi-byte partners. If you set it to 4, all the "ereg" functions get rerouted. You can combine these together as you please by simply adding them—for example, for "mail" and "str" rerouting, you add 1 and 2, giving 3, so you set `mbstring.func_overload` to 3 to overload these two. To overload everything, set it to 7, which is 1 ("mail") + 2 ("str") + 4 ("ereg").

abs( )

> `number abs ( number num )`

The `abs()` function returns the absolute value of the parameter you pass to it. By absolute, I mean that it leaves positive values untouched, and converts negative values into positive values. Thus:

```
abs(50); // 50
abs(-12); // 12
```

You can either send a floating-point number or an integer to `abs()`, and it will return the same type:

```
abs(50.1); // 50.1
abs(-12.5); // 12.5
```

The `abs()` function is helpful for handling user input, such as "How many t-shirts would you like to buy?" While you could write code to check for values equal to or under 0, and issue warnings if appropriate, it is easier to put all quantity input through `abs()` to ensure it is positive.

acos( )

> `float acos ( float num )`

The `acos()` function calculates the arc cosine value of the number provided as its only parameter, essentially reversing the operation of `cos()`. The return value is in radians—you should use the `rad2deg()` to convert radians to degrees.

```
$acos1 = acos(0.4346);
$acos2 = acos(cos(80));
```

addslashes( )

> `string addslashes ( string str )`

There are many situations where single quotes ('), double quotes ("), and backslashes (\) can cause problems—databases, files, and some protocols require that you escape them with \, making \', \", and \\ respectively. In these circumstances, you should use the `addslashes()` function, which takes a string as its only parameter and returns the same string with these offending characters escaped so that they are safe for use.

In *php.ini*, there is a `magic_quotes_gpc` option that you can set to enable "magic quotes" functionality. If enabled, PHP will automatically call `addslashes()` on every piece of data sent in from users, which can sometimes be a good thing. However, in reality it is often annoying—particularly when you plan to use your variables in other ways.

Note that calling addslashes( ) repeatedly will add more and more slashes, like this:

```
$string = "I'm a lumberjack and I'm okay!";
$a = addslashes($string);
$b = addslashes($a);
$c = addslashes($b);
```

After running that code, you will have the following:

```
$a: I\'m a lumberjack and I\'m okay!
$b: I\\\'m a lumberjack and I\\\'m okay!
$c: I\\\\\\\'m a lumberjack and I\\\\\\\'m okay!
```

The reason the number of slashes increases so quickly is because PHP will add a slash before each single and double quote, as well as slashes before every existing slash.

The addslashes( ) function has a counterpart, stripslashes( ), that removes one set of slashes.

 If you can, use a database-specific escaping function instead of addslashes( ). For example, if you're using MySQL, use mysql_escape_string( ).

asin( )

```
float asin ( float num )
```

The asin( ) function calculates the arc sine value of the number provided as its only parameter, essentially reversing the operation of sine( ). The return value is in radians—you should use the rad2deg( ) to convert radians to degrees.

```
$asin1 = asin(0.4346);
$asin2 = asin(sin(80));
```

atan( )

```
float atan ( float num )
```

The atan( ) function calculates the arc tangent value of the number provided as its only parameter, essentially reversing the operation of tan( ). The return value is in radians—you should use the rad2deg( ) to convert radians to degrees.

```
$atan1 = atan(0.4346);
$atan2 = atan(tan(80));
```

base_convert( )

```
string base_convert ( string num, int from_base, int to_base )
```

It is impractical for PHP to include separate functions to convert every base to every other base, so they are grouped into one function: base_convert( ). This takes three parameters: a number to convert, the base to convert from, and the base to convert to. For example, the following two lines are identical:

```
print decbin(16);
print base_convert("16", 10, 2);
```

The latter is just a more verbose way of saying "convert the number 16 from base 10 to base 2." The advantage of using base_convert( ) is that we can now convert binary directly to hexadecimal, or even crazier combinations, such as octal to duodecimal (base 12) or hexadecimal to vigesimal (base 20).

The highest base that base_convert( ) supports is base 36, which uses 0–9 and then A–Z. If you try to use a base larger than 36, you will get an error.

bindec( )

```
number bindec ( string binary_num )
```

The bindec( ) function converts a binary number into a decimal number. It takes just one parameter, which is the number to convert. For example:

```
print decbin("10000"); // 16
```

call_user_func( )

```
mixed call_user_func ( function callback [, mixed param1 [, mixed ...]] )
```

The call_user_func( ) function is a special way to call an existing PHP function. It takes the function to call as its first parameter, with the parameters to pass into the variable function as multiple parameters to itself. For example:

```
$func = "str_replace";
$output_single = call_user_func($func, "monkeys", "giraffes", "Hundreds and
thousands of monkeys\n");
```

In that example, "monkeys", "giraffes", and "Hundreds of thousands of monkeys" are the second, third, and fourth parameters to call_user_func( ), but get passed into str_replace( ) (the function in $func) as the first, second, and third parameters.

An alternative to this function is call_user_func_array( ), where the parameters to be passed are grouped in an array.

call_user_func_array( )

```
mixed call_user_func_array ( function callback, array params )
```

The call_user_func_array( ) function is a special way to call an existing PHP function. It takes a function to call as its first parameter, then takes an array of parameters as its second parameter.

```
$func = "str_replace";
$params = array("monkeys", "giraffes", "Hundreds and thousands of monkeys\
n");
$output_array = call_user_func_array($func, $params);
echo $output_array;
```

ceil( )

```
float ceil ( float num )
```

The ceil( ) function takes a floating-point number as its only parameter and rounds it to the nearest integer above its current value. If you provide an integer, nothing will happen. For example:

```
$number = ceil(11.9); // 12
$number = ceil(11.1); // 12
$number = ceil(11); // 11
```

chr( )

```
string chr ( int ascii_val )
```

To convert an ASCII number to its character equivalent, use the chr( ) function. This takes an ASCII value as its parameter and returns the character equivalent, if there is one.

```
$letter = chr(109);
print "ASCII number 109 is equivalent to $letter\n";
```

That would output "ASCII number 109 is equivalent to m". The ord( ) function does the opposite of chr( ): it takes a string and returns the equivalent ASCII value.

connection_status( )

```
int connection_status ( void )
```

The connection_status( ) function takes no parameters and returns 0 if the connection is live and execution is still taking place; 1 if the connection is aborted; 2 if the connection has been aborted; and 3 if the connection has been aborted and subsequently timed out.

The last situation is only possible if ignore_user_abort(true) has been used, and the script subsequently timed out. The values 0, 1, 2, and 3 evaluate to the constants CONNECTION_NORMAL, CONNECTION_ABORTED, CONNECTION_TIMEOUT, and CONNECTION_ABORTED | CONNECTION_TIMEOUT (a bitwise OR of the previous two).

This script can tell the difference between shutdown occurring because the script finished or because script timeout was reached:

```
function say_goodbye( ) {
        if (connection_status( ) == CONNECTION_TIMEOUT) {
                print "Script timeout!\n";
        } else {
                print "Goodbye!\n";
        }
}

register_shutdown_function("say_goodbye");
set_time_limit(1);
print "Sleeping...\n";
sleep(2);
print "Done!\n";
```

cos( )

```
float cos ( float num )
```

The cos( ) function calculates the cosine value of the number provided as its only parameter. The parameter should be passed as radians—you should use deg2rad( ) to convert degrees to radians.

```
$cos1 = cos(10);
$cos2 = cos(deg2rad(80));
```

count_chars( )

```
mixed count_chars ( string str [, int mode] )
```

The count_chars( ) function takes a string parameter and returns an array containing the letters used in that string and how many times each letter was used.

Using count_chars( ) is complicated by the fact that it actually returns an array of exactly 255 elements by default, with each number in there evaluating to an ASCII code. You can work around this by passing a second parameter to the function. If you pass 1, only letters with a frequency greater than 0 are listed; if you pass 2, only letters with a frequency equal to 0 are listed. For example:

```
$str = "This is a test, only a test, and nothing but a test.";
$a = count_chars($str, 1);
print_r($a);
```

That will output the following:

```
Array ( [32] => 11 [44] => 2 [46] => 1 [84] => 1 [97] => 4 [98] => 1 [100]
=> 1 [101] => 3 [103] => 1 [104] => 2 [105] => 3 [108] => 1 [110] => 4 [111]
=> 2 [115] => 5 [116] => 8 [117] => 1 [121] => 1)
```

In that output, ASCII codes are used for the array keys, and the frequencies of each letter are used as the array values.

date( )

```
string date ( string date_format [, int timestamp] )
```

Users like to have their dates in a variety of formats, so PHP lets you convert timestamps into different types of strings using the date( ) function.

You can send two parameters to date( ), with the second one being optional, as with strtotime( ). Parameter one is a special string containing formatting codes for how you want the timestamp converted, and parameter two is the timestamp you want to convert. If you do not supply the second parameter, PHP assumes you want to convert the current time.

Parameter one is tricky: it is a string of letters from a predefined list of 31 possibles. You can use other characters in the string, and these are copied directly into the formatted date. If you are trying to put words into the date format that you do not want to be converted into their date equivalent, you need to escape them with a backslash, \. To make things even more confusing, if your escaped letter is an existing escape sequence, then you need to escape it again!

The complete list of date format characters is shown in Table 7-1. Be careful, as they are case-sensitive!

Table 7-1. Format characters for use in date( )

Format character	Description	Example
a	Lowercase am/pm	am or pm
A	Uppercase am/pm	AM or PM
B	Swatch Internet Time	000 to 999
c	ISO 8601 date, time, and time zone	2004-06-18T09:26:55+01:00
d	2-digit day of month, leading zeros	01 to 31
D	Day string, three letters	Mon, Thu, Sat
F	Month string, full	January, August
g	12-hour clock hour, no leading zeros	1 to 12
G	24-hour clock hour, no leading zeros	0 to 23
h	12-hour clock hour, leading zeros	01 to 12
H	24-hour clock hour, leading zeros	00 to 23
i	Minutes with leading zeros	00 to 59
I	Is daylight savings time active?	1 if yes, 0 if no
j	Day of month, no leading zeros	1 to 31
l	Day string, full	Monday, Saturday
L	Is it a leap year?	1 if yes, 0 if no
m	Numeric month, leading zeros	01 to 12
M	Short month string	Jan, Aug
n	Numeric month, no leading zeros	1 to 12
O	Difference from GMT	200
r	RFC-822 formatted date	Sat, 22 Dec 1979 17:30 +0000
s	Seconds, with leading zeros	00 to 59
S	English ordinal suffix for day number	st, nd, rd, or th
t	Number of days in month	28 to 31
T	Time zone for server	GMT, CET, EST
U	Unix Timestamp	1056150334
w	Numeric day of week	0 (Sunday), 6 (Saturday)
W	ISO-8601 week number of year	30 (30th week of the year)
y	Two-digit representation of year	97, 02
Y	Four-digit representation of year	1997, 2002
z	Day of year	0 to 366
Z	Time zone offset in seconds	-43200 to 43200

This first example of date( ) is very basic and prints out the current time in 24-hour clock format:

```
print date("H:i");
```

It's possible to mix the output of date( ) with a text string to get a natural-looking statement, like this:

```
print "The day yesterday was " . date("l", time( ) - 86400);
```

Note that on very specific occasions (particularly when daylight savings time kicks in), the above script will be incorrect. If you need absolute precision, either check for DST or subtract a whole day using mktime( ).

This next example outputs the date in the format of 31st of August 2005. Notice that we have the word of in the date format, and it has been passed through to the output instead of being converted. The reason for this is that lowercase O and lowercase F do not have any formatting purpose in the date function (although this may be changed in the future), so they are just copied straight into output:

```
print date("jS of F Y");
```

In the next example, our date( ) function is embedded between two other strings, which makes for particularly neat output:

```
print "My birthday is on a " . date("l", strtotime("22 Dec 2004")) . " this
year.";
```

decbin( )

```
string decbin ( int num )
```

The decbin( ) function converts a decimal number into a binary number. It takes just one parameter, which is the number to convert. For example:

```
print decbin(16); // "10000"
```

dechex( )

```
string dechex ( int num )
```

The dechex( ) function converts a decimal number into a binary number. It takes just one parameter, which is the number to convert. For example:

```
print dechex(232); // "e8"
```

decoct( )

```
string decoct ( int num )
```

The decoct( ) function converts a decimal number into an octal number. It takes just one parameter, which is the number to convert. For example:

```
print decoct(19); // "23"
```

deg2rad( )

```
float deg2rad ( float num )
```

The deg2rad( ) function converts degrees to radians. Radians are calculated as being $degrees multiplied by the mathematical constant pi, then divided by 180.

```
$sin1 = sin(deg2rad(80));
```

die( )

```
void exit ( [mixed status] )
```

The die( ) function terminates execution of a script, and is an alias of the exit( ) function.

```
$db = open_database( ) OR die("Couldn't open database!");
```

dl( )

```
int dl ( string extension_name )
```

Use the dl( ) function to load an extension at runtime, passing the name of the extension to load as its only parameter. Note that there are cross-platform considerations to using dl( ) that are discussed later. The downside to using dl( ) is that it needs to dynamically load and unload the extension each time your scripts run—this ends up being a great deal slower than running PHP as a web server module, where the extensions are loaded just once and kept in memory.

One last warning: using dl( ) with multithreaded web servers (such as Apache 2) will simply not work; you will need to use the static method of editing your *php.ini* file and restarting the server.

Here is an example of dl( ) on both Windows and Unix:

```
dl('php_imap.dll'); // Windows
dl('imap.so'); // Unix
```

empty( )

```
bool empty ( mixed var )
```

The empty( ) function returns true if its parameter has a false value. This is not the same as the isset( ): if a variable was set and had a false value (such as 0 or an empty string), empty( ) would return false, and isset( ) would return true.

```
$var1 = "0";
$var2 = "1";
$var3 = "";

if (empty($var1)) print "Var1 empty\n";
if (empty($var2)) print "Var2 empty\n";
if (empty($var3)) print "Var3 empty\n";
if (empty($var4)) print "Var4 empty\n";
```

That would print "Var1 empty", "Var3 empty", then "Var4 empty".

escapeshellcmd( )

```
string escapeshellcmd ( string command )
```

The escapeshellcmd( ) function is used to escape special characters in shell commands that may otherwise trick your script into running malicious code. If you ever plan to allow users to execute a program on your server—in itself a major security risk—you should always pass their variables through this function first. For example:

```
$_GET["search"] = escapeshellcmd($_GET["search"]);
passthru("grep {$_GET["search"] /var/www/meetinglogs/*");
```

eval( )

```
mixed eval ( string code )
```

You can execute the contents of a string as if it were PHP code using the eval( ) function. This takes just one string parameter and executes that string as PHP. For example:

```
$str = '$i = 1; print $i;';
eval($str);
```

That script assigns two PHP statements to $str, then passes $str into eval( ) for execution.

The eval( ) function allows you to store your PHP code in a database, or to build it at runtime, which gives you a lot more flexibility.

 If you are considering using eval( ), bear in mind these words from the creator of PHP, Rasmus Lerdorf: "If eval( ) is the answer, you're almost certainly asking the wrong question." That is, you should be able to achieve your goals without resorting to eval( ).

exec( )

```
string exec ( string command [, array &output [, int &return_val]] )
```

The exec( ) function runs an external program, specified in the first parameter. It sends back the last line outputted from that program as its return value, unlike passthru( ), which prints out all the output the program generates.

```
print exec("uptime");
```

The uptime command is available on most Unix systems and prints out just one line of output—perfect for exec( ).

Calling exec( ) is usually preferred when the output of your program is irrelevant, whereas passthru( ) automatically prints your output.

If you pass a second and third parameter to exec( ), the output of the command will be put into parameter two as an array with one line per element, and the numeric exit status of the command will be put into parameter three. Similarly, if you pass a second parameter to passthru( ), it will be filled with the return value of the command.

For example:

```
exec("dir", $output, $return);
echo "Dir returned $return, and output:\n";
var_dump($output);
```

That example should work fine on Windows, as well as on many versions of Unix.

 PHP's exec( ) is more like the Perl execution operator (`...`) than the Perl exec( ) function.

exit( )

```
void exit ( [mixed status] )
```

The exit( ) function takes just one optional parameter and immediately terminates execution of the script. If you pass it a parameter, this is used as the script exit code. If it is a string, it is printed out. The function die( ) is an alias of exit( ) and works the same way.

Use exit( ) wherever you need to end a script with no further work. For example:

```
if ($password != "frosties") {
        print "Access denied.";
        exit( ); // note: ( ) is optional
}
```

The exit( ) function takes a maximum of one parameter, which can either be a program return number or a string. Many programs return numbers so that they can be chained to other programs and their output properly judged. In this case, 0 usually means "Everything went OK," and everything else means "Something went wrong." Using exit( ) with a string causes PHP to output the string and then terminate the script—a behavior commonly used by programmers with exit( )'s alias, die( ), like this:

```
do_some_func( ) OR die("do_some_func( ) returned false!");
```

In that situation, do_some_func( ) will be called and, if it returns false, die( ) will be called to terminate the script.

floor( )

```
float floor ( float num )
```

The floor( ) function takes a floating-point number as its only parameter and rounds it to the nearest integer below its current value. If you provide an integer, nothing will happen. For example:

```
$number = floor(11.1); // 11
$number = floor(11.9); // 11
$number = floor(11); // 11
```

The floor( ) function converts a positive floating-point number to an integer in the same way as typecasting, except typecasting is faster. This is not true for negative numbers, where the two will produce different results because floor( ) rounds down (e.g., -3.5 becomes -4) and typecasting knocks off the non-integer data (e.g., -3.5 becomes -3).

function_exists( )

```
bool function_exists ( string function_name )
```

If you're working with functions that are not part of the PHP core (i.e., that need to be enabled by users), it's a smart move to use the function_exists( ) function. This takes a function name as its only parameter and returns true if that function (either built-in or one you've defined yourself) is available for use. It only checks whether the function is available, not whether it will work—your system may not be configured properly for some functions. Here is how it looks in code:

```
if (function_exists("imagepng")) {
        echo "You have the GD extension loaded.";
} else {
        echo "Can't find imagepng() - do you have GD loaded?";
}
```

 If you ever want to know whether you have a function available to you, use the function_exists() function. This takes one string parameter that is the name of a function and returns true if the function exists or false if it does not. Many people use function_exists() to find out whether they have an extension available, by calling function_exists() on a function of that extension. However, this is accomplished more easily with the extension_loaded() function, covered in the next section.

get_extension_funcs( )

array get_extension_funcs (string *extension_name*)

The get_extension_funcs() function takes the name of an extension and returns an array of the functions available inside that extension. This is often combined with a call to get_loaded_extensions(), like this:

```
$extensions = get_loaded_extensions();

foreach($extensions as $extension) {
        echo $extension;
        echo ' (', implode(', ', get_extension_funcs($extension)), ')<br/>';
}
```

Breaking that down, it retrieves the names of all extensions currently loaded and cycles through them using a foreach loop. For each extension, it calls get_extension_funcs() to get the functions made available by that extension, then implodes that array into a string separated neatly by commas, then surrounds the whole thing in parentheses. For example, if you have the *wddx* extension installed, you should see the following line somewhere in your output:

```
wddx (wddx_serialize_value, wddx_serialize_vars, wddx_packet_start, wddx_
packet_end, wddx_add_vars, wddx_deserialize)
```

get_loaded_extensions( )

array get_loaded_extensions (void)

The get_loaded_extensions() function takes no parameters and returns an array of the names of all extensions you have loaded.

```
$extensions = get_loaded_extensions();
echo "Extensions loaded:\n";
foreach($extensions as $extension) {
        echo " $extension\n";
}
```

If you just want to check whether a specific extension is loaded or not, without having to go through the fuss of sifting through the return value of get_loaded_extensions( ), you can use the simple shortcut function extension_loaded( ), which takes an extension name as its only parameter and returns true if it has loaded or false if not.

hexdec( )

number hexdec (string *hex_string*)

The hexdec( ) function converts a hexadecimal number into a decimal number. It takes just one parameter, which is the number to convert. For example:

print hexdec(e8); // 232

html_entities( )

string html_entities (string *html* [, int *options* [, string *charset*]])

The html_entities( ) function converts characters that are illegal in HTML, such as &, <, and ", into their safe equivalents: &, <, and ", respectively.

```
$flowerpot_men = "Bill & Ben";
$safe_flowerpots = htmlentities($flowerpot_men);
// it's now "Bill &amp; Ben"
```

This method of encoding is often referred to as *&-escaping*. You can reverse this conversion using the html_entity_decode( ) function.

html_entity_decode( )

string html_entity_decode (string *html* [, int *options* [, string *charset*]])

The html_entity_decode( ) function converts an &-escaped string into its original format, reversing the operation of html_entities( ).

```
$flowerpot_men = "Bill & Ben";
$safe_flowerpots = htmlentities($flowerpot_men);
// it's now "Bill &amp; Ben"
$unsafe_flowerpots = html_entity_decode($safe_flowerpots);
// back to "Bill & Ben"
```

ignore_user_abort( )

int ignore_user_abort ([bool *enable*])

The ignore_user_abort( ) function allows your script to carry on working after the user has cancelled her request. Passing true as its only parameter will instruct PHP that the script is not to be terminated, even if your end user closes her browser, has navigated away to another site, or has clicked Stop. This is useful if you have some important processing to do and you do not want to stop it even if your users click cancel, such as running a payment through on a credit card. You can also pass false to ignore_user_abort( ), thereby making PHP exit when the user closes the connection.

```
ignore_user_abort(true);
// carry on if user clicks Stop in their browser
```

ini_get( )

string ini_get (string *varname*)

The ini_get( ) function allows you to read a value from the *php.ini* file without altering it. It takes the name of the value to read as its only parameter and returns the value. Boolean values returned by ini_get( ) should be typecasted as integer; otherwise, false values will be returned as an empty string. For example:

```
print "Display_errors is turned on: ";
print (int) ini_get("display_errors");
```

Many numerical values in *php.ini* are represented using M for megabyte and other shortcuts. These are preserved in the return value of ini_get( ), which means you should not rely on these values to be plain numbers.

ini_set( )

string ini_set (string *varname*, string *value*)

The ini_set( ) function allows you to change system attributes that affect the way your script is executed. Changes only affect the current script, and will revert back when the script ends.

To use ini_set( ), pass it the value you want to change as its first parameter, and the new value to use as its second parameter. If it is successful, it will return the previous value. For example:

```
print ini_set("max_execution_time", "300") . "<br />";
print ini_set("display_errors", "0") . "<br />";
print ini_set("include_path", "/home/paul/include") . "<br />";
```

Many variables cannot be changed using ini_set( ), because they have already been used. For example, magic_quotes_gpc decides whether PHP should automatically send all HTTP input through the addslashes( ) function before giving it to you. Although you can change this using ini_set( ), it is pointless to do so: it will be changed *after* PHP has already modified the variables.

is_callable( )

bool is_callable (mixed *var* [, bool *check_syntax_only* [, string &*proper_name*]])

The is_callable( ) function takes a string as its only parameter and returns true if that string contains a function name that can be called using a variable function. For example:

```
$func = "sqrt";
if (is_callable($func)) {
        print $func(49);
}
```

Function
Reference

isset( )

```
bool isset ( mixed var [, mixed var [, ...]] )
```

The isset( ) function returns true if its parameter has already been set in your script. This is not the same as the empty( ): if a variable was set and had no value, isset( ) would return true, and empty( ) would return false.

To check for "variable not set," use the not operator !, as in if (!isset($foo)).

ltrim( )

```
string ltrim ( string str [, string trim_chars] )
```

The ltrim( ) function works like the normal trim( ), except it only trims whitespace from the lefthand side of a string.

```
$string = ltrim(" testing ");
// $string is "testing "
```

md5( )

```
string md5 ( string str [, bool raw_output] )
```

Although the sha1( ) function is recommended for checksumming data securely, another popular algorithm is MD5, where the "MD" stands for Message Digest. The md5( ) function produces a data checksum in exactly the same way as sha1( ); the difference is that it is only 32-bytes long. Because sha1( ) is longer, it is less likely to have a "collision"—a situation where two different strings share the same checksum. However, md5( ) has a slight speed advantage. Unless you're trying to serve your website from a 386 or have been asked to use a particular algorithm, stick with sha1( ).

Using md5( ) is the same as using sha1( ):

```
$md5hash = md5("My string");
print $md5hash;
```

Note that if you are thinking that having fewer bits in MD5 makes it less secure, you are correct—but only just. An MD5 checksum is 32 bytes long, which is equal to 128 bits. That is, an MD5 checksum can be made up of 3.402823669209384634-6337460743177e+38 different possibilities, more commonly referred to as 2 to the power of 128. This an enormous number of varieties, and it is quite secure for most purposes.

microtime( )

```
mixed microtime ( [bool float_output] )
```

The microtime( ) function returns a highly accurate reading of the current time. When called without any parameters, this returns the current system time in seconds and microseconds, ordered microseconds first. For example: 0.82112000 1174676574. If you pass true to microtime( ), PHP will return the time in the more useful format of seconds.microseconds, like this: 1174676587.5996

When using microtime( ), keep in mind that the return value is a floating-point number. There is a setting in your *php.ini* file called precision that sets the number of significant digits to show in floating-point numbers, which means your return value from `microtime( )` may not be as precise as you want. Above, for example, you can see we only have four decimal places returned—this is because *php.ini* defaults precision to 14 significant digits, and there are 10 digits before the decimal place.

If you increase the value of precision to 18 and run `microtime( )` again, you will get results that are more accurate: 1174677004.8997819.

mktime( )

```
int mktime ( [int hour [, int minute [, int second [, int month
[, int day [, int year [, int is_dst]]]]]]] )
```

It's common practice to store year, month, and day in separate variables in order to make comparison easier, and the `mktime( )` function is used to reassemble the components into one Unix timestamp.

Of all the functions in PHP, this one has the most unusual parameter order: hour, minute, second, month, day, year, Is_Daylight_Savings_Time. Note that the hour should be in 24-hour clock time.

So, to pass in 10:30 p.m. on the 20th of June 2005, you would use `mktime( )` like this:

```
$unixtime = mktime(22, 30, 0, 6, 20, 2005, -1);
```

The only parameter that might not make sense is the last one, which is where you tell PHP whether daylight savings time (DST) should be in effect. If this seems odd to you—surely PHP should know whether DST was in effect?—consider the difficulties there are in calculating it. Each country enters DST at its own time, with some countries even having various times inside itself. Other countries, such as Germany, have only been using the DST system since 1980, which further complicates the matter. So, PHP gives you the option: pass 1 as the last parameter to have DST on, pass 0 to have it off, and pass -1 to let PHP take its best guess.

Using `mktime( )` is a great way to do date arithmetic, as it will correct crazy dates quite well. For example, if we wanted to add 13 months to the function call above without having to figure out the new settings, we could just add 13 to the month parameter (currently 6), like this:

```
$unixtime = mktime(10, 30, 0, 19, 20, 2005, -1);
```

Clearly there are not 19 months in the year, so PHP will add one to the year value, subtract 12 from the months value, and calculate the date from there. Similarly you could add 9990 to the hours value and PHP will jump ahead by 416 days.

 All the parameters to `mktime( )`, if less than 10, should not be expressed with a leading zero. The reason for this is that numbers with a leading zero are interpreted by PHP as being octal numbers, and this is likely to cause unforeseen results.

mt_rand( )

```
int mt_rand ( [int min, int max] )
```

The `mt_rand( )` function returns random numbers, similar to the `rand( )`. However, it uses the Mersenne Twister algorithm to generate "better" random numbers (i.e., more random), and is often preferred.

If you supply no parameters, mt_rand( ) will return a number between 0 and mt_getrandmax( ). If you supply it with two parameters, mt_getrandmax( ) will use those as the upper and lower limits for the random number it generates. The limits are inclusive: if you specify 1 and 3, your random number could be 1, 2, or 3.

```
$mtrand = mt_rand( );
$mtrandrange = mt_rand(1,100);
```

The maximum value that can be generated by mt_rand( ) varies depending on the system you use, but on both Windows and Unix, the default is 2,147,483,647.

nl2br( )

```
string nl2br ( string str )
```

The nl2br function inserts a HTML line break (<br />) before all new line characters. You should note that it does not *replace* the line breaks—the \n breaks are left intact. For example:

```
$mystr = "This is a test\nYes it is.";
$brstr = nl2br($mystr);
// set to "This is a test<br />\nYes it is."
```

number_format( )

```
string number_format ( float num [, int decimals
[, string decimal_point, string thousands_sep]] )
```

The number_format( ) function rounds numbers and adds commas as a thousands separator. You can pass it either one, two, or four parameters:

- number_format($n) rounds $n to the nearest whole number and adds commas in between thousands. For example:

    ```
    $total = 12345.6789;
    echo "Total charge is \$", number_format($total), "\n";
    ```

    That will output Total charge is $12,346, because it rounds up to the nearest decimal place.

- number_format($n,$p) rounds $n to $p decimal places, adding commas between thousands. For example:

    ```
    echo "Total charge is \$", number_format($total, 2), "\n";
    ```

    This time the output is 12,345.68, as it has been rounded to two decimal places.

- number_format($n, $p, $t, $d) rounds $n to $p decimal places, using $t as the thousands separator and $d as the decimal separator. For example:

    ```
    echo "Total charge is ", number_format($total, 2, ".", ","), " Euros";
    ```

    The output is now 12.345,68, which swaps the period and comma, as is the norm in many European countries.

octdec( )

```
number octdec ( string octal_string )
```

The octdec( ) function converts an octal number into a decimal number. It takes just one parameter, which is the number to convert. For example:

```
print decoct("23"); // 19
```

ord( )

```
int ord ( string str )
```

The ord( ) function takes a string and returns the equivalent ASCII value. For example:

```
$mystr = "ASCII is an easy way for computers to work with strings\n";
if (ord($mystr{1}) == 83) {
        print "The second letter in the string is S\n";
} else {
        print "The second letter is not S\n";
}
```

That code should output The second letter in the string is S. The chr( ) function does the opposite of ord( ): it takes an ASCII value and returns the equivalent character.

parse_str( )

```
void parse_str ( string str [, array &arr] )
```

QUERY_STRING is the literal text sent after the question mark in a HTTP GET request, which means that if the page requested was *mypage.php?foo=bar&bar=baz*, QUERY_STRING is set to foo=bar&bar=baz. The parse_str( ) function is designed to take a query string like that one and convert it to variables in the same way that PHP does when variables come in. The difference is that variables parsed using parse_str( ) are converted to global variables, as opposed to elements inside $_GET. So:

```
if (isset($foo)) {
        print "Foo is $foo<br />";
} else {
        print "Foo is unset<br />";
}

parse_str("foo=bar&bar=baz");

if (isset($foo)) {
        print "Foo is $foo<br />";
} else {
        print "Foo is unset<br />";
}
```

That will print out Foo is unset followed by Foo is bar, because the call to parse_str( ) will set $foo to bar and $bar to baz. Optionally, you can pass an array as the second parameter to parse_str( ), and it will put the variables into there. That would make the script look like this:

```
$array = array( );

if (isset($array['foo'])) {
        print "Foo is {$array['foo']}<br />";
} else {
        print "Foo is unset<br />";
}

parse_str("foo=bar&bar=baz", $array);
```

```
if (isset($array['foo'])) {
        print "Foo is {$array['foo']}<br />";
} else {
        print "Foo is unset<br />";
}
```

That script has the same output as before, except that the variables in the query string are placed into $array. As you can see, the variable names are used as keys in the array, and their values are used as the array values.

passthru( )

void passthru (string *command* [, int &*return_var*])

The passthru( ) function runs an external program, specified in the first parameter. It prints everything output by that program to the screen, unlike the exec( ), which prints out only the final line of output that the program generates.

```
passthru("who");
```

This function is helpful if you don't want to worry about how many lines the program returned. For example, many sites use the Unix command fortune with passthru("fortune") to get a quick and easy random quote for the bottom of their pages.

Taking user input and passing it into passthru( ) functions (or any other program execution function) is very dangerous. If you really must use user data as input to your program calls, pass it through the special function escapeshellcmd( ) first—it takes your input, and returns it in a safe format that can be used.

For example, you might have a script that allows people to search files in a directory for a word they enter into a web form, with the crux of the script looking something like this:

```
passthru("grep {$_GET["search"] /var/www/meetinglogs/*");
```

That works fine as long as you can trust the people calling the script, but it's very easy for them to send "nonexistent; cat /etc/ passwd; #" as the search field, which causes your grep command to run on an existing file and then print out the contents of your system password file. The # symbol is a shell comment, causing the rest of your original command to be ignored. To solve this problem, stop people from running multiple commands by escaping their input:

```
$_GET["search"] = escapeshellcmd($_GET["search"]);
passthru("grep {$_GET["search"] /var/www/meetinglogs/*");
```

That said, no matter how many precautions you take, it's really not worth running the risk of people executing arbitrary commands, so you should try to avoid using user input for command execution.

pow( )

```
number pow ( number base, number exponent )
```

The pow( ) function takes two parameters: a base and a power to raise it by. That is, supplying 2 as parameter two will multiply parameter one by itself, and supplying 3 will multiply parameter one by itself twice, like this:

```
print pow(10,2); // 100
print pow(10,3); // 1000
print pow(10,4); // 10000
print pow(-10, 4); // 10000
```

The first three lines show the result of 10 * 10, 10 * 10 * 10, then 10 * 10 * 10 * 10. On line four, we have -10 as the first parameter, and it is converted to a positive number in the result. This is basic mathematical theory: "a negative multiplied by negative makes a positive."

You can also send negative powers for the second parameter to pow( ) to generate roots. For example, pow(10, -1) is 0.1, pow(10, -2) is 0.01, pow(10, -3) is 0.001, etc. The values used as parameters one and two need not be integers: pow(10.1,2.3) works fine.

printf( )

```
int printf ( string format [, mixed argument [, mixed ...]] )
```

The printf( ) function may not be a function you will use often, but many people do, so it is good for you to be aware of it. This function is the standard C way to format text, and it has been copied wholesale into PHP for those who want to make use of it. It is not easy to use, but if you are doing a lot of code formatting, it will produce shorter code.

This function takes a variable number of parameters: a format string is always the first parameter, followed by zero or other parameters of various types. Here is a basic example:

```
$animals = "lions, tigers, and bears";
printf("There were %s - oh my!", $animals);
```

That will put together the string "There were lions, tigers, and bears—oh my!" and send it to output. The %s is a special format string that means "string parameter to follow," which means that $animals will be treated as text inside the string that printf( ) creates.

Here is another example, slightly more complicated this time:

```
$foo = "you";
$bar = "the";
$baz = "string";

printf("Once %s've read and understood %s previous section, %s should be
able to use %s bare minimum %s control functions to help %s make useful
scripts.", $foo, $bar, $foo, $bar, $baz, $foo);
```

This time we have several %s formatters in there, and the corresponding number of variables after parameter one. PHP replaces the first %s with parameter two, the second %s with parameter three, the third %s with parameter four, and so on. We have both $foo and $bar appearing more than once in the format list, which is perfectly acceptable.

There is a variety of other format strings for printf( ) as well as %s; a complete list is shown in Table 7-2.

Table 7-2. Format strings for use in printf( )

Format	Meaning
%%	A literal percent character; no matching parameter is required
%b	Parameter is an integer; express it as binary
%c	Parameter is an integer; express it as a character with that ASCII value
%d	Parameter is a positive integer; express it as decimal
%f	Parameter is a float; express it as a float
%o	Parameter is an integer; express it as octal
%s	Parameter is a string; express it as a string
%x	Parameter is an integer; express it as hexadecimal with lowercase letters
%X	Parameter is an integer; express it as hexadecimal with uppercase letters

If you specify one type but use another in its place, PHP will treat it as the type you specified, not as the type it actually is. For example, if you specify %d but provide a float, PHP will ignore the decimal part of the number; if you specify a number inside a string, PHP will treat it as a number. This works well, because you can't always be sure what type a variable is, yet you can always be sure what kind of variable you would *like* it to be.

```
$number = 123;
printf("123 in binary is: %b", $number);
printf("123 in hex is: %h", $number);
printf("123 as a string is: %s", $number);
printf("%% allows you to print percent characters");
```

Putting strings for parameter one separate from the printf( ) call means that you can change languages at the drop of a hat. Furthermore, it means you don't need to add new variables to your script to perform conversions—printf( ) will do them all for you, thanks in particular to an extra piece of functionality it has, revolving around the use of . (a period). For example:

```
$number = 123.456;
$formatted = number_format($number, 2) . "\n";
print "Formatted number is $formatted\n";
printf("Formatted number is %.2f\n", $number);
```

In that code, lines two and three round a float to two decimal places and then print out the result. The same thing is accomplished in line three: %f is the format term meaning float, but by preceding the F with .2 printf( ), it rounds the float to two decimal places. We could have used %.1f for one decimal place, %.8f for eight decimal places, etc.

rad2deg( )

float rad2deg (float *num*)

The rad2deg( ) function converts radians to degrees. Radians are calculated as being $degrees multiplied by the mathematical constant pi, then divided by 180.

    $atan_deg = rad2deg(atan(0.4346));

rand( )

int rand ([int *min*, int *max*])

The rand( ) function returns random numbers. If you call it with no parameters, it will return a number between 0 and the value returned by getrandmax( ).

If you supply it with two parameters, rand( ) will use those numbers as the upper and lower limits of the random number, inclusive of those values. That is, if you specify 1 and 3, the value could be 1, 2, or 3.

    $random = rand( );
    $randrange = rand(1,10);

Using rand( ) is very quick but not very "random"—the numbers it generates are more predictable than using the mt_rand( ) function.

The maximum value that can be generated by rand( ) varies depending on the system you use: on Windows, the highest default value is usually 32,767; on Unix, the value is 2,147,483,647. That said, your system may be different, which is why the getrandmax( ) is available.

rawurldecode( )

string rawurldecode (string *str*)

The rawurldecode( ) function converts a %-escaped string into its original format, reversing the operation of rawurlencode( ).

    $name = 'Paul "Hudzilla" Hudson';
    $safe_name = rawurlencode($name);
    // it's now Paul%20%22Hudzilla%22%20Hudson

    $unsafe_name = rawurldecode($name);
    // back to 'Paul "Hudzilla" Hudson'

rawurlencode( )

string rawurlencode (string *str*)

The rawurlencode( ) function converts non-alphabetic symbols into numerical equivalents preceded by a percent sign, such as %28 for "(", %29 for ")", and %27 for double quotes. This is most commonly used for passing data over URLs.

    $name = 'Paul "Hudzilla" Hudson';
    $safe_name = rawurlencode($name);
    // it's now Paul%20%22Hudzilla%22%20Hudson

This method of encoding is often referred to as *%-escaping*. You can reverse this conversion using the rawurldecode( ) function.

register_shutdown_function( )

```
void register_shutdown_function ( function callback
[, mixed param [, mixed ...]] )
```

The register_shutdown_function( ) function allows you to register with PHP a function to be run when script execution ends. Take a look at this example:

```
function say_goodbye( ) {
        echo "Goodbye!\n";
}

register_shutdown_function("say_goodbye");
echo "Hello!\n";
That would print out the following:
Hello!
Goodbye!
```

You can call register_shutdown_function( ) several times passing in different functions, and PHP will call all of the functions in the order you registered them when the script ends. If any of your shutdown functions call exit, the script will terminate without running the rest of the functions.

One very helpful use for shutdown functions is to handle unexpected script termination, such as script timeout, or if you have multiple exit( ) calls scattered throughout your script and want to ensure that you clean up no matter what. If your script times out, you have just lost control over whatever you were doing, so you either need to back up and undo whatever you have just done, or you need to clean up and terminate cleanly. Either way, shutdown functions are perfect: register a clean-up function near the start of the script and, when script timeout happens, the clean-up function will automatically run.

For example, the following script will print out "Sleeping...Goodbye!":

```
function say_goodbye( ) {
        print "Goodbye!\n";
}

register_shutdown_function("say_goodbye");
set_time_limit(1);
print "Sleeping...\n";
sleep(2);
print "Done!\n";
```

The "Done!" print line will never be executed, because the time limit is set to 1 and the sleep( ) function is called with 2 as its parameter, so the script will sleep for 2 seconds. As a result, "Sleeping..." gets printed, probably followed by a warning about the script going over its time limit, and then the shutdown function gets called.

round( )

```
float round ( float num [, int precision] )
```

The round( ) function takes a floating-point number as its parameter and rounds it to the nearest integer to its current value. If a number is exactly halfway between two integers, round( ) will always round up. If you provide an integer, nothing will happen. For example:

```
$number = round(11.1); // 11
$number = round(11.9); // 12
$number = round(11.5); // 12
$number = round(11); // 11
```

You can also provide the number of decimal places to round to:

```
$a = round(4.4999); // 4
$b = round(4.123456, 3); // 4.123
$c = round(4.12345, 4); // 4.1235
$d = round(1000 / 160); // 6
```

The last example is a common situation encountered by people using round( ). Imagine you were organizing a big trip to the countryside, and 1000 people signed up. You need to figure out how many buses you need to hire, so you take the number of people, 1000, and divide it by the capacity of your buses, 160, then round it to get a whole number. You find the result is 6.

Where is the problem? Well, the actual result of 1000/160 is 6.25—you need 6.25 buses to transport 1000 people, and you will only have ordered 6 because round( ) rounded toward 6 rather than 7, since it was closer. As you cannot order 6.5 buses, what do you do? The solution is simple: in situations like this, you use ceil( ).

rtrim( )

```
string rtrim ( string str [, string trim_chars] )
```

The rtrim( ) function works like the normal trim( ), except it only trims whitespace from the righthand side of a string.

```
$string = rtrim(" testing ");
// $string is " testing"
```

set_time_limit( )

```
void set_time_limit ( int seconds )
```

The set_time_limit( ) function lets you set how long a script should be allowed to execute. This value is usually set inside *php.ini* under the max_execution_time setting; however, you can override that here. The function takes one parameter, which is the number of seconds you want the script to have. Or you can pass 0, which means "Let the script run as long as it needs." This example sets the script execution time to 30 seconds:

```
set_time_limit(30);
```

When you use this function, the script timer is reset to 0; if you set 50 as the time limit, then after 40 seconds set the time limit to 30, the script will run for 70 seconds in total. That said, most web servers have their own time limit over and above PHP's. In Apache, this is set under Timeout in *httpd.conf*, and defaults to 300 seconds. If you use set_time_limit( ) to a value greater than Apache's timeout value, Apache will stop PHP before PHP stops itself. PHP may let some scripts go over the time limit if control is outside the script. For example, if you run an external program that takes 100 seconds and you have set the time limit to 30 seconds, PHP will let the script carry on for the full 100 seconds and terminate immediately afterwards. This also happens if you use the sleep( ) function with a value larger than the amount of time the script has left to execute.

The script time limit specified in *php.ini* or using set_time_limit( ) is also used to specify the number of seconds shutdown functions have to run. For example, if you have a time limit set to 30 seconds and have used register_shutdown_function( ) to set up functions to be called on script end, you will get an additional 30 seconds for all your shutdown functions to run (as opposed to 30 seconds for *each* of your shutdown functions).

sha1( )

```
string sha1 ( string str [, bool raw_output] )
```

SHA stands for the "Secure Hash Algorithm," and it is a way of converting a string of any size into a 40-bit hexadecimal number that can be used for verification. Checksums are like unidirectional (one-way) encryption designed to check the accuracy of input. By *unidirectional*, I mean that you cannot run $hash = sha1($somestring), then somehow decrypt $hash to get $somestring—it is just not possible, because a checksum does not contain its original text.

Checksums are a helpful way of storing private data. For example, how do you check whether a password is correct?

```
if ($password == "Frosties") {
        // ........
}
```

While that solution works, it means that whoever reads your source code gets your password. Similarly, if you store all your users' passwords in your database and someone cracks it, you will look bad. If you have the passwords of people on your database, or in your files, then malicious users will not be able to retrieve the original password.

The downside of that is that authorized users will not be able to get at the passwords either—whether or not that is a good thing varies from case to case, but usually having checksummed passwords is worthwhile. People who forget their password must simply reset it to a new password as opposed to retrieving it.

Checksumming is also commonly used to check whether files have downloaded properly—if your checksum is equal to the correct checksum value, then you have downloaded the file without problem.

The process of checksumming involves taking a value and converting it into a semi-meaningless string of letters and numbers of a fixed length. There is no way—no way whatsoever—to "decrypt" a checksumming to obtain the original value. The only way to hack a checksum is to try all possible combinations of input, which, given that the input for the checksum can be as long as you want, can take millions of years.

Consider this script:

```
print sha1("hello") . "\n";
print sha1("Hello") . "\n";
print sha1("hello") . "\n";
print sha1("This is a very, very, very, very, very, very, very long test");
```

Here is the output I get:

```
aaf4c61ddcc5e8a2dabede0f3b482cd9aea9434d
f7ff9e8b7bb2e09b70935a5d785e0cc5d9d0abf0
```

aaf4c61ddcc5e8a2dabede0f3b482cd9aea9434d
66f52c9f1a93eac0630566c9b82b26f91d727001

There are three key things to notice there: first, all the output is exactly 40 characters in length, and always will be. Second, the difference between the checksum of "hello" and the checksum of "Hello" is gigantic, despite the only difference being a small caps change. Finally, notice that there is no way to distinguish between long strings and short strings—because the checksum is not reversible (that is, you cannot extract the original input from the checksum), you can create a checksum of strings of millions of characters in just 40 bytes.

If you had stored your users' passwords checksummed in your database, then you need to checksum the passwords they provide before you compare them to the values in your database. One thing that is key to remember is that sha1( ) will always give the same output for a given input.

 If you set the optional second parameter to true, the SHA1 checksum is returned in raw binary format and will have a length of 20.

sin( )

    float sin (float num)

The sin( ) function calculates the sine value of the number provided as its only parameter. The parameter should be passed as radians—you should use deg2rad( ) to convert degrees to radians.

    $sin1 = sin(10);
    $sin2 = sin(deg2rad(80));

sleep( )

    int sleep (int seconds)

The sleep( ) function pauses execution for a set number of seconds, determined by the parameter you provide it. For example:

    sleep(4);
    echo "Done\n";

The maximum script execution time is 30 seconds by default (although you may have changed this by altering the max_execution_time setting inside *php.ini*), but you can use sleep( ) to make your scripts go on for longer than that because PHP does not have control during the sleep operation.

sqrt( )

    float sqrt (float num)
    To obtain the square root of a number, use the sqrt( ) function, which takes
    as its parameter the value you wish to calculate the square root of:
    print sqrt(25);
    print sqrt(26);

That will output 5 as the result of line one, then 5.0990195135928 for line two.

str_pad( )

string str_pad (string *input*, int *length* [, string *padding* [, int *type*]])

The str_pad( ) function makes a given string (parameter one) larger by X number of characters (parameter two) by adding on spaces. For example:

```
$string = "Goodbye, Perl!";
$newstring = str_pad($string, 2);
```

That code would leave " Goodbye, Perl! " in $newstring, which is the same string from $string, except with a space on either side, equalling the two we passed in as parameter two.

There is an optional third parameter to str_pad( ) that lets you set the padding character to use, so:

```
$string = "Goodbye, Perl!";
$newstring = str_pad($string, 10, 'a');
```

That would put "aaaaaGoodbye, Perl!aaaaa" into $newstring.

We can extend the function even more by using its optional fourth parameter, which allows us to specify which side we want the padding added to. The fourth parameter is specified as a constant, and you either use STR_PAD_LEFT, STR_PAD_RIGHT, or STR_PAD_BOTH:

```
$string = "Goodbye, Perl!";
$a = str_pad($string, 10, '-', STR_PAD_LEFT);
// $a is "----------Goodbye, Perl!"

$b = str_pad($string, 10, '-', STR_PAD_RIGHT);
// $b is "Goodbye, Perl!----------",

$c = str_pad($string, 10, '-', STR_PAD_BOTH);
// $c is "-----Goodbye, Perl!-----"
```

Note that HTML only allows a maximum of one space at any time. If you want to pad more, you will need to use   the HTML code for a non-breaking space.

str_replace( )

mixed str_replace (mixed *needle*, mixed *replace*, mixed *haystack* [, int &*count*])

The str_replace( ) function replaces parts of a string with new parts you specify and takes a minimum of three parameters: what to look for, what to replace it with, and the string to work with. It also has an optional fourth parameter, which will be filled with the number of replacements made, if you provide it. Here are examples:

```
$string = "An infinite number of monkeys";
$newstring = str_replace("monkeys", "giraffes", $string);
print $newstring;
```

With that code, $newstring will be printed out as "An infinite number of giraffes". Now consider this piece of code:

```
$string = "An infinite number of monkeys";
$newstring = str_replace("Monkeys", "giraffes", $string);
print $newstring;
```

This time, $newstring will not be "An infinite number of giraffes", as you might have expected. Instead, it will remain "An infinite number of monkeys", because the first parameter to str_replace( ) is Monkeys rather than "monkeys", and the function is case-sensitive.

There are two ways to fix the problem: either change the first letter of "Monkeys" to a lowercase M, or, if you're not sure which case you will find, you can switch to the case-insensitive version of str_replace( ): str_ireplace( ).

```
$string = "An infinite number of monkeys";
$newstring = str_ireplace("Monkeys", "giraffes", $string);
print $newstring;
```

When used, the fourth parameter is passed by reference, and PHP will set it to be the number of times your string was found and replaced:

```
$string = "He had had to have had it.";
$newstring = str_replace("had", "foo", $string, $count);
print "$count changes were made.\n";
```

The above code should output 3 in $count, as PHP will replace had with foo three times.

str_word_count( )

```
mixed str_word_count ( string str [, int count_type [, string char_list]] )
```

The str_word_count( ) function returns the number of words in a string. You can pass a second parameter to str_word_count( ) to make it do other things, but if you only pass the string parameter by itself, then it returns the number of unique words that were found in the string. If you pass 1 as the second parameter, it will return an array of the words found; passing 2 does the same, except the key of each word will be set to the position where that word was found inside the string.

Here are examples of the three options:

```
$str = "This is a test, only a test, and nothing but a test.";
$a = str_word_count($str, 1);
$b = str_word_count($str, 2);
$c = str_word_count($str);
print_r($a);
print_r($b);
echo "There are $c words in the string\n";
```

That should output the following:

```
Array ( [0] => This [1] => is [2] => a [3] => test [4]
=> only [5] => a [6] => test [7] => and [8] =>
nothing [9] => but [10] => a [11] => test )

Array ( [0] => This [5] => is [8] => a [10] => test [16]
=> only [21] => a [23] => test [29] => and [33] =>
nothing [41] => but [45] => a [47] => test )

There are 12 words in the string
```

In the first line, the array keys are irrelevant, but the array values are the list of the words found—note that the comma and period are not in there, as they are not considered words. In the second line, the array keys mark where the first letter of the word in the value was found, thus "0" means "This" was found at the beginning of the string. The last line shows the default word-counting behavior of str_word_count( ).

strcasecmp( )

>   int strcasecmp (string *str1*, string *str2*)

This is a case-insensitive version of the strcmp( ).

> $result = strcasecmp("Hello", "hello");

That will return 0, because PHP will ignore the case difference. Using strcmp( ) instead would have returned -1: "Hello" would come before "hello".

strcmp( )

>   int strcmp (string *str1*, string *str2*)

The strcmp( ) function, and its case-insensitive sibling, strcasecmp( ), is a quick way of comparing two words and telling whether they are equal, or whether one comes before the other. It takes two words for its two parameters, and returns -1 if word one comes alphabetically before word two, 1 if word one comes alphabetically after word two, or 0 if word one and word two are the same.

```
$string1 = "foo";
$string2 = "bar";
$result = strcmp($string1, $string2);

switch ($result) {
        case -1: print "Foo comes before bar"; break;
        case 0: print "Foo and bar are the same"; break;
        case 1: print "Foo comes after bar"; break;
}
```

It is not necessary for us to see that "foo" comes after "bar" in the alphabet, because we already know it does; however, you would not bother running strcmp( ) if you already knew the contents of the strings—it is most useful when you get unknown input and you want to sort it.

If the only difference between your strings is the capitalization of letters, you should know that capital letters come before their lowercase equivalents. For example, "PHP" will come before "php."

strip_tags( )

>   string strip_tags (string *html_text* [, string *allowed_tags*])

You can strip HTML and PHP tags from a string using strip_tags( ). Parameter one is the string you want stripped, and parameter two lets you specify a list of HTML tags you want to keep.

This function can be very helpful if you display user input on your site. For example, if you create your own message board forum on your site, a user could post a title along the lines of: <H1>THIS SITE SUCKS!</H1>, which, because you would display the titles of each post on your board, would display their unwanted message in huge letters on your visitors' screens.

Here are two examples of stripping out tags:

```
$input = "<blink><strong>Hello!</strong></blink>";
$a = strip_tags($input);
$b = strip_tags($input, "<strong><em>");
```

After running that script, $a will be set to "Hello!", whereas $b will be set to `<strong>`
`Hello!</strong>` because we had `<strong>` in the list of acceptable tags. Using this
method, you can eliminate most users from adversely changing the style of your site;
however, it is still possible for users to cause trouble if you allow a list of certain
HTML tags. For example, we could abuse the allow `<strong>` tag using CSS: `<strong`
`style="font: 72pt Times New Roman">THIS SITE SUCKS!</strong>`, a situation shown in
Figure 7-1.

Figure 7-1. Not what you want to see—strip_tags( ) gone wrong

If you allow `<strong>` tags, you allow *all* `<strong>` tags, regardless of whether they have
any extra unwanted information in there, so it is best not to allow any tags at all—not
`<strong>`, not `<img>`, etc.

This sort of attack is commonly referred to as Cross-Site Scripting (XSS), as it allows
people to submit specially crafted input to your site to load their own content. For
example, it's fairly easy for malicious users to make their username a piece of
JavaScript that redirects visitors to a different site, passing along all their cookies from
your site. Be careful: make sure to put strip_tags( ) to good use.

stripslashes( )

string stripslashes (string *str*)

The stripslashes( ) function is the opposite of addslashes( ): it removes one set of
\-escapes from a string. For example:

```
$string = "I'm a lumberjack and I'm okay!";
$a = addslashes($string);
// string is now "I\'m a lumberjack and I\'m okay!"

$b = stripslashes($a);
// string is now "I'm a lumberjack and I'm okay!"
```

strlen( )

```
int strlen ( string str )
```

The strlen( ) function takes just one parameter (the string), and returns the number of characters in it:

```
print strlen("Foo") . "\n"; // 3
print strlen("Goodbye, Perl!") . "\n"; // 14
```

Behind the scenes, strlen( ) actually counts the number of bytes in your string, as opposed to the number of characters. It is for this reason that multibyte strings should be measured with mb_strlen( ).

strpos( )

```
int strpos ( string haystack, mixed needle [, int offset] )
```

The strpos( ) function, and its case-insensitive sibling, stripos( ), returns the index of the beginning of a substring's first occurrence within a string. This is easiest to understand in code:

```
$string = "This is a strpos() test";
print strpos($string, "s") . "\n";
```

That will return 3, because the first lowercase S character in "This is a strpos( ) test" is at index 3. Remember that PHP considers the first letter of a string to be index 0, which means that the S strpos( ) found is actually the *fourth* character.

You can specify whole words in parameter two, which will make strpos( ) return the first position of that word within the string. For example, strpos($string, "test") would return 19—the index of the first letter in the matched word.

You should be aware that if the substring sent in parameter two is not found in parameter one, strpos( ) will return false (as opposed to -1). This is very important, as shown in this script:

```
$string = "This is a strpos() test";
$pos = strpos($string, "This");
if ($pos == false) {
        print "Not found\n";
} else {
        print "Found!\n";
}
```

That will output "Not found", despite "This" quite clearly being in $string. This time, the problem is that "This" is the first thing in $string, which means that strpos( ) will return 0. However, PHP considers 0 to be the same value as false, which means that our if statement cannot tell the difference between "Substring not found" and "Substring found at index 0."

If we change our if statement to use === rather than ==, PHP will check the value of 0 and false and find they match (both false), then check the types of 0 and false, and find that they do not match—the former is an integer, and the latter is a boolean. So, the corrected version of the script is this:

```
$string = "This is a strpos() test";
$pos = strpos($string, "This");
if ($pos === false) {
        print "Not found\n";
```

```
} else {
       print "Found!\n";
}
```

There is a third parameter to strpos( ) that allows us to specify where to start searching from. For example:

```
$string = "This is a strpos() test";
$pos = strpos($string, "i", 3);
if ($pos === false) {
       print "Not found\n";
} else {
       print "Found at $pos!\n";
}
```

Using 3 as the third parameter forces strpos( ) to start its search after the "i" of "This", meaning that the first match is the "i" of "is". Therefore, it returns the value 5.

strstr( )

string strstr (string *haystack*, string *needle*)

The strstr( ) function and its case-insensitive cousin, stristr( ), is a nice and easy function that finds the first occurrence of a substring (parameter two) inside another string (parameter one), and returns all characters from the first occurrence to the end of the string. This next example will match the "www" part of the URL *http://www.example.com/mypage.php*, then return everything from the "www" until the end of the string:

```
$string = "http://www.example.com/mypage.php";
$newstring = strstr($string, "www");
```

strtolower( )

string strtolower (string *str*)

The strtolower( ) function takes one string parameter and returns that string entirely in lowercase characters.

```
$string = "I like to program in PHP";
$a = strtolower($string);
```

In that example, $a will be set to "i like to program in php".

strtotime( )

int strtotime (string *time* [, int *now*])

The strtotime( ) function converts strings to a timestamp and takes two parameters: the string time to convert, and a second optional parameter that can be a relative timestamp. Parameter one is important; we will come back to parameter two shortly. Consider this script:

```
print strtotime("22nd December 1979");
print strtotime("22 Dec. 1979 17:30");
print strtotime("1979/12/22");
```

Here, there are three ways of representing the same date with the second also including a time. If you run that script, you will see PHP output an integer for each one, with the first and third being the same, and the second one being slightly higher. These numbers are the Unix timestamps for the dates we passed into strtotime( ), so it successfully managed to convert them.

You must use American-style dates (i.e., month, day, year) with strtotime( ); if it finds a date like 10/11/2003, it will consider it to be October 11th as opposed to November 10th.

If PHP is unable to convert your string into a timestamp, it will return -1. This next example tests whether date conversion worked or not:

```
$mydate = strtotime("Christmas 1979");
if ($mydate == -1) {
        print "Date conversion failed!";
} else {
        print "Date conversion succeeded!";
}
```

The strtotime( ) function has an optional second parameter, which is a timestamp to use for relative dates. This is because the date string in the first parameter to strtotime( ) can include relative dates such as "Next Sunday," "2 days," or "1 year ago." In this situation, PHP needs to know what these relative times are based on, and this is where the second parameter comes in—you can provide any timestamp you want, and PHP will calculate "Next Sunday" from that timestamp. If no parameter is provided, PHP assumes you are referring to the current time.

For example, this next line of code will print the timestamp for the next Sunday (that is, not the upcoming Sunday, but the one after):

```
print strtotime("Next Sunday");
```

You can pass in custom timestamps with your relative dates. For instance, this next line uses time( ) minus two days as its second parameter, and "2 days" for its first parameter, which means it returns the current timestamp:

```
print strtotime("2 days", time() - (86400 * 2));
```

This final example subtracts a year from a given timestamp, and works as expected:

```
print strtotime("1 year ago", 123456789);
```

Converting textual dates to usable dates is not always easy, and you should experiment with various dates to see what you can get to work and what you cannot.

 Be wary of dates such as this one: August 25, 2003, 10:26 a.m. Although this may look well formed, strtotime( ) is not able to handle it because it has commas. If you have dates with commas in them, be sure to strip them out using the str_replace( ) function, covered earlier in this chapter.

strtoupper( )

string strtoupper (string *str*)

The strtoupper( ) function takes one string parameter and returns that string entirely in uppercase characters.

```
$string = "I like to program in PHP";
$a = strtoupper($string);
```

In that example, $a will be set to "I LIKE TO PROGRAM IN PHP".

substr( )

```
string substr ( string str, int start_pos [, int length] )
```

The substr( ) function allows you to read just part of a string and takes a minimum of two parameters: the string to work with, and where you want to start reading from. There is an optional third parameter to specify how many characters you want to read. Here are some examples of basic usage:

```
$message = "Goodbye, Perl!";
$a = substr($message, 1);
// $a contains "oodbye, Perl!" - strings and arrays start at 0
// rather than 1, so it copied from the second character onwards.

$b = substr($message, 0);
// $b contains the full string because we started at index 0

$c = substr($message, 5);
// $c copies from index 5 (the sixth character),
// and so will be set to "ye, Perl!"

$d = substr($message, 50);
// $d starts from index 50, which clearly does not exist.
// PHP will return an empty string rather than an error.

$e = substr($message, 5, 4);
// $e uses the third parameter, starting from index five
// and copying four characters. $e will be set to "ye, ",
// a four-letter word with a space at the end.

$f = substr($message, 10, 1);
// $f has 1 character being copied from index 10, which gives "e"
```

You can specify a negative number as parameter three for the length, and PHP will consider that number the amount of characters you wish to omit from the end of the string, as opposed to the number of characters you wish to copy:

```
$string = "Goodbye, Perl!";
$a = substr($string, 5, 5);
// copies five characters from index five onwards, giving "ye, P"

$b = substr($string, 5, -1);
// copies five characters from the end, except the last character,
// so $b is set to "ye, Perl",

$c = substr($string, 0, -7);
// $c is set to "Goodbye"
```

Using negative lengths allows you to say "copy everything but the last three characters," for example.

You can also use a negative start index, in which case, you start copying *start* characters from the end. You can even use a negative length with your negative start index, like this:

```
$string = "Goodbye, Perl!"
$a = substr($string, 5);
// copy from character five until the end
```

```
$b = substr($string, 5, 5);
// copy five characters from character five

$c = substr($string, 0, -1);
// copy all but the last character

$d = substr($string, -5);
// $d is "Perl!", because PHP starts 5 characters from the end, then copies
from there to the end

$e = substr($string, -5, 4);
// this uses a negative start and a positive length; PHP starts five
characters from the end of the string ("P"), then copies four characters, so
$e will be set to "Perl"

$f = substr($string, -5, -4);
// start five characters from the end, and copy everything but the last four
characters, so $f is "P"
```

tan( )

```
float tan ( float num )
```

Calculates the tangent value of the number provided as its only parameter. The parameter should be passed as radians—you should use deg2rad( ) to convert degrees to radians.

```
$tan1 = tan(10);
$tan2 = tan(deg2rad(80));
```

time( )

```
int time ( void )
```

PHP represents time as the number of seconds that have passed since January 1st 1970 00:00:00 GMT, a date known as the start of the Unix epoch; hence, this date format is known as *epoch time* or a *Unix timestamp*. This might be a peculiar way to store dates, but it works well—internally, you can store any date since 1970 as an integer, and convert to a human-readable string wherever necessary.

The basic function to get the current time in epoch format is time( ). This takes no parameters and returns the current timestamp representing the current time on the server. Here is an example script:

```
print time( );
$CurrentTime = time( );
print $CurrentTime;
```

As you can see, we can either print the return value of time( ) directly, or we can store it away in a variable and then print the contents of the variable—the result is identical.

Working in Unix time means you are not tied down to any specific formatting, which means you need not worry about whether your date has months before days (or vice versa), whether long months are used, whether day numbers or day words (Saturday, Tuesday, etc.) are used, and so on. Furthermore, to add one to a day (to get tomorrow's date), you can just add one day's worth of seconds to your current timestamp: $60 \times 60 \times 24 = 86400$.

For more precise time values, use the microtime( ) function.

trim( )

        string trim (string *str* [, string *trim_chars*])

You can use the trim( ) function to strip spaces, new lines, and tabs (collectively called *whitespace*) from either side of a string variable. That is, if you have the string " This is a test " and pass it to trim( ) as its first parameter, it will return the string "This is a test"—the same thing, but with the surrounding spaces removed.

You can pass an optional second parameter to trim( ) if you want, which should be a string specifying the individual characters you want it to trim( ). For example, if we were to pass to trim the second parameter " tes" (that starts with a space), it would output "This is a"—the test would be trimmed, as well as the spaces. As you can see, trim( ) is again case-sensitive—the T in "This" is left untouched.

There are two minor variants to trim( )—ltrim( ) and rtrim( )—which do the same thing, but only trim from the left and right respectively.

Here are examples:

```
$a = trim(" testing ");
// $a is "testing"

$b = trim(" testing ", " teng");
// $b is is "sti"
```

ucfirst( )

        string ucfirst (string *str*)

The ucfirst( ) function takes one string parameter and converts the first letter of the string to an uppercase character, leaving the others untouched.

```
$string = "i like to program in PHP";
$a = strtoupper($string);
```

In that example, $a will be set to "I like to program in PHP".

ucwords( )

        string ucwords (string *str*)

The ucwords( ) function takes one string parameter and converts the first letter of each word in the string to an uppercase character, leaving the others untouched.

```
$string = "i like to program in PHP";
$a = strtoupper($string);
```

In that example, $a will be set to "I Like To Program In PHP".

unset( )

```
void unset ( mixed var [, mixed var [, mixed ...]] )
```

The unset( ) function deletes a variable so that isset( ) will return false. Once deleted, you can recreate a variable later on in a script.

```
$name = "Paul";
if (isset($name)) print "Name is set\n";
unset($name);
if (isset($name)) print "Name is still set\n";
```

That would print out "Name is set", but not "Name is still set", because calling unset( ) has deleted the $name variable.

usleep( )

```
void usleep ( int microseconds )
```

The usleep( ) is similar to the sleep( ), which pauses script execution, except that it uses microseconds (millionths of a second) for its sleep time rather than seconds. It is so named because "u" is similar in style to the Greek character Mu that is associated with "micro." It takes the amount of time to pause execution as its only parameter.

```
usleep(4000000);
echo "Done\n";
```

The maximum script execution time is 30 seconds by default (although you may have changed this by altering the max_execution_time setting inside *php.ini*), but you can use usleep( ) to make your scripts go on for longer than that because PHP does not have control during the sleep operation.

 The use of usleep( ) is not advised if you want backward compatibility, because it wasn't available on Windows prior to PHP 5.

virtual( )

```
bool virtual ( string filename )
```

The virtual( ) function performs a virtual request to the local Apache web server for a file, almost as if your script were a client itself. This request is processed and its output is sent back to your script. Note that you must be running Apache as the web server—this function does not work on other servers.

Using this method you can, for example, execute a Perl script from your PHP script or, for real weirdness, execute another PHP script from your PHP script. Although, for that purpose, you should probably use include( ) or require( ).

```
// run a page counter Perl script
virtual("counter.pl");
```

wordwrap( )

```
string wordwrap ( string str [, int line_length
[, string break_char [, bool cut]]] )
```

Although web pages wrap text automatically, there are two situations when you might want to wrap text yourself:

- When printing to a console as opposed to a web page, text does not wrap automatically. Therefore, unless you want your users to scroll around, it is best to wrap text for them.

- When printing to a web page that has been designed to exactly accommodate a certain width of text, allowing browsers to wrap text whenever they want will lead to the design getting warped.

In either of these situations, the wordwrap( ) function comes to your aid. If you pass a sentence of text into wordwrap( ) with no other parameters, it will return that same string wrapped at the 75-character mark using "\n" for new lines. However, you can pass both the size and new line marker as parameters two and three if you want to, like this:

```
$text = "Word wrap will split this text up into smaller lines, which makes
for easier reading and neater layout.";
$text = wordwrap($text, 20, "<br />");
print $text;
```

Running that script will give you the following output:

```
Word wrap will split<br />this text up into<br />smaller lines, which<br />
makes for easier<br />reading and neater<br />layout.
```

As you can see, wordwrap( ) has used <br />, a HTML new line marker, and split up words at the 20-character mark. Note that wordwrap( ) always pessimistically wraps words—that is, if you set the second parameter to 20, wordwrap( ) will always wrap when it hits 20 characters or under—not 21, 22, etc. The only exception to this is if you have words that are individually longer than 20 characters—wordwrap( ) will not break up a word, so it may return larger chunks than the limit you set.

If you really want your limit to be a hard maximum, you can supply 1 as a fourth parameter, which enables "cut" mode—words over the limit will be cut up if this is enabled. Here is an example of cut mode in action:

```
$text = "Micro-organism is a very long word.";
$text = wordwrap($text, 6, "\n", 1);
print $text;
```

That will output the following:

```
Micro-
organi
sm is
a very
long
word.
```

8

Object-Oriented PHP

Before PHP 5 came along, object-oriented programming (OOP) support in PHP was more of a hack than a serious attempt. As a result, the few who used it often regretted the choice, and it is not surprising that the whole system got a full rewrite in PHP 5. It is now much more advanced and flexible and should please just about everyone.

> If you have used OOP in PHP 4, I strongly recommend you read this entire chapter from start to finish—OOP has been massively redesigned in PHP 5 and is much more functional and feature-rich now.

Conceptual Overview

OOP was designed to allow programmers to more elegantly model their programs upon real-world scenarios. It allows programmers to define things (objects) in their world (program), set a few basic properties, then ask them to do things. Consider an object of type Dog—there are many dogs in the world, but only one animal "dog." As such, we could have a blueprint for dogs, from which all dogs are made. While dogs have different breeds that vary a great deal, at the end of the day they all have four legs, a wet nose, and a dislike of cats and squirrels.

So, we have our dog blueprint, from which we might create a Poodle breed, a Chihuahua breed, and an Alsatian breed. Each of these is also a blueprint, but they are all based upon the Dog blueprint. From our Poodle breed, we can then create a Poodle, which we will call Poppy. Poppy is an actual dog, based upon the Poodle breed, and therefore also based upon the Dog blueprint. We can create other Poodles (or Chihuahuas or Alsatians) simply by creating an instance of that breed.

As all dogs are able to bark, we can add a bark( ) function (known as a "method," as it is inside a class) to our dog blueprint, which, in turn, means that the Poodle breed has a bark( ) method. Therefore, Poppy can bark( ) too. We can also define variables (known as "properties" inside objects) inside the dog blueprint, such as $Name, $Age, and $Friendliness. These also become available in the Poodle breed, which stems from the dog animal, and therefore into Poppy. Each object of type Poodle would have its own set of properties—its own $Name, its own $Age, etc.

Because the breeds stem from the Dog blueprint, we can also add methods and properties to breeds individually without having them in the Dog blueprint. For example, Poodles come in three general sizes: standard, miniature, and toy. Last time I checked, you don't get toy Alsatians, so putting a $Size property into the Dog blueprint would just create a property that is not used in a third of the dogs.

If you are still with me, then you are on the way to fully understanding how object-oriented code works.

Classes

The blueprints of dog breeds and animals are known as *classes*—they define the basic architecture of the objects available in our programs. Each class is defined as having a set of methods and properties, and you can inherit one class from another—our Breed classes, for example, inherited from the Dog class, thereby getting all the Dog methods and properties available. Inheriting is often referred to as *subclassing*—Poodle would be a subclass of Dog.

Some languages, such as C++, allow you to inherit from more than one class, which is known as *multiple inheritance*. This technique allows you to have a class Bird and a class Horse, then create a new class called FlyingHorse—which inherits from both Bird and Horse—to give you animals like the mythical Pegasus. PHP does not allow you to do this because it generally makes for very confusing programs, and is quite rare, even in C++.

PHP allows you to inherit from precisely one parent class, and you can inherit as many times as you want. For example, the Dog class could inherit from the class Carnivora, which would contain Cat, Dog, Bear, etc. Carnivora could inherit from Mammalia, holding all mammals, which could in turn inherit from Vertebrata, holding all animals with a backbone, etc.—the higher up you go, the more vague the classes become. This is because each class inherits methods and properties from its parent class, as well as adding its own.

 People often use the terms *parent, child, grandparent,* etc., to define their class structure. A child class is one that inherits from another—Poodle is a child of Dog, and would be a grandchild of Carnivora. Carnivora would be the parent of Dog and grandparent of Poodle—this will make more sense later, when you are creating your own classes and sub-classing freely.

Defining a Class

Given the class structure of dogs and breeds discussed above, it is time to take a look at how that translates into PHP code. Here is the PHP code necessary to define a very basic Dog class:

```
class dog {
        public function bark() {
                print "Woof!\n";
        }
}
```

Here the Dog class has just one method, bark( ), which outputs "Woof!". Don't worry about the public part for now—that just means "can be called by anyone" and we'll be looking at that later. If we create an object of type Dog, we could call its bark( ) method to have it output the message.

 Class naming conventions follow the same rules as variable naming, excluding the dollar sign at the beginning. You can use any name for your methods, except stdClass and __PHP_Incomplete_ Class—both of these are reserved by PHP.

How to Design Your Class

When designing your classes, there is one golden rule: keep to real-world thinking. However, although that one rule sounds simple, it's nebulous—what exactly *is* real-world thinking? Fortunately there are a number of more simple rules you can follow that will help keep your code particularly readable:

- Start or end local properties with a special character, so that you are always clear about what variable is being set. The most common method is to start local properties with an underscore, e.g., _Name, _Age, etc.

- To follow OOP guidelines strictly, nearly all of your properties should be either private or protected—they should not be accessible from outside of an object. More on this later.

- Write accessor methods to set and get private properties. These methods should be how you interface with the object. To get a property called _Age, write a method Age( ). To set a property called _Age, write a method SetAge( ).

- Always put properties and methods as low in your inheritance as they can go without repetition. If you find one object has properties and methods it is not supposed to have, you have gone wrong somewhere. For example, while dolphins can swim, gorillas cannot, so do not put a swim( ) method into a Mammal class just to save time.

If you are wondering why it is that accessor methods should be used to read and write properties, it is because OOP practice dictates that objects should be self-contained. That is, other parts of your program should be able to work with them using simple method calls, so that they do not need implicit knowledge of an object's internal structures and operations.

Basic Inheritance

To extend the Dog class to breeds, the extends keyword is needed, like this:

```
class Dog {
        public function bark( ) {
                print "Woof!\n";
        }
}

class Poodle extends Dog {
        // nothing new yet
}
```

Overriding Methods

PHP allows us to redefine methods in subclasses, which means we can make the Poodle class have its own version of bark( ). This is done by redefining the method inside the child class, making the Poodle class look like this:

```
class Poodle extends Dog {
        public function bark( ) {
                print "Yip!\n";
        }
}
```

We'll come back to inheritance after we look at objects—actual instances of our classes.

The Scope Resolution Operator

The scope resolution operator is ::—two colons next to each other. It is used in object-oriented programming when you want to access static or overridden methods of a class. For example, if you have a method sayhello( ) as well as a sayhello( ) method of a Person object, you would use Person::sayhello( )—you resolve which sayhello( ) you mean by using the class name and the scope resolution operator.

The most common use for scope resolution is with the pseudo-class parent. For example, if you want a child object to call its parent's __construct( ) method, you would use parent::__construct( ). This is shown later in this chapter, in the section "Parent Constructors."

 Internally to PHP, the scope resolution operator is called "paamayim nekudotayim," which is Hebrew for "double colon."

Objects

Classes are mere definitions. You cannot play fetch with the definition of a dog; you need a real, live, slobbering dog. Naturally, we cannot create live animals in our PHP scripts, but we can do the next best thing: creating an instance of our class.

In our earlier example, "Poppy" was a dog of type Poodle. We can create Poppy by using the following syntax:

```
$poppy = new Poodle;
```

That creates an instance of the class Poodle, and places it into the property $poppy. Poppy, being a Dog, can bark by using the bark( ) method, and to do this, you need to use the special -> operator. Here is a complete script demonstrating creating objects—note that the method override for bark( ) is commented out.

```
class Dog {
        public function bark( ) {
                print "Woof!\n";
        }
}

class Poodle extends Dog {
        /* public function bark( ) {
                print "Yip!\n";
        } */
}

$poppy = new Poodle;
$poppy->bark( );
```

Execute that script, and you should get "Woof!". Now try taking out the comments around the bark( ) method in the Poodle class; running it again, you should see "Yip!" instead.

Properties

In the next code block, the line public $Name; defines a public property called $Name that all objects of class Dog will have. PHP allows you to specify how each property can be accessed, and we will be covering that in depth soon—for now, we will just be using public.

```
class Dog {
        public $Name;

        public function bark( ) {
                print "Woof!\n";
        }
}
```

We can now set Poppy's name by using this code:

```
$poppy->Name = "Poppy";
```

Notice that -> is used again to work with the object $poppy, and also that there is no dollar sign before Name. The following would be incorrect:

```
$poppy->$Name = "Poppy";
// danger!
```

While that will work, it won't access the Name property of $poppy. Instead, it will look for the $Name variable in the current scope, and use the contents of that variable as the name of the property to read from $poppy. That might be what you want, but otherwise, this will cause silent bugs in your code.

Each object has its own set of properties that are independent of other objects of the same type. Consider the following code:

```
$poppy = new Poodle;
$penny = new Poodle;
$poppy->Name = "Poppy";
$penny->Name = "Penny";
print $poppy->Name;
```

That will still output "Poppy", because Penny's properties are separate from Poppy's.

PHP allows you to dynamically declare new properties for objects. For example, saying "$poppy->YippingFrequency = 52820;" would create a new public property for $poppy called $YippingFrequency, and assign it the value 52820. It would create the property only for $poppy, and not for any other instances of the same class.

The 'this' Variable

Once inside an object's method, you have complete access to its properties, but to set them you need to be more specific than just using the property name you want to work with. To specify you want to work with a local property, you need to use the special $this variable, which always points to the object you are currently working with. For example:

```
function bark( ) {
        print "{$this->Name} says Woof!\n";
}
```

When calling an object method, PHP automatically sets the $this variable that contains that object—you do not need to do anything to have access to it.

Objects Within Objects

You can use objects inside other objects in the same way as other variable types. For example, we could define a DogTag class and give each Dog a DogTag object like this:

```
class DogTag {
        public $Words;
}

class Dog {
        public $Name;
        public $DogTag;

        public function bark( ) {
                print "Woof!\n";
        }
```

```
    }

    // definition of Poodle...
```

Accessing objects within objects is as simple as using -> again:

```
$poppy = new Poodle;
$poppy->Name = "Poppy";
$poppy->DogTag = new DogTag;
$poppy->DogTag->Words = "My name is Poppy. If you find me, please call 555-
1234";
```

The $DogTag property is declared like any other, but needs to be created with new
once $poppy has been created.

Access Control Modifiers

There are a number of keywords you can place before a class, a method definition, or a property to alter the way PHP treats them. Here's the full list, along with
what each of them does:

- Public: This property or method can be used from anywhere in the script
- Private: This property or method can be used only by the class or object it is
  part of; it cannot be accessed elsewhere
- Protected: This property or method can be used only by code in the class it is
  part of, or by descendants of that class
- Final: This property, method, or class cannot be overridden in subclasses
- Abstract: This method or class cannot be used directly—you have to sub-
  class this

The problem with public properties is that they allow methods to be called and
properties to be set from anywhere within your script, which is generally not a
smart thing. One of the benefits of properly programmed OOP code is *encapsula-
tion*, which can be thought of as similar to data hiding. That is, if your object
exposes all its properties to the world, programmers using those objects need to
understand how your classes work. In an encapsulated word, other programmers
would only need to know the specification for your class, such as "call function X,
and you'll get Y" back. They wouldn't—and shouldn't—have to know how it all
works internally.

To give an example of this, we had a DogTag object $DogTag inside each dog object,
as well as a $Name property, but they contained repeated information. If someone
had changed the $Name property, the $DogTag information would have remained
the same. The programmer can't really be blamed for changing $Name: it was
publicly accessible, after all. The solution is to make all the variables private to the
object using either private or protected, and to provide accessor methods like
setName() to stop unknowing programmers from changing variables directly.
These accessors are written by us, so we can have them do all the necessary work,
such as changing the name on the dog tag when a dog's name changes.

Generally speaking, most of the variables in a class should be marked as either protected or private. Sometimes you will need to use public, but those times are few and far between.

Public

Public properties and methods are accessible from anywhere in your script, which makes this modifier the easiest to use. In PHP 4, all object properties were declared with var and were essentially public, but using this terminology is deprecated and may generate compiler warnings. Take a look at the following code:

```
class Dog {
        public $Name;

        public function bark( ) {
                print "Woof!\n";
        }
}

class Poodle extends Dog {
        public function bark( ) {
                print "Yip!\n";
        }
}

$poppy = new Poodle;
$poppy->Name = "Poppy";
print $poppy->Name;
```

That code works in precisely the same way as before; the public keyword has not made any difference. This is because, by default, all class methods are public; before PHP 5, there was no way to make them anything else.

While the public keyword is not needed, I recommend you use it anyway—it is a good way to remind people who read your code that a given method is indeed public. It is also possible that class methods without an access modifier may be deprecated in the distant future.

You always need to specify an access modifier for properties. Previous versions of PHP used the var keyword to declare properties, again because it had no concept of access modifiers. You should avoid this, and be more specific with public or one of the other keywords.

Private

Private properties are accessible only inside the methods of the class that defined them. If a new class inherits from it, the properties will not be available in the methods of that new class; they remain accessible only in the functions from the original class. For example:

```
class Dog {
        private $Name;
        private $DogTag;
```

```
        public function setName($NewName) {
            // etc
        }
}
```

Both $Name and $DogTag are private, which means no one can access them unless they are doing so in a method that is part of the class, such as setName(). This remains public because we want this to be accessible by anyone.

Now if our nosey programmer comes along and tries to set $Name directly, using code like $poppy->Name, he will not get what he was expecting: PHP will give him the error message: "Cannot access private property Dog::$Name". However, if that private property were inherited from another class, PHP will try to accommodate his request by having a private property and a public property. Yes, this is confusing; however, the following code should clear things up:

```
class Dog {
        private $Name;
}

class Poodle extends Dog { }

$poppy = new Poodle;
$poppy->Name = "Poppy";
print_r($poppy);
```

Running that script will output the following:

```
poodle Object
(
[Name:private] =>
[Name] => Poppy
)
```

Notice that there are two Name properties—one that is private and cannot be touched, and another that PHP creates for local use as requested. Clearly this is confusing, and you should try to avoid this situation, if possible.

Keep in mind that private methods and properties can only be accessed by the exact class that owns them; child classes cannot access private parent methods and properties. If you want to do this, you need the protected keyword instead.

Protected

Properties and methods marked as protected are accessible only through the object that owns them, whether or not they are declared in that object's class or have descended from a parent class. Consider the following code:

```
class Dog {
        public $Name;
        private function getName() {
                return $this->Name;
        }
}

class Poodle extends Dog {
```

```
        public function bark( ) {
                print "'Woof', says " . $this->getName( );
        }
}

$poppy = new Poodle;
$poppy->Name = "Poppy";
$poppy->bark( );
```

In that code, the class Poodle extends from class Dog, class Dog has a public property $Name and a private method getName( ), and class Poodle has a public method called bark( ). So, we create a Poodle, give it a $Name value of "Poppy" (the $Name property comes from the Dog class), then ask it to bark( ). The bark( ) method is public, which means we can call it as shown above, so this is all well and good.

However, the bark( ) method calls the getName( ) method, which is part of the Dog class and was marked private—this will stop the script from working, because private properties and methods cannot be accessed from inherited classes. That is, we cannot access private Dog methods and properties from inside the Poodle class.

Now try changing getName( ) to protected, and all should become clear—the property is still not available to the world as a whole, but handles inheritance as you would expect, meaning that we *can* access getName( ) from inside Poodle.

Final

The final keyword is used to declare that a method or class cannot be overridden by a subclass. For example:

```
class Dog {
        private $Name;
        private $DogTag;
        final public function bark( ) {
                print "Woof!\n";
        }
        // etc
```

The Dog bark( ) method is now declared final, which means it cannot be overridden in a child class. If we have bark( ) redefined in the Poodle class, PHP outputs a fatal error message: "Cannot override final method dog::bark( )". Using the final keyword is optional, but it makes your life easier by acting as a safeguard against people overriding a method you believe should be permanent.

For stronger protection, the final keyword can also be used to declare a class uninheritable—that is, that programmers cannot extend another class from it. For example:

```
final class Dog {
        private $Name;
        public function getName( ) {
                return $this->Name;
        }
}

class Poodle extends Dog {
```

Object-Oriented PHP

```php
        public function bark( ) {
                print "'Woof', says " . $this->getName( );
        }
}
```

Attempting to run that script will result in a fatal error, with the message: "Class Poodle may not inherit from final class (Dog)".

Abstract

The abstract keyword is used to say that a method or class cannot be created in your program as it stands. This does not stop people inheriting from that abstract class to create a new, non-abstract (concrete) class.

Consider this code:

```php
$poppy = new Dog;
```

The code is perfectly legal—we have a class Dog, and we're creating one instance of that and assigning it to $poppy. However, given that we have actual breeds of dog to choose from, what this code actually means is "create a dog with no particular breed." Even mongrels have breed classifications, which means that a dog without a breed is impossible and should not be allowed. We can use the abstract keyword to enforce this in code:

```php
abstract class Dog {
        private $Name;
// etc

$poppy = new Dog;
```

The Dog class is now abstract, and $poppy is now being created as an abstract dog object. PHP now halts execution with a fatal error message: "Cannot instantiate abstract class Dog".

As mentioned already, you can also use the abstract keyword with methods, but if a class has at least one abstract method, the class itself must be declared abstract. Also, you will get errors if you try to provide any code inside an abstract method, which makes this illegal:

```php
abstract class Dog {
        abstract function bark( ) {
                print "Woof!";
        }
}
```

It even makes *this* illegal:

```php
abstract class Dog {
        abstract function bark( ) { }
}
```

Instead, a proper abstract method should look like this:

```php
abstract class Dog {
        abstract function bark( );
}
```

If it helps you understand things better, you can think of abstract classes as being similar to interfaces, which are discussed later in this chapter.

Iterating Through Object Properties

We can treat an object as an array with the foreach loop, and it will iterate over each of the properties inside that object that are accessible. That is, private and protected properties will not be accessible in the general scope. Take a look at this script:

```
class Person {
        public $FirstName = "Bill";
        public $MiddleName = "Terence";
        public $LastName = "Murphy";
        private $Password = "Poppy";
        public $Age = 29;
        public $HomeTown = "Edinburgh";
        public $FavouriteColor = "Purple";
}

$bill = new Person( );

foreach($bill as $var => $value) {
        echo "$var is $value\n";
}
```

That will output this:

```
FirstName is Bill
MiddleName is Terence
LastName is Murphy
Age is 29
HomeTown is Edinburgh
FavouriteColor is Purple
```

Note that the $Password property is nowhere in sight, because it is marked Private and we're trying to access it from the global scope. If we re-fiddle the script a little so that the foreach loop is called inside a method, we should be able to see the property:

```
class Person {
        public $FirstName = "Bill";
        public $MiddleName = "Terence";
        public $LastName = "Murphy";
        private $Password = "Poppy";
        public $Age = 29;
        public $HomeTown = "Edinburgh";
        public $FavouriteColor = "Purple";

        public function outputVars( ) {
                foreach($this as $var => $value) {
```

```
                        echo "$var is $value\n";
                }
            }
    }

    $bill = new Person( );
    $bill->outputVars( );
```

Now the output is this:

```
    FirstName is Bill
    MiddleName is Terence
    LastName is Murphy
    Password is Poppy
    Age is 29
    HomeTown is Edinburgh
    FavouriteColor is Purple
```

Now that it's the object itself looping through its properties, we can see private properties just fine. Looping through objects this way is a great way to handwrite serialization methods—just remember to put the code inside a method; otherwise, private and protected data will get ignored.

Object Type Information

Inheriting from class to class is a powerful way to build up functionality in your scripts. However, very often it is easy to get lost with your inheritance—how can you tell what class a given object is?

PHP comes to the rescue with a special keyword, instanceof, which is an operator. Instanceof will return true if the object on the lefthand side is of the same class, or a descendant of, the class given on the righthand side. You can also use the instanceof keyword to see whether an object implements an interface. For example, given the code $poppy = new Poodle;:

```
    if ($poppy instanceof poodle) { }
    if ($poppy instanceof dog) { }
```

Both of those if statements would evaluate to be true, because $poppy is an object of the Poodle class and also a descendant of the Dog class.

Java programmers will be happy to know that instanceof is the same old friend they've grown used to over the years.

If you only want to know whether an object is a descendant of a class, and not of that class itself, you can use the is_subclass_of( ) method. This takes an object as its first parameter, a class name string as its second parameter, and returns either true or false depending on whether the first parameter is descended from the class specified in the second parameter.

Understanding the difference between instanceof and is_subclass_of( ) is crucial—this script should make it clear:

```
class Dog { }
class Poodle extends Dog { }
$poppy = new Poodle( );
print (int)($poppy instanceof Poodle);
print "\n";
print (int)is_subclass_of($poppy, "Poodle");
```

That should output a 1, then a 0. Typecasting to int is used because boolean false is printed out as "" (blank). But by typecasting to an integer, this becomes 0. Using instanceof reports true that $poppy is either a Poodle or a Dog, whereas is_subclass_of( ) reports false because $poppy is not descended from the class Poodle—it *is* a Poodle.

 New versions of PHP 5 (after 5.0.2) will allow you to specify a string as parameter one of is_subclass_of( ), and check whether the class named in that string is a subclass of parameter two.

Class Type Hints

Although PHP remains a loosely typed language—which means that properties are not explicitly either string, integer, or boolean—PHP 5 introduces class type hints, which allow you to specify what class of object should be passed into a method. These are not required, and are also not checked until the script is actually run; they aren't strict, by any means. Furthermore, they only work for classes right now—you can't specify, for example, that a parameter should be an integer or a string. Having said that, future versions will likely introduce the ability to request that arrays be passed in.

Here is an example of a type hint in action:

```
class Dog {
        public function do_drool( ) {
                echo "Sluuuuurp\n";
        }
}

class Cat { }

function drool(Dog $some_dog) {
        $some_dog->do_drool( );
}

$poppy = new Cat( );
drool($poppy);
```

The drool( ) method will accept one parameter, $some_dog, but that parameter name is preceded by the class hint—I have specified that it should only accept a parameter of type Dog. In the example, I have made $poppy a Cat object, and that will give the following output:

```
Fatal error: Argument 1 must be an instance of dog in C:\home\classhint.php
on line 12
```

Providing a class hint for a class type that does not exist will cause a fatal error. Class hints are essentially a way for you to skip having to use the instanceof keyword again and again to verify that your methods have received the right kind of objects. Using a class hint is essentially an implicit call to instanceof, without the extra code.

 As with the instanceof keyword, you can specify an interface as the class hint, and only classes that interface will be allowed through.

Constructors and Destructors

If you think back to the example where each dog had a DogTag object in it, this led to code like the following:

```
$poppy = new Poodle;
$poppy->Name = "Poppy";
$poppy->DogTag = new DogTag;
$poppy->DogTag->Words = "If you find me, call 555-1234";
```

Using that method, if we had other objects inside each Poodle object, we would need to create the Poodle plus all its other associated objects by hand.

Another way to do this is to use *constructors*. A constructor is a special method you add to classes that is called by PHP whenever you create an instance of the class. For example:

```
class DogTag {
        public $Words;
}

class Dog {
        public $Name;
        public $DogTag;

        public function bark( ) {
                print "Woof!\n";
        }

        public function __construct($DogName) {
                print "Creating a Dog: $DogName\n";
                $this->Name = $DogName;
                $this->DogTag = new DogTag;
                $this->DogTag->Words = "My name is $DogName. If you find me,
                                        please call 555-1234";
        }
}

class Poodle extends Dog {
        public function bark( ) {
                print "Yip!\n";
        }
}
```

```
$poppy = new Poodle("Poppy");
print $poppy->DogTag->Words . "\n";
```

Note the __construct( ) method in the Dog class, which takes one variable—that is our constructor. Whenever we instantiate a Poodle object, PHP calls the relevant constructor.

There are three other important things to note:

- The constructor is not in the Poodle class, it's in the Dog class. When PHP looks for a constructor in Poodle, and fails to find one there, it goes to its parent class (where Poodle inherited from). If it fails to find one there, it goes up again, and up again, *ad infinitum,* until it reaches the top of the class structure. As the Dog class is the top of our class structure, PHP does not have far to go.

- PHP only ever calls *one* constructor for you. If you have several constructors in a class structure, PHP will only call the first one it finds.

- The __construct( ) method is marked public, which is not by accident. If you don't mark the constructor as public, you can instantiate objects of a class only from within the class itself, which is almost an oxymoron. If you make this private, you need to use a static method call, which is discussed later in this chapter.

Parent Constructors

Take a look at this code:

```
class Poodle extends Dog {
        public function bark( ) {
                print "Yip!\n";
        }

        public function __construct($DogName) {
                print "Creating a poodle\n";
        }
}
```

If you replace the original Poodle definition with this new one and try running the script again, you will get the error message: "Trying to get property of non-object" on the line where we have print $poppy->DogTag->Words. This is because DogTag is defined as being an instance of our DogTag class only in the Dog class constructor, and, as PHP will only ever call one constructor for us, the Dog class constructor is not called because PHP finds the Poodle constructor first.

The fact that PHP always calls the "nearest" constructor—that is, if there is no child constructor, it will call the parent constructor and not the grandparent constructor—means that we need to call the parent constructor ourselves. We can do this by using the special method call parent::__construct( ). The "parent" part means "get the parent of this object, and use it," and the __construct( ) part means "Call the construct method." So the whole line means "Get the parent of this object and then call its constructor."

The call to the parent's __construct() is just a normal method call, and the dog constructor needs a dog name as its parameter. So, to make the poodle Class work properly, we would need the following:

```
class Poodle extends Dog {
        public function bark() {
                print "Yip!\n";
        }

        public function __construct($DogName) {
                parent::__construct($DogName);
                print "Creating a poodle\n";
        }
}
```

The output should be this:

```
Creating Poppy
Creating a poodle
My name is Poppy. If you find me, please call 555-1234
```

Note that "Creating Poppy" is output before "Creating a poodle", which might seem backward, but it makes sense given that we call the Dog constructor before we do any Poodle code. It is always best to call parent::__construct() first from the constructor of a child class, in order to make sure all the parent's properties are set up correctly before you try and set up the new stuff.

Destructors

Constructors are very useful, as I am sure you will agree, but there is more: PHP also allows you to define class *destructors*—a method to be called when an object is deleted. PHP calls destructors as soon as objects are no longer available, and the destructor method, __destruct(), takes no parameters. For example:

```
public function __destruct() {
        print "{$this->Name} is no more...\n";
}
```

If you add that method into the Poodle class, all Poodles created will have that method called before being destroyed. Add that into the same script as the constructor we just defined for poodles, and run it again—here's what it outputs:

```
Creating Poppy
Creating a poodle
My name is Poppy. If you find me, please call 555-1234
Poppy is no more...
```

Like constructors, destructors are only called once—you need to use parent::__destruct(). The key difference is that you should call parent::__destruct() after the local code for the destruction, so that you are not destroying properties before using it. For example:

```
public function __destruct() {
        print "{$this->Name} is no more...\n";
        parent::__destruct();
}
```

Deleting Objects

So far, our objects have been automatically destroyed at the end of the script they were created in, thanks to PHP's automatic garbage collection. However, you will almost certainly want to arbitrarily delete objects at some point in time, and this is accomplished using unset( ) in the same way as you would delete an ordinary property.

It is important to note that calling unset( ) on an object will call its destructor before deleting the object, as you would expect.

Copying Objects

From PHP 5 onward, objects are always handled as references. This means that when you pass an object into a function, any changes you make to it in there are reflected outside the function. For example:

```
function namechange($dog) {
        $dog->Name = 'Dozer';
}

namechange($poppy);
print $poppy->Name . "\n";
```

Here we define a function that accepts one variable, $dog, then changes its name to Dozer. We then pass our $poppy dog into the function, and output its name—unsurprisingly, it outputs "Dozer" rather than "Poppy". Sometimes it is important to only work on copies of objects, particularly if you don't want to affect the state of the original. To do this, we use the built-in keyword clone, which performs a complete copy of the object. For example, we could use the namechange( ) function above like this:

```
namechange(clone $poppy);
```

That would create a copy of $poppy and pass it into namechange( ), leaving the original $poppy untouched. Here is the output of the code now:

```
Creating Poppy
Creating a poodle
My name is Poppy. If you find me, please call 555-1234
Dozer is no more...
Poppy
Poppy is no more...
```

Note that Dozer is still mentioned—that is because the copied object passed into namechange( ) gets its name changed to Dozer; then, when the function ends, the copied object is automatically destroyed by PHP, and its destructor is called. However, $poppy lives on untouched, as you can see from the last two lines.

Internally, the clone keyword copies all the properties from the first object to a new object, then calls a magic method __clone( ) for the class it is copying. You can override __clone( ) if you want, thereby giving you the flexibility to perform extra actions when a property is copied—you can think of it as a constructor for a copied object. For example:

```
public function __clone() {
        $this->Name .= '++';
}
```

That method will be called on the copied object, and will set the copied object to have the same name as the original, with ++ tacked onto the end. So, rather than the clone being called Poppy, it will be called Poppy++. If we clone the clone, it will be called Poppy++++, and so on.

For really advanced functionality, you can also call parent::__clone() to work your way up the inheritance chain and call the __clone() method of the parent class. Again, all the copying of data is already done, so all the __clone() method would be required to do is make any last-minute tweaks to the copy. Here's how that looks:

```
abstract class Dog {
        public function __clone() {
                echo "In dog clone\n";
        }
}

class Poodle extends Dog {
        public $Name;
                public function __clone() {
                echo "In poodle clone\n";
                parent::__clone();
        }
}

$poppy = new Poodle();
$poppy->Name = "Poppy";

$rover = clone $poppy;
```

Comparing Objects with == and ===

When comparing objects, == and === may not work quite as you expect them to. If you were comparing two integers of the same value (e.g., 5), then == and === would both return true; however, with objects, == compares the objects' contents and === compares the objects' handles.

There is a difference there, and it's crucial: if you create an object and clone it, its clone will have exactly the same values. It will, therefore, return true for == as the two objects are the same in terms of their values. However, if you use ==, you will get false back, because it compares the handles of the objects and finds them to be different. This code example demonstrates this:

```
class Employee { }

$Bob = new Employee();
$Joe = clone $Bob;
```

```
print (int)($Bob == $Joe) . "\n";
print (int)($Joe === $Joe) . "\n";
```

That will output a 1, then a 0. Apart from basic comparison differences, this also matters because versions of PHP at 5.0.2 and earlier can encounter problems when doing a == comparison in very specific objects, like this:

```
class Employee {
        public function __construct() {
                $this->myself = $this;
        }
}

$Bob = new Employee();
$Joe = clone $Bob;

print (int)($Bob == $Joe) . "\n";
print (int)($Bob === $Joe) . "\n";
```

There is a class that puts a reference to itself in the $myself property on construction. Naturally, this is a silly thing to do, but the example is simplified—in a real scenario, it might store a reference to another object that has a reference back to itself, which would cause the same problem. If you execute that script, you won't get 1 and 0. Instead, you'll get "PHP Fatal error: Nesting level too deep - recursive dependency?" because with ==, PHP compares each individual value of the object. So it looks at the value of $myself, finds it to be an object, looks inside it, finds $myself, looks inside it, finds $myself, etc., and carries on looping.

The solution to this is to use === in the comparison, which will allow PHP to compare object handles and, therefore, immediately tell that the two objects are identical. This has been fixed in newer versions of PHP.

Saving Objects

Previously, we covered how to save arrays in PHP using serialize(), unserialize(), urlencode(), and urldecode(). Saving objects works in the same way—you serialize() them into a string to make a format that can be saved, then urlencode() them to get a format that can be passed across the web without problem.

For example:

```
$poppy = new Poodle('Poppy');
$safepoppy = urlencode(serialize($poppy));
```

There is one special feature with saving objects: when serialize() and unserialize() are called, they will look for a __sleep() and __wakeup() method on the object they are working with, respectively. These methods, which you have to provide yourself if you want them to do anything, allow you to keep an object intact during its hibernation period (when it is just a string of data).

For example, when __sleep() is called, a logging object should save and close the file it was writing to, and when __wakeup() is called, the object should reopen the file and carry on writing. Although __wakeup() need not return any value, __sleep()

must return an array of the values you wish to have saved. If no __sleep() method is present, PHP will automatically save all properties, but you can mimic this behavior in code by using the get_object_vars() method—more on that soon.

In code, our logger example would look like this:

```
class Logger {
        private function __sleep() {
                $this->saveAndExit();
                // return an empty array
                return array();
        }

        private function __wakeup() {
                $this->openAndStart();
        }

        private function saveAndExit() {
                // ...[snip]...
        }
```

Any objects of this class that are serialized would have __sleep() called on them, which would in turn call saveAndExit()—a mythical clean-up method that saves the file and such. When objects of this class are unserialized, they would have their __wakeup() method called, which would in turn call openAndStart().

To have PHP save all properties inside a __sleep() method, you need to use the get_object_vars() function. This takes an object as its only parameter and returns an array of all the properties and their values in the object. You need to pass the properties to save back as the values in the array, so you should use the array_keys() function on the return value of get_object_vars(), like this:

```
private function __sleep() {
        // do stuff here
        return array_keys(get_object_vars($this));
}
```

Magic Methods

Whenever you see a method name start with a double underscore, it is a "magic" method—one that PHP has provided that you have not declared yourself. PHP reserves all methods starting with __ as magic, which means although you can use them yourself, you may find that a later version of PHP uses them as a magic method and causes conflict.

So far, we've seen the following: __sleep(), __wakeup(), __clone(), __construct(), and __destruct()—methods that give you special control over your objects that you would not otherwise be able to have. In order to have a full understanding of OOP in PHP there several more you should know: __autoload(), __get(), __set(), __call(), and __toString().

__autoload( )

This global function is called whenever you try to create an object of a class that hasn't been defined. It takes just one parameter, which is the name of the class you have not defined. If you try to construct an object of a class that PHP does not recognize, PHP will run this function, then try to re-create the object and give you a second chance to load the right class.

As a result, you can write scripts like this:

```php
function __autoload($Class) {
        print "Bar class name: $Class!\n";
        include "barclass.php";
}

$foo = new Bar;
$foo->wombat();
```

Here we try and create a new object of type Bar, but it doesn't exist. Therefore, the __autoload( ) function is called, with "Bar" being passed in as its first parameter. This then include( )s the file *barclass.php*, which contains the class definition of Bar. PHP will again try and create a new Bar, and this time it will succeed, which means we can work with $foo as normal.

When creating more advanced scripts, you might try include( )ing the parameter passed into __autoload( )—that way you just need to define each class in a file of its own, with the file named after the class. This has been optimized so that calls to __autoload( ) are cached—don't be afraid to make good use of this technique. At O'Reilly's Open Source Conference in 2004, one of the lead developers of PHP, Andi Gutmans, said, "After having written many examples and worked with it for some time, I'd only ever code this way"—as firm an endorsement as anyone could ask for!

__get( )

This is the first of three unusual magic methods, and allows you to specify what to do if an unknown property is read from within your script. For example:

```php
class Dog {
        public $Name;
        public $DogTag;
        // public $Age;

        public function __get($var) {
                print "Attempted to retrieve $var and failed...\n";
        }
}

$poppy = new Dog;
print $poppy->Age;
```

Our Dog class has $Age commented out, and we attempt to print out the Age value of $poppy. When this script is called, $poppy is found to not to have an $Age property, so __get( ) is called for the Dog class, which prints out the name of the property that was requested—it gets passed in as the first parameter to __get( ). If you try uncommenting the public $Age; line, you will see __get( ) is no longer called, as it is only called when the script attempts to read a property that does not exist.

From a practical point of view, this means values can be calculated on the fly without the need to create and use accessor methods—not quite as elegant, perhaps, but easier to read and write.

__set( )

The __set( ) magic method complements __get( ), in that it is called whenever an undefined property is set in your scripts. Here is one example of how you could use __set( ) to create a very simple database table class and perform ad hoc queries as if they were members of the class:

```
class MyTable {
        public $Name;

        public function __construct($Name) {
                $this->Name = $Name;
        }

        public function __set($var, $val) {
                mysql_query("UPDATE {$this->Name} SET $var = '$val';");
        }

        // public $AdminEmail = 'foo@bar.com';
}

$systemvars = new MyTable("systemvars");
$systemvars->AdminEmail = 'telrev@somesite.net';
```

In that script, $AdminEmail is commented out, and therefore does not exist in the MyTable class. As a result, when $AdminEmail is set on the last line, __set( ) is called, with the name of the property being set and the value it is being set to passed in as parameters one and two, respectively. This is used to construct an SQL query in conjunction with the table name passed in through the constructor. While this might seem like an odd way to solve the problem of setting key database values, it is pretty hard to deny that the last line of code ($systemvars->AdminEmail...) is actually very easy to read.

This system could be extended to more complicated objects as long as each object knows its own ID number.

 PHP lets you set arbitrary values in objects, even if their classes don't have that value defined. If this annoys you (if you used OPTION EXPLICIT in your old Visual Basic scripts, for example) you can simulate the behavior by using __get( ) and __set( ) to print errors.

__call( )

The __call( ) magic method is to methods what __get( ) is to properties—if you call meow( ) on an object of class Dog, PHP will fail to find the method and check whether you have defined a __call( ) method. If so, your __call( ) is used, with the name of the method you tried to call and the parameters you passed being passed in as parameters one and two, respectively.

Here's an example of __call( ) in action:

```
class Dog {
        public $Name;
        public function bark( ) {
                print "Woof!\n";
        }

        // public function meow( ) {
        //        print "Dogs don't meow!\n";
        // }

        public function __call($function, $args) {
                $args = implode(', ', $args);
                print "Call to $function() with args '$args' failed!\n";
        }
}

$poppy = new Dog;
$poppy->meow("foo", "bar", "baz");
```

Again, note that the meow( ) method is commented out—if you want to be sure that __call( ) is not used if the method already exists, remove the comments from meow( ).

__toString( )

The last magic method you need to know about is __toString( ), which allows you to set a string value for the object that will be used if the object is ever used as a string. This is a fairly simple magic method, and works like this:

```
class Cat {
        public function __toString( ) {
                return "This is a cat\n";
        }
}

$toby = new Cat;
print $toby;
```

Making this work in PHP 5 caused quite a lot of headaches for the PHP developers—getting the balance right, as to when objects should be converted and when they should not, took a lot of debating. This feature is quite likely to change in future releases, and if it were not for the fact that it is perfect for use with the SimpleXML extension, I doubt it would have made it into PHP 5 at all. However, for now (2005), this is how it works.

Static Class Methods and Properties

You can declare methods and properties from a class as static, meaning that they are available to the class as well as to individual objects. For example, if we wanted to define a function, nextID( ), that returned the next available employee ID, we could declare it static. That way, we could call nextID( ) directly from the script without the need for any Employee objects. This allows you to use a helpful class method without needing to instantiate an object first.

You can also make properties static, which results in there being only one of that property for the entire class—all objects share that one property. So, rather than using the nextID( ), we could just have a static property $NextID that holds the next available employee ID number. When we create a new employee, it takes $NextID for its own $ID, then increments it by one.

To declare your properties and methods as being static, use the static keyword. Here is an example:

```
class Employee {
        static public $NextID = 1;
        public $ID;

        public function __construct( ) {
                $this->ID = self::$NextID++;
        }

        public function NextID( ) {
                return self::$NextID;
        }
}

$bob = new Employee;
$jan = new Employee;
$simon = new Employee;

print $bob->ID . "\n";
print $jan->ID . "\n";
print $simon->ID . "\n";
print Employee::$NextID . "\n";
print Employee::NextID( ) . "\n";
```

That will output 1 2 3 4, which are the employee IDs of Bob, Jan, and Simon, respectively, as well as the next available ID number, 4. Note that the scope resolution operator, ::, is used to read the static property from the Employee class.

The use of self inside the constructor refers to the class of the current object, just as earlier on we used parent to refer to the parent class of the current object.

There are some additional special rules to using static methods and properties. First, because static method calls are actually resolved at compile time, you may not use the contents of a variable as the class name, like this:

```
$foo = "Employee";
print $foo::$NextID;
// will not work
```

You cannot access static class variables from objects of that class outside of their methods, which means "$bob->NextID" will not work. You may, however, access static class methods as you would access any other method.

Helpful Utility Functions

There are three particular OOP-related functions that will make your life easier, and these are class_exists(), get_class(), and get_declared_classes(). In order, class_exists() returns true if the specified class has been declared, get_class() returns the class name of the object you pass to it, and get_declared_classes() returns an array of all classes of which you can currently create an object.

Here are some examples:

```
if ($foo == $bar) {
        $sam = new Employee;
} else {
        $sam = new Dog;
}

print "Sam is a " . get_class($sam) . "\n";
print "Class animal exists: " . class_exists("animal") . "\n\n\n\n";
print "All declared classes are: " . get_declared_classes() . "\n";
```

The most common use for get_class() is when one object can be of several possible types, as in the code above. C++ users will be familiar with the concept of Runtime Type Information (RTTI), and this is pretty much the same thing.

Interfaces

If you had a Boat class and a Plane class, how would you implement a Boatplane class? The methods found in Boat would be helpful to give you code such as sink(), scuttle(), dock(), etc., and the methods found in Plane would be helpful to give you code such as takeoff(), land(), and bailout(). What is really needed here is the ability to inherit from both the Boat class *and* the Plane class, a technique known as *multiple inheritance*.

Sadly, PHP has no support for multiple inheritance, which means it is a struggle to implement this particular scenario. The solution is to use *interfaces*, which can be thought of as abstract classes where you can define sets of abstract methods that will be used elsewhere. If we were to use interfaces in the above example, both boat and plane would be interfaces, and class Boatplane would implement both of these interfaces. A class that implements an interface has to have concrete methods for each of the abstract methods defined in the interface, so by making a class implement an interface, you are in fact saying, "This class is able to do everything the interface says it should." In essence, using interfaces is a way to form contracts with your classes—they must implement methods A, B, and C; otherwise, they will not work.

The above example could be written using interfaces like this:

```
interface Boat {
        function sink();
        function scuttle();
        function dock();
}

interface Plane {
        function takeoff();
        function land();
        function bailout();
}

class Boatplane implements Boat, Plane {
        public function sink() { }
        public function scuttle() { }
        public function dock() { }
        public function takeoff() { }
        public function land() { }
        public function bailout() { }
}

$obj = new Boatplane();
```

There are no access modifiers for the methods in the interface: they are all public by default, because it doesn't make sense to have them as anything else. Similarly, you shouldn't try to use abstract or static modifiers on your interfaces—if you get an error like "PHP Fatal error: Access type for interface method boat::sink() must be omitted", you know you've gone wrong somewhere.

Try commenting out the bailout() method in the Boatplane class, so that it only has five methods as opposed to six. Now run the script again. PHP should quit with the fatal error, "Fatal error: Class Boatplane contains 1 abstract methods and must therefore be declared abstract (plane::bailout)".

Our Boatplane class, by implementing both the boat and plane interfaces, has essentially promised PHP it will have a method bailout(). Therefore, PHP gives it one by default—the bailout() method from the plane interface. However, as interfaces and their methods are entirely abstract, and by commenting out that one line, we have not re-implemented bailout() in the Boatplane class. The abstract method will be used and will thereby make the entire Boatplane class abstract—hence the error. What this has proved is that when a class implements an interface, it makes an unbreakable contract with PHP that it will implement each method specified in that interface.

Uncomment the bailout() method in the Boatplane class, and try commenting out both the Boat and Plane interfaces, as well as rewriting the Boatplane class so that you remove the "implements" part. This time the script should run fine, just as it did the first time around. Essentially, there is nothing different—the Boatplane class has all the same methods as it did before, so why bother with interfaces at all? The key is the "unbreakable contract" aspect, because by having a class implement an interface, you know for a fact that it must implement *all* the methods specified in the interface and not just one or two.

The use of interfaces should be considered in the same light as the use of access modifiers—declaring a property private changes nothing, really, except that it forces other programmers (and perhaps yourself) to live up to various expectations about the object of that class. The same applies to interfaces and, although they are perhaps likely to remain one of the more niche aspects of PHP, they are certainly here to stay.

 There is one situation in which interfaces actually make a concrete difference to your code, and that's with the Standard PHP Library (SPL), which is a set of reusable interfaces and classes that solve basic programming problems. When trying to use functionality from the SPL, you must always implement the appropriate interfaces—just implementing the methods isn't good enough.

The function get_declared_interfaces( ) will return an array of all the interfaces currently available to you, and it takes no parameters.

If you really want to delve deep into the world of interfaces, you can also have one interface inheriting from another using the same syntax you would use to inherit classes. As a result, this next script is the same as the previous one, as the plane interface inherits from the boat interface, and the Boatplane class implements the Plane interface:

```
interface Boat {
        function sink( );
        function scuttle( );
        function dock( );
}

interface Plane extends Boat {
        function takeoff( );
        function land( );
        function bailout( );
}

class Boatplane implements Plane {
        public function sink( ) { }
        public function scuttle( ) { }
        public function dock( ) { }
        public function takeoff( ) { }
        public function land( ) { }
        public function bailout( ) { }
}

$obj = new Boatplane( );
```

 It's important to note that although interfaces can extend other interfaces, and classes can implement interfaces, interfaces cannot extend classes. If you try this, you'll get an error along the lines of "Fatal error: boat cannot implement dog - it is not an interface".

Dereferencing Object Return Values

If you call a function that returns an object, you can treat the return value of that function as an object from the calling line and access it directly. For example:

```
$lassie = new Dog( );
$collar = $lassie->getCollar( );
echo $collar->Name;

$poppy = new Dog( );
echo $poppy->getCollar( )->Name;
```

In the first example, we need to call getCollar( ) and save the returned value into $collar, before echoing out the Name property of $collar. In the second example, we use the return value from getCollar( ) immediately from within the same line of code, and echo out Name without an intermediate property like $collar.

> For now at least, return value dereferencing only applies to objects. If you have a function someFunc( ) that returns an array, for example, using $obj->someFunc( )[3] to access an element in the return value will cause a parse error—you need to store the return value in another property, then access it.

9

HTML Forms

PHP was originally designed for use on the Internet, and although you can now use it for command-line applications and GUIs, its main purpose remains working on the Web. When it comes to the Web, HTML has ruled unchallenged for some years as the de facto standard for displaying information, even more so now that WAP usage has evaporated. This means that if you want to write a frontend for your PHP web applications, you need to understand HTML.

HTML is a very simple markup language that offers its users a great deal of flexibility. While this might make it easy to learn and write in, it makes the job of web browsers such as Internet Explorer and Mozilla much harder, because they need to be able to cope with thousands of exceptions.

The problem with HTML is that it became used to express style instead of just information. For example, designers would use HTML to specify the font of a piece of text, as opposed to what that the text *was*. With content and style so irretrievably mixed inside HTML, computers were not able to extract information about a document simply by reading through the HTML tags used.

A movement was started to redefine how web pages are designed so that HTML would contain only content information, with a new language, CSS (cascading style sheets) storing the style information. There were also some recommending that XML was the way forward for data, and that HTML could be eliminated altogether. While the XML argument made sense, many realized that there were simply too many HTML-based web sites in existence to be able to just drop HTML, so the standard "XHTML" was born—a modification of HTML that makes it XML-compliant.

The code you see in this book is all XHTML-compliant, and I recommend you keep to this in your own work. You may notice that all HTML attributes are surrounded by quotes, and all HTML tags used in this book are closed either by using `</tag>` or `<tag/>`—these are two of the rules enforced in XHTML. While teaching HTML and/or XHTML is outside the scope of this book, we are at least going to look at creating HTML forms, which are the primary means of sending data to PHP.

What Does It Mean to Be Dynamic?

Before Perl and PHP became widespread on the web site scene, the vast majority of sites were classed as "static"—they would only change when the original author(s) uploaded new content to them. This was fine for the time, because the Internet's primary aim was for many years to be a tool to allow universities and research institutes to share information and learning.

When the Web first started to be used by the masses in the mid-90s, the number of uses it could be put to grew very quickly, and people wanted to do everything online—reserving tickets for a gig, shopping, and downloading music. In order to be able to properly communicate with users, dynamic sites became popular because they could get feedback from users, allow users to influence content on sites by adding their own information and views, and form communities of people who all share the same goal.

Designing a Form

A "form" on the Web is considered to be zero or more form elements, plus a submit button. These forms are designed to electronically replicate the forms we've all filled in hundreds of times before in real life—signing up for a bank account, a passport, etc. You start your form using the <form> HTML tag, and you end with </form>. By separating forms like this, you can have multiple forms on one page.

Given the above definition, here is the most basic form in HTML:

```
<form>
<input type="submit" />
</form>
```

That will simply show a button with "Submit" written on it, which will not submit any data when clicked. Figure 9-1 shows how it looks in Konqueror running on Linux:

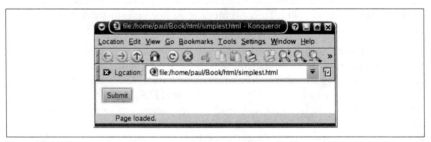

Figure 9-1. The most basic form is just a Submit button by itself

There are two attributes to the <form> tag that you should be aware of and use: action and method. Action sets the location of the page that will handle the results of the form—the place where the variables should be sent. Method describes how the data should be submitted, and you have two options: GET and POST.

GET and POST

When defining the method a web browser should use to send variables to the page specified by your action, you either use GET or POST. Both send variables across to a page, but they do so in different ways.

GET sends its variables in the URL of your visitors' web browsers (shown in Figure 9-2), which makes it easy to see what was sent. However, it also makes it very easy for visitors to change what was sent, and, moreover, there is usually a low limit on the number of characters that can be sent in a URL—often fewer than 250. As a result, if you send long variables using GET, you are likely to lose large amounts of them.

Figure 9-2. HTTP GET sends data in the URL in a very obvious manner

POST sends its variables behind the scenes, which means it is much harder to mimic, cannot be changed without some effort on your visitors' behalf, and has a much higher limit (usually several megabytes) on the amount of data that can be sent. The downside to using POST is that browsers will not automatically resend post data if your user clicks her Back button, leading to messages like "The data on this page needs to be resent", which often confuse users. This does not happen with GET, because browsers consider GET URLs the same as any other URL, and happily resend data as needed.

You can set how much data PHP should accept by editing the post_max_size entry in your *php.ini* file—it is usually set to 8M by default, allowing your users to transfer up to 8 megabytes.

Given this newfound knowledge, here's the same form again, this time using action and method. It will still look the same as our previous effort, but this time it will use POST to send data to *someform.php*:

```
<form action="someform.php" method="post">
<input type="submit" />
</form>
```

Available Elements

There are many types of elements you can place into your forms. The most important of these are shown in Table 9-1.

Table 9-1. HTML elements for use in forms

Element	Description
input type="checkbox"	A checkbox that lets users select multiple options.
input type="file"	A text box plus a button that opens a file selection dialog.
input type="hidden"	A hidden form element where you set the value.
input type="password"	A text box where the text is replaced by a password character (usually asterisk *).

Table 9-1. HTML elements for use in forms (continued)

Element	Description
input type="radio"	A radio button. Radio buttons are like grouped checkboxes—you can only select one at a time.
input type="reset"	A button to clear the form. It's one of the weird oddities of the Web that this still exists—do *you* know anyone who uses it?
input type="submit"	A button to submit the form.
input type="text"	A text box.
option	An option in a SELECT element.
select	A listbox; can also be a drop-down list box.
textarea	Multiline text box.

There are four elements worthy of particular note: file elements actually upload files to the server, and can take quite a long time to transfer if the connection speed is slow—handling file uploads is covered later. Hidden elements don't appear on your user's screen; they are useful when keeping information across forms and pages, or simply just to force input for certain fields.

Password elements hide the password on the client side by using *s or something similar, but it is important to note that the password is still sent in plain text—no encryption is done. Finally, textarea elements need a closing tag, with the text in between forming their content, i.e., <textarea>Some text</textarea>.

A Working Form

We now have enough information to construct a working form, so here goes:

```
<form action="someform.php" method="post">
Name: <input type="text" name="Name" value="Jim" /><br />
Password: <input type="password" name="Password" /><br />
Age: <input type="text" name="Age" /><br />
<input type="submit" />
</form>
```

That will submit three variables to *someform.php*: Name, Password, and Age. Form variables are given names using the name attribute—the names you use here will be used in the PHP script that receives the variables. The default value of a field can be set using the value attribute, which means that the Name text box will be set to Jim by default.

This new form is shown in Figure 9-3.

The Age field, which will presumably contain numbers like 18, 34, etc., is the same type as the Name field, which is likely to contain strings like "Bob," "Sarah," etc. HTML does not have any way to say "restrict this field to numbers only," which means users can enter their age as "Elephant," if they wish. Never trust input from users!

And now a more complicated form, using various other types:

```
<form action="someform.php" method="get">
Name: <input type="text" name="Name" value="Jim" /><br />
```

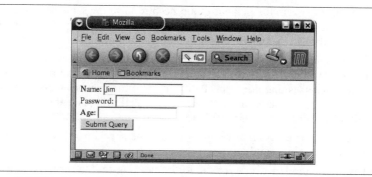

Figure 9-3. This time the form is more advanced—note the default value for the Name field

```
Password: <input type="password" name="Password" maxlength="10" /><br />
Age range: <select name="Age">
<option value="Under 16">Under 16</option>
<option value="16-30" selected="selected">16-30</option>
<option value="31-50">31-50</option>
<option value="51-80">51-80</option>
</select><br /><br />
Life story:<br /> <textarea name="Story" rows="10" cols="80">
Enter your life story here</textarea><br /><br />
<input type="radio" name="FaveSport" value="Tennis" /> Tennis
<input type="radio" name="FaveSport" value="Cricket" /> Cricket
<input type="radio" name="FaveSport" value="Baseball" /> Baseball
<input type="radio" name="FaveSport" value="Polo" /> Polo
<br />
<input type="checkbox" name="Languages[ ]" value="PHP" checked="checked" />
PHP
<input type="checkbox" name="Languages[ ]" value="CPP" /> C++
<input type="checkbox" name="Languages[ ]" value="Delphi" /> Delphi
<input type="checkbox" name="Languages[ ]" value="Java" /> Java
<br /><input type="submit" />
</form>
```

There are several pieces of particular importance in there, so you should read through carefully:

- maxlength="10" is one of the attributes for the Password element—this can be used in normal text boxes too, and acts to restrict the number of characters that can be typed in to the value of maxlength (10, in the example).

- Age is now a drop down list box—note how the name attribute is placed inside the select element, but each individual option element has its own value. The text inside the value attribute is what is submitted to the form handler specified in the form's action attribute. The text after each option and before the next option is the text the user will see.

- selected is specified as an attribute of one of the option elements, which means that that option will be the default selection of the parent select list.

- Life story is a textarea element. Note that it has attributes rows and cols to specify the size of the text area in characters.

- All members of a radio element group need to have the same name attribute. The name attribute is used to inform the browser which group each radio element is part of so that users can select only one at a time.

- All members of a checkbox group need to have the same name attribute, and that name attribute needs square brackets [ ] at the end. The reason for the square brackets is that it informs PHP that the value may be an array of information—users can select multiple values, and PHP will place them all into an array of the value of the name attribute.

- checked is specified as an attribute of one of the checkboxes, which means it will be checked by default.

- GET is the method attribute for the form, meaning that the information sent through to the handler page (*someform.php*) will be sent in the location bar of the browser as a normal URL. This will allow you to see how easy it is to change variables in the location bar and, by entering lots of text into the Story textarea element, how easy it is to have too much data for GET to handle.

Figure 9-4 shows how the form should look.

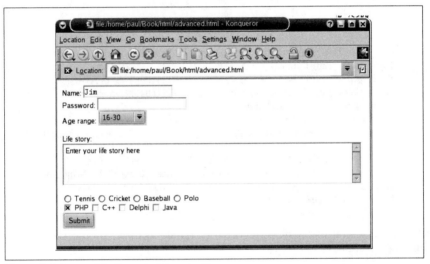

Figure 9-4. Some of the form elements on offer

Hundreds of books have been published on HTML programming, and if you want to carry on learning more about HTML, you will do best to pick up one of them. If you're not sure where to start, try *HTML & XHTML: The Definitive Guide* by Musciano and Kennedy (O'Reilly).

Handling Data

Handling data coming in from HTML pages is by far the most common task in PHP, and many might say it deserves a whole chapter to itself! In this section, we will be looking at how variables get into your scripts, and also at how you can distinguish between where those variables come from.

register_globals

Prior to PHP 4.1, variables submitted from external sources—such as session variables, cookies, form fields, etc.—were automatically converted to variables inside PHP, as long as register_globals was enabled in the *php.ini* file, which it was by default. These variables were also accessible through the arrays $HTTP_POST_VARS, $HTTP_COOKIE_VARS, $HTTP_SESSION_VARS, etc.

Imagine the following situation: you have a secure site, where members are identified by logon names, such as "Administrator," "Joe," and "Peter." The pages on this site track the username by way of the variable UserID, which is stored in a cookie on the computer when the user authenticates to the site. With register_globals enabled, $UserID is available as a variable to all scripts on your site, which, while helpful, is a security hole.

Here is a URL that demonstrates the problem: *http://www.yoursite.com/secure.php?UserID=root*. When register_globals is enabled, all variables sent by GET and POST are also converted to variables, and are indistinguishable from variables from other sources. The result of this is that a hacker could, by using the URL above, impersonate someone else—like root!

This was clearly a critical situation, and it was worryingly common. As such, the decision was made to recommend that all users disable register_globals. In PHP 4.2, this was pushed further by having the default value of register_globals changed to off, and this is how it has remained in PHP 5. Register_globals is not likely to be changed back to on for its default value, which means that it is best to learn the proper way of doing things: using the superglobals.

Working Around register_globals

In order to provide a middle ground for users who did not want to use the superglobals but also did not want to enable register_globals, the function import_request_variables() was introduced. This copies variables from the superglobal arrays into variables in their own right, and takes two parameters: a special string of which types of variables to convert, and the prefix that should be added to them.

The special string can contain "g" for GET variables, "p" for POST, "c" for cookies, or any combination of them. The prefix works in almost the same way as the prefix to extract() does, except that it does not add an underscore, which means that scripts relying on older functionality can use import_request_variables() to get back to the old manner of working. As with the prefix used in extract(), the string is appended to the beginning of the names of each variable created to ensure there is no naming clash with existing data.

Here are some examples:

```
import_request_variable("p", "post");
import_request_variable("gp", "gp");
import_request_variable("cg", "cg");
```

Note that the order of the letters in the first parameter matters—in gp, for example, any POST variables that have the same names as GET variables will overwrite the GET variables. In other words, the GET variables are imported first, then the POST variables. If we had used pg, it would have been POST and then GET, so the ordering is crucial.

Once import_request_variables( ) is used, you can use the new variables immediately, like this:

```
print $_GET['Name'];
import_request_variables("g", "var");
print $varName;
```

If you don't specify a prefix, or if the prefix is empty, you will get a notice to warn you of the security issue.

It is strongly recommended that you avoid using import_request_variables( ) unless you cannot live without it. Importing external data into the global variable namespace is dangerous; the superglobal arrays are much safer.

Magic Quotes

PHP has a special *php.ini* setting called magic_quotes_gpc, which means that PHP will automatically place backslashes (\) before all quotes and other backslashes for GET, POST, and COOKIE data (GPC)—the equivalent of running the addslashes( ) function. These slashes are required to make user input safe for database entry. Without them, strings are likely to be interpreted incorrectly.

This functionality is usually turned on by default, which means that all GPC data coming into your script is safe for database entry. But it also means that if your data is not destined for a database, you need to disable magic quotes in your *php.ini* file.

I prefer to turn off magic quotes and handle the slashes myself, as this leads to much more predictable and easily understood behavior. Changing your execution environment at runtime to enable magic quotes will have no effect on the script, as the variables are already parsed and ready for use by the time your code is executed. So, the only way to do this is to set magic_quotes_gpc to off in your *php.ini* file.

Handling Our Form

You now know enough to be able to program a script to handle the advanced form presented previously. Our variables will be coming in using the GET method. In the real world, you would use POST because it is possible that users will submit large quantities of data in the "Life story" field; however, using GET here lets you see how it all works. Because we're using the GET method, we should be reading our variables from $_GET.

The first two fields sent are Name and Password, which will both contain string data. Remember that the password HTML form element transmits its data as plain text, which means that both Name and Password can be handled the same way. As they are coming in via GET, the values entered by our visitors will be in $_ GET['Name'] and $_GET['Password']—note that the cases have been preserved from the form exactly and that, as per usual, PHP considers $_GET['name'] to be different from $_GET['Name'].

The next input is the select list box Age, which will return a string value—either "Under 16", "16-30", "31-50", or "51-80". From the PHP point of view, this is no different from handling input from a text box other than that we can, to a certain extent, have an idea about what the values will be. That is, under normal circumstances, we will always know what the values will be, as our users have to pick one option from a list we present. However, it takes only a little knowledge to "hack" the page so that users can input what they like—just remember the golden rule: "Never trust user input."

The Story text area element submits data in the same way as a normal text box does, with the difference that it can contain new line characters \n. The chances are that you want to HTML line breaks (the <br /> tag) as well as the \n line breaks, so you should use nl2br( ), like this:

```
$_GET['Story'] = nl2br($_GET['Story']);
```

Next we get to our radio buttons, FaveSport. As radio buttons can only submit one value, this one value will be available as a normal variable in $_ GET['FaveSport']. This is in contrast to the checkbox form elements that follow— they have the name Languages[ ], which will make PHP convert them into a single array of values, available in $_GET['Languages'].

We can put the whole script together using the above information, plus the other techniques we've covered in previous chapters. This script parses the form properly:

```
$_GET['Languages'] = implode(', ', $_GET['Languages']);
$_GET['Story'] = str_replace("\n", "<br />", $_GET['Story']);

print "Your name: {$_GET['Name']}<br />";
print "Your password: {$_GET['Password']}<br />";
print "Your age: {$_GET['Age']}<br /><br />";
print "Your life story:<br />{$_GET['Story']}<br /><br />";
print "Your favorite sport: {$_GET['FaveSport']}<br />";
print "Languages you chose: {$_GET['Languages']}<br />";
```

The entire script to handle the HTML form we created is just eight lines long, of which six are just print statements reading from the $_GET array. The first two lines aren't anything special either: line one converts the Languages array created from the checkboxes into one string using implode( ), and line two converts the new line characters in the Story text area into HTML line breaks.

However, the script above contains a bug. What happens if our users *don't* check any boxes for languages? The answer is that browsers *will not* send any languages information, which means that $_GET['Languages'] will not be set, which in turn means that the first line in the script will cause an error. The solution is simple: use if (isset($_GET['Languages'])) to check whether there is a value set. If there is, use implode( ) to make it a string, and if not, put a dummy text string in there like, "You didn't select any languages!" The final output of this form is shown in Figure 9-5.

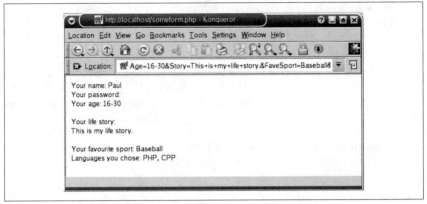

Figure 9-5. The finished form handler—note the variables being passed in the URL bar because we used GET

Splitting Forms Across Pages

Very often it is necessary to split up one long form into several smaller forms, placed across several pages. When this is the case, you can pass data from page to page by using hidden form elements, storing answers in session values, or storing answers in a database.

Of the three, you are most likely to find using hidden form elements the easiest to program and the easiest to debug. As long as you are using POST, data size will not be a problem, and the advantage is that you can view the HTML source code at any time to see if things are working as planned. Of course, that also means that hackers can view the source code (and make changes to it), so you should really only resort to hidden fields if you can't use sessions for some reason.

If our existing form was part one of a larger set of forms, we would need to append the following HTML to the bottom of part two of the forms so that the values are carried over to part three:

```
<input type="hidden" name="Name" value="<?php print $_GET['Name']; ?>" />
<input type="hidden" name="Password" value="<?php print $_GET['Password'];
?>" />
```

You'd need to have all the others there also, but it works in the same way, so there is no point repeating them all here.

Validating Input

Any sensible site should include server-side validation of variables, because they are much harder to hack, and they will work no matter what browsers your visitors are using.

Basic input validation in PHP is done using the functions is_string( ), is_numeric( ), is_float( ), is_array( ), and is_object( ). Each of these functions take just one parameter, a variable of their namesake, and return true if that variable is of the appropriate type. For example, is_numeric( ) will return true if the variable passed to it is a number, and is_object( ) will return true if its variable is an object. There is one other function of this type that works the same way but is useless for validation, and that is is_resource( )—it's mentioned here for the sake of completeness.

The three basic validation checks you should conduct on input are whether you have each of your required variables, whether they have a value assigned, and whether they are of the type you were expecting. From there, you can conduct more complicated checks, such as whether the integer values are in the range you would expect, whether the string values have enough characters, whether the arrays have enough elements, etc.

Here are some examples:

```
// is the $Age variable set with a numeric value between 18 and 30?
if (isset($Age)) {
        if (is_numeric($Age)) {
                if (($Age > 18) && ($Age < 30)) {
                        // input is valid
                } else {
                        print "Sorry, you're not the right age!";
                }
        } else {
                // empty or non-numeric
                print "Age is incorrect!"
        }
} else {
        print "Please provide a value for Age.";
}


// is $SpouseAge either unset, blank, or between 18 and 120?
if (isset($SpouseAge) && $SpouseAge != "") {
        if (is_numeric($SpouseAge)) {
                if (($SpouseAge >= 18) && ($SpouseAge < 120)) {
                        // input is valid
                } else {
                        print "Spouse is not the right age!";
                }
        } else {
                print "Spouse Age is incorrect!";
        }
} else {
        // input is valid; no spouse
        print "You have no spouse.";
}


// is $Income non-negative?
if (isset($Income)) {
        if (is_numeric($Income)) {
                if ($Income >= 0) {
                        // input is valid
```

```
            } else {
                    print "Your income is negative!";
            }
        } else {
                print "Please provide a numeric value for Income.";
        }
    } else {
            print "Please valid a value for Income.";
    }
```

 There is a function confusingly similar to is_numeric( ), called is_int( ). This returns true if the variable passed in is an integer, which may sound similar to is_numeric( ). However, data passed in through a form, even if numeric in content, is of type string, which means that is_int( ) will fail. On the other hand, is_numeric( ) returns true if the variable is a number or a string containing a number. This same problem applies to is_float( ), as floating-point values set from user input are typed as strings.

For more specific parsing of character types in a variable, the CTYPE library is available. There are eleven CTYPE functions in total, all of which work in the same way as is_numeric( ): you pass a variable in, and get either true or false back.

Table 9-2 categorizes what each function matches.

Table 9-2. The CTYPE functions and what they match

ctype_alnum( )	Matches A–Z, a–z, 0–9
ctype_alpha( )	Matches A–Z, a–z
ctype_cntrl( )	Matches ASCII control characters
ctype_digit( )	Matches 0–9
ctype_graph( )	Matches values that can be represented graphically
ctype_lower( )	Matches a–z
ctype_print( )	Matches visible characters (not whitespace)
ctype_punct( )	Matches all non-alphanumeric characters (not whitespace)
ctype_space( )	Matches whitespace (space, tab, new line, etc.)
ctype_upper( )	Matches A–Z
ctype_xdigit( )	Matches digits in hexadecimal format

The matches are absolute, which means that ctype_digit( ) will return false for the value "123456789a" because of the "a" at the end, as this script shows:

```
$var = "123456789a";
print (int)ctype_digit($var);
```

Similarly, "123 " will fail the ctype_digit( ) test because it has a space after the number. There is no match for floating-point numbers available, as ctype_digit( ) matches 0–9 without also matching the decimal point. As a result, it will return false for 123.456. For this purpose you need to use is_float( ).

Form Design

As mentioned already, forms are the primary way for users to send data to your scripts, so it's essential that you get them right. Above and beyond the coding aspect of forms, there are a number of basic usability guidelines you should follow in your design:

- Use stylesheets or tables to lay your elements out neatly. This makes the form easier to read, and it is also easier to report individual errors on fields.

- If there is an error within a field, put a notice next to it and a message at the top of the page; otherwise, people may not realize there's a problem. You should also consider changing the color of the problem field to make it obvious which one is bad.

- Mark required fields either with bold text or, more commonly, an asterisk *.

- If your database has a field length limit, put a size limit on a text box to stop people from entering too much text and later finding out their data has been trimmed by your database.

- Don't make your forms too long—they confuse people and make them feel threatened.

- If you split your form across pages, let your visitors know how far they are in the process of form submission, e.g., "Page 2 of 5." This lets people know where they stand at all times, without leaving them wondering, "Will this next button take money out of my account, or are there more pages to come?"

Summary

- If you are using PHP to handle form input data—and let's face it, you probably will do so some day, if you are not already—make sure you do not make any assumptions about the reliability of the data. Remember, it came from users, and we don't trust users, do we?

- If you are inserting form data into your database, try turning magic quotes on. Then turn it back off again once you realize it's evil, and switch to something like `mysql_escape_string( )`.

- Users already have a hard enough time *before* they get in contact with your forms, so do not make them more complicated than they need to be. Split forms across pages if possible, keep selections to a minimum, lay options out neatly using HTML tables, and mark required fields clearly.

HTML Forms

10

Cookies and Sessions

HTTP is a stateless protocol, which means that any data you have stored is forgotten when the page has been sent to the client and the connection is closed. Eventually, Netscape invented the *cookie*—a tiny bit of information that a web site could store on the client's machine that was sent back to the web site each time the page was requested. Each cookie could only be read by the web site that had written it, meaning that it was a secure way to store information across pages.

Cookies earned a bad name at first, because they allowed people to track how often a visitor came to their site and what they did while there, and many people believed that cookies signalled the end of privacy on the Web. Urban myths popped up saying that cookies could read any information from your hard drive, and people were encouraged to disable cookies across the board. The reality is that cookies are harmless, and fortunately for us, are now commonly accepted.

Sessions grew up from cookies as a way of storing data on the server side, because the inherent problem of storing anything sensitive on clients' machines is that they are able to tamper with it if they wish. In order to set up a unique identifier on the client, sessions still use a small cookie that holds a value that identifies the client to the server, and corresponds to a datafile on the server.

Cookies Versus Sessions

Both cookies and sessions are available to you as a PHP developer, and both accomplish the same task of storing data across pages on your site. However, there are differences between the two.

Cookies can be set to a long lifespan, which means that data stored in a cookie can be stored for months, if not years. Cookies, having their data stored on the client, work smoothly when you have a cluster of web servers, whereas sessions are stored on the server, meaning if one of your web servers handles the first request, the other web servers in your cluster will not have the stored information. Cookies can also be manipulated on the client side, using JavaScript, whereas sessions cannot.

Sessions are stored on the server, which means clients do not have access to the information you store about them. This is particularly important if you store shopping baskets or other information you do not want your visitors to be able to edit by hacking their cookies. Session data, being stored on your server, does not need to be transmitted with each page; clients just need to send an ID, and the data is loaded from the local file. Finally, sessions can be any size you want because they are held on your server, whereas many web browsers have a limit on how big cookies can be to stop rogue web sites chewing up gigabytes of data with meaningless cookie information. Sessions rely upon a client-side cookie to store the session identifier—without this, PHP must resort to placing the identifier in the URL, which is insecure. If a cookie is used, it is set to expire as soon as the user closes his browser.

Cookies versus sessions usually comes down to one choice: do you want your data to work when your visitor comes back the next day? If so, then your only choice is cookies. If you are storing sensitive information, store it in a database and use the cookie to store an ID number to reference the data. If you do not need semi-permanent data, then sessions are generally preferred—they are a little easier to use, do not require their data to be sent in entirety with each page, and are also cleaned up as soon as your visitor closes his web browser.

 Because cookies are stored on your visitor's computer, they can easily be changed by the visitor. This presents a serious security problem: if you store a user ID in a cookie to allow people to automatically log in when they visit your site, that user could edit the cookie to a different ID number and thus impersonate anyone. It's problems like this that make sesssions preferable for secure data; cookies are hard to secure without resorting to security through obscurity.

Using Cookies

The setcookie( ) call needs to be before the HTML form because of the way the web works. HTTP operates by sending all "header" information before it sends "body" information. In the header, it sends things like server type (e.g., "Apache"), page size (e.g., "29019 bytes"), and other important data. In the body, it sends the actual HTML you see on the screen. HTTP works in such a way that header data cannot come after body data—you must send all your header data before you send any body data at all.

Cookies come into the category of header data. When you place a cookie using setcookie( ), your web server adds a line in your header data for that cookie. If you try and send a cookie after you have started sending HTML, PHP will flag serious errors and the cookie will not get placed.

There are two ways to correct this:

- Put your cookies at the top of your page. By sending them before you send anybody data, you avoid the problem entirely.
- Enable output buffering in PHP. This allows you to send header information such as cookies wherever you like—even after (or in the middle of) body data. Output buffering is covered in depth in the following chapter.

The setcookie() function itself takes three main parameters: the name of the cookie, the value of the cookie, and the date the cookie should expire. For example:

```
setcookie("Name", $_POST['Name'], time() + 31536000);
```

 Cookies are sent to the server each time a user visits a page. So, if you set a cookie in a script, it does not become available until your user visits the next page (or hits refresh)—this often confuses people who are desperately hunting for a bug.

In the example code, setcookie() sets a cookie called Name to the value set in a form element called Name. It uses time() + 31536000 as its third parameter, which is equal to the current time in seconds plus the number of seconds in a year, so that the cookie is set to expire one year from the time it was set.

Once set, the Name cookie will be sent with every subsequent page request, and PHP will make it available in $_COOKIE. Users can clear their cookies manually, either by using a special option in their web browser or just by deleting files.

The last three parameters of the setcookie() function allow you to restrict when it's sent, which gives you a little more control:

- Parameter four (*path*) allows you to set a directory in which the cookie is active. By default, this is / (active for the entire site), but you could set it to /messageboards/ to have the cookie only available in that directory and its subdirectories.
- Parameter five (*domain*) allows you to set a subdomain in which the cookie is active. For example, specifying "mail.yoursite.com" will make the cookie available there but not on www.yoursite.com. Use ".yoursite.com" to make the cookie available everywhere.
- Parameter six (*secure*) lets you specify whether the cookie must only be sent through a HTTPS connection or not. The default, 0, has the cookie sent across both HTTPS and HTTP, but you can set it to 1 to force HTTPS only.

Once a cookie has been set, it becomes available to use on subsequent page loads through the $_COOKIE superglobal array variable. Using the previous call to setcookie(), subsequent page loads can have their Name value read like this:

```
print $_COOKIE["Name"];
```

Using Sessions

Sessions store temporary data about your visitors and are particularly good when you don't want that data to be accessible from outside of your server. They are an alternative to cookies if the client has disabled cookie access on her machine, because PHP can automatically rewrite URLs to pass a session ID around for you.

Starting a Session

A session is a combination of a server-side file containing all the data you wish to store, and a client-side cookie containing a reference to the server data. The file and the client-side cookie are created using the function session_start( )—it has no parameters but informs the server that sessions are going to be used.

When you call session_start( ), PHP will check to see whether the visitor sent a session cookie. If it did, PHP will load the session data. Otherwise, PHP will create a new session file on the server, and send an ID back to the visitor to associate the visitor with the new file. Because each visitor has his own data locked away in his unique session file, you need to call session_start( ) before you try to read session variables—failing to do so will mean that you simply will not have access to his data. Furthermore, as session_start( ) needs to send the reference cookie to the user's computer, you need to have it before the body of your web page—even before any spaces.

Adding Session Data

All your session data is stored in the session superglobal array, $_SESSION, which means that each session variable is one element in that array, combined with its value. Adding variables to this array is done in the same way as adding variables to any array, with the added bonus that session variables will still be there when your user browses to another page.

To set a session variable, use syntax like this:

```
$_SESSION['var'] = $val;
$_SESSION['FirstName'] = "Jim";
```

Older versions of PHP used the function session_register( ); however, use of this function is strongly discouraged, as it will not work properly in default installations of PHP 5. If you have scripts that use session_register( ), you should switch them over to using the $_SESSION superglobal, as it is more portable and easier to read.

Before you can add any variables to a session, you need to have already called the session_start( ) function—don't forget!

You cannot store resources such as database connections in sessions, because these resources are unique to each PHP script and are usually cleaned when that script terminates.

Reading Session Data

Once you have put your data away, it becomes available in the $_SESSION super-global array with the key of the variable name you gave it. Here is an example of setting data and reading it back out again:

```
$_SESSION['foo'] = 'bar';
print $_SESSION['foo'];
```

Unlike cookies, session data is available as soon as it is set.

Removing Session Data

Removing a specific value from a session is as simple as using the function unset( ), just as you would for any other variable. It is important that you unset only specific elements of the $_SESSION array, not the $_SESSION array itself, because that would leave you unable to manipulate the session data at all.

To extend the previous script to remove data, use this:

```
$_SESSION['foo'] = 'bar';
print $_SESSION['foo'];
unset($_SESSION['foo']);
```

Ending a Session

A session lasts until your visitor closes her browser—if she navigates away to another page, then returns to your site without having closed her browser, *her session will still exist*. Your visitor's session data might potentially last for days, as long as she keeps browsing around your site, whereas cookies usually have a fixed lifespan.

If you want to explicitly end a user's session and delete his data without him having to close his browser, you need to clear the $_SESSION array, then use the session_destroy( ) function. The session_destroy( ) function removes all session data stored on your hard disk, leaving you with a clean slate.

To end a session and clear its data, use this code:

```
session_start( );
$_SESSION = array( );
session_destroy( );
```

There are two important things to note there. First, session_start( ) is called so that PHP loads the user's session, and second, we use an empty call to the array( ) function to make $_SESSION an empty array—effectively wiping it. If session_ start( ) is not called, neither of the following two lines will work properly, so always call session_start( ).

Checking Session Data

You can check whether a variable has been set in a user's session using isset( ), as you would a normal variable. Because the $_SESSION superglobal is only initial-ized once session_start( ) has been called, you need to call session_start( ) before using isset( ) on a session variable. For example:

```
session_start();

if (isset($_SESSION['FirstName'])) {
        /// your code here
}
```

You can also use empty( ) with session data, or indeed any other function—the $_SESSION array and its data can be used like any other array.

Files Versus Databases

The session-handling system in PHP is actually quite basic at its core, simply storing and retrieving values from flat files based upon unique session IDs handed out when a session is started. While this system works very well for small-scale solutions, it does not work too well when multiple servers come into play. The problem is down to location: where should session data be stored?

If session data is stored in files, the files would need to be in a shared location somewhere—not ideal for performance or locking reasons. However, if the data is stored in a database, that database could then be accessed from all machines in the web server cluster, thereby eliminating the problem. PHP's session storage system was designed to be flexible enough to cope with this situation.

 PHP saves its session data to your /tmp directory by default, which is usually readable by everyone who has access to your server. As a result, be careful what you store in your sessions or, better yet, either change the save location or use a database with finer-grained security controls!

To use your own solution in place of the standard session handlers, you need to call the function session_set_save_handler( ), which takes several parameters. In order to handle sessions, you need to have your own callback functions that handle a set of events, which are:

- Session open (called by session_start( ))
- Session close (called at page end)
- Session read (called after session_start( ))
- Session write (called when session data is to be written)
- Session destroy (called by session_destroy( ))
- Session garbage collect (called randomly)

To handle these six events, you need to create six functions with very specific numbers of functions and return types. Then you pass these six functions into session_set_save_handler( ) in that order, and you are all set. This sets up all the basic functions, and prints out what gets passed to the function so you can see how the session operations work:

```
function sess_open($sess_path, $sess_name) {
        print "Session opened.\n";
        print "Sess_path: $sess_path\n";
        print "Sess_name: $sess_name\n\n";
        return true;
```

```
    }

    function sess_close() {
            print "Session closed.\n";
            return true;
    }

    function sess_read($sess_id) {
            print "Session read.\n";
            print "Sess_ID: $sess_id\n";
            return '';
    }

    function sess_write($sess_id, $data) {
            print "Session value written.\n";
            print "Sess_ID: $sess_id\n";
            print "Data: $data\n\n";
            return true;
    }

    function sess_destroy($sess_id) {
            print "Session destroy called.\n";
            return true;
    }

    function sess_gc($sess_maxlifetime) {
            print "Session garbage collection called.\n";
            print "Sess_maxlifetime: $sess_maxlifetime\n";
            return true;
    }

    session_set_save_handler("sess_open", "sess_close", "sess_read",
                    "sess_write", "sess_destroy", "sess_gc");
    session_start();

    $_SESSION['foo'] = "bar";
    print "Some text\n";
    $_SESSION['baz'] = "wombat";
```

That will give the following output:

```
Session opened.
Sess_path: /tmp
Sess_name: PHPSESSID
Session read.
Sess_ID: m4v94bsp45snd6llbvi1rvv2n5
Some text
Session value written.
Sess_ID: m4v94bsp45snd6llbvi1rvv2n5
Data: foo|s:3:"bar";baz|s:6:"wombat";
Session closed.
```

There are four important things to note in that example:

1. You can, if you want, ignore the parameters passed into sess_open( ). We're going to be using a database to store our session data, so we do not need the values at all.

2. Writing data comes just once, even though our two writes to the session are nonsequential—there is a print statement between them.

3. Reading data is done just once, and passes in the session ID.

4. All the functions return true except sess_read( ).

Item 1 is not true if you actually care about where the user asks you to save files. If you are using your own session filesystem, you might want to actually use $sess_path when it gets passed in—this is your call.

Items 2 and 3 are important, as they show that PHP only does its session reading and writing once. When it writes, it gives you the session ID to write and the whole contents of that session; when it reads, it just gives you the session ID to read and expects you to return the whole session data value.

The last item shows that sess_read( ) is the one function that needs to return a meaningful value to PHP. All the others just need to return true, but reading data from a session needs to either return the data or return an empty string: ''.

If you return true or false from your session read function, it is likely that PHP will crash—always return either the session string or an empty string.

What we're going to do is use MySQL as our database system for session data using the same functions as those above—in essence, we're going to modify the script so that it actually works.

We need to create a table to handle the session data, and here's how it will look:

```
CREATE TABLE sessions (ID INT NOT NULL AUTO_INCREMENT PRIMARY KEY,
SessionID CHAR(26), Data TEXT DEFAULT '', DateTouched INT);
```

The ID field is not required, as it is not likely we will ever need to manipulate the database by hand.

Now, before you try this next code, you need to tweak two values in your *php.ini* file: session.gc_probability and session.gc_maxlifetime. The first one, in tandem with session.gc_divisor, sets how likely it is for PHP to trigger session clean up with each page request. By default, session.gc_probability is 1 and session.gc_divisor is 1000, which means it will execute session clean up once in every 1000 scripts. As we're going to be testing our script out, you will need to change session.gc_probability to 1000, giving us a 1000/1000 chance of executing the garbage collection routine. In other words, it will always run.

The second change to make is to lower session.gc_maxlifetime. By default, it is 1440 seconds (24 minutes), which is far too long to wait to see if our garbage collection routine works. Set this value to 20, meaning that when running our garbage collection script, we should consider everything older than 20 seconds to be unused and deletable. Of course, in production scripts, this value needs to be set back to 1440 so that people do not get their sessions timing out before they can even read a simple web page!

With that in mind, here's the new script:

```
mysql_connect("localhost", "phpuser", "alm65z");
mysql_select_db("phpdb");

function sess_open($sess_path, $sess_name) {
        return true;
}

function sess_close() {
        return true;
}

function sess_read($sess_id) {
        $result = mysql_query("SELECT Data FROM sessions WHERE SessionID
                = '$sess_id';");
        $CurrentTime = time();
        if (!mysql_num_rows($result)) {
                mysql_query("INSERT INTO sessions (SessionID, DateTouched)
VALUES
                ('$sess_id', $CurrentTime);");
                return '';
        } else {
                extract(mysql_fetch_array($result), EXTR_PREFIX_ALL,
'sess');
                mysql_query("UPDATE sessions SET DateTouched = $CurrentTime
WHERE
                        SessionID = '$sess_id';");
                return $sess_Data;
        }
}

function sess_write($sess_id, $data) {
        $CurrentTime = time();
        mysql_query("UPDATE sessions SET Data = '$data', DateTouched =
                $CurrentTime WHERE SessionID = '$sess_id';");
        return true;
}

function sess_destroy($sess_id) {
        mysql_query("DELETE FROM sessions WHERE SessionID = '$sess_id';");
        return true;
}

function sess_gc($sess_maxlifetime) {
        $CurrentTime = time();
        mysql_query("DELETE FROM sessions WHERE DateTouched + $sess_
maxlifetime
                < $CurrentTime;");
        return true;
}
```

```
session_set_save_handler("sess_open", "sess_close", "sess_read",
        "sess_write", "sess_destroy", "sess_gc");
session_start();

$_SESSION['foo'] = "bar";
$_SESSION['baz'] = "wombat";
```

As that script starts, it forms a connection to the local SQL server, which is used through the script for the session-handling functions. When a session is read, sess_read( ) is called and given the session ID to read. This is used to query our sessions table—if the ID exists, its value is returned. If not, an empty session row is created with that session ID and an empty string is returned. The empty row is put in there so that we can later say UPDATE while writing and will not need to bother with whether the row exists already; we'll know we created it when reading. The sess_write( ) function updates the session with ID $sess_id so that it holds the data passed in with $data.

The last function of interest is sess_gc( ), which is called randomly to handle dele- tion of old session information. We edited *php.ini* so that *randomly* means "every time" right now, and this function receives the lifespan in seconds of session data, and deletes all rows that have not been read or updated in that time. We can tell how long it has been since a row was last read/written because both sess_read( ) and sess_write( ) update the DateTouched field to the current time. Therefore, to tell whether or not a record was touched after the garbage collection time limit, we simply take DateTouched and add the time limit $sess_maxlifetime to it—if that value is under the current time, the session data is no longer valid.

It is interesting to note that you need not use databases *or* files to store your sessions. As we've seen, you get to define the storage and retrieval method for your system, so if you really wanted, you could write your own extension called PigeonStore that sends and retrieves session data through pigeons. It really doesn't matter, because PHP just calls the functions you tell it to; what you do in there is up to you, so use it wisely.

Storing Complex Data Types

You can use sessions to store complex data types such as objects and arrays simply by treating them as standard variables, as this code shows:

```
$myarr["0"] = "Sunday";
$myarr["1"] = "Monday";
$myarr["2"] = "Tuesday";
$myarr["3"] = "Wednesday";
$myarr["4"] = "Thursday";
$myarr["5"] = "Friday";
$myarr["6"] = "Saturday";

$_SESSION["myarr"] = $myarr;
```

You can also use the serialize( ) and unserialize( ) functions to explicitly convert to and from a string. If you do not call serialize( ) yourself, PHP will do it for you when the session data is written to disk—many do rely on this, but I would say it's best to be explicit and serialize( ) data yourself.

If you are trying to store objects in your session and you find it is not restoring the class name properly, it is probably because you started the session before you had the class defined. This problem is often encountered by people who use the session.auto_start directive in *php.ini*.

11

Output Buffering

Without output buffering, PHP sends data to your web server as soon as it is ready. Not only is this slow because of the need to send lots of little bits of data, but it also means you are restricted in the order you can send data. Output buffering cures these ills by enabling you to store up your output and send it when you are ready to—or to not send it at all, if you so decide.

Why Use Output Buffering?

Output buffering lets you "send" cookies at any point in your script, ignoring the "headers first" HTTP rule. Internally, it causes PHP to store the cookies separate from the HTML data and then send them together at the end, in the correct order.

Once you are using output buffering, you can compress content before you send it. HTML is made up of lots of simple, repeating tags, and normal text on a site is easy to compress, which means that compressing your pages can drastically cut the amount of bandwidth your site (and your visitor!) uses, as well as how long it takes to transfer a page.

One final advantage is that output buffers are stackable, meaning that you can have several buffers working on top of each other, sending whichever ones you want to output.

Output buffering generally will not affect the speed of your web server by any great amount, unless you choose to compress your content. Compression takes up extra CPU time; however, the amount of page bandwidth you use will be cut by about 40%, which means your server will spend less time sending data across the network. Your compression mileage may vary—if you have lots of pictures, this will matter less; if you are sending lots of XML, your savings will be higher.

Getting Started

There are two ways to start buffering output: through a *php.ini* setting to enable output buffering for all scripts, or by using a function call on a script-by-script basis. The latter is preferred, as it makes your code more portable and also gives you greater flexibility in how you use output buffering.

To create a new output buffer and start writing to it, call ob_start( ). There are two ways to end a buffer: ob_end_flush( ) and ob_end_clean( ). The former ends the buffer and sends all data to output, and the latter ends the buffer without sending it to output. Every piece of text written while an output buffer is open is placed into that buffer, as opposed to being sent to output. For example:

```
ob_start( );
print "Hello First!\n";
ob_end_flush( );

ob_start( );
print "Hello Second!\n";
ob_end_clean( );

ob_start( );
print "Hello Third!\n";
```

That script will output "Hello First" because the first text is placed into a buffer and then flushed with ob_end_flush( ). The "Hello Second" will not be printed out, though, because it is placed into a buffer that is cleaned using ob_end_clean( ) and not sent to output. Finally, the script will print out "Hello Third" because PHP automatically flushes open output buffers when it reaches the end of a script.

Reusing Buffers

The functions ob_end_flush( ) and ob_end_clean( ) are complemented by ob_flush( ) and ob_clean( ), which do the same jobs but don't end the output buffer. We could rewrite the previous script like this:

```
ob_start( );
print "Hello First!\n";
ob_flush( );
print "Hello Second!\n";
ob_clean( );
print "Hello Third!\n";
```

This time the buffer is flushed but left open, then cleaned and still left open, and finally, automatically closed and flushed by PHP as the script ends. This saves creating and destroying output buffers, which is about 60% faster than opening and closing buffers all the time.

Stacking Buffers

Multiple output buffers can be open simultaneously, in which case, PHP writes to the most recently opened buffer. For example:

```
ob_start( );
print "Hello first!\n";

ob_start( );
print "Hello second!\n";

ob_clean( );
```

That script will print out "Hello first!". The first buffer is started and filled with "Hello first", then a second buffer is started on top of the previous buffer, leaving the original still intact (though just out of reach for the time being). The new buffer is filled with "Hello second", but ob_clean( ) is called, clearing the most recent buffer and leaving the first untouched. The original buffer is then automatically sent by PHP when the script terminates.

Stacking output buffers becomes more important when you remember that it's generally smart to make your whole page buffered in a master buffer. Without stackable buffers, you would be unable to use any other buffers inside the main page.

Flushing Stacked Buffers

When you have no output buffers open, any text you print out goes straight to your user. When you have an output buffer, that text is stored away until you choose to flush it. When you have stacked output buffers, your buffers flush data up one level as opposed to going directly to output. For example:

```
ob_start( );
print "In first buffer\n";

ob_start( );
print "In second buffer\n";
ob_end_flush( );

print "In first buffer\n";
ob_end_flush( );
```

That will output the following:

```
In first buffer
In second buffer
In first buffer
```

As you can see, the second buffer gets flushed into the first buffer where it was left off, as opposed to directly to output—it literally gets copied into the parent buffer. Take a look at the following script:

```
ob_start( );
print "In first buffer\n";

ob_start( );
print "In second buffer\n";
ob_end_flush( );

print "In first buffer\n";
ob_end_clean( );
```

It is the same as the previous script, with the only difference being the last line—ob_end_clean( ) is used rather than ob_end_flush( ). That script outputs nothing at all, because the second buffer gets flushed into the first buffer and then the first buffer gets cleaned, which means the clients receives none of the text.

As long as you keep in mind that output buffers are stacked, not parallel, this functionality will work in your favor—you can progressively build up your content by opening up new buffers and flushing in content to a parent buffer as you go.

Reading Buffers

Output buffers are two-way affairs, which means you can read from them as well as write to them. So far we have only covered writing data; reading that data back is done by using the ob_get_contents( ) function.

The ob_get_contents( ) function takes no parameters and returns the full contents of the most recently opened buffer. For example:

```
$result = mysql_query("SELECT * FROM EmployeeTable WHERE ID = 55;");

while ($row = mysql_fetch_assoc($result)) {
        extract($row);
        print "Some info A: $SomeInfoA\n";
        print "Some info B: $SomeInfoB\n";
        print "Some info C: $SomeInfoC\n";
        // ...[snip]...
        print "Some info Z: $SomeInfoZ\n";
}
```

That script sends its data (presumably lots of employee data) to the screen. With output buffering, we can change it to save to a file, like this:

```
ob_start( )
$result = mysql_query("SELECT * FROM EmployeeTable WHERE ID = 55;");

while ($row = mysql_fetch_assoc($result)) {
        extract($row);
        print "Some info A: $SomeInfoA\n";
        print "Some info B: $SomeInfoB\n";
        print "Some info C: $SomeInfoC\n";
        //...[snip]...
        print "Some info Z: $SomeInfoZ\n";
}

$output = ob_get_contents( );
ob_end_clean( );
file_put_contents("employee.txt", $output);
```

That scripts treats output like a scratch pad, saving it to a file rather than sending it to output.

Other OB Functions

The ob_get_length( ) and ob_get_level( ) functions both take no parameters and return a number. For ob_get_length( ), the return value is the number of bytes held in the buffer, and for ob_get_level( ), it is the *nest count*. This returns 0 if you are not within an output buffer, 1 if you have one open, 2 if you have two, etc.

Using ob_get_level( ), it is possible to recursively close and flush/clean all open buffers if you have an error. The ob_get_length( ) function is helpful if you want to send a custom HTTP Content-Length header—although that is for advanced users only!

Finally, the ob_list_handlers( ) function takes no parameters and returns an array of any output handlers currently in effect. If output buffering is turned on, you should get back an array containing the default output handler; if you're using gzip to compress your buffer, you should get "ob_gzhandler"; and if you've used URL rewriting, you should get "URL-Rewriter".

Flushing Output

If you aren't using output buffer, you can still use the flush( ) to send all output immediately, without waiting for the end of the script. You can call flush( ) as often as you want, and it makes your visitor's browser update with new content. For example:

```
<html>
<body>
This page is loading...<br />
<?php sleep(2); ?>
Almost there...<br />
<?php sleep(2); ?>
Done.<br />
</body>
</html>
```

 Internet Explorer has an "optimization" that makes it render a page only after it has received the first 256 bytes, whether or not you use flush( )—you might find these example scripts do not work in IE as described. To make the scripts work, make them output at least 256 characters before the first call flush( ).

If you try that, you will see that the page appears all at once, having taken a little over four seconds to load—not a very helpful progress monitor! Now consider the following script, making use of flush( ):

```
<html>
<body>
This page is loading.<br />
<?php flush( ); sleep(2); ?>
Almost there...<br />
<?php flush( ); sleep(2); ?>
```

```
Done.<br />
</body>
</body>
```

This time, you will literally see the page loading—each line will appear one by one, as seen in Figures 11-1, 11-2, and 11-3.

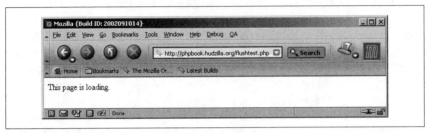

Figure 11-1. Loading...

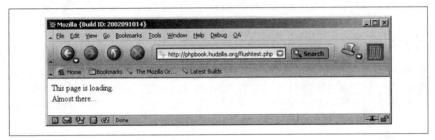

Figure 11-2. ...loading...

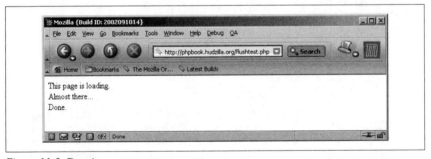

Figure 11-3. Done!

You can use JavaScript to alter what has been output already, like this:

```
<html>
<body>
<div id="flushme">
Hello, world!
</div>
<?php flush(); sleep(2); ?>
<script>
d = document.getElementById("flushme");
d.innerHTML = "Goodbye, Perl!";
```

```
</script>
<?php flush( ); sleep(2); ?>
<script>
d.innerHTML = "Goodnight, New York!";
</script>
</body>
</html>
```

The JavaScript locates the DIV HTML element on the page, then sets its innerHTML property to different messages as the script loads—a simple yet effective way to handle keeping users up-to-date while a script loads.

Using flush( ) is good for all sorts of things, but as you have seen, it is particularly good when you are executing a long script and want to keep users informed. It takes very little work to print out "Please wait - generating your file" and call flush( ) before creating a 500MB file—you can even follow up with printing out "File created - click here to download," so that your scripts feel much more interactive.

Compressing Output

Output buffering allows you to compress the HTML you send to your visitors, which makes your site load faster for your users and also allows you to make more use of the bandwidth allocated to your server.

Whenever a visitor connects to your site, she sends along information such as the last page she visited, the name of the web browser she is using, and what content and encoding she accepts. The encoding part is what we're interested in—if a browser supports compressed HTML, it sends word of this to the web server each time it requests a page. The web server can then send back compressed HTML if told to do so—this is important, because browsers that *do not* support compressed HTML will always get plain HTML back, so this works for everyone.

Compressed HTML is literally the zipped version of the normal HTML a browser would otherwise have received; the client unzips it, then reads it as normal. As zipping information requires that you must know all the information before you compress it, output buffering is perfect—you send all your data to a buffer, zip the buffer, and send it off to your users.

As the tie between output buffering and output compression is so close, the code to make it work is equally close. To enable it, just pass the ob_gzhandler parameter to ob_start( ); that will automatically check whether content compression is supported, and enable it, if it is. For example:

```
ob_start("ob_gzhandler")
// output content for compression here
ob_end_flush( );
```

From the client's point of view, nothing will have changed, except the fact that the site might load a little quicker. If he clicks "View Source" from his web browser, he'll see normal HTML because the process is entirely transparent.

Content compression works only on the contents of the output buffer—it does not compress pictures, CSS files, or other attachments to your HTML.

You're only allowed one compressed buffer with PHP because of the need to compress content all at once; be careful when stacking more than one buffer at a time.

URL Rewriting

The two functions output_add_rewrite_var( ) and output_reset_rewrite_vars( ) cause your URLs, forms, and frames to be rewritten so that they will pass in variables and values of your choosing. They do this by using output buffering and parsing any HTML A elements (links) plus any FORM elements and FRAMES elements and appending fields to URLs contained therein. For example:

```php
<?php
  output_add_rewrite_var('foo', 'baz');
  echo '<a href="mypage.php">Click here!</A><br />';
  output_add_rewrite_var('bar', 'baz');
  echo '<a href="mypage.php">Click here!</A><br />';

  echo '<form action="mypage.php" method="post">';
  echo '<input type="button" value=" Click here! " />';
  echo '</form>';
?>

<a href="mypage.php">Click here!</a>
```

When you run that, you should find that the URLs have been rewritten to point to *http://localhost/mypage.php?foo=baz&bar=baz*. What's more, both links are the same: the fact that you printed out one link before adding the second variable is irrelevant, thanks to output buffering. The form will have extra hidden fields in there for your values, effectively giving the same result. The best part is that PHP always leaves the forms and URLs working as they did before: any fields in your forms or variables in your URLs will remain there, untouched.

The output_reset_rewrite_vars( ) function undoes the effects of your calls to output_add_rewrite_var( ). One call to output_reset_rewrite_vars( ) wipes out any variables you've added to URLs and FORMs—it goes back and changes them all to be without the added variables.

Here's the same script again, except this time with output_reset_rewrite_vars( ) tacked on the end:

```php
<?php
  echo '<a href="mypage.php">Click here!</a><br />';
  output_add_rewrite_var('foo', 'baz');
  echo '<a href="mypage.php">Click here!</a><br />';
  output_add_rewrite_var('bar', 'baz');
  echo '<a href="mypage.php">Click here!</a><br />';

  echo '<form action="mypage.php" METHOD="POST">';
  echo '<input type="button" value=" Click here! " />';
  echo '</form>';
?>

<a href="mypage.php">Click here!</a>
```

```php
<?php
  output_reset_rewrite_vars();
?>
```

That will print out all URLs and the form as written, without the foo and bar variables.

12

Security

The Internet is not a safe place, thanks to a small percentage of its users who feel the need to attack other users electronically. The reasons for the attacks vary—sometimes it is for monetary gain, where attackers find holes in your code that they can exploit to their advantage, and other times it is just for fun.

If your PHP scripts run on an Internet-facing server, they are accessible to hackers and you need to take extra care. Many PHP projects—particularly the larger ones, such as PostNuke—have had major exploits published that allow hackers to take control of a web server remotely. This chapter contains tips and advice to help you avoid falling victim to the next hacker that comes your way.

Security Tips

The easiest way for hackers to find holes in your web site is to scan for strings that give away a known vulnerability. This can be done with a client-side tool that simply hits IP addresses again and again until it finds something it recognizes, but many modern hackers utilize Google to search for data.

As a result, it has never been more important to keep a tight control over what files are on your web site and what information you give to visitors.

Put Key Files Outside Your Document Root

Your document root is the root directory of your web server. That is, if your site is *example.com*, the root directory would be the directory that *http://www.example.com/* points to. For example, on Linux this is often */var/www/html*, and on Windows this is often *c:\inetpub\wwwroot*.

As long as you have the permissions set up correctly, PHP can read from any file you want inside scripts. However, unless you configure Apache to do otherwise, users will not be able to load files from outside of the document root directly through their web browsers. That is, if you place your files in */var/www*, and the "highest" directory your visitors can get to is */var/www/html*, then the files are safe.

Remember That Most Files Are Public

When you have files in your public HTML directory, people can get at them—it is that simple. There was a silly craze a while ago to use the file extension *.inc* for PHP include files—scripts that only served to be included into other scripts. While this might make sense, and allows you to see how a script works simply by looking at its name, it is actually a major security hole.

For example, if you save your database connection info in a file and then include( ) that file into every script you write, that file would probably be called something like *dbconnect.inc*. Now, what happens if someone were to type *www.example.com/dbconnect.inc* directly into his web browser? Your web server would load the *.inc* file, and send it as plain text because it does not end in a PHP-handled file extension, which means that someone accessing the *.inc* file directly would see your source code.

A much better solution, if you particularly want to mark your files as include files, is to use the extension *.inc.php*—this way, they *will* be parsed by PHP before being sent to people directly, and therefore will not reveal your source code.

Hide Your Identity

Most web servers, by default, send out information about themselves with each request served. For example, a default installation of Mandrake Linux 9.1 returns the following information with each file served:

```
Server: Apache/2.0.48 (Win32) PHP/5.0.2-dev
```

From that, we can ascertain that the machine is running Apache 2.0.48 on Windows, a CVS version of PHP 5.0.2.

Now, all an attacker has to do is check for known bugs in Apache 2.0.49, PHP 5.0.2 or, worse, Windows, and exploit them—we have, in effect, given him a head start.

Editing your *httpd.conf* file, look for the two directives ServerSignature and ServerTokens—both of these control what information Apache gives out about itself. ServerSignature is used to define what Apache prints at the bottom of server-generated pages, such as 404 error pages. Similarly, with ServerTokens set to full (the default), the same information is sent along with every request. To change this, set ServerSignature to Off and ServerTokens to Prod—this will stop it printing anything out for error messages, and restrict the information sent with each request to just Apache. A big step forward—at least now your site will not appear if people are scanning for certain Apache versions.

Here is how that same Windows Apache server describes itself with these changes in place:

```
Server: Apache
```

Much better!

Hiding PHP

By default, PHP is set to announce its presence whenever anyone asks—this is usually through the web server. You can turn this functionality off by editing your *php.ini* file and changing expose_php to Off.

If you do this, as well as using a different file extension, your use of PHP is mostly hidden. However, if your code generates any error messages, your use of PHP will become immediately obvious. To get around this, and thereby truly hide PHP, you should force PHP not to display error messages—edit your *php.ini* file and set display_errors to Off.

This will make debugging a little harder, but be sure to set log_errors to On—this will make sure that whenever your script generates an error, it will be stored away in the error log file so that you can analyze the problem.

As an alternative to changing the file extension, why not just drop it altogether? Tim Berners-Lee wrote a famous article called "Cool URIs Don't Change" (available from *http://www.w3.org/Provider/Style/URI.html*) that says, among other things, that you should consider stripping off file extensions just in case you decide to change technology later—good advice.

Encryption

Practicing the art of encryption, both for data you store locally and for data you send to and from your clients and other data consumers, is not only *recommended*, but it is a staple *requirement* for anything done in conjunction with the Internet.

Encryption is undoubtedly the most complicated topic PHP programmers have to face, partially because encryption is inherently complex, and partially because the PHP extension designed to handle encryption seems to have been designed for encryption experts to use, as opposed to normal people!

Encrypting Data

To encrypt data, you need to use seven different functions, which are: mcrypt_module_open( ), mcrypt_create_iv( ), mcrypt_enc_get_iv_size( ), mcrypt_enc_get_key_size( ), mcrypt_generic_init( ), mcrypt_generic( ), mcrypt_generic_deinit( ), and finally, mcrypt_module_close( ).

The easiest way to learn these functions is just to use them, because they accept limited input and give limited output. This script is a good place to start:

```
srand((double)microtime( )*1000000 );
$td = mcrypt_module_open(MCRYPT_RIJNDAEL_256, '', MCRYPT_MODE_CFB, '');
$iv = mcrypt_create_iv(mcrypt_enc_get_iv_size($td), MCRYPT_RAND);
$ks = mcrypt_enc_get_key_size($td);
$key = substr(sha1('Your Secret Key Here'), 0, $ks);
mcrypt_generic_init($td, $key, $iv);
$ciphertext = mcrypt_generic($td, 'This is very important data');
mcrypt_generic_deinit($td);
mcrypt_module_close($td);
```

```
print $iv . "\n";
print trim($ciphertext) . "\n";
```

The script starts with the random number generator seeded with a random value, which is important because our initialization vector (or IV, a seed for random encryption and decryption) will be created by calling the random number generator. The first function called is mcrypt_module_open( ), which opens an encryption algorithm for use. It takes four parameters; however, most people will want to leave them as the same values seen in the script because they are more than enough, even in very secure environments.

Moving on, the next function called is mcrypt_create_iv( ), which creates an IV for our encryption. IVs aren't used to make the key any more difficult to guess. Instead, their purpose is to make the plaintext more innocuous—a process referred to as *whitening*, because the goal of the IV is to make your plaintext look more like white noise by randomizing it a little before encryption.

The mcrypt_create_iv( ) function takes two parameters: the size of IV to create and the method to use to create the IV. The first parameter is filled with the return value from mcrypt_enc_get_iv_size( ), which returns the length the IV should be for the encryption algorithm passed in as its only parameter. The second parameter can be one of MCRYPT_RAND, MCRYPT_DEV_RANDOM, or MCRYPT_DEV_URANDOM. The first generates the IV using a software randomizer; the second uses the Unix device */dev/random*; and the third uses the Unix device */dev/urandom*. For maximum portability, use *MCRYPT_RAND*—it is not as random as the other two, but it will work wherever you put it. If you use *MCRYPT_RAND*, remember to seed the random number generated with srand( )!

The function returns an IV for the algorithm we selected with mcrypt_module_open( ). Next we call mcrypt_enc_get_key_size( ) to get the maximum key size our algorithm (parameter one) will take, then we create a key for that algorithm using substr( ) and sha1( ). The return value of mcrypt_enc_get_key_size( ) is the largest key this algorithm accepts, so we pass a plaintext key into sha1( ) to get a hashed value, then copy as many characters from it as the algorithm method will accept.

The next two functions, mcrypt_generic_init( ), and mcrypt_generic( ), initialize the encryption engine with the algorithm, IV, and key we selected, then perform the encryption. The first takes three parameters, which are the algorithm resource to use, the IV we created with mcrypt_create_iv( ), and the key we created using sha1( ) and substr( ). Mcrypt_generic takes two parameters, which are the algorithm resource and the data we actually want to encrypt—it returns the encrypted value, our ciphertext, which we store in $ciphertext.

So, after lots of function calls, we have finally performed encryption with the function mcrypt_generic( ). To end the script, we need to do some clean up, which is where mcrypt_generic_deinit( ) and mcrypt_module_close( ) come in—both take the algorithm resource as their only parameter and clean up the module.

It's possible to perform encryption using the mcrypt library with fewer functions. Generally speaking, this is not recommended: using an IV and doing things properly ensures the data is secured properly. Please remember that the only thing worse than not being secured is not being secured and thinking you *are* secured!

To recap, we select an encryption algorithm and block cipher, create an IV to whiten our plaintext a little, create a secret key that encrypts our data, initialize the algorithm to use our IV and key, run the encryption itself to get our ciphertext, then clean up.

Symmetric Decryption

Once you have mastered encryption, decryption is fairly easy, as it shares most of the same concepts. Here is the same script again; this time, it encrypts and then decrypts the information:

```
srand((double)microtime( )*1000000 );
$td = mcrypt_module_open(MCRYPT_RIJNDAEL_256, '', MCRYPT_MODE_CFB, '');
$iv = mcrypt_create_iv(mcrypt_enc_get_iv_size($td), MCRYPT_RAND);
$ks = mcrypt_enc_get_key_size($td);
$key = substr(sha1('Your Secret Key Here'), 0, $ks);

mcrypt_generic_init($td, $key, $iv);
$ciphertext = mcrypt_generic($td, 'This is very important data');
mcrypt_generic_deinit($td);

mcrypt_generic_init($td, $key, $iv);
$plaintext = mdecrypt_generic($td, $ciphertext);
mcrypt_generic_deinit($td);
mcrypt_module_close($td);

print $iv . "\n";
print trim($ciphertext) . "\n";
print trim($plaintext) . "\n";
```

Note that we actually call mcrypt_generic_deinit( ) and then mcrypt_generic_init( ) immediately afterwards—this is important for the encryption to work properly, and you must not forget to do this.

It is crucial that you do not forget to deinit( ) after you encrypt, then call init( ) again when you want to decrypt.

The above scripts use a very strong form of encryption; however, even they can be broken in seconds if someone cracks your key—keep it secret at all costs. Your IV need not be kept secure, but there's no harm in doing so.

13

Files

Files can store all sorts of information. However, most file formats (e.g., picture formats such as PNG and JPEG) are binary, and very difficult and/or impossible to write using normal text techniques—in these situations, you should use the library designed to cope with each format.

One reminder: if you are using an operating system that uses backslash (\) as the path separator (e.g., Windows), you need to escape the backslash with another backslash, making (\\). Owing to this, handling files can be quite different for Windows and Unix users. Both operating systems are covered here.

Reading Files

There are several ways to open and display files, and each has its uses. You don't need to know all the ways to read files—it is probably best to learn one and stick with it for your own code. However, you will almost certainly come across each of these methods in other people's code, because everyone has her own method of getting things done.

readfile( )

If you want to output a file to the screen without doing any form of text processing on it whatsoever, readfile( ) is the easiest function to use. When passed a filename as its only parameter, readfile( ) will attempt to open it, read it all into memory, then output it without further question. If successful, readfile( ) will return an integer equal to the number of bytes read from the file.

If unsuccessful, readfile( ) will return false, and there are quite a few reasons why it may fail. For example, the file might not exist, or it might exist with the wrong permissions.

Here is an example script:

```
$testfile = @readfile("/home/paul/test.txt");
// OR "@readfile("c:\\boot.ini");" if you are using Windows
if (!$testfile) {
        print "Could not open file.\n";
}
```

If readfile( ) fails to open the file, it will print an error message to the screen. You can suppress this by placing an @ symbol before the function call.

The advantages to using readfile( ) are clear: there is no fuss, and there is little way for it to go wrong. However, the disadvantage is equally clear: you have no control over the text that comes out.

 From here on, I will use the variable $filename to signify a filename you have chosen. This is to avoid having to keep printing separate examples for Windows and Unix.

file_get_contents( ) and file( )

The next evolutionary step up from readfile( ) is called file_get_contents( ), and it also takes one parameter for the filename to open. This time, however, it does not output any data. Instead, it will return the contents of the file as a string, complete with new line characters \n where appropriate. For example:

```
$filestring = file_get_contents($filename);
if ($filestring) {
        print $filestring;
} else {
        print "Could not open $filename.\n";
}
```

The file_get_contents( ) function opens $varname and places its contents into $filestring. Effectively, that piece of code is the same as our call to readfile( ), but only because we're not doing anything with $filestring once we have it.

If you want your file to be converted into an array, with each line an element inside that array, you should use the file( ) function:

```
$filearray = file($filename);

if ($filearray) {
        while (list($var, $val) = each($filearray)) {
                ++$var;
                $val = trim($val);
                print "Line $var: $val<br />";
        }
} else {
        print "Could not open $filename.\n";
}
```

That script iterates over the file array, outputting one line at a time with line numbers. Array indexes start at 0, so we need ++$var to make sure that it starts at line 1 rather than line 0. We call trim( ) on $val because each element in the array still has its new line character \n at the end, and trim( ) will take that off.

fopen( ) and fread( )

For many people, fopen( ) is a fiendishly complex function. This is because it is another one of those functions lifted straight from C, and is not as user-friendly as most PHP functions. On the flip side, fopen( ) is an incredibly versatile function that you are likely to come to love for its ability to manipulate files just as you want it to.

It has two key parameters: the file to open, and how you would like it opened. The first parameter is $filename, as with the other examples. Parameter two is what makes fopen( ) so special: you specify letters in a string that define whether you want to read from (r), write to (w), or append to (a) the file specified in parameter one.

There is also a fourth option, b or t, which opens the file in binary mode or text mode—the latter of which is designed to allow Windows to translate Unix-style line returns (\n) into Windows-style line returns (\r\n). PHP will enable binary mode by default on Windows in newer versions of PHP, but not on Unix, and not on older versions of PHP. This naturally causes great confusion, but the solution is simple: if you want binary mode, specify it. If you don't want binary mode, specify text mode with a t. Do not leave it to the default.

Take a look at the following usages:

```
$fh_flowers = fopen("kinds_of_flowers.txt", "r")
    OR die ("Can't open flowers file!\n");

$fh_logfile = fopen("$appname-log.log", "w")
    OR die ("Log file not writeable!\n");
```

The fopen( ) function returns a file handle resource, which is a pointer to the location of the contents of the file. You cannot output it directly, e.g., print fopen($filename), but all fopen( )-related functions accept file handles as the file to work with. You should store the return value of fopen( ) in a variable for later use:

```
$handle = fopen($filename, "a");
if (!$handle) {
        print "Failed to open $filename for appending.\n";
}
```

If the file cannot be opened, fopen( ) returns false. If the file is successfully opened, a file handle is returned and you can proceed. Once the file handle is ready, we can call other functions on the opened file, depending on how the file was opened (the second parameter to fopen( )). To read from a file, the function fread( ) is used; to write to a file, fwrite( ) is used. For now we're interested in reading, so you should use rb for the second parameter to fopen( ).

The fread( ) function takes two parameters: a file handle to read from (this is the return value from fopen( )) and the number of bytes to read. When combined with the feof( ), which takes a file handle as its only parameter and returns true if you are at the end of the file or false otherwise, it becomes easier to work with files of several megabytes or, indeed, hundreds of megabytes. For example:

```
$huge_file = fopen("VERY_BIG_FILE.txt", "r");
while (!feof($huge_file)) {
        print fread($huge_file, 1024);
}
fclose($huge_file);
```

This use of fread() is also good for when you only care about a small part of the file. For example, Zip files all start with the letters "PK", so we can do a quick check to ensure a given file is a Zip file with this code:

```
$zipfile = fopen("data.zip", "r");
if (fread($zipfile, 2) != "PK") {
  print "Data.zip is not a valid Zip file!";

}
fclose($zipfile);
```

To instruct PHP to use fread() to read in the entire contents of a file, you need to specify the exact file size in bytes as the second parameter to fread(). PHP comes to the rescue again with the filesize() function, which takes the name of a file to check and returns its filesize in bytes—precisely what we're looking for.

 Don't worry about specifying a number in the second parameter that is larger than the file—PHP will stop reading when it hits the end of the file or the number of bytes in the second parameter, whichever comes first.

When reading a file, PHP uses a file pointer to determine which byte it is currently up to—like the array cursor. Each time you read in a byte, PHP advances the file pointer by one place. Reading in the entire file at once advances the pointer to the end of the file.

So, to use fread() to read in an entire file, we can use the following line:

```
$contents = fread($handle, filesize($filename));
```

Notice that fread()'s return value is the text it read in, and in the above situation, that is the entire file. To finish off using fread(), it is necessary to close the file as soon as you are done with it.

 Using fclose() immediately closes a file handle (although PHP will automatically close any file handles when your script finishes).

To close a file you have opened with fopen(), use fclose(). This takes the file handle we got from fopen() and returns true if it was able to close the file successfully. We have now got enough to use fopen() to fully open and read in a file, then close it:

```
$handle = fopen($filename, "rb");
$contents = fread($handle, filesize($filename));
```

```
fclose($handle);
print $contents;
```

You will need to set $filename to be the location of a file on your system that you have access to. In that example, fopen( ) is called with rb as the second parameter, for "read-only, binary-safe". Also, filesize( ) is being used to fread( ) in all of $filename's contents. The call to fclose( ) is made before $contents is printed, so that it is closed as soon as $handle is no longer needed.

Reading by line using fgets( )

In the same way that fread( ) is good for reading large files piece by piece, fgets( ) is good for reading large files line by line. Accessing by line means that you don't need to load the entire file into RAM at once, and it also lets you process each line as it arrives. To use fgets( ), pass it a file handle as its only parameter, and it will send back the next line as its return value.

For example, the next code block reads a large log line by line, only printing the lines that start with the word "Error":

```
$access_log = fopen("access_log", "r");
while (!feof($access_log)) {
        $line = fgets($access_log);
        if (preg_match("/^Error:/", $line)) {
                print $line;
        }
}
fclose($access_log);
```

 You can find more information about the preg_match( ) in Chapter 15.

Creating and Changing Files

Like reading files, creating and changing files can also be done in more than one way. There are just two options this time: file_put_contents( ) and fwrite( ). Both of these functions complement functions we just looked at, which are file_get_contents( ) and fread( ), respectively, and they mostly work in the same way.

file_put_contents( )

This function writes to a file with the equivalent of fopen( ), fwrite( ) (the opposite of fread( )), and fclose( )—all in one function, just like file_get_contents( ). It takes two parameters: the filename to write to and the content to write, respectively, with a third optional parameter specifying extra flags that we will get to in a moment. If file_put_contents( ) is successful, it will return the number of bytes written to the file; otherwise, it will return false.

Here is an example:

```
$myarray[ ] = "This is line one";
$myarray[ ] = "This is line two";
```

```
$myarray[ ] = "This is line three";
$mystring = implode("\n", $myarray);
$numbytes = file_put_contents($filename, $mystring);
print "$numbytes bytes written\n";
```

That should output "52 bytes written", which is the sum total of the three lines of text plus the two new line characters used to implode( ) the array. Remember that the new line character is, in fact, just one character inside files, whereas PHP represents it using two: \ and n.

You can pass in a third parameter to file_put_contents( ) which, if set to FILE_ APPEND, will append the text in your second parameter to the existing text in the file. If you do not use FILE_APPEND, the existing text will be wiped and replaced.

fwrite( )

The opposite of fread( ) is fwrite( ), which also works with the file handle returned by fopen( ). This takes a string to write as a second parameter, and an optional third parameter where you can specify how many bytes to write. If you do not specify the third parameter, all of the second parameter is written out to the file.

 As with fread( ), PHP will stop writing when it reaches the end of the string or when it has reached the number of bytes specified in this length parameter, whichever comes first—you don't need to worry about specifying more bytes than you have in the string.

Here is an example using the variable $mystring from the previous example to save space:

```
$handle = fopen($filename, "wb");
$numbytes = fwrite($handle, $mystring);
fclose($handle);
print "$numbytes bytes written\n";
```

If I had added 10 as the third parameter to the fwrite( ) call, only the first 10 bytes of $mystring would have been written out. Note again that fclose( ) is called immediately after the file handle is finished with, which is always the best practice.

The fwrite( ) function uses a file pointer in the same way as fread( ). As you write out data, PHP moves the file pointer forward so that you always write to the end of a file (unless you move the file pointer yourself).

Moving, Copying, and Deleting Files

PHP has simple functions to handle all moving, copying, and deleting of files. Unix users will know there is no command for "rename," because renaming a file is essentially the same as moving it. Thus, you use the move (mv) command—it is the same in PHP.

Files are moved using rename( ), copied using copy( ), and deleted using unlink( ). This is so named because Unix systems consider filenames to be "hard links" to the actual files themselves—to unlink a file is to delete it.

All three functions will operate without further input from you. If you choose to pass an existing file to the second parameter of rename( ), it will rename the file in parameter one to the file in parameter two, overwriting the original file. The same applies to copy( )—you will overwrite all files without question, as long as you have the correct permissions.

Moving Files with rename( )

Used for both renaming and moving files, rename( ) takes two parameters: the original filename and the new filename you wish to use. The function can rename/move files across directories and drives, and will return true on success or false otherwise.

Here is an example:

```
$filename2 = $filename . '.old';
$result = rename($filename, $filename2);
if ($result) {
        print "$filename has been renamed to $filename2.\n";
} else {
        print "Error: couldn't rename $filename to $filename2!\n";
}
```

If you had $filename set to *c:\\windows\\myfile.txt*, the above script would move that file to *c:\\windows\\myfile.txt.old*.

The rename( ) function should be used to move ordinary files, and not files uploaded through a form. This is because there is a special function, called move_uploaded_file( ), which checks to make sure the file has indeed been uploaded before moving it. This stops people trying to hack into your server by making private files visible. You can perform this check yourself, if you like, by calling the is_uploaded_file( ) function.

Copying Files with copy( )

Like rename( ), copy( ) also takes two parameters: the filename you wish to copy from and the filename you wish to copy to. The difference between rename( ) and copy( ) is that calling rename( ) results in the file being in only one place, the destination, whereas copy( ) leaves the file in the source location and places a new copy of the file into the destination.

```
$filename2 = $filename . '.old';
$result = copy($filename, $filename2);
if ($result) {
        print "$filename has been copied to $filename2.\n";
} else {
```

```
            print "Error: couldn't copy $filename to $filename2!\n";
    }
```

The result of that script is that there will be a file $filename and also a $filename.
old, e.g., *c:\\windows\\myfile.txt* and *c:\\windows\\myfile.txt.old*.

> This function will not copy empty (zero-length) files—to do that,
> you need to use the function touch( ).

Deleting Files with unlink( )

To delete files, pass a filename string as the only parameter to unlink( ). This
function only deals only with files—to delete directories, you need rmdir( ).

```
if (unlink($filename)) {
        print "Deleted $filename!\n";
} else {
        print "Delete of $filename failed!\n";
}
```

> If you have a file opened with fopen( ), you need to fclose( ) it
> before you call unlink( ).

Other File Functions

There are three functions that allow you to work more intimately with the contents
of a file: rewind( ), fseek( ), and fwrite( ). We already looked at fwrite( ), but the
other two functions are new. The first, rewind( ), is a helpful function that moves
the file pointer for a specified file handle (parameter one) back to the beginning.
That is, if you call rewind($handle), the file pointer of $handle gets reset to the
beginning. This allows you to reread a file or write over whatever you have already
written.

The second, fseek( ), allows you to move a file handle's pointer to an arbitrary
position, specified by parameter two, with parameter one being the file handle to
work with. If you do not specify a third parameter, fseek( ) sets the file pointer to
the start of the file, meaning that passing 23 will move to the 24th byte of the file
(files start from byte 0, remember). For the third parameter, you can either pass
SEEK_SET, the default, which means "from the beginning of the file," SEEK_CUR,
which means "relative to the current location," or SEEK_END, which means "from
the end of the file." For example:

```
$handle = fopen($filename, "w+");
fwrite($handle, "Mnnkyys\n");
rewind($handle);
fseek($handle, 1);
fwrite($handle, "o");
fseek($handle, 2, SEEK_CUR);
fwrite($handle, "e");
fclose($handle);
```

The first byte of a file is byte 0, and you count upward from there—the second byte is at index 1, the third at index 2, etc.

To begin with, the string "Mnnkyys" is written to $handle, but rewind( ) is then called to move the file pointer back to the beginning of the file (the letter "M"). The fseek( ) function is then called, with 1 as the second parameter, to move the file pointer to offset 1 in the file, which is currently the first of two letter "n"s. The fwrite( ) function is called again, writing an "o"—this will replace the current letter "n" at that offset with an "o". Next, fseek( ) is called once more, passing in 2 and SEEK_CUR, which means "Move to the byte 2 ahead of the current byte," which happens to be the first of two letter "y"s. Then fwrite( ) is called for the last time, replacing that "y" with an "e", and finally the file is closed.

Checking Whether a File Exists

The act of checking whether a file exists is one of the most basic file-related tasks you'll want to do, and file_exists( ) makes it as easy as it should be. Specify the filename to check as the only parameter, and it returns true if the file exists and false otherwise. For example:

```
if (file_exists("snapshot1.png")) {
        print "Snapshot1.png exists!\n";
} else {
        print "Snapshot1.png does not exist!\n";
}
```

The result of file_exists( ) is cached, which means you first need to call the clearstatcache( ) function if you want to be absolutely sure a file exists.

Retrieving File Time Information

Most filesystems store the time that each file was last accessed and last modified, often referred to as "atime" for the last access time and "mtime" for the last modification time. These are accessible through the PHP functions fileatime( ) and filemtime( ). These return a Unix timestamp for the time, which you then need to convert using a call to date( ), like this:

```
$contacts = "contacts.txt";
$atime = fileatime($contacts);
$mtime = filemtime($contacts);

$atime_str = date("F jS Y H:i:s", $atime);
$mtime_str = date("F jS Y H:i:s", $mtime);
// eg June 8th 2005 16:04:15

print "File last accessed: $atime_str\n";
print "File last modified: $mtime_str\n";
```

Note that some people disable "atime" on their filesystem as a performance optimization, making this data potentially unreliable. In this situation, you will still get a date and time returned for the "atime"; it is just likely to be out of date.

Dissecting Filename Information

The pathinfo( ) function takes a filename and returns the same filename broken into various components. It takes a filename as its only parameter and returns an array with three elements: dirname, basename, and extension. Dirname contains the name of the directory the file is in (e.g., *c:\windows* or */var/www/public_html*), basename contains the base filename (e.g., *index.html* or *somefile.txt*), and extension contains the file extension, if any (e.g., *html* or *txt*).

You can see this information yourself by running this script:

```
$fileinfo = pathinfo($filename);
var_dump($fileinfo);
```

If $filename were set to */home/paul/sandbox/php/foo.txt*, this would be the output:

```
array(3) {
        ["dirname"]=>
        string(22) "/home/paul/sandbox/php"
        ["basename"]=>
        string(7) "foo.txt"
        ["extension"]=>
        string(3) "txt"
}
```

 In earlier versions of PHP, pathinfo( ) had problems handling directories that had a period (.) in the name, e.g., */home/paul/foo. bar/baz.txt*. This is no longer the case in PHP 5, so pathinfo( ) is safe to use again.

If all you want to do is get the filename part of a path, you can use the basename( ) function. This takes a path as its first parameter and, optionally, an extension as its second parameter. The return value from the function is the name of the file without the directory information. If the filename has the same extension as the one you specified in parameter two, the extension is taken off also.

For example:

```
$filename = basename("/home/paul/somefile.txt");
$filename = basename("/home/paul/somefile.txt", ".php");
$filename = basename("/home/paul/somefile.txt", ".txt");
```

The first line sets $filename to *somefile.txt*, the second also sets it to *somefile.txt* because the filename does not have the extension *.php*, and the last line sets it to *somefile*.

Handling File Uploads

The basis for file uploads lies in a special variety of HTML input element, file, which brings up a file selection dialog in most browsers that allows your visitor to select a file for uploading. You can include this element in a HTML form just like you would any other element—web browsers render it as a text box and a "select" (or "browse") button. When your form is submitted, it will automatically send with it the file.

Here is an example HTML form that allows users to select a file for uploading to your server. Note that we specify enctype in our form in order that our file be transmitted properly, and that the action property of the form is set to point to *upload2.php*, which we will look at in a moment.

```
<form enctype="multipart/form-data" method="post" action="upload2.php">
    Send this file: <input name="userfile" type="file" /><br />
    <input type="submit" value="Send File" />
</form>
```

We give the new file element the name userfile. Now, here is the accompanying PHP script, *upload2.php*, which prints out a little information about the file just uploaded from *upload1.php*:

```
$filename = $_FILES['userfile']['name'];
$filesize = $_FILES['userfile']['size'];
print "Received $filename  - its size is $filesize";
```

If there are file uploads, PHP puts information in the superglobal $_FILES for each one in the form of an array. If you run var_dump( ) on $_FILES, here is how it will look:

```
array(1) {
        ["fileone"]=> array(5) {
                ["name"]=> string(14) "Greenstone.bmp"
                ["type"]=> string(9) "image/bmp"
                ["tmp_name"]=> string(24) "C:\WINDOWS\TEMP\php6.tmp"
                ["error"]=> int(0)
                ["size"]=> int(26582)
        }
}
```

The name element contains the original filename given by the user, type is the MIME file type (if known), tmp_name is the name the file has on your server (this might be something like */tmp/tmp000*)—whether there were any errors or not—and size is the size of the file sent in bytes.

If you find files over a certain size aren't being uploaded properly, you may need to increase the upload_max_filesize setting in your *php.ini* file.

You can move uploaded files using the aptly named move_uploaded_file( ) function. This takes two filenames as its parameters, and returns false if the file you tried to move was either not sent by HTTP upload (perhaps your user was trying to fool your script into touching */etc/passwd?*) or if it couldn't be moved (perhaps owing to permissions problems). In the event that the desination file exists already, it will be overwritten.

The first parameter should be the name of the uploaded file you wish to work with. This corresponds to $_FILES['userfile']['tmp_name'] if you are using userfile as the form element in your upload HTML page. The second parameter is the name of the filename you want the uploaded file to be moved to. If all goes well, PHP returns true, and the file will be where you expect it. Here is the whole operation in action:

```
if (move_uploaded_file($_FILES['userfile']['tmp_name'], "/place/for/file"))
{
        print "Received {$_FILES['userfile']['name']} -
            its size is {$_FILES['userfile']['size']}";
} else {
        print "Upload failed!";
}
```

Note that you will need to edit /place/for/file to somewhere PHP has permission to copy files. As you can see, a call to move_uploaded_file( ) checks security and does all the copying work for you.

Checking Uploaded Files

The move_uploaded_file( ) function is the same as the rename( ) function, with the difference that it only succeeds if the file was just uploaded by the PHP script. This adds extra security to your script by stopping people trying to move secure data, such as password files, into a public directory.

If you want to perform this check yourself, use the is_uploaded_file( ) function. This takes a filename as its sole parameter, and returns true if the file was uploaded by the script and false if not. Here is a simple example:

```
if (is_uploaded_file($somefile)) {
        copy($somefile, "/var/www/userfiles/$somefile");
}
```

If you just want to check whether a file was uploaded before you move it, move_uploaded_file( ) is better.

Locking Files with flock( )

The fopen( ) function, when called on a file, does not stop that same file from being opened by another script. This means you might find one script reading from a file as another is writing or worse, two scripts writing to the same file simultaneously.

The solution to this problem is to use file locking, which is implemented in PHP using the flock( ) function. When you lock a file, you have the option of marking it a read-only lock, thereby sharing access to the file with other processes, or an exclusive lock, allowing you to make changes to the file. On Unix, flock( ) is *advisory*, meaning that the OS is free to ignore it. Windows forces the use of flock( ), whether or not you ask for it.

The flock( ) function takes a file handle as its first parameter and a lock operation as its second parameter. File handles you know already, and the operations are simple: LOCK_SH requests a shared lock, LOCK_EX requests an exclusive lock, and LOCK_UN releases a lock. Calling flock( ) will return true if the file lock was retrieved successfully, or false if it failed. So, for example, flock( ) could be used like this:

```
$fp = fopen( $filename,"w"); // open it for WRITING ("w")
if (flock($fp, LOCK_EX)) {
        // do your file writes here
        flock($fp, LOCK_UN); // unlock the file
} else {
        // flock() returned false, no lock obtained
        print "Could not lock $filename!\n";
}
```

File locking requires a fairly modern file system, which does not include the original version of Microsoft's FAT file system, commonly used on Windows 95 and 98. NTFS, as well as FAT32, are both fine. Furthermore, the Network File System (NFS), commonly used to provide file sharing across Unix boxes, is not suitable for use with flock( ).

The file locking mechanism in PHP automatically makes processes queue up for their locks by default. For example, save this next script as *flock.php*:

```
$fp = fopen("foo.txt", "w");
if (flock($fp, LOCK_EX)) {
        print "Got lock!\n";
        sleep(10);
        flock($fp, LOCK_UN);
}
```

That script attempts to lock the file *foo.txt*, so you must create that file before running the script. The script locks it with LOCK_EX, which means no other program can lock that file. Once the lock is obtained, the script sleeps for 10 seconds, then unlocks the file and quits. If a lock cannot be obtained because another application has a lock, the script waits at the flock( ) call for the lock to be released, then locks it itself and continues.

To test this out, open up two command prompts and run the script twice. The first script run will get a lock immediately and print "Got lock!", then sleep for 10 seconds. If while the first script is sleeping you launch the second script, it will wait ("block") on the flock( ) call and wait for the first script to finish. When the first script finishes, the second script will succeed in getting its lock, print out "Got lock!", then sleep for 10 more seconds until it finally terminates.

Sometimes it is not desirable to have your scripts wait for a file to become unlocked; in this situation, you can add an extra option to the second parameter using the bitwise OR operator, |. If you pass in LOCK_NB ORed with your normal second parameter, PHP will not block when it requests a file lock. This means that if the file lock is not available, flock( ) will return immediately with false rather than wait for a lock to become available.

Here is how that looks in code:

```
$fp = fopen("foo.txt", "w");
if (flock($fp, LOCK_EX | LOCK_NB)) {
```

```
        echo "Got lock!\n";
        sleep(10);
        flock($fp, LOCK_UN);
} else {
        print "Could not get lock!\n";
}
```

This time, the first script will get the lock and print "Got lock!", whereas the second will fail to get the lock, return immediately, and print "Could not get lock!".

If you intend to have several users accessing the same file frequently, locking as shown above is not sufficient to guarantee data consistency. The problem is that between the call to fopen( ) and flock( ), there is a race condition: it is possible that another user may get in and change our file before we have locked it. Of course, we can't lock a file without opening it first, so the solution is to use a lock file—often called a semaphore file. To write to our real file, we must first successfully lock the matching semaphore file; without that lock, we ought not to write to the real file. A semaphore file is just a normal file like any other—if you want to get permission to lock *myfile.txt*, create an empty semaphore file called *myfile.txt. sem* and have people lock that first.

Reading File Permissions and Status

If you're sick of getting errors when you try to work with a file for which you have no permissions, there is a solution: is_readable( ) and its cousin functions, is_writeable( ), is_executable( ), is_file( ), and is_dir( ). Each takes a string as its only parameter and returns true or false. The functions work as you might expect: is_readable( ) will return true if the string parameter is readable, is_dir( ) will return false if the parameter is not a directory, etc.

For example, to check whether a file is readable:

```
$filename = 'c:\boot.ini'; // Windows
$filename = '/etc/passwd'; // Unix

if (is_readable($filename)) {
        print file_get_contents($filename);
} else {
        print 'File not readable!';
}
```

Or to check whether a file is writable:

```
if (is_file($filename) && is_writeable($filename)) {
        $handle = fopen($filename, "w+");
        // ...[snip]...
}
```

The is_readable( ) function and friends have their results cached for speed purposes. If you call is_file( ) on a filename several times in a row, PHP will calculate it the first time around then use the same value again and again in the future. If you want to clear this cached data so that PHP will have to check is_file( ) properly, you need to use the clearstatcache( ) function.

Calling clearstatcache( ) wipes PHP's file information cache, forcing it to recalculate is_file( ), is_readable( ), and such afresh. This function is, therefore, particularly useful if you are checking a file several times in a script and are aware that that file might change status during execution. It takes no parameters and returns no value.

 The is_readable( ), is_writeable( ), is_executable( ), is_file( ), and is_dir( ) functions will all fail to work for remote files, as the file/directory to be examined must be local to the web server so that it can check it properly.

To read the owner of a file, use the fileowner( ) function, which takes a filename as its only parameter and returns the ID of the file's owner, like this:

```
$owner = fileowner("/etc/passwd");
if ($owner != 0) {
        print "Warning: /etc/passwd isn't owned by root!";
}
```

Changing File Permissions and Ownership

PHP's chmod( ) function is vaguely similar to the Unix chmod command, but you must always specify the permissions using octal values; you can specify just one filename; and you specify that filename before the permission setting. As you are using octal values, you need to precede the security level with a 0. This function takes two parameters: the file to set and the value to set it to.

The chmod( ) function is available only to those using PHP on a Unix-like operating system. This is because Windows has a vastly different security system than Unix, where privileges are handed out by user and user group. Whereas Unix users can say "Read only for user, read-write for group," Windows users on Windows 95, 98, and ME can only say "Read only" or "Not read only." PHP does not support the fine-grained Windows NT/2000/XP/2003 access model.

Here are two examples:

```
chmod("/var/www/myfile.txt", 0777);
chmod("/var/www/myfile.txt", 0755);
```

Line one sets the file to readable, writable, and executable by all users, whereas line two sets the file to readable, writable, and executable by owner, and just readable and writable by everyone else.

The chown( ) function is quite rarely used in PHP, as you must have administrator privileges to change the ownership of a file. However, on the command line chown( ) is sometimes helpful, and it attempts to change the file passed in parameter one so that it is owned by the user specified in parameter two. On success, true is returned; otherwise, false. The second parameter can either be a username or a user ID number. For example:

```
if (chown("myfile.txt", "sally")) {
        print "File owner changed.\n";
} else {
```

```
        print "File ownership change failed!\n";
    }
```

Note that both chmod( ) and chown( ) only work on local filesystems.

Working with Links

Unix links come in two types: hard links, which are files, and symlinks (also known as soft links), which are pointers to other files. The difference is crucial: if you delete a hard link, you delete the file (unless there are other hard links pointing to the same file), whereas if you delete a symlink, the original file remains untouched.

You can create hard links and symlinks in PHP using the link( ) and symlink( ) functions, both of which take a target and a link name as their only two parameters and return true if they were successful or false otherwise. For example:

```
$result = link("/home/paul/myfile.txt", "/home/andrew/myfile.txt");
if (!$result) {
        echo "Hard link could not be created!\n";
} else {
        $result = symlink("/home/paul/myfile.txt", "/home/andrew/myfile.
txt");
        if (!$result) {
                echo "Symlink could not be created either!\n";
        }
}
```

PHP also gives you the readlink( ) function that takes a link name as its only parameter and returns the target that the link points to. For example:

```
$target = readlink("/home/andrew/myfile.txt");
print $target;
// prints /home/paul/myfile.txt
```

Working with Directories

Now that you have mastered working with individual files, it is time to take a look at the larger file system—specifically, how PHP handles directories. Let's start with something simple—listing the contents of a directory. There are three functions we need to perform this task: opendir( ), readdir( ), and closedir( ). The first of the three takes one parameter, which is the directory you wish to access. If it opens the directory successfully, it returns a handle to the directory, which you should store away somewhere for later use.

The readdir( ) function takes one parameter, which is the handle that opendir( ) returned. Each time you call readdir( ) on a directory handle, it returns the filename of the next file in the directory in the order in which it is stored by the file system. Once it reaches the end of the directory, it will return false. Here is a complete example of how to list the contents of a directory:

```
$handle = opendir('/path/to/directory');

if ($handle) {
```

```
        while (false !== ($file = readdir($handle))) {
            print "$file<br />\n";
        }
        closedir($handle);
    }
```

At first glance, the while statement might look complicated—!== is the PHP operator for "not equal and not the same type as." The reason we do it this way as opposed to just while ($file = readdir($handle)) is because it is sometimes possible for the name of a directory entry to evaluate to false, which would end our loop prematurely. In that example, closedir( ) takes our directory handle as its sole parameter, and it just cleans up after opendir( ).

Creating Directories

Making a new directory in PHP is done using the mkdir( ) function, which takes a directory name as its first parameter, a permission mode as its second, and true or false as its third, depending on whether you also want to create parent directories (defaults to false). The function returns true if the directory was created successfully or false otherwise. For example:

```
mkdir("/path/to/my/directory", 0777);
// if /path/to/my exists, this should return true if PHP has the right
permissions

mkdir("/path/to/my/directory", 0777, true);
// will create /path, /path/to, and /path/to/my if needed and allowed
```

Deleting Directories

PHP has the function rmdir( ) that takes a directory name as its only parameter and will delete the specified directory. However, there is a minor catch—the directory must be empty; otherwise, the call will fail. There is no functionality in PHP to allow you to delete non-empty directories, which means you need to resort to more cunning methods—many people use complex scripts to go through each directory, deleting files as they go. When it is empty, they use rmdir( ).

I would not recommend that—a far easier method is simply to execute the local directory-deleting program, e.g., deltree on Windows, or rm -rf on Unix. However, blindly deleting whole directories using scripts is not recommended—if you are sure you want a directory and all its subdirectories gone, check over it one last time and then delete it by hand.

Reading and Changing the Working Directory

When working from the command line, it is a common requirement to be able to change the current working directory—the directory that your PHP script is operating in. To find the current working directory, use getcwd( ). You can then change the working directory using chdir( ), like this:

```
$original_dir = getcwd( );
// something like /home/paul
chdir("/etc");
```

```
// now we're in /etc
$passwd = fopen("passwd", "r");
// open the /etc/passwd file
fclose($passwd);
chdir($original_dir);
```

Both getcwd( ) and chdir( ) return true on success or false on failure.

One Last Directory Function

The scandir( ) function is a neat function that takes a minimum of one parameter with an optional second. Parameter one is the path of a directory you want to work with—scandir( ) returns an array of all files and directories in the directory you specify here. Parameter two, if included and set to 1, will sort the array returned reverse-alphabetically—if it is not set, the array is returned sorted alphabetically.

This next script prints out a list of all the files and directories in the current directory, with reverse sorting:

```
$files = scandir(".", 1);
var_dump($files);
```

Using scandir( ) is a quick alternative to calling readdir( ) repeatedly, and is particularly helpful when you use the second parameter.

Remote Files

The fopen( ) function allows you to manipulate any files for which you have permission. However, its usefulness is only just beginning, because you can specify remote files as well as local files—even files stored on HTTP and FTP servers. PHP automatically opens a HTTP/FTP connection for you, returning the file handle as usual. For all intents and purposes, a file handle returned from a remote file is good for all the same uses as a local file handle.

This example displays the Slashdot web site through your browser:

```
$slash = fopen("http://www.slashdot.org", "r");
$site = fread($slash, 200000);
fclose($slash);
print $site;
```

The r mode is specified because web servers do not allow writing through HTTP (without WebDAV), and some will even deny access for reading if you are an anonymous visitor, as PHP normally is.

 If you are looking to find a quick way to execute an external script, try using fopen( ). For example, to call *foo.php* on *example.com*, use fopen("www.example.com/foo.php", "r"). You need not bother reading in the results—simply opening the connection is enough to make the server on *example.com* process the contents of *foo.php*.

File Checksums

PHP's sha1_file( ) function creates a checksum hash value using the SHA1 algorithm. To use it, pass the filename and capture the return value, like this:

```
$sha1 = sha1_file($filename);
```

For MD5 hashing, you can use the function md5_file( ). It works in exactly the same way as sha1_file( ), except that it returns the MD5 hash as opposed to the SHA1 hash.

Parsing a Configuration File

If you have created a complex application in PHP, you will want to save your data so that you have a persistent store for application configuration options. The Windows .ini file format is a very simple way to store data in a structured manner, and looks like this:

```
; this is a comment

[Main]
LastRun = 1076968318
User = "Paul"

[Save]
SavePath = /home/paul
AutoSave = yes
SaveType = BINARY
```

Lines that start with a semicolon (;) and blank lines are ignored. Lines that contain a string surrounded by square brackets, such as [Main] above, are section titles. Sections are just there for organizational reasons, as you will see shortly—above, you can see that the LastRun and User keys are under the Main section, and the SavePath, AutoSave, and SaveType keys are under the Save section.

Each key in the .ini file has a value that follows the equals sign, and the value can either be a string (such as the value for User), a constant (such as the value for AutoSave and SaveType), or a number (such as the value for LastRun). You can use strings without quotes if you want to, as shown in the SavePath value—the quotes are just syntactic sugar that helps differentiate between a string and a constant. However, if your string contains nonalphanumeric characters such as—, the quotes are mandatory to avoid confusion.

Because you can specify strings without quotes, if they are fairly simple strings, the value for SaveType is actually interpreted as a string and sent back as such to PHP. However, PHP's .ini file reader, parse_ini_file( ), will compare the value of each key against the list of constants in the system and replace any constants it finds with the value of the constant. You can override this by putting quotes around the string—this is helpful if you don't want "yes" to be converted to 1 by PHP. While this might seem irrelevant, consider that the country code for Norway is "NO" which, if not surrounded by quotes, will be interpreted by PHP as the constant "no" and set to false.

By default, parse_ini_file( ) ignores section headers and returns each *.ini* key and its value as an associative array. However, if you pass true as the second parameter, it makes each section header an element in the return value, and the values in that section as subelements in that array.

We can use parse_ini_file( ) to parse the previous *.ini* file like this:

```
define("BINARY", "Save was binary");
$inifile = parse_ini_file("my.ini");
var_dump($inifile);
$inifile = parse_ini_file("my.ini", true);
var_dump($inifile);
```

As you can see, it parses the file twice: once ignoring section headers, and once not. Here is the output:

```
array(5) {
        ["LastRun"]=>
        string(10) "1076968318"
        ["User"]=>
        string(4) "Paul"
        ["SavePath"]=>
        string(10) "/home/paul"
        ["AutoSave"]=>
        string(1) "1"
        ["SaveType"]=>
        string(15) "Save was binary"
}

array(2) {
        ["Main"]=>
        array(2) {
                ["LastRun"]=>
                string(10) "1076968318"
                ["User"]=>
                string(4) "Paul"
        }

        ["Save"]=>
        array(3) {
                ["SavePath"]=>
                string(10) "/home/paul"
                ["AutoSave"]=>
                string(1) "1"
                ["SaveType"]=>
                string(15) "Save was binary"
        }
}
```

In both calls to var_dump( ), BINARY gets recognized as a constant and replaced by its value, "Save was binary". Also notice that */home/paul* was recognized as a string, despite it not being enclosed in quotation marks.

As you can see, the first printout has all the *.ini* values in one array, whereas the second has a top-level array containing the section headers, and each section header element is itself an array containing the section values.

There are several reserved words for *.ini* file keys that you cannot use, such as "yes," "no," and "null."

Using *.ini* files for configuration data is easy, but remember that storing sensitive data in there may cause security headaches. Many people name *.ini* files with the *.php* extension so that their web server parses it as PHP. They then add a line to the top, like this:

```
; <?php exit; ?>
```

This is because the semicolon is an *.ini* file comment, so parse_ini_file( ) will ignore it. However, it is not a comment in PHP, so PHP will call the exit( ) function and terminate the script. As a result, it is not possible to call the script directly through a browser—only through parse_ini_file( ).

While this idea has merit, it is simply asking for trouble. What if a new version of Apache or PHP is installed and, temporarily, stops the *.php* extension from working? Yes, it is an ulikely scenario, but why bother taking the risk? Your best bet is just to place the *.ini* file outside of your public HTML folder so that only local users can access it.

Files

14

Databases

This chapter covers how to interact with your database manager using PHP, and how to format that data for output. The database systems used are MySQL 4, PEAR::DB, and SQLite.

Using MySQL with PHP

Working with MySQL through PHP is easy, as long as you have a working knowledge of SQL. This book does not attempt to teach SQL; if you are new to it, you should stop reading now, purchase a book on SQL, and then return after having read it.

Connecting to a MySQL Database

The mysql_connect() and mysql_select_db() functions connect to a database, then select a working database for use in the connection. The former usually takes three arguments, which are the IP address of a MySQL server to connect to, the username you wish to log on as, and the password for that username, like this:

```
mysql_connect("db.hudzilla.org", "username", "password");
```

Future examples in this book will always use the username "phpuser" and the password "alm65z"; choose something more secure in your own scripts.

By default, the MySQL queries you run in PHP will be executed on the most recent connection you open in your script. Each script needs to open its own database connection through which to execute its database queries; although, by using a persistent connection, they can be made to share connections. This is discussed later in this chapter.

The first parameter in mysql_connect() can either be an IP address or a hostname. Most operating systems also allow you to use "localhost" as the local computer and have MySQL connect directly through a local socket. Alternatively, you can specify 127.0.0.1, which is also the local computer, and have MySQL connect through TCP/IP, which is a little slower. To connect to a remote server, just enter either the hostname (e.g., *www.microsoft.com*) or the IP address (e.g., 212.113. 192.101) as the first parameter, and your data will be sent transparently over the Internet.

Once you have a connection open, call mysql_select_db( )—it takes just one argument, which is the name of the database you wish to use. Once you select a database, all queries you run are on tables in that database until you select another database, so it is like the USE statement in MySQL. Examples in this book will always use the database "phpdb"—again, you should change this for your own purposes, for security reasons.

Like mysql_connect( ), you generally use this function only once per script. Once both are done, you have a connection to your database with a database selected—you are all set to perform queries.

```
$connection = mysql_connect("localhost", "phpuser", "alm65z");
if ($connection) {
        $db = mysql_select_db("phpdb");
        if (!$db) print "Failed to select 'phpdb'.\n";
} else {
        print "Failed to connect to database.\n";
}
```

Once you are connected, you can use the function mysql_ping( ) to check whether the server is alive. It automatically uses the most recently opened database connection—so you need not pass it any parameters—and returns true if the server was contacted or false if the connection appears to be lost.

The last two parameters aren't used all that often, but are worth knowing about. Calling mysql_connect( ) for the first time will open a new connection to the MySQL server, but calling it again in the same script, with the same arguments as the first call, will just return the previous connection. If you specify parameter four as true (or 1, as is most common), PHP will always open a new connection each time you call mysql_connect( ).

The last parameter allows you to specify additional connection options, of which the only really useful one is MYSQL_CLIENT_COMPRESS, which tells the server that it may use data compression to save network transfer time. This is a smart move if your web server and database server are on different machines.

Querying and Formatting

The majority of your interaction with MySQL in PHP will be done using the mysql_query( ) function, which takes the SQL query you want to perform as its parameter. It will then perform that query and return a special resource known as a MySQL result index, which contains a pointer to all the rows that matched your query. "Result index" is nothing more than a fancy term for a MySQL resource type, but you will see it used in MySQL error messages.

This result index is the return value of mysql_query( ), and you should save it in a variable for later use. Whenever you want to extract rows from the results, count the number of rows, or perform other operations on the results from the query, you need to use this value.

One other helpful function is mysql_num_rows( ), which takes a result index as its parameter and returns the number of rows inside that result—this is the number of rows that matched the query you sent in mysql_query( ). With the two together, we can write a basic database-enabled script:

```
mysql_connect("localhost", "phpuser", "alm65z");
mysql_select_db("phpdb");
$result = mysql_query("SELECT * FROM usertable");
$numrows = mysql_num_rows($result);
print "There are $numrows people in usertable\n";
```

That captures the return value of mysql_query( ) inside $result, then uses it on the very next line. This MySQL result index is used often, so it is important to keep track of it. The exception to this is when you are executing a write query in MySQL, where you don't want to know the result.

The mysql_query( ) function will return false if the query is syntactically invalid (if you have used a bad query). This means that very often, it is helpful to check the return value even if you are writing data: if the data was not written successfully, mysql_query( ) will tell you so with the return value. Similarly, an empty result will return true, which may mean you executed a dumb query by accident—something like SELECT * FROM people WHERE Age > 500 will return no rows (and hence, true) unless you're programming a fantasy adventure!

Disconnecting from a MySQL Database

It is not necessary to explicitly disconnect from your MySQL server or to free the space allocated to your SQL results by hand. However, if you have a popular script that takes more than five seconds to execute, you should do all you can to conserve resources. Therefore, it is smart to explicitly free up your MySQL resources rather than wait to let PHP do it on your behalf.

There are two functions for this purpose: mysql_free_result( ) and mysql_close( ). The first is used to deallocate memory that was used to store the query results returned by mysql_query( ). If you have big queries being returned, you should be calling mysql_free_result( ) if there is much time between you finishing with the data and your script finishing execution. Here is how it works:

```
$result = mysql_query("SELECT * FROM really_big_table;");
// ...[snip]...
mysql_free_result($result);
```

The purpose of mysql_close( ) is to save computer resources, but another important reason for using it is that there is a limited number of connections that a MySQL server can accept. If you have several clients holding connections open for no reason, then the server may well need to turn away other clients who are waiting to connect to the database. The actual number of connections a database server can accept is set by the database administrator, but if you plan to have no more than 100, you should be OK. As with mysql_free_result( ), it is good to call mysql_close( ) if you think there will be some time between your last database use and your script ending.

Using mysql_close( ) is simple: you do not need to supply any parameters to it, as it will automatically close the last-opened MySQL connection. Of course, if you captured the return value from mysql_connect( ), you can supply that to mysql_close( ) and it will close a specific connection—handy if you have multiple MySQL connections open for some reason.

Here's a simple example of mysql_close( ) in action:

```
mysql_connect("localhost", "phpuser", "alm65z");
mysql_select_db("phpdb");
// ...[snip]...
mysql_close( );
```

In the example above, the call to mysql_close( ) is not needed—the script ends immediately after, and any open MySQL connections that aren't permanent connections will be closed automatically.

Reading in Data

To read data from a MySQL result index, use the mysql_fetch_assoc( ) function. This takes one row from a MySQL result and converts it to an associative array, with each field name as a key and the matching field value as the value. The function increments its position each time it is called, so calling it for the first time reads the first row, the second time the second row, etc., until you run out of rows—in which case, it returns false. In this respect, it works like the each( ) array function we looked at previously.

To extend our previous script to output nicely formatted data, we would need to make it use mysql_fetch_assoc( ) to go through each row returned by the query, printing out all fields in there:

```
mysql_connect("localhost", "phpuser", "alm65z");
mysql_select_db("phpdb");
$result = mysql_query("SELECT * FROM usertable");

if ($result && mysql_num_rows($result)) {
        $numrows = mysql_num_rows($result);
        $rowcount = 1;
        print "There are $numrows people in usertable:<br /><br />";

        while ($row = mysql_fetch_assoc($result)) {
                print "Row $rowcount<br />";

                foreach($row as $var => $val) {
                        print "<B>$var</B>: $val<br />";
                }

                print "<br />";
                ++$rowcount;
        }
}
```

Figure 14-1 shows how that script looks when viewed through a web browser.

Figure 14-1. The contents of our table printed out through PHP

That script connects to the local MySQL database server and selects the phpdb database for use. It then runs a basic query on our usertable table and stores the result index in $result. The next line checks that $result is true and that there is at least one row in there—if so, it stores the number of rows in $numrows, sets the $rowcount variable to 1, then outputs the number of rows it found.

The next section is the new part: $row is set to the return value of mysql_fetch_ assoc( ), which means it will be set to an array containing the data from the next row in the result. If mysql_fetch_assoc( ) has no more rows to return, it sends back false and ends the while loop. Each time we have a row to read, $rowcount is outputted and then the script goes through the array stored in $row (sent back from mysql_fetch_assoc( )), outputting each key and its value.

Finally, $rowcount is incremented, and the while loop goes around again.

 As an alternative to mysql_fetch_assoc( ), many programmers use mysql_fetch_array( ). The difference between the two is that, by default, mysql_fetch_array( ) returns an array of the row data with numerical field indexes (i.e., 0, 1, 2, 3) as well as string field indexes (i.e., Name, Age, etc.). Unless you need both indexes, stick with mysql_fetch_assoc( ).

Mixing in PHP Variables

Because the parameter for mysql_query( ) is a string, you can use variables as you would in any other string. For example:

```
$result = mysql_query("SELECT ID FROM webpages WHERE Title =
'$SearchCriteria';");
$numhits = mysql_num_rows($result);
print "Your search for $SearchCriteria yielded $numhits results";
```

You can use PHP variables wherever you want inside SQL queries, as long as you end up with a valid SQL query; otherwise, mysql_query( ) will return false. For example:

```
function simplequery($table, $field, $needle, $haystack) {
        $result = mysql_query("SELECT $field FROM $table WHERE
                $haystack = $needle LIMIT 1;");

        if ($result) {
                if (mysql_num_rows($result)) {
                        $row = mysql_fetch_assoc($result);
                        return $row[$field];
                }
        } else {
                print "Error in query<br />";
        }

}
```

That function allows you to pass in the name of the table you want to read, the field you are interested in, and the criteria it should match. Then it executes the appropriate query and sends the requested value back as its return value. This function can, therefore, be used like this:

```
$firstname = simplequery("usertable", "firstname", "ID", $UserID);
```

The advantage to this is that you can program all sorts of error checking into simplequery( ) without making your scripts any more cluttered to read.

Although mixing PHP variables into your MySQL calls is powerful, you must be careful not to allow your users to abuse your scripts to hack into your systems. The first defense in this fight is the function mysql_escape_string( ), which is designed to make PHP variables more safe when used inside MySQL queries. To use this function, pass in the string that you wish to make safer, and it will return the new value. The function works by escaping all potentially dangerous characters in the string you pass in, including single quotes—be wary about using this function in combination with addslashes( ).

Reading Auto-Incrementing Values

When creating your MySQL tables, you can specify fields as INT AUTO_INCREMENT PRIMARY KEY, which means that MySQL will automatically assign increasingly higher integers to the field as INSERT queries are sent.

There are two ways to read the last-used auto-increment value: using a query or calling a function. The query option relies on the special MAX( ) function of MySQL. As MySQL will assign increasingly higher numbers to the ID field, the way to find the most recently assigned number is to run code like this:

```
mysql_query("SELECT MAX(ID) AS ID FROM dogbreeds;");
```

The smart alternative is to use the function mysql_insert_id( ), which will return the last ID auto-inserted by the current connection. There is a subtle difference there, and one that makes it important enough for you to learn both methods of retrieving auto-incrementing values. The difference lies in the fact that mysql_insert_id( ) returns the last ID number that MySQL issued for this connection, regardless of what other connections are doing. Furthermore, mysql_insert_id( ) only stores one value—the last ID number that MySQL issued for this connection on any table. On the other hand, using the SQL query allows you to check the very latest ID that has been inserted, even if you have not run any queries or if it has been 20 minutes since your last query. Furthermore, you can use the query on any table you like, which makes it even more useful.

Unbuffered Queries for Large Data Sets

Using mysql_query( ) for large queries has several serious disadvantages:

- PHP must wait while the entire query is executed and returned before it can start processing.
- In order to return the whole result to PHP at once, all the data must be held in RAM. Thus, if you have 100MB of data to return, the PHP variable to hold it all will be 100MB.

The disadvantages of mysql_query( ) are the advantages of mysql_unbuffered_query( ), which also queries data through SQL:

- The PHP script can parse the results immediately, giving immediate feedback to users.
- Only a few rows at a time need to be held in RAM.

One nice feature of mysql_unbuffered_query( ) is that, internally to PHP, it is almost identical to mysql_query( ). As a result, you can almost use them interchangeably inside your scripts. For example, this script works fine with either mysql_query( ) or mysql_unbuffered_query( ):

```php
<?php mysql_connect("localhost", "php", "alm65z");
    mysql_select_db("phpdb");
    $result = mysql_unbuffered_query("SELECT ID, Name FROM
conferences;");

        while ($row = mysql_fetch_assoc($result)) {
            extract($row, EXTR_PREFIX_ALL, "conf");
            print "$conf_Name\n";
        }
?>
```

Before you rush off to make all your queries unbuffered, be aware that there are drawbacks to using mysql_unbuffered_query( ) that can make it no better than mysql_query( ):

- You *must* read all rows from the return value, as MySQL will not allow you to run fresh queries until you have done so. If you're thinking of using this as a quick way to find something and then stop processing the rows part of the way through, you're way off track—sorry!
- If you issue another query before you finish processing all the rows from the previous query, PHP will issue a warning. SELECTs within SELECTs are not possible with unbuffered queries.

- Functions such as mysql_num_rows( ) return only the number of rows read so far. This will be 0 as soon as the query returns, but as you call mysql_fetch_assoc( ), it will increment until it has the correct number of rows at the end.

- Between the time the call to mysql_unbuffered_query( ) is issued and your processing of the last row, the table remains locked by MySQL and cannot be written to by other queries. If you plan to do time-consuming processing on each row, this is not good.

If you're not sure which of the two is best, use mysql_query( ).

PEAR::DB

PEAR::DB is an advanced, object-oriented database library that provides full database abstraction—that is, you use the same code for all your databases. If you want your code to be as portable as possible, PEAR::DB provides the best mix of speed, power, and portability. However, if your scripts are only ever going to run locally, there is no compelling reason to use PEAR::DB.

PEAR::DB works by abstracting not only the calls neccessary to work with the databases (such as mysql_connect( ), pgsql_query( ), etc.), but also clashes with SQL syntax, such as the LIMIT clause. In PHP 5.1, there's a new extension called *PHP Data Objects* (PDO) that abstracts only the functions, which is halfway between PEAR::DB and using normal DB calls. PEAR::DB is likely to be updated to use PDO, as it's much more efficient.

This script below provides a good demonstration of how PEAR::DB works:

```
include_once('DB.php');

$conninfo = "mysql://username:password@localhost/phpdb";
$db = DB::connect($conninfo);

if (DB::isError($db)) {
        print $db->getMessage( );
        exit;
}

$result = $db->query("SELECT * FROM people;");

while ($result->fetchInto($row, DB_FETCHMODE_ASSOC)) {
        extract($row);
        print "$Name:  $NumVisits\n";
}

$result->free( );
$db->disconnect( );
```

PEAR::DB uses a URL-like connection string, often called a Data Source Name (DSN), to define its connection. This is the same method as seen in JDBC, so it should already be familiar to Java developers. The string can be broken down into parts, as shown in Table 14-1.

Table 14-1. The different parts of a PEAR::DB connection string

mysql://	Connection type
Username	Your username
Password	Your password
@localhost	The address of your server
/phpdb	The database name to use

If any part of your DSN contains characters that might be confused for separators (such as :, @, or /), you should use `rawurlencode()` to %-escape them. For example:

```
$username = "paul";
$password = "p|trp@tr";

$username = rawurlencode($username);
// does nothing; our username is safe

$password = rawurlencode($password);
// $password is now p%7Ctrp%40tr

$conninfo = "mysql://$username:$password@localhost/phpdb";
```

The connection type is the kind of server you are connecting to. You can choose from the list shown in Table 14-2.

Table 14-2. Database providers for PEAR::DB

fbsql	FrontBase
ibase	InterBase
ifx	Informix
msql	Mini SQL
mssql	Microsoft SQL Server
mysql	MySQL
oci8	Oracle 7/8/8i
odbc	ODBC (Open Database Connectivity)
pgsql	PostgreSQL
sqlite	SQLite
sybase	SyBase

Once the DSN is prepared, you must pass it into a call to `DB::connect()` as its first parameter. This will return a reference to the object you can use for querying. `PEAR::DB` is object-oriented, which means you need to hang on to the return value from `DB::connect()`.

The `DB::isError()` function is a special function call that takes the value to check as its parameter, and returns true if that value is one of `PEAR::DB`'s error types. In our example, $db is passed in so we can check whether `DB::connect()` failed. On the off chance that an error has occurred, it will be stored in the getMessage( ) function of your database connection.

However, if things go well, you can start querying the system using the query( ) function of our $db object. This takes the SQL query to perform as its only parameter, and returns another kind of object that contains the result information. To cycle through the result information, a while loop is used, taking advantage of the fetchInto( ) PEAR::DB function. This will return false if it cannot return any more rows, and takes two parameters: where it should send the data it fetches, and how it should store the data there. Using DB_FETCHMODE_ASSOC means that PEAR::DB will set up $row to be an associative array of one row in the result set, recursively iterating through the rows with each while loop.

At the end of the script, we call the free( ) and disconnect( ) functions to clean up.

Quick PEAR::DB Calls

PEAR::DB has the getOne( ), getRow( ), and getCol( ) functions for making easy queries, and each takes an SQL query to execute as its parameter. The first executes the query and then returns the first row of the first column of that query, the second returns all columns of the first row in the query, and the last returns the first column of all rows in the query. The getOne( ) function returns just one value, whereas getRow( ) and getCol( ) both return arrays of values.

Here is an example demonstrating each of these functions in action, using a table of people:

```
include_once('DB.php');
$db = DB::connect("mysql://phpuser:alm65z@localhost/phpdb");

if (DB::isError($db)) {
        print $db->getMessage( );
        exit;
} else {
        $maxage = $db->getOne("SELECT MAX(Age) FROM people;");
        print "The highest age is $maxage<br />";
        $allnames = $db->getCol("SELECT Name FROM people;");
        print implode(', ', $allnames) . '<br />';
        $onecol = $db->getRow("SELECT * FROM people WHERE Name =
'Ildiko';");
        var_dump($onecol);
}

$db->disconnect( );
```

Query Information

Because PEAR::DB smooths over the differences between database servers, it is very helpful for measuring the effects of queries. Three particularly helpful functions are numRows( ), numCols( ), and affectedRows( ), which return information about what a query actually did—numRows( ) returns how many rows were returned from a SELECT statement, numCols( ) returns how many columns (fields) were returned from a SELECT statement, and affectedRows() returns how many rows were altered by an UPDATE, INSERT, or DELETE statement. For example, if we have three rows with Age 35 in our people table and execute the query UPDATE people SET Name = 'xxx' WHERE Age = 35, affectedRows() would return 3.

Here is an example of these functions in action:

```
include_once('DB.php');
$db = DB::connect("mysql://phpuser:alm65z@localhost/phpdb");

if (DB::isError($db)) {
        print $db->getMessage();
        exit;
} else {
        $result = $db->query("SELECT * FROM people;");
        print 'Query returned ' . $result->numRows() . ' rows\n';
        print 'Query returned ' . $result->numCols() . ' cols\n';
        print 'Query affected ' . $db->affectedRows() . ' rows\n';
        $db->query("INSERT INTO people VALUES ('Thomas', 36);");
        print 'Query returned ' . $result->numRows() . ' rows\n';
        print 'Query returned ' . $result->numCols() . ' cols\n';
        print 'Query affected ' . $db->affectedRows() . ' rows\n';
        $result->free();
}

$db->disconnect();
```

The first PEAR::DB query is a SELECT statement, which means that it will return values for numRows() and numCols(). The affectedRows() function is *not* a function of the PEAR::DB query result object—numRows() is $result->numRows(), numCols() is $result->numCols(), but affectedRows() is $db->affectedRows().

This is because SELECT statements are read from the database and return a result object from $db->query(). INSERT, UPDATE, and DELETE statements only return success or failure, and because affectedRows() only returns a meaningful value when used with these types of statements, it would be pointless to put affectedRows() into the query() result.

This is illustrated in the next block of code—this time, we insert a new person into the table, and again print out the three functions. Note that we do not capture the return value of the function, because it does not return anything useful in this script. This time around, printing out numRows() and numCols() returns the same values as before, because the $result object is unchanged from the previous call.

Calling $db->affectedRows() should return 1, because we inserted a row. To illustrate the situation with the return value of query(), try editing the code to this:

```
$result = $db->query("INSERT INTO people VALUES ('Thomas', 0);");
```

This time, you should get the following error when you try to run the script:

```
Fatal error: Call to a member function on a non-object
```

This is because the return value from query( ) will be true if it succeeds, and an error otherwise. As a result, calling $result->numRows( ) is calling a function on true, which will not work.

Use numRows( ) and numCols( ) only with SELECT queries, and use affectedRows( ) only with INSERT, UPDATE, and DELETE queries.

Advanced PEAR::DB: Prepared Statements

PEAR::DB is capable of *prepared statements*—a technique to handle repetitive SQL statements. Prepared statements let you treat an SQL query somewhat like a function—you define roughly what the query will do, without actually passing it any values, then later you "call" the query and pass it the values to use.

Prepared statements are easy to use and eliminate much of the fuss of SQL, because you no longer need long and complicated queries to achieve your goals. Most importantly, you don't need to worry about escaping quotes and the like.

A prepared statement looks something like this:

```
INSERT INTO people VALUES (?, ?);
```

Once you have the prepared statement ready, it can be called later by providing the values previously filled with question marks:

```
include_once('DB.php');
$db = DB::connect("mysql://phpuser:alm65z@localhost/phpdb");

if (DB::isError($db)) {
        print $db->getMessage( );
        exit;
} else {
        $data = array(
                array("Gabor", 25),
                array("Elisabeth", 39),
                array("Vicky", 19)
        );

        $prep = $db->prepare("INSERT INTO people VALUES (?, ?);");

        while(list($var, $val) = each($data)) {
                print "Adding element $var\n";
                $db->execute($prep, $val);
        }
}

$db->disconnect( );
```

The $data array has three elements, each arrays in their own right. Look down to the line $db->execute( )—this function takes two parameters: the prepared statement to execute and the array of values to pass to it. When PEAR::DB fills in the question marks in the prepared statement passed in parameter one of execute( ), it iterates through the array passed as parameter two—element zero of the array is used for the first question mark, element one is used for the second, etc.

Going back to the $data array, you should now realize that the reason it is an array of arrays is because each child array holds one complete set of values for the prepared statement, ready to be passed into $db->execute( ) later on. The first set of values is "Gabor" and 25, which will be turned into this:

```
INSERT INTO people VALUES ('Gabor', 25);
```

The $db->prepare( ) function is what actually sets up the prepared statement. It takes the SQL statement to use as its parameter, with question marks being used wherever values need to be provided later. You can mix hard-coded values and question marks freely, and you should take advantage of this so that you need to do as little work as possible.

Calling prepare( ) returns the index number of the prepared statement to use, which is an integer. This needs to be stored away in a variable so that you can specify which prepared statement you want to use when you call execute( ).

The actual execution of the prepared statement is inside a while loop. The loop iterates through each element in the $data array, extracting its key and value into $var and $val, respectively; each time we have an element, we call execute( ). This takes two parameters: the prepared statement to execute and the values to pass to it. In the example code above, the return value from the $db->prepare( ) line is used as parameter one, and the $val value extracted from the $data array is sent in as parameter two. That will execute the prepared statement three times, as we have three sets of data to be inserted.

SQLite

SQLite is a fully functional relational database system that does not use the traditional client/server database architecture. For example, MySQL has a server running on a machine somewhere, and a client (in the form of PHP, in our examples) connects to that server to perform queries. SQLite, on the other hand, works on local files, with no database server required—when you run queries using SQLite, they are translated into operations on the local files.

From PHP 5 onward, SQLite is bundled and enabled by default, which means that everyone, everywhere, will have it by default. If you are writing an application that needs a data store, you no longer need to worry whether they have Oracle or Microsoft SQL Server installed or, indeed, whether they have any database server installed at all.

Before You Begin

SQLite uses a file for every database you create, which means that it is very easy to keep track of your data, particularly if you want to back up and restore information. However, it also means that this file must be easily available, preferably local—using remote file systems, such as NFS, is not recommended.

There are some unique aspects to SQLite that you should be aware of—the most important is its handling of field types. SQLite does not distinguish between data types beyond "string" and "number"—CHAR(255), for example, is the same as VARCHAR(20), which is the same as TEXT, which makes it typeless like PHP. This boils down to "If your data type has CHAR, TEXT, BLOB, or CLOB in it, it is text; otherwise, it is a number." This is fuzzy matching—VARCHAR has "CHAR" in it; thus, it is considered to be a text field.

There is one exception to this state of affairs, and that is when you want an autoincrementing primary key value. If you define a field as being INTEGER PRIMARY KEY, it must contain a 32-bit signed integer—equivalent to an INT data type in MySQL—and, if you do not fill this value when you insert a row, SQLite will automatically fill it with an integer one higher than the highest in there already. If the value is already at 2147483647, which is the highest number it can hold, SQLite will hand out random numbers. Note that the data type must be INTEGER and not INT—INT will be treated as a normal number field.

Finally, because SQLite stores its data in files, it is not able to handle multiple simultaneous writes to the same table. Essentially, when a write query comes in, SQLite locks the database (a file), performs the write, then unlocks the file— during the locked time, no other queries can write to that database. This is a problem if you want your database to scale, or if you are using a system that does not have a reliable file locking mechanism, such as NFS.

Getting Started

Working with SQLite is similar to working with other databases. The syntax is slightly different, and you invariably need to pass in an exact database connection with each call to the library; however, there should be no problem if you have already mastered another SQL dialect.

 There's an object-oriented version of SQLite for people who like that sort of thing.

The four key functions to use are sqlite_open( ), sqlite_close( ), sqlite_query( ), and sqlite_fetch_array( ), and they work almost exactly like their MySQL equivalents. The connection function is sqlite_open( ), not sqlite_connect( ), reflecting the lack of client/server architecture.

Here is an example script:

```
$dbconn = sqlite_open('phpdb');

if ($dbconn) {
        sqlite_query($dbconn, "CREATE TABLE dogbreeds
                (Name VARCHAR(255), MaxAge INT);");
        sqlite_query($dbconn, "INSERT INTO dogbreeds VALUES ('Doberman',
15)");
        $result = sqlite_query($dbconn, "SELECT Name FROM dogbreeds");
        var_dump(sqlite_fetch_array($result, SQLITE_ASSOC));
} else {
        print "Connection to database failed!\n";
}
```

Connecting to an SQLite database is simply a matter of providing the filename to use as the parameter to sqlite_open( ). Some programmers have adopted the convention of using the filename extension *.sqlite* for their databases, but you are free to do as you please, as this convention has yet to catch on.

After opening the database, you will notice that sending queries requires passing the database connection as the first parameter, with the query as the second parameter. The queries themselves are standard SQL, so you should be able to take your existing SQL skillset and apply it directly here. There is no sqlite_fetch_assoc( ) function at this time, so the sqlite_fetch_array( ) function is used, specifying SQLITE_ASSOC as parameter two. If you do not do this, sqlite_fetch_array( ) will return each field of data twice—once with its numeric index, and again with its field name string index.

Other than the minor differences listed above, SQLite works much like MySQL. The advantage of absolute cross-platform compatibility, regardless of whether people have a database server running, makes SQLite a great tool to keep handy in your toolkit.

 When calling sqlite_open( ), you can pass in :memory: as the filename to have SQLite create its database in memory. This is substantially faster than working with a disk, but it will be deleted when your script terminates.

Advanced Functions

There are three extra functions for SQLite that you are likely to find helpful. First, the equivalent function of mysql_insert_id( ) is sqlite_last_insert_rowid( ), which requires the connection resource as its only parameter. Creating auto-incrementing fields in SQLite requires you to declare them as "INTEGER PRIMARY KEY"—the AUTO_INCREMENT keyword is *not* required. The sqlite_last_insert_rowid( ) function will return the auto-increment ID number that was used for the last INSERT query you sent.

Second, the functional equivalent of PEAR::DB's getOne( ) is sqlite_fetch_single( ). This will return the first column of the first row of the result of your query, and you pass the return value of sqlite_query( ) into sqlite_fetch_single( ) as its only parameter.

Finally, the function sqlite_array_query( ) is a very powerful function that returns an array of all the rows returned. For example:

```
$dbconn = sqlite_open('phpdb');

if ($dbconn) {
        // this assumes you created the dogbreeds table using the previous
        script!
        sqlite_query($dbconn, "INSERT INTO dogbreeds VALUES
                ('Poodle', 14)");
        sqlite_query($dbconn, "INSERT INTO dogbreeds VALUES
                ('Jack Russell', 16)");
        sqlite_query($dbconn, "INSERT INTO dogbreeds VALUES
```

```
                        ('Yorkshire Terrier', 13)");
            var_dump(sqlite_array_query($dbconn, "SELECT * FROM
                        dogbreeds", SQLITE_ASSOC));
    } else {
            print "Connection to database failed!\n";
    }
```

The first three INSERT queries make the data more interesting. The key line is where sqlite_array_query( ) is called. The function basically works as a combination of sqlite_query( ) and repeated calls to sqlite_fetch_array( ), so it requires the database connection as parameter one, and the query to execute as parameter two. In the example, SQLITE_ASSOC is also passed in, as we would normally do when calling sqlite_fetch_array( ).

Here is the output that script generates, when used immediately after the script that created the dogbreeds table:

```
array(4) {
        [0]=>
        array(2) {
                ["Name"]=>
                string(8) "Doberman"
                ["MaxAge"]=>
                string(2) "15"
        }

        [1]=>
        array(2) {
                ["Name"]=>
                string(6) "Poodle"
                ["MaxAge"]=>
                string(2) "14"
        }

        [2]=>
        array(2) {
                ["Name"]=>
                string(12) "Jack Russell"
                ["MaxAge"]=>
                string(2) "16"
        }

        [3]=>
                array(2) {
                ["Name"]=>
                string(17) "Yorkshire Terrier"
                ["MaxAge"]=>
                string(2) "13"
        }
}
```

Each row in the table became an element in the returned array value, and each element was, in fact, an array in its own right, containing the names and values of each of the fields of that array. Using sqlite_array_query( ) is a very fast, very optimized way to extract lots of data from your database with just one call.

Mixing SQLite and PHP

It is possible to make PHP and SQLite work together to filter data. For example, this next code creates a PHP function that gets used in an SQLite query:

```
mysql_connect("localhost", "phpuser", "alm65z");
mysql_select_db("phpdb");

mysql_query("CREATE TABLE sqlite_test (ID INT NOT NULL AUTO_INCREMENT
        PRIMARY KEY, Name VARCHAR(255));");
mysql_query("INSERT INTO sqlite_test (Name) VALUES ('Peter Hutchinson');");
mysql_query("INSERT INTO sqlite_test (Name) VALUES ('Jeanette Shieldes');");

$conn = sqlite_open("employees");
sqlite_query($conn, "CREATE TABLE employees (ID INTEGER NOT NULL PRIMARY
KEY, Name VARCHAR(255));");
sqlite_query($conn, "INSERT INTO employees (Name) VALUES ('James
Fisher');");
sqlite_query($conn, "INSERT INTO employees (Name) VALUES ('Peter
Hutchinson');");
sqlite_query($conn, "INSERT INTO employees (Name) VALUES ('Richard
Hartis');");

function ExistsInBoth($name) {
        $result = mysql_query("SELECT ID FROM sqlite_test WHERE Name =
'$name';");
        if (mysql_num_rows($result)) {
                return 1;
        } else {
                return 0;
        }
}

sqlite_create_function($conn, "EXISTS_IN_BOTH", "ExistsInBoth");

$query = sqlite_query($conn, "SELECT Name FROM employees WHERE EXISTS_IN_
BOTH(Name)");

while($row = sqlite_fetch_array($query, SQLITE_ASSOC)) {
        extract($row);
        print "$Name is in both databases\n";
}
```

The call to sqlite_create_function( ) takes an SQLite connection as its first parameter, the name you want to give the function inside SQLite as its second, and the actual PHP function name as its third.

Persistent Connections

You can switch to persistent connections in MySQL by changing the function call from mysql_connect( ) to mysql_pconnect( ). They both take the same parameters, with the difference being that mysql_connect( ) will always open a new connection, whereas mysql_pconnect( ) will open a new connection only if there is not one already available. Otherwise, it will just use the existing connection. Similarly, the SQLite function `sqlite_open()` has a persistent counterpart, `sqlite_popen()`.

In the per-process Apache module (`prefork`), persistent resources such as persistent MySQL connections are stored per process. This means if you have 150 Apache children running, you'll need 150 MySQL permanent connections—even if some of those processes aren't using MySQL right now.

MySQL Improved

New with PHP 5 is the MySQLi extension, which is "MySQL Improved." This is an all new extension designed to take advantage of the new features available from MySQL 4.1 and upward, and includes new functionality such as native commit and rollback, as well as prepared statements. As the MySQLi extension is only designed to work with MySQL 4.1 and upward, it isn't likely to see any widespread use for some time.

If you are an early adopter of MySQL 4.1 and want to jump in headfirst with some testing, the MySQLi functions work similarly to the MySQL functions—you just need to add an "i" after "mysql" in your code. For example, `mysql_connect()` becomes `mysqli_connect()`, `mysql_query()` becomes `mysqli_query()`, etc. That said, there are *some* differences between MySQL and MySQLi code. For example, `mysqli_connect()`'s fourth parameter lets you specify the default database to use, letting you skip the call to `mysqli_select_db()`. If you still want to use it, `mysqli_select_db()` itself is also different, now taking the return value of `mysqli_connect()` as its first parameter, and the database to select as its second parameter.

At the time of writing, three MySQLi functions had potentially serious incompatibilities with their MySQL cousins. All three of `mysqli_fetch_row()`, `mysqli_fetch_array()`, and `mysqli_fetch_assoc()` return null when there are no more rows to be found, as opposed to the false that the MySQL extension would have returned. If you want to keep your code easily portable between MySQL and MySQLi, do not try to differentiate between false and null.

If you want to install support for both MySQL and MySQLi when compiling PHP, just point --with-mysql and --with-mysqli to the MySQL 4.1 client library on your system.

15

Regular Expressions

Regular expressions, usually referred to as regexps, offer you more power over your strings, but are tricky to learn because they use complicated syntax. Regexps can:

- Replace text
- Test for a pattern within a string
- Extract a substring from within a string

We'll be looking at all three of these uses in this chapter, as well as providing a comprehensive list of the different expressions you can use to work with all kinds of strings.

You should know that the set of string functions covered in Chapter 7 are faster, easier to read, and less hassle to use than regular expressions; you should only use regular expressions if you have a particular need. PHP contains two ways to perform regular expressions, known as POSIX-extended and Perl-Compatible Regular Expressions (PCRE). The PCRE functions are more powerful than the POSIX ones, and faster too, so we will be using the PCRE functions here.

Basic Regexps with preg_match( ) and preg_match_all( )

The basic regexp function is preg_match( ) and it takes two parameters: the pattern to match and the string to match it against. It will apply the regular expression in parameter one to the string in parameter two and see whether it finds a match—if it does, it will return 1; otherwise, 0. The reason it returns 1 is because regular expressions return the number of matches found, but preg_match( ), for speed reasons, returns as soon as it finds the first match—this means it is very quick to check whether a pattern exists in a string. An alternative function, preg_match_all( ), does not exit after the first match; we will get to that later in this chapter.

Regular expressions are formed by starting with a forward slash /, followed by a sequence of special symbols and words to match, then another slash and, optionally, a string of letters that affect the expression. Table 15-1 shows a list of very basic regular expressions and strings, and whether or not a match is made.

Table 15-1. preg_match() calls and what they match

Function call	Result
preg_match("/php/", "php")	True
preg_match("php/", "php")	Error; you need a slash at the start
preg_match("/php/", "PHP")	False; regexps are case-sensitive
preg_match("/php/i", "PHP")	True; /i means "case-insensitive"
preg_match("/Foo/i", "FOO")	True

The i modifier makes regexps case-insensitive.

The preg_match( ) returns true if there is a match, so you can use it like this:

```
if (preg_match("/php/i", "PHP")) {
        print "Got match!\n";
}
```

Regexp Character Classes

Regular expressions allow you to form *character classes* of words using brackets [and]. For example, you can define a character class [Ff] that will match "F" or "f". You can also use character classes to accept ranges; for example, [A-Z] will accept all uppercase letters, [A-Za-z] will accept all letters, whether uppercase or lowercase, and [a-z0-9] will accept lowercase letters and numbers only. At the beginning of a character class, the caret symbol ^ means "not," therefore [^A-Z] will accept everything that is not an uppercase letter, and [^A-Za-z0-9] will accept symbols only—no uppercase letters, no lowercase letters, and no numbers.

There is a list of regular expressions using character classes, along with the string they match—and whether or not a match is made—in Table 15-2.

Table 15-2. Regular expressions using character classes

Function call	Result
preg_match("/[Ff]oo/", "Foo")	True
preg_match("/[^Ff]oo/", "Foo")	False; the regexp says "Anything that is not F or f, followed by "oo". This would match "too", "boo", "zoo", etc.
preg_match("/[A-Z][0-9]/", "K9")	True
preg_match("/[A-S]esting/", "Testing")	False; the acceptable range for the first character ends at S
preg_match("/[A-T]esting/", "Testing")	True; the range is inclusive
preg_match("/[a-z]esting[0-9][0-9]/", "TestingAA")	False

Table 15-2. Regular expressions using character classes (continued)

Function call	Result
preg_match("/[a-z]esting[0-9][0-9]/", "testing99")	True
preg_match("/[a-z]esting[0-9][0-9]/", "Testing99")	False; case sensitivity!
preg_match("/[a-z]esting[0-9][0-9]/i", "Testing99")	True; case problems fixed with /i
preg_match("/[^a-z]esting/", "Testing")	True; first character can be anything that is not a, b, c, d, e, etc. (lowercase)
preg_match("/[^a-z]esting/i", "Testing")	False; the range excludes lowercase characters only, so you would think T would be fine. However, the "i" at the end makes it insensitive, which turns [^a-z] into [^a-zA-Z]

The last one is a common mistake, so make sure you understand why it does not match.

Regexp Special Characters

The metacharacters +, *, ?, and { } affect the number of times a pattern should be matched, ( ) allows you to create subpatterns, and $ and ^ affect the position. + means "Match one or more of the previous expression," * means "Match zero or more of the previous expression," and ? means "Match zero or one of the previous expression." For example:

```
preg_match("/[A-Za-z ]*/", $string);
// matches "", "a", "aaaa", "The sun has got his hat on", etc

preg_match("/-?[0-9]+/", $string);
// matches 1, 100, 324343995, and also -1, -234011, etc. The "-?" means
"match exactly 0 or 1 minus symbols"
```

This next regexp shows two character classes, with the first being required and the second optional. As mentioned before, $ is a regexp symbol in its own right; however, here we precede it with a backslash, which works as an escape character, turning the $ into a standard character and not a regexp symbol. We match precisely one symbol from the range A–Z, a–z, and _, then match zero or more symbols from the range A–Z, a–z, underscore, and 0–9. If you're able to parse this in your head, you will see that this regexp will match PHP variable names:

```
preg_match("/\$[A-Za-z_][A-Za-z_0-9]*/", $string);
```

Table 15-3 shows a list of regular expressions using +, *, and ?, and whether or not a match is made.

Table 15-3. Regular expressions using +, *, and ?

Regexp	Result
preg_match("/[A-Z]+/", "123")	False
preg_match("/[A-Z][A-Z0-9]+/i", "A123")	True
preg_match("/[0-9]?[A-Z]+/", "10GreenBottles")	True; matches "0G"
preg_match("/[0-9]?[A-Z0-9]*/i", "10GreenBottles")	True
preg_match("/[A-Z]?[A-Z]?[A-Z]*/", "")	True; zero or one match, then zero or one match, then zero or more means that an empty string matches

Opening braces { and closing braces } can be used to define specific repeat counts in three different ways. First, {*n*}, where *n* is a positive number, will match *n* instances of the previous expression. Second, {*n*,} will match a minimum of *n* instances of the previous expression. Third, {*m,n*} will match a minimum of *m* instances and a maximum of *n* instances of the previous expression. Note that there are no spaces inside the braces.

Table 15-4 shows a list of regular expressions using braces, and whether or not a match is made.

Table 15-4. Regular expressions using braces

Regexp	Result
preg_match("/[A-Z]{3}/", "FuZ")	False; the regexp will match precisely three uppercase letters
preg_match("/[A-Z]{3}/i", "FuZ")	True; same as above, but case-insensitive this time
preg_match("/[0-9]{3}-[0-9]{4}/", "555-1234")	True; precisely three numbers, a dash, then precisely four. This will match local U.S. telephone numbers, for example
preg_match("/[a-z]+[0-9]?[a-z]{1}/", "aaa1")	True; must end with one lowercase letter
preg_match("/[A-Z]{1,}99/", "99")	False; must start with at least one uppercase letter
preg_match("/[A-Z]{1,5}99/", "FINGERS99")	True; "S99", "RS99", "ERS99", "GERS99", and "NGERS99" all fit the criteria
preg_match("/[A-Z]{1,5}[0-9]{2}/i", "adams42")	True

Parentheses inside regular expressions allow you to define subpatterns that should be matched individually. The most common use for these is to specify groups of alternatives for matches, allowing you to match very specific criteria. For example, "the (cat|car) sat on the (mat|drive)" would match "the cat sat on the mat", "the car sat on the mat", "the cat sat on the drive", and "the car sat on the drive". You can use as many alternatives as you want, so "the (car|cat|bat|bull|wool|white paint) sat on the (mat|drive)" could match many sentences.

Table 15-5 shows a list of regular expressions using parentheses, and whether or not a match is made.

Table 15-5. Regular expressions using braces

Regexp	Result
print preg_match("/(Linux|Mac OS X)/", "Linux")	True
print preg_match("/(Linux|Mac OS X){2}/", "Mac OS XLinux")	True
print preg_match("/(Linux|Mac OS X){2}/", "Mac OS X Linux")	False; there's a space in there, which is not part of the regexp
preg_match("/contra(diction|vention)/", "contravention")	True
preg_match("/Windows ([0-9][0-9] +|Me|XP)/", "Windows 2000")	True; matches 95, 98, 2000, 2003, Me, and XP
preg_match("/Windows (([0-9][0-9] +|Me|XP)|Codename (Whistler|Longhorn))/", "Windows Codename Whistler")	True; uses nested subpatterns to match all versions of Windows, but also codenames

Finally, we have the dollar $ and caret ^ symbols, which mean "end of line" and "start of line," respectively. Consider the following string:

```
$multitest = "This is\na long test\nto see whether\nthe dollar\nSymbol\nand
the\ncaret symbol\nwork as planned";
```

As you know, \n means "new line," so that is a string containing the following text:

This is
a long test
to see whether
the dollar
Symbol
and the
caret symbol
work as planned

In order to parse multiline strings, we need the m modifier, so m needs to go after the final slash. Without m, our multiline string is treated as only being one line, with "This" at the start of the line and "planned" at the end. By adding "m" to the regexp, we're asking PHP to match $ and ^ against the start and end of each line wherever the newline (\n) character is. All of these code snippets return true:

```
preg_match("/is$/m", $multitest);
// returns true if 'is' is at the end of a line

preg_match("/the$/m", $multitest);
// returns true if 'the' is at the end of a line

preg_match("/^the/m", $multitest);
// returns true if 'the' is at the end of a line

preg_match("/^Symbol/m", $multitest);
// returns true if 'Symbol' is at the start of a line
```

```
preg_match("/^[A-Z][a-z]{1,}/m", $multitest);
// returns true if there's a capital and one or more lowercase letters at
// line start
```

As explained, without the m modifier, the $ and ^ metacharacters only match the start and end of the entire string. With m, $ and ^ match the start and end of each new line. If you want to get the start and end of the string when m is enabled, you should use \A and \z, like this:

```
preg_match("/\AThis/m", $multitest);
// returns true if the string starts with "This" (true)
```

```
preg_match("/symbol\z/m", $multitest);
// returns true if the string ends with "symbol" (false)
```

Words and Whitespace Regexps

While there are many other patterns for use in regular expressions, they generally aren't very common. So far we've looked at all but five of the most common ones, which leaves us with . (a period), \s, \S, \b, and \B.

The pattern . will match any single character except \n (new line). Therefore, c.t will match "cat," but not "cart."

The next two, \s and \S, equate to "Match any whitespace" and "Match any non-whitespace," respectively. That is, if you specify [\s\S], your regular expression will match any single character, regardless of what it is; if you use [\s\S]*, your regular expression will match anything. For example:

```
$string = "Foolish child!";
preg_match("/[\S]{7}[\s]{1}[\S]{6}/", $string);
```

That matches precisely seven non-whitespace characters, followed by one whitespace character, followed by six non-whitespace characters—the exact string.

The last two patterns, \b and \B, equate to "On a word boundary" and "Not on a word boundary," respectively. That is, if you use the regexp /oo\b/, it will match "foo," "moo," "boo," and "zoo," because the "oo" is at the end of the word, but not "fool," "wool," or "pool," because the "oo" is inside the word. The \B pattern is the opposite, which means it would match only patterns that aren't on the edges of a word—using the previous example, "fool," "wool," and "pool" would be matched, whereas "foo," "moo," "boo," and "zoo" would not.

For example:

```
$string = "Foolish child!";

if (preg_match("/oo\b/i", $string)) {
        // we will not get here
}

preg_match("/oo\B/i", $string);
// opposite of previous search; returns true
```

```
preg_match("/no\b/", "he said 'no!'");
// returns true; \b is smart enough to know that !, ', ?, and other symbols
aren't part of words

preg_match("/royalty\b/", "royalty-free photograph");
// returns true; \b considers hyphenated words to be separate
```

Storing Matched Strings

The preg_match( ) function has a fourth parameter that allows you to pass in an array for it to store a list of matched strings. Consider this script:

```
$a = "Foo moo boo tool foo!";
preg_match("/[A-Za-z]oo\b/i", $a, $matches);
```

The regexp there translates to "Match all words that start with an uppercase or lowercase letter followed by "oo" at the end of a word, case-insensitive." After running, preg_match( ) will place all the matched patterns in the string $a into $matches, which you can then read for your own uses.

The preg_match( ) function returns as soon as it finds its first match, because most of the time we only want to know whether a string exists, as opposed to how often it exists. As a result, our fourth parameter is not working as we hoped quite yet—we need another function, preg_match_all( ), to get this right. This works just like preg_match( )—it takes the same parameters (except in very complicated cases you are unlikely to encounter), and returns the same values. Thus, with no changes, the same code works fine with the new function:

```
$a = "Foo moo boo tool foo!";
preg_match_all("/[A-Za-z]oo\b/i", $a, $matches);
var_dump($myarray);
```

This time, $matches is populated properly—but what does it contain? Many regexp writers write complicated expressions to match various parts of a given string in one line, so $matches will contain an array of arrays, with each array element containing a list of the strings the preg_match_all( ) found.

Line three of the script calls var_dump( ) on the array, so you can see the matches preg_match_all( ) picked up. The var_dump( ) function simply outputs the contents of the variable(s) passed to it for closer inspection, and is particularly useful with arrays and objects. You can read more on var_dump( ) later on.

Regular Expression Replacements

Using regular expressions to accomplish string replacement is done with the function preg_replace( ), and works in much the same way as preg_match( ).

The preg_replace( ) function takes a regexp as parameter one, what it should replace each match with as parameter two, and the string to work with as parameter three. The second parameter is plain text, but can contain $n to insert the text matched by subpattern n of your regexp rule. If you have no subpatterns, you should use $0 to use the matched text, like this:

```
$a = "Foo moo boo tool foo";
$b = preg_replace("/[A-Za-z]oo\b/", "Got word: $0\n", $a);
print $b;
```

That script would output the following:

```
Got word: Foo
Got word: moo
Got word: boo
tool Got word: foo
```

If you *are* using subpatterns, $0 is set to the whole match, then $1, $2, and so on are set to the individual matches for each subpattern. For example:

```
$match = "/the (car|cat) sat on the (drive|mat)/";
$input = "the cat sat on the mat";
print preg_replace($match, "Matched $0, $1, and $2\n", $input);
```

In that example, $0 will be set to "the cat sat on the mat", $1 will be "cat", and $2 will be "mat".

There are two further uses for preg_replace( ) that are particularly interesting: first, you can pass arrays as parameter one and parameter two, and preg_replace( ) will perform multiple replaces in one pass—we will be looking at that later. The other interesting functionality is that you can instruct PHP that the match text should be executed as PHP code once the replacement has taken place. Consider this script:

```
$a = "Foo moo boo tool foo";
$b = preg_replace("/[A-Za-z]oo\b/e", 'strtoupper("$0")', $a);
print $b;
```

This time, PHP will replace each match with strtoupper("*word*") and, because we have appended an e (for "eval" or "execute") to the end of our regular expression, PHP will execute the replacements it makes. That is, it will take strtoupper(word) and replace it with the result of the strtoupper( ) function, which is, of course, *WORD*. It is essential to put the $0 inside double quotes so that it is treated as a string—without the quotes, it will just read strtoupper(foo), which is probably not what you meant.

Here is the output:

```
FOO MOO BOO tool FOO
```

Optionally you can also pass a fourth parameter to preg_replace( ) to specify the maximum number of replacements you want to make. For example:

```
$a = "Foo moo boo tool foo";
$b = preg_replace("/[A-Za-z]oo\b/e", 'strtoupper("$0")', $a, 2);
print $b;
```

Now the output is this:

```
FOO MOO boo tool foo
```

Only the first two matches have been replaced, thanks to the fourth parameter being set to 2.

Regular Expression Syntax Examples

Table 15-6 is a comprehensive table of all the regular expressions we've covered. Column one contains example expressions, and column two contains what each expression will match.

Table 15-6. Complete list of regular expression examples

Expression	Will match...
foo	The string "foo"
^foo	"foo" at the start of a line
foo$	"foo" at the end of a line
^foo$	"foo" when it is alone on a line
[Ff]oo	"Foo" or "foo"
[abc]	a, b, or c
[^abc]	d, e, f, g, V, %, ~, 5, etc.—everything that is not a, b, or c (^ is "not" inside character classes)
[A-Z]	Any uppercase letter
[a-z]	Any lowercase letter
[A-Za-z]	Any letter
[A-Za-z0-9]	Any letter or number
[A-Z]+	One or more uppercase letters
[A-Z]*	Zero or more uppercase letters
[A-Z]?	Zero or one uppercase letters
[A-Z]{3}	Three uppercase letters
[A-Z]{3,}	A minimum of three uppercase letters
[A-Z]{1,3}	One, two, or three uppercase letters
[^0-9]	Any non-numeric character
[^0-9A-Za-z]	Any symbol (not a number or a letter)
(cat|sat)	Matches either "cat" or "sat"
([A-Z]{3}|[0-9]{4})	Matches three letters or four numbers
Fo*	F, Fo, Foo, Fooo, Foooo, etc.
Fo+	Fo, Foo, Fooo, Foooo, etc.
Fo?	F, Fo
.	Any character except \n (new line)
\b	A word boundary; e.g. te\b matches the "te" in "late" but not the "te" in "tell."
\B	A non-word boundary; "te\B" matches the "te" in "tell" but not the "te" in "late."
\n	Newline character
\s	Any whitespace (new line, space, tab, etc.)
\S	Any non-whitespace character

The Regular Expressions Coach

Although there is no doubt that regular expressions are incredibly useful, they also easily get out of hand when trying to match complex strings. Furthermore, anything past twelve or so characters gets hard to read and understand, which is a common source of bugs.

To work around this problem, I suggest you use a program called the Regex Coach (pictured in Figure 15-1), available from *http://www.weitz.de/regex-coach*— it is free to use non-commercially, and it is able to help you check that your regular expressions are correct by visually highlighting strings that match. The Coach is fully compatible with all the options shown here, including string replacement, and can even break down a regexp and describe it in plain English.

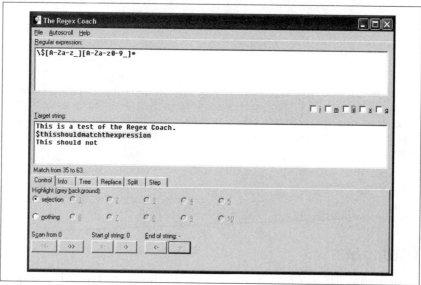

Figure 15-1. Use the Regex Coach to try out regular expressions and get instant feedback

16

Manipulating Images

Lots of people stereotype PHP as only being suitable for outputting text, but that's not true—you can use PHP to create complex and dynamic pictures using the GD image extension. This chapter covers many of the GD functions that will allow you to make your own images for your site, either from scratch or by using existing images.

For image manipulation purposes, PHP ships with its own copy of the popular GD library. You used to have to get your own copy of GD and hope it was compatible with your PHP version. This is no longer the case. The copy of GD that ships with PHP will work with that version of PHP.

Getting Started

An important PHP function when working with images is header(). This outputs a HTTP header of your choice; in this situation, we will be sending the content-type header, which tells web browsers what kind of content they can expect through the connection. Popular content types include text/plain for plain text documents; text/html for most web pages; and image/*, where the * is *png*, *jpeg*, *gif*, or MIME types for other picture formats.

As header() sends HTTP headers, it must be used before you send any content through. This is a core HTTP rule—no headers can be sent after content. This is the same thing that stops you from using cookies after you have sent content. The header() function is covered in more detail in Chapter 20, but for now, we will just work with this one aspect of it.

Creating a new image is done with the imagecreate() function, which has two parameters: the height and width of the image you wish to create. This will return false if it failed to create an image, which is usually the result of a lack of memory; otherwise, it will return the image as a resource for you to use in other image functions. To free up this image's memory, pass that resource into imagedestroy() as its only parameter.

Once you have your image resource, it is yours to play with all you want. PHP provides a selection of functions for you to use to manipulate the image. When you are done, you just choose your output format and the picture is finished.

To output the picture, you call one of several functions. If you want to convert it to PNG format, you call imagepng( ). This function takes two parameters, which are the image resource to use and a filename to save the picture as (optional). If you don't provide the second parameter, imagepng( ) sends the PNG-formatted picture straight to output, which is usually a visitor to your site.

To choose JPEG, you call the imagejpeg( ) function, which takes three parameters—the same two as imagepng( ), plus the quality you wish to use for the picture. The quality, a number between 0 (lowest quality, smallest file) and 100 (highest quality, largest file), is optional, as is the filename parameter. If you want to set the quality without specifying a filename, just provide an empty string (''') as the filename.

The most basic image script looks like this:

```
$image = imagecreate(400,300);
// do stuff to the image
imagejpeg($image, '', 75);
imagedestroy($image);
```

Save that as *picture1.php*. As most of your pictures will probably be referenced from a web page, we will also make a companion web page. Save this as *phppicture.html*:

```
<html>
<title>PHP Art</title>
<body>
PHP woz 'ere:
<img src="picture1.php" />
</body>
</html>
```

Open up your web browser and load in *phppicture.html*—you should see a large black box for the image, as shown in Figure 16-1.

 Be sure not to have anything outside the PHP code block, not even an empty line or a space. Everything outside the PHP block is sent to the browser as part of the picture, and even having a single space character at the end of the file will cause problems.

The next step is to add a little color in place of the "do stuff to the image" comment, so we need imagecolorallocate( ) (note that you must use U.S. spellings for these function names). This new function takes four parameters: the image resource you are choosing a color for, then three integers between 0 and 255—one each for the red value, then green value, and the blue value of the color. You can also specify these colors in hexadecimal format (e.g., 0xff) rather than decimal.

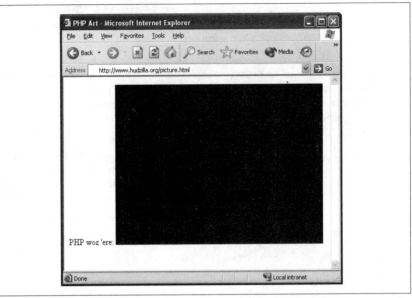

Figure 16-1. Our first picture using PHP is a big square colored entirely black—not exactly a stunner, but a good start

The first color you allocate is automatically used as the background color for your image, so this next piece of code is a minor modification of the last script to include color information:

```
$image = imagecreate(400,300);
$gold = imagecolorallocate($image, 255, 240, 00);
imagepng($image);
imagedestroy($image);
```

Save that over *picture1.php*, and refresh *phppicture.html*—you should see the black square replaced by a yellow square.

Don't worry about deallocating colors, as they are just numbers and not resources, meaning they don't use up any special memory. If you really want to deallocate a color (perhaps if you're working with a paletted image), use the imagecolordeallocate( ) function.

Choosing a Format

For high-quality images with many colors or a lot of detail, the JPEG format is preferred. JPEG saves in true color and allows you to set the compression ratio in order to get the best trade-off between size and quality. PNGs, on the other hand, work best as a replacement for GIFs, and as such, work well using limited colors. They also offer alpha transparency and quite small file sizes.

So, put as simply as possible: for photographs, prefer JPEGs, and for everything else, prefer PNGs. Just as an aside, and at the risk of starting a flame war, the colorcorrect pronunciations are "ping," "jay-peg," and "jif." Note that WBMP is not Windows Bitmap, as you might have first thought—it stands for Wireless Bitmap and is designed for use in limited bandwidth situations.

Getting Arty

The imagefilledrectangle( ) function takes six parameters in total, which are, in order: an image resource to draw on, the top-left X coordinate, the top-left Y coordinate, the bottom-right X coordinate, the bottom-right Y coordinate, and a color to use. There is a similar function called imagerectangle( ), which takes the same parameters but only draws the *outline* of the rectangle, whereas imagefilledrectangle( ) fills the shape with color.

In order to draw a rectangle in such a way as to make it stand out, we need to allocate another color and then draw the rectangle. Here is how that is done:

```
$white = imagecolorallocate($image, 255, 255, 255);
imagefilledrectangle($image, 10, 10, 390, 290, $white);
```

Put those two lines just after the definition of $gold, then save the modified script and refresh *phppicture.html*.

This function becomes more interesting when used in a loop, like this:

```
$image = imagecreate(400,300);
$gold = imagecolorallocate($image, 255, 240, 00);
$white = imagecolorallocate($image, 255, 255, 255);
$color = $white;

for ($i = 400, $j = 300; $i > 0; $i -= 4, $j -= 3) {
        if ($color == $white) {
                $color = $gold;
        } else {
                $color = $white;
        }

        imagefilledrectangle($image, 400 - $i, 300 - $j, $i, $j, $color);
}

imagepng($image);
imagedestroy($image);
```

That script calls imagefilledrectangle( ) each iteration of the loop, slowly making the rectangle smaller and smaller as $i and $j decrease in value. Your output should look like Figure 16-2.

 In place of a plain color, it is possible to fill your shapes with a tiled image using the imagesettile( ) function.

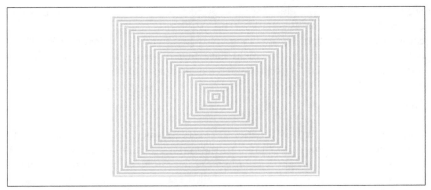

Figure 16-2. Using a simple loop, we've turned our simple rectangle into a series of concentric rectangles

More Shapes

Using three new functions, we can make a much more complicated image. These are: imagecreatetruecolor( ), imagefilledellipse( ), and imagefilledarc( ).

Here is a script using these new functions:

```
header("content-type: image/png");

$image = imagecreatetruecolor(400,300);
$blue = imagecolorallocate($image, 0, 0, 255);
$green = imagecolorallocate($image, 0, 255, 0);
$red = imagecolorallocate($image, 255, 0, 0);

imagefilledellipse($image, 200, 150, 200, 200, $red);
imagefilledellipse($image, 200, 150, 180, 180, $blue);
imagefilledellipse($image, 200, 150, 50, 50, $red);
imagefilledarc($image, 200, 150, 200, 200, 345, 15, $green, IMG_ARC_PIE);
imagefilledarc($image, 200, 150, 200, 200, 255, 285, $green, IMG_ARC_PIE);
imagefilledarc($image, 200, 150, 200, 200, 165, 195, $green, IMG_ARC_PIE);
imagefilledarc($image, 200, 150, 200, 200, 75, 105, $green, IMG_ARC_PIE);

imagepng($image);
imagedestroy($image);
```

The output from that script is shown in Figure 16-3.

Figure 16-3. Ellipses and circles

Using imagecreatetruecolor( ) is the same as imagecreate( )—it takes the same two parameters, and returns an image resource that is freed using imagedestroy( ). The difference between the two is that imagecreatetruecolor( ) returns an image with a true-color palette, whereas an image made by imagecreate( ) cannot contain more than 256 colors. Furthermore, the image resource returned by imagecreatetruecolor( ) automatically has a black background, so you needn't worry about the first allocated color being used as the image background color.

The two new shape functions take several parameters, so you may need to keep the list at hand when working with them. The parameters for imagefilledellipse( ) are: image resource, center of ellipse (X coordinate), center of ellipse (Y coordinate), height, width, and color. As there are more parameters required to draw an arc, imagefilledarc( ) is more complicated again: image resource, center X, center Y, height, width, then the start and end points of the arc specified in degrees, followed by color and, finally, the type of arc to draw.

The start and end points for arcs are specified from 0 to 359 degrees, with 0 pointing directly to the right, or 3 o'clock if you think in clock faces. To draw a complete circle rather than just a section, as in the example, you would specify 0 and 359 as the start and end points; although, in this case, it is easier just to use imagefilledellipse( ). The final parameter to imagefilledarc( ) is the type of arc to draw, and you have the choice of the following:

- IMG_ARC_PIE, as in the previous example, which draws a filled wedge shape with a curved edge

- IMG_ARC_CHORD, which draws a straight line between the starting and ending angles

- IMG_ARC_NOFILL, which draws the outside edge line without drawing the two lines toward the center of the arc

- IMG_ARC_EDGED, which draws an unfilled wedge shape with a curved edge

You can combine these four together in various ways to make your own style of arc, with the exception of IMG_ARC_CHORD and IMG_ARC_PIE, which cannot be combined together because they conflict geometrically. Some examples:

```
imagefilledarc($image, 200, 150, 200, 200, 345, 15, $green,
    IMG_ARC_CHORD | IMG_ARC_NOFILL);
imagefilledarc($image, 200, 150, 200, 200, 345, 15, $green,
    IMG_ARC_EDGED | IMG_ARC_NOFILL);
```

If we use those to replace the first and third calls from the previous script, they should make the righthand arc become a straight line on the outside edge of the arc, and make the lefthand arc become an unfilled wedge. This is pictured in Figure 16-4.

So far, we've only been looking at the filled shapes, but there are unfilled varieties too: imageellipse( ) complements imagefilledellipse( ), imagearc( ) complements imagefilledarc( ), and imagerectangle( ) complements imagefilledrectangle( ). The first and last of these work the same, whether they are filled or otherwise, but imagefilledarc( ) is slightly different—you don't need the last parameter, because the arc is always the equivalent of IMG_ARC_NOFILL.

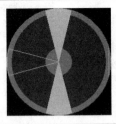

Figure 16-4. Now we've tweaked the last parameter to imagefilledarc() for the first and third calls

Complex Shapes

Rectangles, ellipses, and arcs are inherently easy to use because they have predefined shapes, whereas polygons are multisided shapes of arbitrary geometry and are more complicated to define.

The parameter list is straightforward and the same for both imagefilledpolygon() and imagepolygon(): the image resource to draw on, an array of points to draw, the number of total points, and the color. The array is made up of pairs of X,Y pixel positions. PHP uses these coordinates sequentially, drawing lines from the first (X,Y) to the second, to the third, etc., until drawing a line back from the last one to the first.

The easiest thing to draw is a square, and we can emulate the functionality of imagefilledrectangle() like this:

```
$points = array(
        20, // x1, top-left
        20, // y1

        230, // x2, top-right
        20, // y2

        230, // x3, bottom-right
        230, // y3

        20, // x4, bottom-left
        230 // y4
);

$image = imagecreatetruecolor(250, 250);
$green = imagecolorallocate($image, 0, 255, 0);
imagefilledpolygon($image, $points, 4, $green );

header('Content-type: image/png');
imagepng($image);
imagedestroy($image);
```

I have added extra whitespace in there to make it quite clear how the points work in the $points array—see Figure 16-5 for how this code looks in action. For more advanced polygons, try writing a function that generates the points for you.

Figure 16-5. A square drawn using imagefilledpolygon() as opposed to imagefilled-rectangle()—as long as you get the numbers right, it should look exactly the same

PHP draws the polygon by iterating sequentially through the points array, and if your shape crosses itself, it is interpreted as a hole in the polygon. If you re-cross the hole, it becomes filled again, and so on.

Outputting Text

To output text using PHP, you first need fonts. PHP allows you to use TrueType (TTF) fonts, PostScript Type 1 (PS) fonts, or FreeType 2 fonts, with TTF tending to be the most popular, due to the availability of fonts. If you are running Windows, you probably have at least 20 TTF fonts already installed that you can use—check in the "Fonts" subdirectory of your Windows directory to see what is available. Many Unix distributions come with TTF fonts installed also—either check in */usr/share/fonts/truetype*, or run a search for them. Alternatively, if you have a Windows CD around, you can borrow some from there. Some distributions (including Debian and SUSE) allow you to install Microsoft's Core Fonts for the Web. The Free Software Foundation has a set of free fonts that you can grab from its web site.

For this next example, I used the font Arial, which is stored in the same directory as my PHP script. Save this code as *addingtext.php*:

```
$image = imagecreate(400,300);
$blue = imagecolorallocate($image, 0, 0, 255);
$white = ImageColorAllocate($image, 255,255,255);

if(!isset($_GET['size'])) $_GET['size'] = 44;
if(!isset($_GET['text'])) $_GET['text'] = "Hello, world!";

imagettftext($image, $_GET['size'], 15, 50, 200, $white,
        "ARIAL", $_GET['text']);
header("content-type: image/png");
imagepng($image);
imagedestroy($image);
```

The two isset() lines in that example are there to make sure there is a default font size, 44, and default text, "Hello, world!" for our image. These are set only if you do not pass values using *addingtext.php?size=26&text=Foobarbaz*.

Next comes the important function, imagettftext(), which takes eight parameters in total: the image resource to draw on, font size to use, angle to draw at, X coordinate, Y coordinate, color, font file, and the text to write. A few of those parameters are the same as parameters we've used in other functions, but font size in points, angle, name of font, and the text to print are all new. The X and Y coordinates might fool you at first, because they should be set to the position in which you want the lower-left corner of the first character to appear.

The angle parameter works almost in the same manner as the angle parameters used in imagefilledarc(), with the difference being that it works in the opposite direction—the angles in imagefilledarc() work in a clockwise direction from 3 o'clock, whereas imagettftext() works counter-clockwise. That is, specifying 15 as the angle will make the text rotate 15 degrees so that it slants upward.

The font name parameter needs to point to the TTF file you want to use. If this filename does not begin with /, PHP will automatically add .ttf to the end and search locally. On Unix machines, you may find that PHP searches in /usr/share/fonts/truetype. As you can see in the example, "ARIAL" is specified, so ARIAL.TTF will be loaded and used for printing the text.

The final parameter for the function is the text to print, and you should be sure to specify any new lines as \n\r, not one or the other. You may find that certain fonts do not have various special characters—in this situation, you will see empty boxes drawn rather than the special characters.

The output from this script is shown in Figure 16-6.

Figure 16-6. Any TrueType font at any size, any angle, and any color—all through one easy function

 If you do not want your text to be anti-aliased (smooth-edged), put a minus sign before your color, e.g., -$white.

Fitting text into an exact space is a complex art, particularly when you rotate the text too. PHP makes the job easier with the function imagettfbbox(), which will return an array containing the coordinates of a bounding box around the text—literally, how big it is in each of its dimensions. The complication here is that it is tricky to get the coordinate system right, as the numbers returned seem easier to use than they actually are.

To call imagettfbbox(), you need to pass in four parameters: font point size, rotation angle, font name, and text string to measure. This is essentially a cut-down version of imagettftext(), so you can just copy your existing call to that and remove the unnecessary parameters.

What you will get back is an array of eight elements, which are shown in Table 16-1.

Table 16-1. The eight elements in the array returned by imagettfbox( )

0	Lower-left corner, X coordinate
1	Lower-left corner, Y coordinate
2	Lower-right corner, X coordinate
3	Lower-right corner, Y coordinate
4	Upper-right corner, X coordinate
5	Upper-right corner, Y coordinate
6	Upper-left corner, X coordinate
7	Upper-left corner, Y coordinate

Each of those coordinates are relative to the text itself, viewed horizontally. That is, although 0 should be the lower-left corner of our first letter, it's unlikely that either the lower-left X or the lower-left Y will be 0, particularly if your text is rotated. For example, in our previous example we rotated text 15 degrees counter-clockwise, which would put the lower-left corner of our rotated text to the right and above the lower-left corner of the horizontal text. Add to that the fact that the numbers are frequently a little off, especially if you use large fonts, and you should be ready for problems!

However, if you are not rotating your text, or if you are rotating only a little (under about 20 degrees), you are not likely to encounter any problems, and you can use a fairly simple script like this next one to get your image fitting your text closely:

```
if(!isset($_GET['size'])) $_GET['size'] = 44;
if(!isset($_GET['text'])) $_GET['text'] = "Hello, world!";

$size = imagettfbbox($_GET['size'], 0, "ARIAL", $_GET['text']);
$xsize = abs($size[0]) + abs($size[2]);
$ysize = abs($size[5]) + abs($size[1]);

$image = imagecreate($xsize, $ysize);
$blue = imagecolorallocate($image, 0, 0, 255);
$white = ImageColorAllocate($image, 255,255,255);
imagettftext($image, $_GET['size'], 0, abs($size[0]), abs($size[5]), $white,
        "ARIAL", $_GET['text']);

header("content-type: image/png");
imagepng($image);
imagedestroy($image);
```

Note the use of the abs( ) function to convert negative numbers to positive. The value abs($size['5']) is used as the Y coordinate for the text because imagettfbbox( ) returns its values from the lower-left corner of the baseline of the text string, not the absolute lower-left corner. The baseline of a letter is where it would sit if you were handwriting it on lined paper—for example, the letter "a" sits on the line, whereas the letter "y" sits below the line, with the "v" part of the letter resting on the baseline. The baseline problem is illustrated in Figures 16-7 and 16-8.

This text is sitting on the bottom

Figure 16-7. This text uses the image height to align the text to the bottom of the picture; note how the "g" in "sitting" is cut off because it falls below the baseline

This text is not sitting on the bottom

Figure 16-8. This text aligns to the top of the picture, as our code does, so that the baseline is no longer right at the bottom and the "g" is fully visible

Loading Existing Images

Some of the best ways to use the image functions in PHP are with existing images. For example, you can write a script to dynamically create buttons by first loading a blank button image from your hard drive and overlaying text on top. Loading images takes the form of a call to imagecreatefrom*( ), where the * is *png*, *jpeg*, or various other formats. These functions take just one parameter, which is the file to load, and return an image resource for use as we've been doing already.

The first step in creating a customizable button script is to create a blank button (as in Figure 16-9) using the art package of your choice.

Figure 16-9. A blank button saved in PNG format is easy to load into PHP for dynamic modification

Adding text to this button is largely the same as our existing text code, with a few minor changes:

- The $blue color is no longer needed, and we will not be using imagecreate( ).
- We need to center the text in the middle of the button.
- The font size needs to come down a little in order to fit the button.

With that in mind, here's the new script:

```
if(!isset($_GET['size'])) $_GET['size'] = 26;
if(!isset($_GET['text'])) $_GET['text'] = "Button text";

$size = imagettfbbox($_GET['size'], 0, "ARIAL", $_GET['text']);
$xsize = abs($size[0]) + abs($size[2]);
$ysize = abs($size[5]) + abs($size[1]);
```

```
$image = imagecreatefrompng("button.png");
$imagesize = getimagesize("button.png");
$textleftpos = round(($imagesize[0] - $xsize) / 2);
$texttoppos = round(($imagesize[1] + $ysize) / 2);
$white = ImageColorAllocate($image, 255,255,255);

imagettftext($image, $_GET['size'], 0, $textleftpos, $texttoppos, $white,
"ARIAL", $_GET['text']);
header("content-type: image/png");
imagepng($image);
imagedestroy($image);
```

The new function in that script is getimagesize( ), which returns the width and height of the image specified in its parameter as an array, with elements 0 and 1 being the width and height, respectively. In addition, element 2 is the type of the picture, and will be set to either IMAGETYPE_BMP, IMAGETYPE_GIF, IMAGETYPE_JPEG, IMAGETYPE_PNG, IMAGETYPE_PSD, IMAGETYPE_SWF, among other values. This element is particularly helpful when used with image_type_to_mime_type( ).

Running that script without any parameters generates the picture shown in Figure 16-10, although you can send "text" and "size" if you want to play around. With this script in place, you can generate a whole toolbar of buttons for a web site using this one script, simply by changing the "text" value you pass in. Of course, it is not very efficient to keep regenerating the same buttons each time a page is loaded, so if I were you, I would save each generated picture as a file named after the text used—that way, you can use file_exists( ) to attempt to load the existing picture and save the extra work.

Figure 16-10. An empty button overlaid with rendered text

With just a little work, we can even add a simple shadow to the text, as shown in Figure 16-11. To do this, allocate a new color for the shadow (such as black), then call imagettftext( ) twice—once for the shadow, and again for the text itself. Offset the shadow by +1 on X and Y, and the text by -1 on X and Y, completing the effect.

Figure 16-11. Drawing text twice to get a shadow

Color and Image Fills

The function imagefill( ) takes four parameters: an image resource, the X and Y coordinates to start the fill at, and the color with which to fill. The fill will automatically flood your image with color outward from the point specified by your X and Y parameters until it encounters any other color.

Put this `imagefill()` function call into your *addingtext.php* script, just after `imagettftext()`:

```
$red = imagecolorallocate($image, 255, 0, 0);
imagefill($image, 0, 0, $red);
```

With that function, our red color is used to fill in the image starting from (0,0), which is the top-left corner. If you load the script into your web browser, you will see the fill has left some parts of the blue behind—the parts it couldn't "reach" inside the text. Also, you will notice there is a bluish fringe around the text, where the white text was anti-aliased (smoothed) against the blue background, producing a blue-white edge to the text. Figure 16-12 shows how the fill looks with the blue areas that could not be reached inside letters. Figure 16-13 shows a close-up of the letter "o," where you can see the anti-aliasing in action. As our fill starts on blue, it will not fill over any other shade of blue, which is why this fringe has been left there.

Figure 16-12. Our first fill leaves blue areas inside letters, and also a blue fringe around each of the letters

![Close-up of the letter o showing anti-aliasing]

Figure 16-13. Anti-aliasing has made PHP blend the blue and white together on the edges of the letters to get a smooth effect—our fill leaves these intact

There is a similar function, `imagefilltoborder()`, where the color to fill is the fifth parameter, and the new fourth parameter is the color at which the fill should stop "flowing." That is, the fill will keep flooding outward until it hits the border color. If we change our `imagefill()` call to `imagefilltoborder()` and specify `$white` as the color at which to stop, it should eliminate the anti-aliasing fringe around the letters. Replace the `imagefill()` call with this:

```
imagefilltoborder($image, 0, 0, $white, $red);
```

Whereas the `imagefill()` function will fill the image with color until it encounters any other color, the `imagefilltoborder()` function call shown above will fill the image with color and continue until it finds pixels colored with `$white`. When you look at it in your browser, you will notice the text has become very jagged, because our red fill has taken away all the blue-white smoothing.

The imagesettile() function allows you to use an existing image as the picture for your fill in place of a color, which PHP will tile across your image as it fills. This function takes just two parameters: the image you want to change and the image to use as a tile fill.

In order to use a tiled image for your fills rather than a color, pass the constant IMG_COLOR_TILED where you would usually pass a color. Thus, we can alter the *addingtext.php* script to look like this:

```
if(!isset($_GET['size'])) $_GET['size'] = 44;
if(!isset($_GET['text'])) $_GET['text'] = "Hello, world!";
$size = imagettfbbox($_GET['size'], 0, "ARIAL", $_GET['text']);
$xsize = abs($size[0]) + abs($size[2]);
$ysize = abs($size[5]) + abs($size[1]);

$image = imagecreate($xsize, $ysize);
$blue = imagecolorallocate($image, 0, 0, 255);
$white = ImageColorAllocate($image, 255,255,255);
imagettftext($image, $_GET['size'], 0, abs($size[0]), $ysize, $white,
"ARIAL", $_GET['text']);

$bg = imagecreatefrompng("button_mini.png");
imagesettile($image, $bg);
imagefill($image, 0, 0, IMG_COLOR_TILED);
header("content-type: image/png");

imagepng($image);
imagedestroy($image);
imagedestroy($bg);
```

You can use imagesettile() as many times as you need in order to do several fills using different images. As an added bonus, once you have used imagesettile(), you can also use IMG_COLOR_TILED wherever you create filled shapes—just use it in place of the color and you can create tiled polygons, ellipses, and other shapes.

Adding Transparency

Specifying the part of an image that should be transparent is as simple as picking the color to use as transparent and passing it into the imagecolortransparent() function. As the support for transparency in some browsers (notably with Internet Explorer and PNG transparency) is limited, this function is most useful when the transparent image is used as part of a larger image so that the transparency can be seen.

```
$image = imagecreatetruecolor(400,400);

$black = imagecolorallocate($image, 0, 0, 0);
imagecolortransparent($image, $black);

/// rest of picture here
```

Using Brushes

In the same way that imagesettile( ) allows you to use a picture for filling, imagesetbrush( ) allows you to use a picture for an outline. While this could be a premade picture you've just loaded, you can get nice effects by using handmade pictures that are swept around basic shapes.

Figure 16-14 shows a picture of a lot of dots ranging in color from red to yellow—not very interesting, but great for using as a brush.

Figure 16-14. The picture we'll be using as our brush

Those dots were created with this script:

```
$brush = imagecreate(100,100);

$brushtrans = imagecolorallocate($brush, 0, 0, 0);
imagecolortransparent($brush, $brushtrans);

for ($k = 1; $k < 18; ++$k) {
        $color = imagecolorallocate($brush, 255, $k * 15, 0);
        imagefilledellipse($brush, $k * 5, $k * 5, 5, 5, $color);
}

imagepng($brush);
imagedestroy($brush);
```

The next step is to create a larger image, recreate that brush, and use it as the outline for a shape. Here's the code:

```
$pic = imagecreatetruecolor(600,600);
$brush = imagecreate(100,100);

$brushtrans = imagecolorallocate($brush, 0, 0, 0);
imagecolortransparent($brush, $brushtrans);
```

```
for ($k = 1; $k < 18; ++$k) {
        $color = imagecolorallocate($brush, 255, $k * 15, 0);
        imagefilledellipse($brush, $k * 5, $k * 5, 5, 5, $color);
}

imagesetbrush($pic, $brush);
imageellipse($pic, 300, 300, 350, 350, IMG_COLOR_BRUSHED);

imagepng($pic);
imagedestroy($pic);
imagedestroy($brush);
```

The new line in there is the call to imagesetbrush( )—note that it takes the image you're changing as the first parameter, and the brush to use as the second. To actually use the brush that has been set, we need to pass the special constant IMG_COLOR_BRUSHED as the color parameter for our shape.

That's pretty much it. The only other thing is the call to imagecolortransparent( ), which is there so that the black part of the brush (most of it!) doesn't overlay itself.

The result of that script is shown Figure 16-15—not bad for such a simple script, particularly as only one ellipse is actually drawn in the code.

Figure 16-15. Drawing an ellipse with our dots gives us a brightly colored Mobius strip

Once you've used your brush, you can change it for something else, and do so as many times as you want. Figure 16-16 shows the output of this next script, which uses ellipses drawn several times in different colors by re-creating the brush as necessary:

```
$pic = imagecreatetruecolor(400,400);

$bluecol = 0;
```

```
for ($i = -10; $i < 410; $i += 80) {
        for ($j = -10; $j < 410; $j += 80) {
                $brush = imagecreate(100,100);

                $brushtrans = imagecolorallocate($brush, 0, 0, 0);
                imagecolortransparent($brush, $brushtrans);

                for ($k = 1; $k < 18; ++$k) {
                        $color = imagecolorallocate($brush, 255,
                                $k * 15, $bluecol);
                        imagefilledellipse($brush, $k * 2, $k * 2,
                                1, 1, $color);
                }

                imagesetbrush($pic, $brush);
                imageellipse($pic, $i, $j, 50, 50, IMG_COLOR_BRUSHED);

                imagedestroy($brush);
        }

        $bluecol += 40;
}

imagepng($pic);
imagedestroy($pic);
```

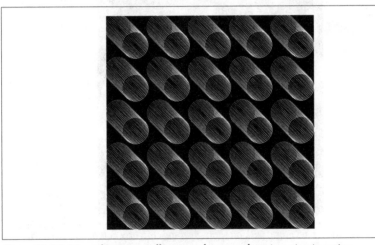

Figure 16-16. Many dots, many ellipses, and many colors: iteration in action

Basic Image Copying

The two functions imagecopy( ) and imagecopymerge( ) are similar in that they copy one picture into another. Both of their first eight parameters are identical:

- The destination image you're copying to
- The source image you're copying from

- The X coordinate you want to copy to
- The Y coordinate you want to copy to
- The X coordinate you want to copy from
- The Y coordinate you want to copy from
- The width in pixels of the source image you want to copy
- The height in pixels of the source image you want to copy

Parameters three and four allow you to position the source image where you want it on the destination image, and parameters five, six, seven, and eight allow you to define the rectangular area of the source image that you want to copy. Most of the time, you will want to leave parameters five and six at 0 (copy from the top-left corner of the image), and parameters seven and eight at the width of the source image (the bottom-right corner of it) so that it copies the entire source image.

The way these functions differ is in the last parameter: imagecopy( ) always over-writes all the pixels in the destination with those of the source, whereas imagecopymerge( ) merges the destination pixels with the source pixels by the amount specified in the extra parameter: 0 means "Keep the source picture fully," 100 means "Overwrite with the source picture fully," and 50 means "Mix the source and destination pixel colors equally." The imagecopy( ) function is there-fore equivalent to calling imagecopymerge( ) and passing in 100 as the last parameter.

Figures 16-17 and 16-18 show two input images that will be used to test these functions.

Figure 16-17. Our source picture: some stars

Now, to get those two to merge, we need a script like this one:

```
$stars = imagecreatefrompng("stars.png");
$gradient = imagecreatefrompng("gradient.png");
imagecopymerge($stars, $gradient, 0, 0, 0, 0, 256, 256, 60);
header('Content-type: image/png');
imagepng($stars);
imagedestroy($stars);
imagedestroy($gradient);
```

That merges the two at 60%, which gives slightly more prominence to the gradient. The result is shown in Figure 16-19.

Figure 16-18. Our destination picture: a smooth, blue gradient

Figure 16-19. Stars + gradient + some imagination = the night sky

Scaling and Rotating

PHP offers you two different ways to resize an image, and you should choose the right one for your needs. The first option, imagecopyresized( ), allows you to change the size of an image quickly but has the downside of producing fairly low-quality pictures. When an image with detail is resized, aliasing ("jaggies") is usually visible, which makes the resized version hard to read, particularly if the resizing was to an unusual size. The other option is imagecopyresampled( ), which takes the same parameters as imagecopyresized( ) and works in the same way, with the exception that the resized image is smoothed so that it is still visible. The downside here is that the smoothing takes more CPU effort, so the image takes longer to produce.

Here is an example of imagecopyresized( ) in action— save it as *specialeffects.php*:

```
header("content-type: image/png");
$src_img = imagecreatefrompng("complicated.png");
$srcsize = getimagesize("complicated.png");
$dest_x = $srcsize[0] / 1.5;
$dest_y = $srcsize[1] / 1.5;
$dst_img = imagecreatetruecolor($dest_x, $dest_y);

imagecopyresized($dst_img, $src_img, 0, 0, 0, 0,
        $dest_x, $dest_y, $srcsize[0], $srcsize[1]);
imagepng($dst_img);
```

```
imagedestroy($src_img);
imagedestroy($dst_img);
```

There are two images being used in there. The first one, $src_img, is created from a PNG screenshot of the online PHP manual—this contains lots of text, which highlights the aliasing problem with imagecopyresized( ) nicely. The variables $dest_x and $dest_y are set to be the width and height of *complicated.png* divided by 1.5, which will set the destination size to be 66% of the source size. Resizing "exact" values such as 10%, 50%, etc., usually looks better than resizing unusual values such as 66%, 79%, etc.

The second image is then created using imagecreatetruecolor( ) and our destination sizes, and is stored in $dst_img. Now comes the key part: imagecopyresized( ) takes quite a few variables, and you needn't bother memorizing them. They are, in order, the image to copy to, image to copy from, destination X coordinate, destination Y coordinate, source X coordinate, source Y coordinate, destination width, destination height, source width, and source height. Parameters three to six, the coordinates, allow you to copy regions of the picture as opposed to the whole picture—PHP will copy from the specified coordinate to the end of the picture, so by passing in 0, we're using the entire picture. You probably will not ever want to copy regions using these parameters, so just leave them as 0.

Take a screenshot of a web site of your choosing and save it as *complicated.png* in the same directory as your PHP script, then load up *specialeffects.php* in your browser. All being well, you should see something similar to Figure 16-20—the web site picture has been resized down, but as a result, all the text is hard—if not impossible—to read.

Figure 16-20. Using imagecopyresized( ) on a picture is fast, but produces low-quality results

Now, to give you an idea why imagecopyresampled( ) is better, change the imagecopyresized( ) call to imagecopyresampled( ). The parameter list is identical, so just change the function name. This time, you should see a marked difference—the web site is still smaller but should be perfectly legible, as the text should be nicely smoothed. This is shown in Figure 16-21.

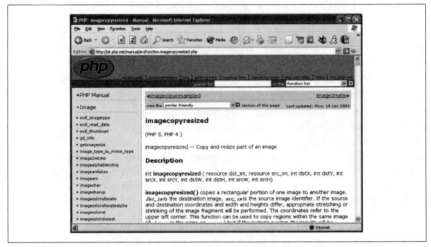

Figure 16-21. Using imagecopyresampled() gives a superior end result

The final special effect we're going to look at is imagerotate( ), which rotates an image. This is much easier to do than resizing and resampling, as it only has three parameters: the image to rotate, the number of degrees counter-clockwise you wish to rotate it, and the color to use wherever space is uncovered. The rotation is performed from the center of the source image, and the destination image will automatically be sized to fit the whole of the rotated image.

The last parameter only really makes sense once you have seen it in action, so try out this script:

```
$image = imagecreatefrompng("button.png");
$hotpink = imagecolorallocate($image, 255, 110, 221);
$rotated_image = imagerotate($image, 50, $hotpink);

header("content-type: image/png");
imagepng($rotated_image);
imagedestroy($image);
imagedestroy($rotated_image);
```

You'll need to put your own file in where I have used *button.png*, but otherwise you should see something like Figure 16-22 when you load the picture in your web browser.

The image has been rotated by 50 degrees, anti-aliased to avoid jagged lines, and resized by the minimum amount so that the outputted picture has just enough space to hold the rotated image. Finally, note that the gaps in the image, effectively the "background," have been colored the hot pink we defined. White is usually preferable, but it would not have been quite so obvious in the screenshot.

Figure 16-22. The button rotated 50 degrees counter-clockwise

Points and Lines

Drawing points is accomplished with the function imagesetpixel( ), which takes four parameters: the image to draw on, the X and Y coordinates, and the color to use. Thus, you can use it like this:

```
$width = 255;
$height = 255;
$image = imagecreatetruecolor($width, $height);

for ($i = 0; $i <= $width; ++$i) {
        for ($j = 0; $j <= $height; ++$j) {
                $col = imagecolorallocate($image, 255, $i, $j);
                imagesetpixel($image, $i, $j, $col);
        }
}

header("Content-type: image/png");
imagepng($image);
imagedestroy($image);
```

In that example, there are two loops to handle setting the green and blue parameters with imagecolorallocate( ), with red always being set to 255. This color is then used to set the relevant pixel to the newly allocated color, which should give you a smooth gradient like the one in Figure 16-23.

Figure 16-23. Smooth gradiants using per-pixel coloring

Drawing lines is only a little more difficult than individual pixels, and is handled by the imageline( ) function. This time, the parameters are the image to draw on, the X and Y coordinates of the start of the line, the X and Y coordinates of the end of the line, and the color to use for drawing. We can extend our pixel script to draw a grid over the gradient by looping from 0 to $width and $height, incrementing by 15 each time, and drawing a line at the appropriate place. $width and $height were both set to 241 in the previous script because that is 255 - 15 + 1, which means it is the largest grid we can draw using the stock 0–255 color range. The +1 is necessary because drawing a line on the 255th row of the picture would be invisible—it would be outside!

Add these lines before the header( ) call:

```
for ($i = 0; $i <= $width; $i += 15) {
        imageline($image, $i, 0, $i, 255, $black);
}

for ($i = 0; $i <= $height; $i += 15) {
        imageline($image, 0, $i, 255, $i, $black);
}
```

The first loop draws the vertical lines, so the X coordinate increments by 15 with each loop, whereas the Y coordinates are always 0 and 255, or from the very top to the very bottom. The second loop does the same for the horizontal lines, so this time it is the Y coordinates that change.

To get the script to work, you will also need to add this line after the call to imagecreatetruecolor( ):

```
$black = imagecolorallocate($image, 0, 0, 0);
```

The output from that script should generate the picture shown in Figure 16-24.

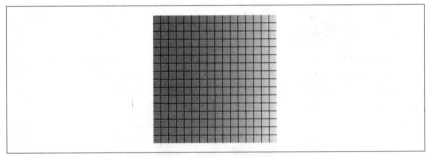

Figure 16-24. Grid lines created with imageline() and loops

The imagesetthickness( ) function allows you to specify the width in pixels of all lines drawn. All lines drawn using imageline( ) are affected, but it also affects rectangles, arcs, etc. To use the function, pass in the image to alter as parameter one, and the width in pixels as parameter two, then simply draw lines. The new thickness remains in place until you change it again or destroy the image.

Special Effects Using imagefilter( )

 The filters described here were written for the PHP-bundled build of GD, and may not be available in other releases.

The best way to explain this function is to describe how it works, then show a code example. Although the function accepts different numbers of parameters that do very different things, the function returns true if the filter was applied successfully and false otherwise.

First up is IMG_FILTER_BRIGHTNESS, which takes a number between -255 and 255 that represents how much you want to brighten or darken the image. Setting it to 0 leaves the picture unchanged, 255 sets it to full white (brightest), and -255 sets it to full black (darkest). Most pictures tend to look almost invisible beyond +200 or -200.

This code example will lighten our space picture just a little:

```
$image = imagecreatefrompng("space.png");
imagefilter($image, IMG_FILTER_BRIGHTNESS, 50);
header("content-type: image/png");
imagepng($image);
imagedestroy($image);
```

Next up is IMG_FILTER_COLORIZE, which takes three parameters between -255 and 255 that respectively represent the red, green, and blue values you want to add or subtract from the image. Setting the blue value to -255 will take all the blue out of all the pixels in the image, whereas setting the red to 128 will add red to them. Setting all three of them to 128 will have the effect of adding white to the picture, brightening it in the same way as IMG_FILTER_BRIGHTNESS.

This code example will make our image look more magenta:

```
$image = imagecreatefrompng("space.png");
imagefilter($image, IMG_FILTER_COLORIZE, 100, 0, 100);
header("content-type: image/png");
imagepng($image);
imagedestroy($image);
```

Moving on, the IMG_FILTER_CONTRAST filter allows you to change the contrast of the image, and takes just one parameter for a contrast value between -255 and 255. Lower values increase the contrast of the picture, essentially reducing the number of colors so that they are more separate and obvious to the eye. Using positive values brings the colors closer together by mixing them with gray until, at 255, you have a full-gray picture.

This code example shows how even a small positive number makes quite a difference to the resulting image:

```
$image = imagecreatefrompng("space.png");
imagefilter($image, IMG_FILTER_CONTRAST, 20);
header("content-type: image/png");
imagepng($image);
imagedestroy($image);
```

The `IMG_FILTER_EDGEDETECT` and `IMG_FILTER_EMBOSS` filters make all the edges in your picture stand out as if they were embossed, and sets everything else to gray. No parameters are needed for either of them, so using them is quite easy.

This next script uses edge detection to grab the edges, then embosses them to make the effect more obvious:

```
$image = imagecreatefrompng("space.png");
imagefilter($image, IMG_FILTER_EDGEDETECT);
imagefilter($image, IMG_FILTER_EMBOSS);
header("content-type: image/png");
imagepng($image);
imagedestroy($image);
```

If you want to blur an image, you have a choice of two filters: `IMG_FILTER_GAUSSIAN_BLUR` and `IMG_FILTER_SELECTIVE_BLUR`. The latter is a generic blur function, and the former is a classic "out-of-focus lens" technique that often actually enhances images. Neither function requires parameters.

Although they're easy to use, there's no harm showing an example—here are both of them in action. Just comment out the one you don't want to see:

```
$image = imagecreatefrompng("space.png");
imagefilter($image, IMG_FILTER_GAUSSIAN_BLUR);
imagefilter($image, IMG_FILTER_SELECTIVE_BLUR);
header("content-type: image/png");
imagepng($image);
imagedestroy($image);
```

There's a similar filter, `IMG_FILTER_SMOOTH`, which gives you a little more control over the output. It takes one parameter, but it takes a little explanation! Unlike the other parameters so far, this isn't a value pertaining to how much you'd like to smooth the image. Instead, it's a *weighting* for an image manipulation matrix, and small changes can affect the output massively.

There isn't enough room here to go into a full discussion of what these manipulation matrices are, but suffice to say you can represent many different transformations—from Gaussian blur to edge detection—using a 3×3 numerical matrix, that defines how the colors of the eight pixels surrounding any given pixel (with the pixel itself being the ninth) should have their RGB values changed. With `IMG_FILTER_SMOOTH`, the parameter you pass is used as the change value for the pixel itself, which means you get to define how much the pixel's own color is used to form its final color.

You're not likely to want values outside of the range -8 to 8, as even one number makes quite a big difference. At about 10, the picture is almost normal, because the original pixel values are given more weight than the combined sum of its neighbors. But you can get some cool effects between -6 to -8.

This code example smooths the picture just a little:

```
$image = imagecreatefrompng("space.png");
imagefilter($image, IMG_FILTER_SMOOTH, 6);
header("content-type: image/png");
imagepng($image);
imagedestroy($image);
```

There are two helpful filters that alter the colors in a simple way, which are IMG_FILTER_GRAYSCALE and IMG_FILTER_NEGATE. Both take no parameters: the first sets the picture to grayscale, and the second sets it to use negative colors.

This code example changes the picture to grayscale, then flips it to negative colors:

```
$image = imagecreatefrompng("space.png");
imagefilter($image, IMG_FILTER_GRAYSCALE);
imagefilter($image, IMG_FILTER_NEGATE);
header("content-type: image/png");
imagepng($image);
imagedestroy($image);
```

Interlacing an Image

Interlacing an image allows users to see parts of it as it loads, and takes different forms depending on the image type. For example, interlaced JPEGs (called "progressive"), GIFs, and PNG files show low-quality versions of the file as they load. In comparison, non-interlaced JPEGs appear line by line. To enable interlacing on your picture, simply call this function with the second parameter set to 1, or set to 0 if you want to disable it.

Interlacing is likely to affect your file size: JPEGs often get smaller when interlaced because progressive JPEGs use a more complicated mathematical formula to compress the picture, whereas PNG files often get larger. Progressive JPEGs are a mixed blessing, however: Internet Explorer doesn't handle them properly, and rather than showing low-quality versions of the JPEG as it loads, it simply downloads the entire picture and shows it all at once. As a result, non-progressive JPEGs (line by line) appear to load faster on Internet Explorer. Other browsers don't display this problem.

This example shows interlacing in action for PNG files. It's not likely to be very noticeable if you run this on a local web server and/or use small files, because it will be decompressed too fast.

```
$image = imagecreatefrompng("space.png");
imagefilter($image, IMG_FILTER_MEAN_REMOVAL);
imageinterlace($image, 1);
header("content-type: image/png");
imagepng($image);
imagedestroy($image);
```

Getting an Image's MIME Type

So far we have been handcrafting the header() function call in each of the image scripts, but many people find MIME types hard to remember and/or clumsy to use. If you fit into this category, you should be using the image_type_to_mime_type() function, as it takes a constant as its only parameter and returns the MIME type string. For example, passing in IMAGETYPE_GIF will return image/gif, passing in IMAGETYPE_JPEG will return image/jpeg, and passing in IMAGETYPE_PNG will return image/png.

If you think these constants sound as hard to remember as the MIME types, you're probably right. However, a while back we looked at the getimagesize( ) function, and I mentioned that the third element in the array returned by that function is the type of file it is. These two functions both use the same constant, which means you can use getimagesize( ) and pass the third element into image_type_to_mime_type( ) to have it get the appropriate MIME type for your image—no memorization of constants required.

```
$info = getimagesize("button.png");
print image_type_to_mime_type($info[2]);
```

17

Creating PDFs

Adobe makes a collection of commercial products to create, view, and modify PDFs, but they invariably come with a hefty price tag and generally are restricted to Windows and Macintosh platforms. Once again, PHP comes to the rescue!

Before you begin, note that measurements are in points, and there are 72 points to an inch. However, this can be altered by changing the output resolution of the produced PDF.

Getting Started

Creating a PDF document is similar to creating a picture in that, to get the desired end result, you state the list of drawing actions required to get there—drawing lines, text, adding fonts, etc. You need to track the PDF document you are working with at all times, because other PDF functions use it.

Even creating a simple PDF takes quite a few functions; this next code block does comparatively little:

```
$pdf = pdf_new( );
pdf_open_file($pdf, "/path/to/your.pdf");
$font = pdf_findfont($pdf, "Times-Roman", "host");

pdf_begin_page($pdf, 595, 842);
pdf_setfont($pdf, $font, 30);
pdf_show_xy($pdf, "Printing text is easy", 50, 750);
pdf_end_page($pdf);

pdf_close($pdf);
pdf_delete($pdf);
```

Starting at line one, we use pdf_new( ) to create a new PDF document and store it in $pdf. This value will be used in all the subsequent functions, so it is important to keep.

The pdf_open_file( ) function is used to open a file for writing. Note that the free version of PDFlib does not allow alteration of existing PDFs; this function merely creates a new PDF of the given filename. Naturally, it will need to be somewhere your web server is able to write to; otherwise, you will receive an error along the lines of "Fatal error: PDFlib error: function 'PDF_set_info' must not be called in 'object' scope in yourscript.php on line XYZ".

The next line uses pdf_findfont( ) to find and load a font for use inside the generated PDF file. In the example, pdf_findfont( ) takes three parameters—the PDF document to work with, the name of the font to use, and which encoding to use. In the example above, $pdf is specified as the first parameter (as always). "Times-Roman" is specified as the font to use, which is one of the 14 standard internal PDFlib fonts. The next parameter can be set to either "winansi" (Windows), "macroman" (Macintosh), "ebcdic" (EBCDIC code page 1047 machines), "builtin" (for symbol fonts), or "host" (winansi for Windows, macroman for Macintosh, etc.; recommended).

When successful, pdf_findfont( ) returns a font resource which is stored in $font. You may wish to add error checking in your own scripts for extra reliability.

At this point, we're ready to start on the main part of PDF generation. The first three lines merely set things up for the document. The next four—lines four to seven—are the page itself. Reading the source, it should be easy to see that line four and line seven encapsulate one page in the generated PDF file. Objects and text outputted between a pdf_begin_page( ) and pdf_end_page( ) will affect that page, and multiple begin/end blocks are used to create multiple pages.

Note that pdf_begin_page( ) takes a second and third parameter: the X and Y point size of this page. The PDF format allows you to make your pages different point sizes from page to page, but you will most often want to choose one size and stick with it.

You need to pass three parameters to pdf_setfont( ): the first is the PDF resource, as usual; the second parameter is the return value from pdf_findfont for the font you wish to use; and the final parameter is the size to use, in points. Immediately afterward, we call pdf_show_xy( ) to place text into our page. Parameter two of pdf_show_xy( ) is the string to use, and parameters three and four are the X and Y coordinates at which to print the text.

 Confusingly, there is a pdf_set_font( ) function that is deprecated—try not to get mixed up!

The last parameter passed to pdf_show_xy( ) is the distance the text should appear above the page baseline in points. That is, setting this parameter to 0 will have the bottom of a lowercase "a" at the very bottom of the page, and the bottom of a lowercase "y" outside the margins of the page.

With pdf_end_page( ) called, the first and only page is completed, and all that is left to do is clean things up. This is done through the help of two functions, which are pdf_close( ) and pdf_delete( ). They may sound somewhat similar, but you do need to call them both: pdf_close( ) cleans up the PDFlib memory and document-related resources, whereas pdf_delete( ) cleans up PHP's reference to $pdf and any other internal resources. Be sure to call them in the order shown above.

When you run that script through your web browser, you won't see any "Success!" message printed out. However, you should find your PDF file has been created and is viewable in your PDF reader of choice.

Adding More Pages and More Style

Adding more pages is done by calling pdf_begin_page( ) and pdf_end_page( ) repeatedly, like this:

```
for ($i = 1; $i < 10; ++$i) {
        pdf_begin_page($pdf, 595, 842);
        pdf_setfont($pdf, $font, 30);
        pdf_show_xy($pdf, "This is page $i", 50, 750);
        pdf_end_page($pdf);
}
```

A good start is to have a selection of typefaces ready for various parts of your document. In our first example, we have just one—Times-Roman is stored in $font. However, that could be easily modified to this:

```
$times = pdf_findfont($pdf, "Times-Roman", "host");
$timesb = pdf_findfont($pdf, "Times-Bold", "host");
$timesi = pdf_findfont($pdf, "Times-Italic", "host");
```

Combined with the use of pdf_setfont( )'s third parameter, we can create headers and subheaders like this:

```
for ($i = 1; $i < 10; ++$i) {
        pdf_begin_page($pdf, 595, 842);

        pdf_setfont($pdf, $times, 24);
        pdf_show_xy($pdf, "This is page $i", 50, 750);

        pdf_setfont($pdf, $timesb, 16);
        pdf_show_xy($pdf, "Subheader", 100, 700);

        pdf_setfont($pdf, $timesi, 16);
        pdf_show_xy($pdf, "This is some standard text.", 100, 700);

        pdf_end_page($pdf);
}
```

We can even throw in the pdf_setcolor( ) function, which takes two text values followed by color values for its fourth, fifth, sixth, and (optionally) its seventh parameters, and uses them to set the color of fills and objects that follow.

Try adding this line just before the first pdf_setfont( )...

```
pdf_setcolor($pdf, "both", "rgb", 1.0 - (0.1 * $i), 0.0, 0.0);
```

And adding this line just before the second pdf_setfont( )...

```
pdf_setcolor($pdf, "both", "rgb", 0.0, 0.0, 0.0 + (0.1 * $i));
```

The "both" in there means "Set both fill and stroke color" (recommended most of the time), and the "rgb" means "We're going to provide red, green, and blue values for the value." If you'd rather provide CMYK, specify "cmyk" instead of "rgb" and add the extra color value. The PDF generated from that code should have a top header that starts off red and fades into black, and a second-level header and main text that starts off black and fades into blue.

Adding Images

PHP provides us with two functions for using images in PDFs: pdf_open_image_file( ) and pdf_place_image( ). The former reads a specified image type (parameter two) of a specified file name (parameter three) and returns an image that can be used in subsequent functions.

The pdf_place_image( ) function then takes the returned image as its second parameter, and also allows you to specify the X coordinate (parameter three), Y coordinate (parameter four), and any scaling (parameter five) you wish to be applied to the image.

For this next example, you will need to find a JPEG, name it *myimage.jpg*, and place it in the same directory as the script before you run the script.

```
$pdf = pdf_new( );
pdf_open_file($pdf, "/path/to/your.pdf");
pdf_begin_page($pdf, 595, 842);

$testimage = pdf_open_image_file($pdf, "jpeg", "myimage.jpg");
pdf_place_image($pdf, $testimage, 0, 0, 0.5);
pdf_end_page($pdf);
pdf_close($pdf);
pdf_delete($pdf);
```

In the above example, we set the scale parameter of pdf_place_image( ) (parameter five) to 0.5, which will show our *myimage.jpg* picture at half its original size. Note that altering the scale value of pictures will not change the final file size of the PDF that you output, because the file is saved unscaled and then scaled at runtime.

Owing to its saving pictures unscaled, the PDF format allows you to reuse images without having to store multiple copies in the file. So, if we go back to our earlier for loop where we had 10 pages being generated, we get something like this:

```
$pdf = pdf_new( );
pdf_open_file($pdf, "/path/to/your.pdf");

$times = pdf_findfont($pdf, "Times-Roman", "host");
$timesb = pdf_findfont($pdf, "Times-Bold", "host");
$timesi = pdf_findfont($pdf, "Times-Italic", "host");

$testimage = pdf_open_image_file($pdf, "jpeg", "myimage.jpg");

for ($i = 1; $i < 10; ++$i) {
        pdf_begin_page($pdf, 595, 842);
        pdf_setcolor($pdf, 0.0, 0.0, 0.0);
```

```
        pdf_setfont($pdf, $times, 24);
        $scaleval = $i * 10 . '%';
        $smallscale = 0.1 * $i;
        pdf_show_xy($pdf, "This is page $i - $scaleval scale", 50, 750);
        pdf_place_image($pdf, $testimage, 0, 0, $smallscale);
        df_end_page($pdf);
    }

    pdf_close($pdf);
    pdf_delete($pdf);
```

The PDF file generated by that script will be only slightly larger than the previous file.

PDF Special Effects

We can further manipulate images through the use of pdf_rotate( ) and pdf_skew( ) —two functions whose purposes you should be able to guess quite easily. Both take a PDF document reference as their first parameter. The pdf_rotate( ) function then takes one extra parameter—how much to rotate the coordinate system, in degrees— whereas pdf_skew( ) takes two extra parameters: how much to skew the coordinate system in the X direction and how much in the Y direction.

Try adding these two lines just after the call to pdf_begin_page( ) inside the loop of the previous script:

```
pdf_skew($pdf, 10, 10);
pdf_rotate($pdf, 5);
```

Adding Document Data

PDFs are designed to be read like normal printed documents, so Adobe incorporated the ability to add notes in the same manner one might scribble in a margin.

These notes, which can be edited and re-edited by readers, can also be created using PHP by calling the function pdf_add_note( ). Here is an example of its use:

```
pdf_add_note($pdf, 100, 500, 700, 600, "You can create notes easily
        using pdf_add_note()", "Sticky notes", "note", 1);
```

The second, third, fourth, and fifth parameters are, respectively, the lower-left X and lower-left Y coordinates, and the upper-right X and upper-right Y coordinates of the note boundaries. The sixth and seventh parameters are the text to put inside the note and the title to place at the top, and the final two parameters decide the icon used to display the note when closed, and whether or not the note starts open. Once the PDF is loaded, your reader is usually free to move these notes around and edit the text inside them.

In the line above, we add a 600x100 note box that is already open (use 1 to specify the note is open, and 0 to specify it is closed). Instead of note as the penultimate parameter, we have various other options: comment, insert, paragraph, newparagraph, key, or help. In several PDF readers, this parameter has no effect and can be just left as note.

Another important facet to improving the usefulness of documents is to provide meta-data regarding who created the document, and when. This can be achieved through the use of pdf_set_info( ), which takes a key and a value as its second and third parameters. The standard keys for use are Subject, Title, Creator, Author, and Keywords, but you are also able to add your own keys, such as Modified, Created, etc.

Now we can finish off our script by adding in some metadata—add these three lines just below pdf_open_file( ):

```
pdf_set_info($pdf, "Creator", "TelRev");
pdf_set_info($pdf, "Title", "PHP PDF 101");
pdf_set_info($pdf, "MyInfo", "You can write what you please here");
```

When you read the PDF generated by the finished script, you should see the note sticking out quite obviously. The metadata will be there too, but it is likely to be hidden away under a menu somewhere.

18

Creating Flash

PHP uses the Ming library for generating Flash movies, which is licensed under the LGPL. The library is also object-oriented and actively developed by the maintainers. In Flash, all values specifying some form of distance, length, height, or size are in *twips*, which means a twentieth of a pixel. Flash movies scale to fit their container, though, so these measurements are entirely arbitrary figures.

A Simple Movie

One of the biggest advantages to Ming is that it is object-oriented, so you create a shape object, tell it what color it should be, then add it to the movie. The same process applies for all the other operations in Ming, which makes the code easy to read. Here is a script that creates a basic movie:

```
$mov = new SWFMovie( );
$mov->setDimension(200,20);

$shape = new SWFShape( );
$shape->setLeftFill($shape->addFill(0xff, 0, 0));
$shape->movePenTo(0,0);
$shape->drawLineTo(199,0);
$shape->drawLineTo(199,19);
$shape->drawLineTo(0,19);
$shape->drawLineTo(0,0);

$mov->add($shape);
header('Content-type: application/x-shockwave-flash');
$mov->output( );
```

Save that script as *ming1.php*.

First we create a new instance of the SWFMovie class and assign it to our $mov variable. An SWFMovie object allows you to manipulate attributes of the movie as a whole —size, color, animation frame rate, etc. It is also used to add other Flash objects to your movie, so you must hold on to the SWFMovie object that was created.

The setDimension() function is an SWFMovie function that allows you to set the height and width of a movie by specifying values in the first and second parameters. Remember that Flash movies generally have their dimensions set in their host application (usually a web browser). The values you specify here are for the movie as you are creating it; however, if the Flash movie is forced to display at a different size, your items will automatically be proportionally scaled to fit the assigned space.

Moving on to the core of the code, we have a new class: SWFShape. Not surprisingly, we use objects of this class to manipulate shapes in Flash movies—the process is simply to create, manipulate, and then add to the parent movie object. If you forget to add your shapes to your movie object, the end result is that they'll be missing from the final output, so be careful.

In the example above, the parameter that SetLeftFill() takes is the return value of an AddFill() call. This is a function of the SWFShape class, and is overloaded (there is more than one version of it). The version used in the example above takes four parameters—the amount of red to use, the amount of blue, then green, and finally, an optional alpha parameter. The fill returned by the AddFill() function is used to supply the first parameter to SetLeftFill(), which is also overloaded. The end result is that the value passed to SetLeftFill() sets the fill on the left-hand side of the edge—in our example above, this is red.

Next we call MovePenTo() and DrawLineTo() several times. The movePenTo() function lifts the drawing "pen" from the canvas and places it down at the X and Y points specified by the first two parameters, respectively. The drawLineTo() function moves the pen in the same sort of way, except that it does not "lift" the pen from the canvas first, meaning that a line is drawn from the last pen location to the X and Y parameters passed into drawLineTo(), respectively. The drawLineTo() function is called a total of four times, giving us a box, and finally we call the Add() function of our SWFMovie object, $mov, passing in our new box as the parameter—this adds the new shape to the final output.

The last two lines are crucial to the whole process, and must be used precisely as seen above. The first of the two calls the header() function, passing in the correct content type to instruct browsers that the information following is a Shockwave Flash movie. The last line calls the Output() function of our SWFMovie object, which sends all the information you have prepared about your Flash movie out to your client. Once you have called this line, your script is complete.

Generally speaking, you will want to embed your Flash movies inside web pages, and that requires inserting the following line somewhere in a HTML page:

```
<embed src="ming1.php" menu="false" quality="best" bgcolor="#FFFFFF"
swLiveConnect="FALSE" WIDTH="200" HEIGHT="200"
TYPE="application/x-shockwave-flash" PLUGINSPAGE="http://www.macromedia.com/
shockwave/download/index.cgi?P1_Prod_Version=ShockwaveFlash" />
```

To view your animation in action, load the HTML page into your browser. If your Flash movie does not load at all, there may be an error in the PHP script. When viewing the HTML page, you will not see any PHP warnings, because the Flash movie is being sent directly to your browser's Flash player as part of a larger page. You can work around this by loading the Flash movie directly into your browser—you should see the errors printed as normal.

Flash Text

Following the rest of the library, text inside your Flash movie is manipulated using objects. The two key classes here are SWFFont and SWFText. The former holds the actual font shape data, whereas the latter holds information about the text as a whole, including color, position, string data, and the instance of SWFFont used to draw the letters.

The code to generate text works differently under Windows and Unix. First up, Linux users:

```
$font = new SWFFont("Impact.fdb");
$text = new SWFText();

$text->setFont($font);
$text->moveTo(200, 400);
$text->setColor(0, 0xff, 0);
$text->setHeight(200);
$text->addString("Text is surprisingly easy");

$movie = new SWFMovie();
$movie->setDimension(6400, 4800);
$movie->add($text);

header('Content-type: application/x-shockwave-flash');
$movie->output();
```

The Windows code isn't far off, and the end result is the same:

```
$font = new SWFFont("Impact");
$text = new SWFTextField(); // new!
$sprite = new SWFSprite(); // new!

$text->setFont($font);
$text->setColor(0, 0xff, 0);
$text->setHeight(200);
$text->addString("Windows is a little harder!");

$spritepos = $sprite->add($text); // new!
$spritepos->moveTo(200, 400); // new!

$movie = new SWFMovie();
$movie->setDimension(6400, 4800);
$movie->add($text);

header('Content-type: application/x-shockwave-flash');
$movie->output();
```

You'll need to alter your HTML file to display the new script, and also change the width and height attributes of the <embed> object so that the Flash movie is larger; otherwise, you will find the text is probably too small to notice.

That code starts with the two new classes, SWFFont and SWFText. The SWFFont class is remarkably easy to use—merely pass the name of the FDB file you want to use as a font, and save the return value for later use. You can create your own FDB fonts using Ming's *makefdb* utility (available from Ming's home page, *http://ming.sourceforge.net*), so you should replace *Impact.fdb* in the example with your own font.

In line two of our script, we create a new SWFText object and store it in a $text variable. This object works in pretty much the same way as our previous SWFShape object—we set various properties of it, then add it to the parent movie once we're done.

The first thing we do with our $text object is call its setFont( ) function, which makes this SWFText object render in the font used to create the SWFFont object specified as the only parameter. In our case, we created our SWFFont object using *Impact.fdb*, so calling setFont( ) using the new SWFText object will draw the text in this object using the Impact font.

Next, we call the moveTo( ) function to place the text neatly inside the movie, and then call the setColor( ) function (the values are in hexadecimal) to set the text to lime green. The setHeight( ) function sets the height of the text in twips, but again, remember that the final size of the text is dependent on the size at which the movie is played back, and also the dimensions of the parent movie object itself—the value you set here is just relative to the rest of the movie.

The most important function we call for our SWFText object is addString( )—this allows us to draw the string passed as parameter one to the position we set with our moveTo( ) call. It is important to note that the pen the text is drawn with is set to the baseline. If you use moveTo( ) to set the position to 0,0, the text drawn will be drawn outside of your movie.

Actions

Through its powerful *ActionScript* language, Flash provides a flexible scripting environment to allow developers to take more direct control over the operation and flow of their script. For example, you can call stop( ) to stop playing the movie, then play( ) to continue; gotoFrame( ) allows you to jump to a particular part of your movie, and getURL( ) allows you to browse to a new web page. There is a large collection of actions available to you, and the PHP documentation has some very good (if long) examples on how to make use of various functions.

This next script gives you a quick start in using ActionScript:

```
function MakeActionBox($red, $green, $blue){
        $shape = new SWFShape( );
        $shape->setLeftFill($shape->addFill($red, $green, $blue));
        $shape->movePenTo(-100,-20);
        $shape->drawLineTo(100,-20);
        $shape->drawLineTo(100,20);
```

```
        $shape->drawLineTo(-100,20);
        $shape->drawLineTo(-100,-20);
        return $shape;
}

$button = new SWFButton();
$button->setUp(MakeActionBox(0xff, 0, 0));
$button->setOver(MakeActionBox(0xff, 0xff, 0));
$button->setDown(MakeActionBox(0, 0, 0xff));
$button->setHit(MakeActionBox(0, 0, 0));
$button->addAction(new SWFAction("getURL('http://www.slashdot.org',
        'slashdot');"), SWFBUTTON_MOUSEUP);

$movie = new SWFMovie();
$movie->setDimension(200,200);

$displayitem = $movie->add($button);
$displayitem->moveTo(100,100);

header("Content-type: application/x-shockwave-flash");
$movie->output();
```

That script uses a custom function, MakeActionBox( ), to handle some of the grunt work you will experience when working with the SWFButton class. The SWFButton class, used for the $button variable, has several "states" that each require a shape—how the button looks when it is up, when the mouse is over it, when the mouse is clicked on it, and where the mouse can be clicked on it. Each of these states requires a complete shape of its own, so their creation is automated by using the function MakeActionBox( ).

Going through the main chunk of code line by line, you can see it creates an instance of SWFButton and stores it in the $button variable. Four functions are then called: setUp( ), setOver( ), setDown( ), and setHit( ). These define how this button should look when the user interacts with it. The example is quite short; you will find it is more visually appealing to have more than just the color change between states!

Next we come to the important function of this particular script: addAction( ). This takes two parameters: the SWFAction object to add and a flag for when the action should execute. Options include SWFBUTTON_MOUSEUP as seen above or, alternatively, SWFBUTTON_MOUSEDOWN, SWFBUTTON_MOUSEOVER, and more—see the documentation for a full list.

As the first parameter to addAction( ), we pass in new SWFAction(...). The constructor of the SWFAction class takes a string that contains the ActionScript code you wish the action to execute. For this action, which will execute when the user clicks the mouse button on the object, we want to execute the GetUrl( ) ActionScript function. In the example, GetUrl( ) is passed two parameters: the URL to load, and the name of the window to load it in. If the named window does not exist, it will be created for you. So, the addAction( ) line translates to "Create a new ActionScript action that will load the Slashdot web site into a new window, then attach that action to our button so that it executes whenever the user clicks the button."

After the ActionScript code, there is a slight change to the normal procedure—we use $movie->add( ) as before, except this time we grab the return value and store it in the $displayitem variable. This is done because, when adding shapes, text, buttons, and sprites to a movie, the add( ) function returns a special type of object—SWFDisplayItem( )—which is a handle to the object inside the movie. This means you can add the same button (or shape, text, etc.) to the movie several times over, and manipulate them individually without much fuss.

This functionality is important because you cannot manipulate the position of an SWFButton object directly—you need to add it to the movie first, then manipulate the position of the returned SWFDisplayItem object. In the line after the add( ) call, we do just that.

Finally, the movie is sent to output as usual. If you would like to make your button more interesting, you might want to try combining the previous code for manipulating text. To make your ActionScript more interesting, try reading the ActionScript documentation, available from *http://www.macromedia.com/support/ flash/action_scripts/*.

Animation

Adding animation to your Flash movies is both fun and taxing. The key to animation is the SWFDisplayItem object returned by the add( ) function of your movie object. SWFDisplayItem objects have a variety of functions that allow you to move, rotate, scale, and skew your objects easily. This next example demonstrates some basic animation:

```
$font = new SWFFont("Impact.fdb");
$text = new SWFText( );
$text->setFont($font);
$text->moveTo(300, 500);
$text->setColor(0, 0xff, 0);
$text->setHeight(200);
$text->addString("Text is surprisingly easy");

$movie = new SWFMovie( );
$movie->setDimension(6400, 4800);

$displayitem = $movie->add($text);

for($i = 0; $i < 100; ++$i) {
        $displayitem->rotate(-1);
        $displayitem->scale(1.01, 1.01);
        $movie->nextFrame( );
}

header('Content-type: application/x-shockwave-flash');
$movie->output( );
```

Although that code is largely the same as a previous script, the $movie-> add($text) line has now changed so that the return value is captured and stored in $displayitem.

The script then runs through a loop 100 times, each time calling rotate( ), scale( ), and nextFrame( ). Animation works by defining the initial state of the movie, advancing the frame, then specifying changes from the previous frame. In practice, this means you use nextFrame( ) each time you want to move forward to the next frame of your Flash animation.

The rotate( ) function takes a single parameter, which is the floating-point value of the amount to rotate your SWFDisplayItem object from its current rotation. In our example, I have used -1, which means it adds -1 of a degree of rotation with each frame. Because of the way Flash rotation works, this means that the text rotates in a clockwise manner.

The scale( ) function takes two parameters: the amount to scale the object's width and the amount to scale its height. Again, this is based on its last state, which means that the scaling is compounded. By adding 0.01% to the size of our text over 100 frames, we are almost tripling the size of the object.

So, the contents of the for loop translate to "Rotate slightly, scale slightly, next frame" 100 times.

19

XML & XSLT

This chapter covers XML parsing and manipulation using PHP, and requires that you have some familiarity with XML, although XML syntax and grammar are not mentioned in detail—the focus is PHP.

SimpleXML

PHP offers several different ways of parsing XML, but as of PHP 5, the most popular way is to use the SimpleXML extension. SimpleXML works by reading in the entire XML file at once and converting it into a PHP object containing all the elements of that XML file chained together in the same way. Once the file has been loaded, you can simply pull data out by traversing the object tree.

The advantage of SimpleXML is that you no longer need to write any complicated code to access your XML—you simply load it, then read in attributes as you would expect to be able to. Consider the following XML file, *employees.xml*:

```
<employees>
        <employee>
                <name>Anthony Clarke</name>
                <title>Chief Information Officer</title>
                <age>48</age>
        </employee>

        <employee>
                <name>Laura Pollard</name>
                <title>Chief Executive Officer</title>
                <age>54</age>
        </employee>
</employees>
```

The base element is a list of employees, and it contains several employee elements. Each employee has a name, a title, and an age. Now take a look at this basic SimpleXML script:

```
$employees = simplexml_load_file('employees.xml');
var_dump($employees);
```

Here is the output:

```
object(simplexml_element)#1 (1) {
        ["employee"]=>
        array(2) {
                [0]=>
                object(simplexml_element)#2 (3) {
                        ["name"]=>
                        string(14) "Anthony Clarke"
                        ["title"]=>
                        string(25) "Chief Information Officer"
                        ["age"]=>
                        string(2) "48"
                }

                [1]=>
                object(simplexml_element)#3 (3) {
                        ["name"]=>
                        string(13) "Laura Pollard"
                        ["title"]=>
                        string(23) "Chief Executive Officer"
                        ["age"]=>
                        string(2) "54"
                }
        }
}
```

From that, you should be able to see that the base element has an array employee, containing two elements—one for each of the employees in the XML file. Each element in that array is another object, containing the name, the title, and the age of each employee. Put simply, each collection of data is made into an array, and each distinct XML element is made into an object.

Now, consider the following script, using the same XML file:

```
$employees = simplexml_load_file('employees.xml');

foreach ($employees->employee as $employee) {
        print "{$employee->name} is {$employee->title} at age {$employee->age}\n";
}
```

This time the script actually does something useful with the XML content, and iterates through the $employees->employee array. As each employee element is read from the array, its information is printed out. Note how easy it is to read information from elements, simply because the XML is all converted to standard PHP variables.

XML Attributes

SimpleXML allows you to access attributes of XML elements as if the element were an array. Here's some very simple XML with attributes:

```
<cakes>
        <cake type="sponge">
                <name language="english">Victoria Cake</name>
        </cake>
</cakes>
```

In that example, the cake element has a type attribute, and the name element has a language attribute. This next script accesses them both:

```
$xml = simplexml_load_file("cakes.xml");
print "{$xml->cake[0]["type"]}\n";
print "{$xml->cake[0]->name["language"]}\n";
```

The $xml->cake[0] part accesses the first cake element, as we have already discussed. However, note that it treats the cake as an array in order to get the type attribute. If we had used $xml->cake[0]->type, it would have looked for a <type> child element of the cake, which doesn't exist.

The next line, $xml->cake[0]->name["language"], gets the first cake, pulls out its <name> child element, then reads the "language" attribute. As long as you remember that elements use -> and attributes use [ ], you'll be OK.

Reading from a String

While simplexml_load_file() loads XML data from a file, simplexml_load_string() loads XML data from a string. This is generally not as useful, but it does allow you to load several XML files into one string, then use that inside one SimpleXML structure.

For example:

```
$employees = <<<EOT
<employees>
<employee ID="2" FOO="BAR">
<name>Anthony Clarke</name>
<title>Chief Information Officer</title>
<age>48</age>
</employee>
<employee ID="2" BAZ="WOM">
<name>Laura Pollard</name>
<title>Chief Executive Officer</title>
<age>54</age>
</employee>
</employees>
EOT;

$employees = simplexml_load_string($employees);

foreach ($employees->employee as $employee) {
```

```
    print "{$employee->name} is {$employee->title} at age {$employee->
age}\n";
    }
```

The majority of that script is just the heredoc-style string assignment that sets up the XML. Then, with a call to simplexml_load_string( ), the XML is parsed into the $employees object, just as with the simplexml_load_file( ) function. The resulting object is no different.

Searching and Filtering with XPath

The standard way to search through XML documents for particular nodes is called *XPath*. Sterling Hughes (the creator of the SimpleXML extension) described it by saying it's "as important to XML as regular expressions are to plain text," which should give you an idea of just how important it is!

Fortunately for us, XPath is much easier than regular expressions for basic usage. Using the same *employees.xml* file, here is an XPath script:

```
$xml = simplexml_load_file('employees.xml');

echo "<strong>Using direct method...</strong><br />";
$names = $xml->xpath('/employees/employee/name');
foreach($names as $name) {
        echo "Found $name<br />";
}
echo "<br />";

echo "<strong>Using indirect method...</strong><br />";
$employees = $xml->xpath('/employees/employee');
foreach($employees as $employee) {
        echo "Found {$employee->name}<br />";
}
echo "<br />";

echo "<strong>Using wildcard method...</strong><br />";
$names = $xml->xpath('//name');
foreach($names as $name) {
        echo "Found $name<br />";
}
```

That pulls out names of employees in three different ways, and the work is all done in the call to the xpath( ) function. This takes a query as its only parameter, and returns the result of that query. The query itself has specialized syntax, but it's very easy. The first example says, "Look in all the employees elements, find any employee elements in there, and retrieve all the names of them." It's very specific because only employees/employee/name is matched.

The second query matches all employee elements inside employees, but doesn't go specifically for the name of the employees. As a result, we get the full employee back, and need to print $employee->name to get the name.

The last one just looks for name elements, but note that it starts with "//"—this is the signal to do a global search for all name elements, regardless of where—or how deeply nested—they are in the document.

XPath can also be used to filter your results according to any values you want. For example:

```
$xml = simplexml_load_file('employees.xml');

echo "<strong>Matching employees with name 'Laura Pollard'</strong><br />";
$employees = $xml->xpath('/employees/employee[name="Laura Pollard"]');

foreach($employees as $employee) {
        echo "Found {$employee->name}<br />";
}

echo "<br />";

echo "<strong>Matching employees younger than 54</strong><br />";
$employees = $xml->xpath('/employees/employee[age<54]');

foreach($employees as $employee) {
        echo "Found {$employee->name}<br />";
}

echo "<br />";

echo "<strong>Matching employees as old or older than 48</strong><br />";
$employees = $xml->xpath('//employee[age>=48]');

foreach($employees as $employee) {
        echo "Found {$employee->name}<br />";
}

echo "<br />";
```

The filter is done between the square brackets, [and]. The first query grabs all employees elements, then all employee elements inside it, and then filters them so that only those that have a name that matches Laura Pollard are retrieved. Once you get that, the other two are quite obvious: <, >, <=, etc., all work as you'd expect in PHP.

If you want to filter by the value of an attribute rather than the value of an element, you need to use the @ symbol. For example, our *cakes.xml* file has cakes that have a "type" attribute. To search for specific types using XPath, you would need to use code like this:

```
$sponge_cakes = $xml->Xpath('//cake[@type="sponge"]');
```

You can grab only part of a query result by continuing on as normal afterward, like this:

```
$ages = $xml->xpath('//employee[age>=48]/age');

foreach($ages as $age) {
        echo "Found $age<BR/>";
}
```

You can even run queries on queries, with an XPath search like this:

```
$employees = $xml->xpath('//employee[age>=49][name="Laura Pollard"]');
```

Going back to selecting various types of elements, you can use the | symbol (OR) to select more than one type of element, like this:

```
echo "<B>Retrieving all titles and ages</B><BR/>";
$results = $xml->xpath('//employee/title|//employee/age');

foreach($results as $result) {
        echo "Found $result<BR/>";
}
```

That will output the following:

```
Found Chief Information Officer
Found 48
Found Chief Executive Officer
Found 54
```

You can combine all of this together to search on more than one value, like this:

```
$names = $xml->xpath('//employee[age<40]/name|//employee[age>50]/name');

foreach($names as $name) {
        echo "Found $name<BR/>";
}
```

For more complex work, you can run calculations using XPath in order to get tighter control over your queries. For example, if you only wanted the names of employees who have an odd age (that is, cannot be divided by two without leaving a remainder), you would use an XPath query like this:

```
$names = $xml->xpath('//employee[age mod 2 = 1]/name');
```

Along with mod (equivalent to % in PHP) there's also div for division, + and -, and ceiling( ) and floor( ) (equivalent to their namesakes in PHP). These are quite advanced and don't get much use in practice. When using "-", you have to keep it from looking like part of an element name, so foo-bar needs to be written as foo - bar so that we don't think we're talking about an element named foo-bar.

Outputting XML

One of the most interesting features about SimpleXML is that it can, at any time, give you a string containing the well-formed XML representation of its data. This essentially does the opposite of simplexml_load_file( ), but incorporates any changes you've made to the data while it was in SimpleXML form.

For example:

```
$xml = simplexml_load_file('employees.xml');
$xml->employee[1]->age = 55;
echo $xml->asXML();
```

That loads our XML file, and changes the second employee to have an age of 55. The call to asXML( ) then outputs the changed data tree, printing this:

```
<?xml version="1.0"?>
<employees>
        <employee>
```

```
        <name>Anthony Clarke</name>
        <title>Chief Information Officer</title>
        <age>48</age>
    </employee>

    <employee>
        <name>Laura Pollard</name>
        <title>Chief Executive Officer</title>
        <age>55</age>
    </employee>
</employees>
```

Note the changed value for Laura's age. However, blindly changing values isn't a smart move: the XML could change quite easily so that Pollard is no longer the second person in there. Instead, you should really combine it with an XPath search, like this:

```
$xml = simplexml_load_file('employees.xml');
echo "\nBefore transformation:\n\n";

echo $xml->asXML();

$xml->employee[1]->age = 55;

$employees = $xml->xpath('/employees/employee[name="Anthony Clarke"]');
$employees[0]->title = "Chairman of the Board, Chief Information Officer";

echo "\n\nAfter transformation:\n\n";
echo $xml->asXML();
```

This time the age is changed by referencing Laura directly, but I've also changed the job title of Anthony Clarke using a smart XPath search for his exact name. Of course, even names can be duplicated by chance, so an employee ID would be even better!

Transforming XML Using XSLT

XSLT is an XML-based language that allows you to manipulate XML documents before outputting them. With one XML document, you can make the same content look vastly different—for example, you could transform it with a WML XSL stylesheet and send it to WAP devices, or parse it with an SQL XSL stylesheet and send it to a database.

Several browsers (most notably Firefox and Internet Explorer) can perform XSL transformation on the client side by downloading an XML document, the XSL stylesheet, and any accompanying CSS files, then combining them all together on your visitor's computer. But someone with an old version of IE, or any other non-XSL-enabled browser, would not get the same experience.

This is where PHP comes in: your visitor types a URL as usual, but it is PHP that loads the XML and the XSL and combines the two together into the output. On the client side, users see no XML or XSL at all, just normal XHTML. Of course, there is nothing stopping that PHP page from analyzing the visitor's user agent and sending content fit for that browser, whether it be HTML 2, XHTML, WAP, or anything else.

An Example XSL Document

Here is an example XSL document designed to work on the *employees.xml* file from before. Save it in the same directory, as *input.xsl*:

```
<?xml version="1.0" encoding="utf-8"?>
<xsl:stylesheet version="1.0" xmlns:xsl="http://www.w3.org/1999/XSL/
Transform"
        xmlns:rdf="http://www.w3.org/1999/02/22-rdf-syntax-ns#"
        xmlns="http://my.netscape.com/rdf/simple/0.9/">
        <xsl:output method="html" indent="no" encoding="utf-8"/>

        <xsl:template match="/">
                <html>
                <head>
                <title>XSLT</title>
                </head>
                <body>

                <xsl:for-each select="/employees/employee">
                        Job Title: <xsl:value-of select="title"/><br/>
                </xsl:for-each>
                </body>
                </html>
        </xsl:template>
</xsl:stylesheet>
```

As this is not a book on XSLT (there are enough of those available already!), we will not spend much time analyzing what that does to our XML.

After the long document type header that is the norm with XML-based languages, we come to the line starting "<xsl:template". This matches the root of our XML input, and prints out some basic HTML to give our page a minimum structure. The "<xsl:for-each" line is basically an array iterator, like the foreach construct in PHP. Here, the array is whatever XML elements are found by pattern matching against the "select" attribute of the for-each, which is /employees/employee in the example.

The for-each loop contains a line that prints out the value of the title attribute of each employee. The foreach code is executed once for every matching element it finds in the input XML, so given our *employees.xml*, it will execute twice.

Adding PHP to the Mix

PHP's XSL support was rewritten for PHP 5, and although you can retrieve the old extension from PECL, it is not recommended.

PHP uses the libxslt library to perform internal XSLT transformations, presenting its functions through an object-oriented interface.

There are two classes you need to know about to use XSLT: DOMDocument, which holds XML data, and XSLTProcessor, which does the transformation. The DOMDocument class is also interesting for more advanced SimpleXML users, as the two extensions can share their XML data.

To perform XSLT transformation, you need two instances of DOMDocument (one for the XML, and one for the XSL) and one instance of XSLTProcessor. You load XML documents into a DOMDocument class by calling its load( ), like this:

```
$xml = new DOMDocument;
$xml->load("employees.xml");
$xsl = new DOMDocument;
$xsl->load("input.xsl");
```

Then, to perform the XSLT transformation, you need to use XSLTProcessor's importStyleSheet( ) function to load your XSL, then its transformToXML( ) function to load your XML and transform it. The transformToXML sends back transformed content as its return value.

The full PHP code looks like this:

```
$xsl = new DOMDocument( );
$xml = new DOMDocument( );

$xsl->load("input.xsl");
$xml->load("employees.xml");

$xsltproc = new XSLTProcessor( );
$xsltproc->importStylesheet($xsl);
echo $xsltproc->transformToXML($xml);
```

20

Network Programming

PHP has a number of ways to work over a network: the most common protocols have special functions to make often-used functionality easy, but it is possible to use PHP to write any kind of data over any kind of protocol.

Sockets

While it is out of the scope of this book to go into detail about network infrastructure, you at least need to know what protocols, ports, and sockets are. Protocols are like languages, defining how two computers can talk to each other, and there are hundreds of protocols to perform all varieties of operations—there is a protocol for file transfer (File Transfer Protocol, or FTP), a protocol for transferring web pages (Hypertext Transfer Protocol, or HTTP), a protocol for network management (Simple Network Management Protocol, or SNMP), and many more.

Each protocol has a set of ports that it uses, which are theoretical openings in your computer's Internet connection that clients can connect to. They are numbered 1 to 65535, of which the first 1023 are considered reserved for administrative users. By default, your PC "listens" to no ports, meaning that it ignores all incoming connections. However, if you run a web server, it will open up port 80—this is the port for HTTP, where your web server will listen for requests for web pages. Many of the first 1023 ports are used already, which means if you want to use a port for a new service you have written, it is best that you use a number above 1024.

Sockets are the literal connectors between a port and a program, sort of how a plug socket connects an appliance to the electricity grid in your house. Management of sockets in PHP comes in two flavors: easy and hard. As per usual, the easy option is not as flexible as the hard option, but it is much faster to get started with. We are going to be covering both here, because both have their own uses.

Sockets Are Files

The simplest way to work with sockets is by using them as if they were files. In fact, if you are using Unix, sockets actually *are* files, whereas in Windows this behavior is just emulated.

PHP works the same way as Unix, which means you can fread( ) and fwrite( ) to sockets as you would a normal file. For example:

```
$fp = fsockopen ("slashdot.org", 80);

if ($fp) {
        fwrite($fp, "GET / HTTP/1.1\r\nHOST: slashdot.org\r\n\r\n");

        while (!feof($fp)) {
                print fread($fp,256);
        }

        fclose ($fp);
} else {
        print "Fatal error\n";
}
```

The fsockopen( ) call above opens a server on the port we specify, then waits for us to specify what to do with it. Using this function, you could send a hand-crafted HTTP request to the server. In contrast, the fopen( ) remote file handler uses PHP's stream functionality to automatically connect to the server and send the HTTP request using the GET method—there is no flexibility.

As it stands, we open a socket for server *slashdot.org* on port 80; then, after checking the fsockopen( ) call has not returned false to signal failure, we write a HTTP GET request to the connection. Our HTTP request has two lines: first, we send the GET request using fwrite( ), asking for /, which is the root of the server. Second, we specify that we want to read from the host *slashdot.org*, which is a requirement for virtually hosted machines and HTTP 1.1.

With the HTTP request sent, we just need to wait for the response (the web page). This is done using a while loop—while there is more to be read from the file (socket), we fread( ) in another 256 bytes and print it out. Once we are at the end of the "file," we close the socket and end the script.

Using fopen( ) would make the socket open line shorter, at the expense of flexibility. For example, the above script could be rewritten to specify that we are able to receive compressed content:

```
$fp = fsockopen ("slashdot.org", 80);

if ($fp) {
        fwrite($fp, "GET / HTTP/1.1\r\nHOST: slashdot.org\r\n
                ACCEPT-ENCODING: gzip\r\n\r\n");

        while (!feof($fp)) {
                print fread($fp,256);
        }
```

```
        fclose ($fp);
} else {
        print "Fatal error\n";
}
```

Slashdot is set up to serve compressed content when requested, so it will respond to our custom request with the compressed web page.

 If you liked persistent database connections, you might also like persistent socket connections—the function pfsockopen( ) takes the same parameters as fsockopen( ), but it remains open over requests.

Creating a Server

The server socket system starts with socket_create_listen( ), which takes a port number to listen on as its only parameter. This function creates a socket, binds it to the port you specify, and returns a pointer to the socket it created or false if it failed. You will need the socket resource it returns for later functions, so you should always save it in a variable. If the function fails, it is probably because the port you specified is already being used, or because you have insufficient privileges to open the port.

The socket_accept( ) function takes the return value of socket_create_listen( ) as its only parameter, and returns a client connection—someone who connected to our port number. It works by examining the queue of people waiting to be served, and taking the first client from there. If there are no clients waiting to be served, socket_accept( ) will wait ("block") until a client *does* become available, at which point it will return that.

You need to provide two parameters to the socket_write( ) function: the client to write to and the value you want to write. This data is then sent through our socket to the client, as you would expect. Its partner, socket_read( ), also takes two parameters, which are the connection to read from and the number of bytes to read. By using socket_write( ) and socket_read( ) together, you can interact with clients connecting to your socket.

Here is an example script that creates a ROT13 server—when people connect to it and send text, it responds with the ROT13 equivalent of their text:

```
$socket = socket_create_listen("12345");

if (!$socket) {
        print "Failed to create socket!\n";
        exit;
}

while (true) {
        $client = socket_accept($socket);
        $welcome = "\nWelcome to the Amazing ROT13 Machine.\n
        Type '!close' to close this connection, or type '!halt'
        to halt the server.\n";

        socket_write($client, $welcome);
```

```
        while (true) {
                $input = trim(socket_read ($client, 256));
                if ($input == '!close') {
                        break;
                }

                if ($input == '!halt') {
                        socket_close ($client);
                        break 2;
                }

                $output = str_rot13($input) . "\n";
                socket_write($client, $output);
                print "Them: $input, Us: $output\n";
        }

        socket_close ($client);
}

socket_close ($socket);
```

Because this is going to serve data over a potentially infinite length of time, it is important that you execute that script using the CLI SAPI, not your web browser. Once you have it running, bring up a new command-line window and enter the following: **telnet localhost 12345**.

That should launch your telnet program, which is useful for forming simple connections to servers. All being well, you should receive the welcome message from the ROT13 server—try it out with a few words, then type **!shutdown** to finish. If you have followed correctly so far, you should see something like Figure 20-1.

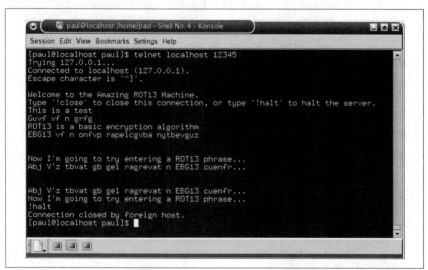

Figure 20-1. Using telnet, we can connect to the ROT13 server and convert text by typing it in

HTTP

Hypertext Transport Protocol is a primarily a basic protocol to handle data transmission, but it is also capable of authentication and more. PHP gives you all the tools you need to manipulate HTTP for your own needs.

Sending Custom Headers

There are several special HTTP headers you can send to instruct the remote client. For example, the "Location" header instructs browsers to request a different URL, the "Content-Type" header tells browsers what kind of content they are about to receive, and the "WWW-Authenticate" header tells browsers that they need to send some authentication information to proceed.

Sending custom headers in PHP is done using the header( ) function, which takes the header to send as its parameter. So, to make a browser go to *www.example.com* when it visits a certain script, this would be used:

```
header("Location: http://www.example.com");
```

Special attention should be paid when using the Location header, however, as it is used to redirect clients from one page to another. When you send a Location header, the rest of your script will still be executed, potentially allowing people to see pages they would otherwise not be able to see. As a result, it's best to call exit immediately after header("Location: ...") to ensure that nothing happens after the redirect notice has been sent.

The headers_sent( ) function, when called with no parameters, returns true if your HTTP headers have been sent or false otherwise. That isn't "whether some headers have been sent" but "whether the header-sending opportunity has passed." That is, if headers_sent( ) returns true, sending more headers will trigger an error because non-header information has already been sent. If you pass in two parameters as references, PHP will fill them with the name of the file and the line number therein where the first output was sent, like this:

```
header("Expires: Sat, 22 Dec 1979 05:30:00 GMT");
echo "This is some text for output.<br />";

if (!headers_sent($filename, $linenum)) {
        // If no headers have been sent, send one.

        // This code will not execute, as we sent the
        // Expires header back in line 1
        header("Location: www.yoursite.com");
        exit;
} else {
        echo "Headers already sent in $filename on line $linenum.";
        exit;
}
```

That will print out the following:

```
This is some text for output.
Headers already sent in C:\home\header.php on line 3.
```

Reading Queued Headers

The headers_sent() takes no parameters, and returns an array that contains a numerically indexed list of the headers that are ready for sending. Using this, we can extend our previous example like this:

```
header("Expires: Sat, 22 Dec 1979 05:30:00 GMT");
echo "This is some text for output.<br />";

if (!headers_sent($filename, $linenum)) {
        // if no headers have been sent, send one
        // this will not execute, as we sent the Expires header.
        header("Location: www.yoursite.com");
        exit;
} else {
        echo "Headers already sent in $filename on line $linenum.<br />";
        echo "Headers sent are:<br /> <UL>";

        $headers = headers_list();
        foreach($headers as $header) {
                echo "<LI>$header</LI>";
        }

        echo "</UL>";

        exit;
}
```

Authentication Over HTTP

HTTP authentication is largely a matter of sending special HTTP headers to your clients, asking them to provide access codes, and it's easy to do with PHP as long as you have configured PHP to run as an Apache module. For example:

```
if (!isset($_SERVER['PHP_AUTH_USER'])) {
        header("WWW-Authenticate: Basic realm=\"Private Area\"");
        header("HTTP/1.0 401 Unauthorized");
        // only reached if authentication fails
        print "Sorry - you need valid credentials granted access
                to the private area!\n";
        exit;
} else {
        // only reached if authentication succeeds
        print "Welcome to the private area, {$_SERVER['PHP_AUTH_USER']}
                - you used {$_SERVER['PHP_AUTH_PW']} as your password.";
}
```

To start the authentication process, we send two HTTP headers using header(). WWW-Authenticate allows us to define the area, or *realm*, to which we are limiting access. It might be "Internet Mail Gateway", "Members Area", or, in our example, "Private Area". This realm name is usually shown to users when they are prompted for their username and password, as shown in Figure 20-2.

Figure 20-2. HTTP authentication is a simple way to keep parts of your site safe from prying eyes

The second header( ) function sends the HTTP status "401", which means "no access". This most often means no username and password have been entered, but it may also mean the details entered were incorrect. Therefore, WWW-Authenticate tells the browser what response is required to authenticate, and the 401 header says "no entry"—you need both to perform authentication.

If your user clicks "Cancel," she should be presented with something other than a blank page. In our example above, we have the print line beginning "Sorry - you need valid..." ready for this eventuality.

The last print statement, "Welcome to the private area", is for people who have authenticated successfully. All it takes to authenticate currently is a username and password—we don't check the values of the data, we just accept whatever they give us.

```
if (!isset($_SERVER['PHP_AUTH_USER'])) {
```

That line forms the crux of authentication with PHP. When users submit authentication, PHP receives the username and password as $_SERVER['PHP_AUTH_USER'] and $_SERVER['PHP_AUTH_PW'], respectively. By checking whether $_SERVER['PHP_AUTH_USER'] is set, we are saying, "Have we received an authentication username from the client?" If we have not, we send a request for authentication using WWW-Authenticate and exit the script.

When our visitors provide a username and password, the script is called again. This time the 'if' statement evaluates to true and we print out our welcome message. Most sites would want to perform some sort of username and password checking in order to make authentication worthwhile, so let us change the script to include simple credentials checking:

```
if (!isset($_SERVER['PHP_AUTH_USER'])) {
        header("WWW-Authenticate: Basic realm=\"Private Area\"");
        header("HTTP/1.0 401 Unauthorized");
        print "Sorry - you need valid credentials to be granted access!\n";
        exit;
} else {
        if (($_SERVER['PHP_AUTH_USER'] == 'paul') &&
                ($_SERVER['PHP_AUTH_PW'] == 'hudson')) {
                print "Welcome to the private area!";
        } else {
                header("WWW-Authenticate: Basic realm=\"Private Area\"");
```

```
                    header("HTTP/1.0 401 Unauthorized");
                    print "Sorry - you need valid credentials to be granted
access!\n";

                    exit;
            }
    }
```

The modified script above now only allows users that provide the username 'paul' and the password 'hudson'.

Sending Mail

The primary function for sending email is mail( ), which takes three basic parameters and one optional one. These parameters are, in order, the email address to send to, the subject of the message, the body of the message, and finally, any extra headers you want to include. Note that this function relies on a working email server that you have permission to use: for Unix machines, this is often Sendmail; Windows machines, you must set the SMTP value in your *php.ini* file.

Here is an example of the most basic type of mail( ) call:

```
mail("a_friend@example.com", "My Subject", "Hello, world!");
```

If you receive mailing errors or don't receive the test mail, you have probably installed PHP incorrectly, or may not have permission to send emails.

You can use variables in place of any of the parameters, like this:

```
$mailaddress = "a_friend@example.com";
$mailsubject = "My Subject";
$mailbody = "Hello, world!";
mail($mailaddress, $mailsubject, $mailbody);
```

To make the email address textual, e.g., "A. Friend" rather than *a_friend@example. com*, you need to add both name and address values into the email address, like this:

```
$mailtoname = "My Best Friend";
$mailtoaddress = "a_friend@example.com";
$mailtocomplete = "$mailtoname <$mailtoaddress>";
mail($mailtocomplete, "My Subject", "Hello, world!");
```

With that new code, the email will appear to have been sent to "My Best Friend", which is much easier to read. The fourth parameter is where you specify any number of additional email headers to send along with the email—these let you affect how the email looks, how it is parsed, and other key information. For example, we can specify who *sent* the email using the From header, we can specify who else should get the email using the CC and BCC headers, or we can specify that the email is to be treated as containing HTML. Each header sent in the third parameter needs to be separated by a carriage return and new line, not just a new line. That is, only \r\n should be used to separate the various parameters, and not any other combination.

Here is a script that sends a HTML mail from a given email address:

```
$message = "<b>This is a <i>test</i></b>";
$headers = "From: foo@bar.com\r\nContent-type: text/html\r\n";
mail("you@yourdomain.com", "Testing", $message, $headers);
```

That should send a message with the text all in bold, and the word "test" in italics. The $headers variable is used to set From so that it appears to be from *foo@bar.com*, then add a carriage return and a new line, and finally send a Content-type header of text/html, which should make the email client display it as HTML. Because HTML emails allow potentially unsafe content, many email clients (such as KMail on Linux) will stop HTML emails being displayed by default, and will instead display a warning—you should be aware of this, and only use HTML email if it is necessary.

MIME Types

The Multipurpose Internet Mail Extensions (MIME) system was designed to allow the formatting of emails so that they can include files, and it is made up of several parts. In order to be able to instruct email clients what types of files are attached, *MIME types* were created—short, textual descriptions of the file types that can be recognized by everyone. MIME types are so popular that they are used across the Web as a whole now, and many operating systems rely on them to decide how to open a file. In emails, attachments are literally copied into the message as an encoded string, with MIME boundary markers being used to tell mail readers where each attachment starts and stops.

There are MIME types for all sorts of formats, from application/zip for zip files to video/quicktime for Quicktime *.mov* files and application/x-tar for tarballs. It is the job of the Internet Assigned Numbers Authority (IANA) to assign official MIME types, and it also keeps a list of all the registered MIME types on its web site. At the time of writing, this list was available at *http://www.iana.org/assignments/media-types*—worth taking a look.

There are hundreds, possibly even thousands, of MIME types out there, simply because there are so many file formats out there. But there are a certain few that stand out as being popular, which are shown in Table 20-1.

Table 20-1. Mime types

application/msexcel	Microsoft Excel data file
application/msword	Microsoft Word data file
application/octet-stream	Generic binary file
application/pdf	Adobe PDF
application/x-shockwave-flash	Macromedia Flash
application/zip	Zip file
audio/mp3	MP3
audio/wav	Wave sound file
audio/x-ogg	Ogg file
font/ttf	TrueType Font
image/bmp	MS Windows .bmp image
image/gif	GIF image

Table 20-1. Mime types (continued)

image/jpeg	JPEG image
image/png	PNG image
image/tiff	TIFF image
image/svg+xml	Scalable Vector Graphic (SVG)
text/html	HTML file
text/plain	Plain text
text/rtf	Rich-Text File
text/tab-separated-values	Tab-Separated Values (TSV)
text/xml	XML
video/mpeg	MPEG video
video/quicktime	Quicktime video

MIME types are used in many places other than in emails—web servers, for example, make very heavy use of MIME types in order to know how to handle files as they are requested, and also so they know what kinds of documents clients can and cannot receive.

It is undesirable to have to keep looking up long lists to find the MIME type you want every time you get a file, but PHP comes to the rescue with a special MIME lookup function, mime_content_type( ). This is based upon the Apache module mod_mime_magic, which itself is based upon the Unix file command. If you have never used this before, the principle is that many types of files have a unique identifier in the first few bytes, referred to as a *magic number*, that specifies what type of file it is. Bitmaps, for example, start with "BM", and MS DOS executables start with "MZ". By having a large lookup table of a selection of these magic numbers, it is quite easy to get an idea what kind of file is being examined, and thus what its MIME type should be.

To enable the MIME magic extension, you must either configure PHP with the switch ---==with-mime-magic (Unix), or enable the extension in your *php.ini* file (Windows). On Windows, you will also need to edit one other entry in your *php. ini* file—mime_magic.magicfile should be set to the directory where PHP was installed, with the subdirectory "*extras*". So if you installed PHP into *c:\php*, this would need to be set to *c:/php/extras/magic.mime*. On Unix, this extension relies on the file "magic," shipped with Apache. If PHP fails to find this for some reason, try setting the *php.ini* entry also.

Once you have the MIME magic extension working, you just need to pass a filename to mime_content_type( ) to get its MIME type as the return value, like this:

```
print mime_content_type("myfiles.zip");
print mime_content_type("poppy.jpg");
```

Given that you actually have those files, that script should output application/zip and image/jpeg.

Easier Mail Sending with PEAR::Mail

Using `PEAR::Mail`, we can write a simple email script like this:

```
include('Mail.php');
$mail = Mail::factory("mail");

$headers = array("From"=>"me@example.com", "Subject"=>"Test Mail");
$body = "This is a test!";
$mail->send("best@friend.com", $headers, $body);
```

The *Mail.php* file is the `PEAR::Mail` script, so it needs to be included before any `PEAR::Mail` functions are used. Line two creates a default instance of `PEAR::Mail`—the parameter `mail` is passed in so that `PEAR::Mail` will use PHP's `mail()` function to send the email. If you pass in `sendmail`, it will send direct via the sendmail program (Unix only).

Alternatively, you can pass in `smtp`, which lets you send a second parameter that is an array containing five keys: host, port, auth, username, and password. Each of these should have a value assigned to it: host should be the SMTP server to connect to, port should be the port number (defaults to 25), auth should be true if you want to authenticate with username and password (defaults to false), and username and password should be set if you want to authenticate. Unless you really want the extra power of connecting directly by hand, it's best to stick with `mail()`.

Line three sets up the headers to use in the email. This time, we need to provide the subject inside a header, as well as the sender information. Here you can use all the techniques we have looked at so far; for example, the From element could have the value `"Me <me@example.com>"` to have the email addresses pretty-printed.

Line four sets the body text to use in the email, which is standard enough. Line five is where the email is actually sent, and you will see that `send()` takes three parameters: address to send to, headers to use, and the content of the email. The first parameter can either be a string with each person's name separated by a comma, or it can be an array.

Sending Mixed-Type Messages with PEAR::Mail_Mime

There is a close cousin of `PEAR::Mail` called `PEAR::Mail_Mime` that has a number of features to make sending attachments very easy.

The first type of attachment we are going to send does not even look like an attachment on the surface. Previous scripts sent HTML mail by adding "Content-type: text/html" to the headers. The problem with this is that people without a HTML mail reader cannot read the message, because they will receive a huge chunk of HTML and will have to dig through it by hand to find the message.

The solution here is to send the message in both plain text and HTML-encoded format, by attaching the HTML message separately. When the email is received by mail readers, they will automatically choose the correct one to display.

When Not To Use HTML Mail

Mailing lists, particularly those attached to the open source community, take a very strong stance against HTML emails. The reason for this is that your message gets sent twice inside the one email—once in plain text and once in HTML. While this is fine for sending personal mails and mails to a controlled list who are willing to receive this, it does waste space in people's email inboxes and also wastes bandwidth for the list host.

We can do this using PEAR::Mail and PEAR::Mail_Mime, as the latter has a very simple way of attaching both a plain text mail and a HTML mail:

```
include('Mail.php');
include('Mail/mime.php');

$message = new Mail_mime();
$text = file_get_contents("mail_text.txt");
$html = file_get_contents("mail_html.html");

$message->setTXTBody($text);
$message->setHTMLBody($html);
$body = $message->get();
$extraheaders = array("From"=>"me@example.com", "Subject"=>"My Subject 7");
$headers = $message->headers($extraheaders);

$mail = Mail::factory("mail");
$mail->send("best@friend.com", $headers, $body);
```

Now the script includes both PEAR::Mail and PEAR::Mail_Mime, as it takes both classes to get the full email sent. Also, rather than handling our message as a text string, the message is an instance of Mail_mime. In the example, the message is stored in the $message variable. Next, both the plain text and HTML messages are retrieved from disk using file_get_contents() and stored in $text and $html, respectively.

Once we have the content loaded, we can put it into the message using the setTxtBody() and setHTMLBody() methods of our $message variable. These both take a string as their only parameter, so just pass in the appropriate return value from file_get_contents().

The body for the message, still stored in $body, now comes from the return value of $message->get(). This retrieves the full message text to send, and is a combination of the HTML and text information all encoded for sending over the Internet. If you want to see how the system works behind the scenes, echo out $body and have a look through.

With the line starting "$extraheaders = ", things begin to get more complicated. The PEAR::Mail->send() function takes its headers as an array and, to accommodate this, PEAR::Mail_Mime also returns its headers as an array. When sending complex emails, you need to have a special set of headers in there that tells the mail reader what to expect. So, once you have your content in place, you just call headers( ) to get the header information. As you still need to use the old headers (from, subject, etc.), you can pass into headers( ) an array of existing headers, and it will add these to the array it returns.

For example, calling headers( ) on its own might return something like this:

```
array(2) {
        ["MIME-Version"]=>
        string(3) "1.0"
        ["Content-Type"]=>
        string(64) "multipart/mixed;
        boundary="=_067d506611ba7a0da2b6106b54282d16""
}
```

However, passing our array $extraheaders in as the only parameter, headers( ) returns this:

```
array(4) {
        ["MIME-Version"]=>
        string(3) "1.0"
        ["From"]=>
        string(14) "me@example.com"
        ["Subject"]=>
        string(12) "My Subject 7"
        ["Content-Type"]=>
        string(64) "multipart/mixed;
        boundary="=_307c199ae5303dac356d5cf48c89fc7c""
}
```

The "boundary" string in Content-Type is randomized, so yours will be different.

Once we have the complete list of headers, this is passed into the send( ) call at the end, which is otherwise unchanged. Now when the mail is received, mail readers should automatically pick the best format for them and display it.

Sending Real Attachments

Using PEAR::Mail_Mime makes it very easy to add attachments to your messages. Add this line after the call to setHTMLBody( ):

```
$message->addAttachment("example.txt");
```

You will, of course, need to change *example.txt* to the name of a file in the same directory as the script. That's all it takes to add an attachment once you are using PEAR::Mail and PEAR::Mail_Mime.

If you run the script again, you should see the attachment has come through properly. However, there is one more thing you can do with PEAR::Mail_Mime and attachments, and that is to attach HTML images. These are essentially the same thing as attachments, except they are not shown as an attachment in most HTML-compliant mail readers; they are shown only in the message body. This makes better sense for HTML pictures, because it would likely confuse people to see a dozen pictures attached to the mail that aren't of importance.

To add a HTML picture, use the addHTMLImage( ) function. As with addAttachment( ), this takes the filename to attach as its only parameter. In order to use this picture, you need to edit the HTML file you are attaching and add the appropriate line, for example:

```
// in the PHP file:
$message->addHTMLImage("button.png");
// and in the HTML file:
<IMG SRC="button.png" />
```

Now when you send the mail, *button.png* should be sent along and displayed inside the message. In Outlook, this results in the first picture file being attached, and the second file being attached (but not listed as an attachment) and shown inside the message—perfect!

Curl

The cURL extension to PHP is designed to allow you to use a variety of web resources from within your PHP script. The name cURL (called Curl from now on, for ease of reading) stands either for "Client for URLs" or "Client URL Request Library," but the function is the same: it lets you use several Internet protocols using one uniform interface, most notably FTP, FTPS, HTTP, HTTPS, and LDAP.

The basic premise to using Curl is that there are four steps: initialize Curl, set your options, execute your query, and close Curl. Steps 1, 3, and 4 are easy, with the majority of the work taking place in step 2. Curl is highly configurable, and there are dozens of options you can set to make it do all sorts of weird and wonderful things. While this is undoubtedly a great advantage, it does make the learning curve a little high.

Installing Curl

If you're using Windows, you can enable Curl support by copying the files *libeay32.dll* and *ssleay32.dll* into your *c:\windows\system32* folder, then enabling the extension in your *php.ini* file. Look for the line ";extension=php_curl.dll" and take the semicolon off from the beginning.

If you're using Unix, you either have to install Curl support through your package manager, or you need to compile it from source. Compiling Curl support into your PHP takes two steps: installing the Curl development libraries on your machine (do this through your package manager), then recompiling PHP with the --with-curl switch in your configure line. As long as you have the *development* version of Curl installed, this should work fine.

Your First Curl Script

The first Curl script we are going to look at is the simplest Curl script that is actually useful: it will load a web page, retrieve the contents, then print it out. So, keeping the four-step Curl process in mind, this equates to:

1. Initialize Curl
2. Set URL we want to load

3. Retrieve and print the URL

4. Close Curl

Here is how that looks in PHP code:

```
$curl = curl_init();
curl_setopt($curl, CURLOPT_URL, "http://www.php.net");
curl_exec($curl);
curl_close($curl);
```

There is a one-to-one mapping of steps to lines of code there—step 1, "Initialize Curl," is done by line one, $curl = curl_init();, etc. There are four functions in that simple script, which are curl_init() for initializing the Curl library, curl_setopt() for setting Curl options, curl_exec() for executing the Curl query, and curl_close() for shutting down the Curl system. As mentioned already, of these four, only the second is complicated—the rest stay as you see them. Curl's functionality is, for the most part, largely manipulated through repeated calls to curl_setopt(), and it is this that distinguishes how Curl operates.

The curl_init() function returns a Curl instance for us to use in later functions, and you should always store it in a variable. It has just one optional parameter: if you pass a string into curl_init(), it will automatically use that string as the URL to work with. In the script above, we use curl_setopt() to do that for clarity, but it is all the same.

You need to provide three parameters to the curl_setopt() function: the Curl instance to use, a constant value for the setting you want to change, and the value you want to use for that setting. There are a huge number of constants you can use for settings, and many of these are listed shortly. In the example we use CURLOPT_URL, which is used to set the URL for Curl to work with, and so the working URL is set to the third parameter.

Calling curl_exec() means, "We're finished setting our options, go ahead and do it," and you need to pass precisely one parameter: the Curl resource to use. The return value of curl_exec() is true/false by default, although we will be changing that soon.

The final function, curl_close(), takes a Curl resource as its only parameter, closes the Curl session, then frees up the associated memory.

Trapping Return Values

To improve on the previous script, it would be good if we actually had some control over the output of our retrieved HTML page. As it is, calling curl_exec() retrieves and outputs the page, but it would be nice to have the retrieved content stored in a variable somewhere for use when we please. There are two ways of doing this. We already looked at how output buffering—and more specifically, the ob_get_contents() function—allows you to catch output before it gets to your visitor and manipulate it as you want. While this might seem like a good way to solve the problem, the second way is even better: Curl has an option specifically for it.

Passing `CURLOPT_RETURNTRANSFER` to `curl_setopt( )` as parameter two and 1 as parameter three will force Curl to not print out the results of its query. Instead, it will return the results as a string return value from `curl_exec( )` in place of the usual true/false. If there is an error, `false` will still be the return value from `curl_exec( )`.

Capturing the return value from `curl_exec( )` looks like this in code:

```
$curl = curl_init( )
curl_setopt($curl, CURLOPT_URL, "http://www.php.net");
curl_setopt($curl, CURLOPT_RETURNTRANSFER, 1);

$result = curl_exec($curl);
curl_close($curl);
print $result;
```

That script will output the same as the previous script, but having the web page stored in a variable before printing gives us more flexibility—we could have manipulated the data in any number of ways before printing.

Alternatively, you can have Curl save its output to a file using `CURLOPT_FILE`, which takes a file handle as its third parameter. This time the script looks like this:

```
$curl = curl_init( );
$fp = fopen("somefile.txt", "w");
curl_setopt ($curl, CURLOPT_URL, "http://www.php.net");
curl_setopt($curl, CURLOPT_FILE, $fp);

curl_exec ($curl);
curl_close ($curl);
```

Using FTP to Send Data

Our next basic script is going to switch from HTTP to FTP so you can see how little difference there is. This next script connects to the GNU FTP server and gets a listing of the root directory there:

```
$curl = curl_init( );
curl_setopt($curl, CURLOPT_URL,"ftp://ftp.gnu.org");
curl_setopt($curl, CURLOPT_RETURNTRANSFER, 1);

$result = curl_exec ($curl);
curl_close ($curl);
print $result;
```

We could have made that script more FTP-specific by providing some FTP options to the script. For example, the `CURLOPT_FTPLISTONLY` option will make PHP return much less information. If you tried the script without this, you would have received read/write information for each of the files and directories, when they were last changed, and so on. `CURLOPT_FTPLISTONLY` changes this so that you only get the file/directory names.

The second FTP option of interest is `CURLOPT_USERPWD`, which makes PHP use the third parameter to `curl_setopt( )` as the username and password used for logging in. As the third parameter contains both the username and the password, you need to split them using a colon, like this: username:password. When logging onto the GNU FTP server, we want to use the anonymous FTP account reserved for guests. In this situation, you generally provide your email address as the password.

With both of these changes implemented, the new script looks like this:

```
$curl = curl_init();
curl_setopt($curl, CURLOPT_URL,"ftp://ftp.gnu.org");
curl_setopt($curl, CURLOPT_FTPLISTONLY, 1);
curl_setopt($curl, CURLOPT_USERPWD, "anonymous:your@email.com");
curl_setopt($curl, CURLOPT_RETURNTRANSFER, 1);

$result = curl_exec ($curl);
curl_close ($curl);
print $result;
```

Try changing the username and password to random values, as this will cause the login to fail. If you run the script again, you will see nothing is printed out—no errors, no warnings; nothing. This is because Curl fails silently, and you need to request Curl's error message explicitly using curl_error( ). As with the other basic functions, this takes just a Curl session handler as its only parameter, and returns the error message from Curl. So, with this in mind, here is our final FTP script:

```
$curl = curl_init();
curl_setopt($curl, CURLOPT_URL,"ftp://ftp.gnu.org");
curl_setopt($curl, CURLOPT_FTPLISTONLY, 1);
curl_setopt($curl, CURLOPT_USERPWD, "foo:barbaz");
curl_setopt($curl, CURLOPT_RETURNTRANSFER, 1);

$result = curl_exec ($curl);
echo curl_error($curl);
curl_close ($curl);
print $result;
```

Note the bad username and password and the extra call to curl_error( ) after curl_exec( ). As long as the GNU team don't change their FTP permissions before you read this, running that script should output "Access denied: This FTP server is anonymous only."

Sending Data Over HTTP

The last Curl script we are going to look at, before we go over a list of the most popular options for curl_setopt( ), shows how to send data out to the Web as opposed to just retrieving it.

First, create the file *posttest.php* in your web server's public directory. Type into the file this code:

```
var_dump($_POST);
```

That simply takes the HTTP POST data that has come in and spits it back out again. Now, create this new script:

```
$curl = curl_init();
curl_setopt($curl, CURLOPT_URL,"http://localhost/posttest.php");
```

```
curl_setopt($curl, CURLOPT_POST, 1);
curl_setopt($curl, CURLOPT_POSTFIELDS, "Hello=World&Foo=Bar&Baz=Wombat");

curl_exec ($curl);
curl_close ($curl);
```

If you are running your *posttest.php* file on a remote server, change "localhost" to the server URL. There are two new values for curl_setopt( ) in there, but otherwise, the script should be clear.

The two new values, CURLOPT_POST and CURLOPT_POSTFIELDS, make our session prepare to send data over HTTP POST and assign the data to send, respectively. CURLOPT_POST just takes a 1 to enable to POST usage, but CURLOPT_POSTFIELDS needs a properly formatted data string to send. The string you use for the third parameter with CURLOPT_POSTFIELDS should be a list of the variables you want to send in the format Variable=Value, with each variable separated by an ampersand, &. Thus, the above script sends three variables over: Hello, Foo, and Baz, with values World, Bar, and Wombat, respectively.

Once the values are sent, Curl captures the response from the server and prints it out directly. Our *posttest.php* script dumps what it got through HTTP POST, so your output should be this:

```
array(3) {
        ["Hello"]=>
        string(5) "World"
        ["Foo"]=>
        string(3) "Bar"
        ["Baz"]=>
        string(6) "Wombat"
}
```

 The field data you pass in as the third parameter to CURLOPT_POSTFIELDS should not have any spaces or special characters. Spaces should be replaced with %20—you can have this and other special characters automatically replaced by using urlencode( ) on the string.

The Abridged List of Curl Options

There are a large number of options available for curl_setopt( )—far too many to cover here. However, of the full list, about half or so are used regularly and, therefore, deserve printing here. They are shown in Table 20-2.

Table 20-2. Curl options

If the 2nd parameter is...	3rd parameter should be...
CURLOPT_COOKIE	A string containing the contents of the cookie data to be set in the HTTP header.
CURLOPT_COOKIEFILE	A string containing the name of the file containing cookie data to be sent.
CURLOPT_CRLF	1 if you want Curl to convert Unix new lines to CR/LF new lines.

Table 20-2. Curl options (continued)

If the 2nd parameter is...	3rd parameter should be...
CURLOPT_FAILONERROR	1 if you want Curl to fail silently if the HTTP code returned is equal to or larger than 300.
CURLOPT_FILE	A string containing the filename where the output of your transfer should be placed. Default is straight to output (STDOUT).
CURLOPT_FOLLOWLOCATION	1 if you want Curl to follow all "Location: " headers that the server sends as part of the HTTP header. You can limit the number of "Location" headers to follow using CURLOPT_MAXREDIRS.
CURLOPT_FTPAPPEND	1 to have Curl append to the remote file instead of overwriting it.
CURLOPT_FTPLISTONLY	1 to list just the names of an FTP directory as opposed to more detailed information.
CURLOPT_HEADER	1 if you want the header to be included in the output. Usually for HTTP only.
CURLOPT_HTTPHEADER	An array of HTTP header fields to be set.
CURLOPT_INFILE	A string containing the filename where the input of your transfer comes from.
CURLOPT_INFILESIZE	The size of the file being uploaded to a remote site.
CURLOPT_MAXREDIRS	The number of "Location:" headers Curl should follow before erroring out. This option is only appropriate if CURLOPT_FOLLOWLOCATION is used also.
CURLOPT_NOBODY	1 to tell Curl not to include the body part in the output. For HTTP(S) servers, this is equivalent to a HEAD request—only the headers will be returned.
CURLOPT_POST	1 if you want Curl to do a regular HTTP POST.
CURLOPT_POSTFIELDS	A string containing the data to post in the HTTP "POST" operation.
CURLOPT_REFERER	A string containing the "referer" header to be used in an HTTP request. This is only necessary if the remote server relies on this value.
CURLOPT_RESUME_FROM	A number equal to the offset, in bytes, that you want your transfer to start from.
CURLOPT_RETURNTRANSFER	1 if you want Curl to return the transfer data instead of printing it out directly.
CURLOPT_STDERR	A string containing the filename to write errors to instead of normal output.
CURLOPT_TIMEOUT	A number equal to the maximum time in seconds that Curl functions can take.
CURLOPT_UPLOAD	1 if you want PHP to prepare for a file upload.
CURLOPT_URL	A string containing the URL you want Curl to fetch.
CURLOPT_USERPWD	A string formatted in the username:password manner, for Curl to give to the remote server if requested.
CURLOPT_USERAGENT	A string containing the "user-agent" header to be used in a HTTP request.
CURLOPT_VERBOSE	1 if you want Curl to give detailed reports about everything that is happening.
CURLOPT_WRITEHEADER	A string containing the filename to write the header part of the output into.

There is a large selection available online at *http://curl.haxx.se/libcurl/c/curl_easy_setopt.html*.

Debugging Curl

Because it works with so many different network protocols, it is very easy to make mistakes when using Curl. You can speed up your debugging efforts by using CURLOPT_VERBOSE to have Curl output detailed information about its actions.

To give you an idea of how CURLOPT_VERBOSE affects the output of your script, here is a script we used earlier, rewritten to add CURLOPT_VERBOSE:

```
$curl = curl_init( );
curl_setopt ($curl, CURLOPT_URL, "http://www.php.net");
curl_setopt($curl, CURLOPT_RETURNTRANSFER, 1);
curl_setopt($curl, CURLOPT_VERBOSE, 1);

curl_exec ($curl);
curl_close ($curl);
```

Note that CURLOPT_RETURNTRANSFER was used but the output from curl_exec( ) was ignored—this is because the extra data provided by CURLOPT_VERBOSE is actually sent straight to the browser, irrespective of CURLOPT_RETURNTRANSFER. By ignoring the output of curl_exec( ), the script will only print out the debugging information. Here is what you should get:

```
* About to connect( ) to www.php.net:80
* Connected to php.net (64.246.30.37) port 80
> GET / HTTP/1.1 Host: www.php.net Pragma: no-cache Accept: image/gif,
        image/x-xbitmap, image/jpeg, image/pjpeg, */*
< HTTP/1.1 200 OK < Date: Fri, 06 Feb 2004 22:13:29 GMT
< Server: Apache/1.3.26 (Unix) mod_gzip/1.3.26.1a PHP/4.3.3-dev
< X-Powered-By: PHP/4.3.3-dev
< Last-Modified: Fri, 06 Feb 2004 22:14:38 GMT
< Content-language: en
< Set-Cookie: COUNTRY=GBR%2C213.152.58.41; expires=Fri,
        13-Feb-04 22:13:29 GMT; path=/; domain=.php.net
< Connection: close
< Transfer-Encoding: chunked
< Content-Type: text/html;charset=ISO-8859-1
* Closing connection #0
```

Note that lines that start with > are headers sent by Curl, lines that start with < are headers sent by the responding server, and lines that start with * are Curl informational messages.

21

Distributing Your Code

Once you have your ideal scripts written, very often you will want to give them to other people. Perhaps you have written code to generate graphs or predict the weather, or perhaps you have just written Yet Another Forum (YAF)—it does not matter what you write, because there are few feelings quite as nice as watching people take your code and use it.

Cross-Platform Code 1: Loading Extensions

The dl( ) function lets you load PHP extensions at runtime, which is a simple way of making sure a particular extension is available to your script. Of course, it is best to have the extension loaded in the *php.ini* file, because it's a lot faster; however, that is not always possible.

The problem with dl( ) is that it requires the filename and extension of the extension you want to include, and extensions differ across platforms. PHP extensions on Windows start with php_ and end with .dll, whereas PHP extensions on Unix just end with .so. For example, the IMAP extension is called *php_imap.dll* on Windows, and just *imap.so* on Unix. The dl( ) function needs that full filename, so we need to add some special code to check which to load.

Luckily, PHP has a special constant value, PHP_SHLIB_SUFFIX, which contains the file extension of PHP extensions on that platform. As such, the code below works around the problems of dl( ) by choosing how to load the extension based upon the platform:

```
function useext($extension) {
        if (!extension_loaded('$extension')) {
                if (PHP_SHLIB_SUFFIX == 'dll') {
                        dl('php_$extension.dll');
                } else {
                        dl('$extension.' . PHP_SHLIB_SUFFIX);
                }
```

```
        }
    }

    useext("imap");
```

The non-Windows code uses `PHP_SHLIB_SUFFIX` for platforms that do not use `.so` as their extension, such as NetWare, which uses *.nlm*.

Cross-Platform Code 2: Using Extensions

In order to be most flexible, PHP offers several extensions that are not cross-platform. For example, the COM extension is only available for Windows, and the process control extension is only available for Unix. This is a necessary evil: it is often better to have something that works for just a few people than to have nothing at all.

If you need to make use of OS-specific extensions, you have two options: inform your users that they need to use a specific OS, or edit your source code to forcefully bail out if you find it being run on the wrong OS. The first option relies on people actually reading your documentation before using the script, but the second option means that each script needs to do unnecessary work to make sure the right OS is being used.

Your best bet is usually to add text everywhere you have the chance: documentation, *readme*, FAQ, on the web site, etc., and leave the script with no checking. When it does not work because a specific extension does not exist, people will look for the answer and hopefully find it wherever you put it.

Cross-Platform Code 3: Path and Line Separators

Each OS has a different way of representing path and line separators for files. Unix and modern Mac OS versions use / as a path separator and \n as a line separator, whereas Windows uses \ or / as a path separator and \r\n as a line separator. Just to make things even more confusing, some old Mac OS versions use \r as a line separator and : as a path separator, so all three are different!

You can make your life easier by using forward slashes (/) everywhere, because Windows accepts both \ and / as path separators. If you are able to refrain from using OS-specific path names like *c:/home/website/index.php*, then do—very often, just */home/website/index.php* will work just fine everywhere.

Line separators are slightly trickier and, if you don't have PHP 5.0.2 or higher, the easiest way to handle them is to put a few lines of code into your shared code library that checks the OS and stores the appropriate line end character in a variable—you can then reuse that variable throughout your other scripts. If you *do* have PHP 5.0.2 or higher, the constant `PHP_EOL` is available to you and represents the appropriate newline character for the current OS.

Using the OS-specific newline character, e.g., \r\n on Windows, is not a smart move if you want the generated files to be portable to other platforms. This is because a script running on Windows will load and save files with \r\n as line ends, whereas the same script on Unix will use just \n. So, if you run a script on Windows that saves a file, it will use \r\n as line ends, but if you try to load that using a Unix machine, it will just look for \n. If you want the files to be portable, always use a consistent newline character. If you're not sure what newline type a file is using, try Sean Burke's "whatnewline" utility from *http://interglacial.com/~sburke/pub/whatnewline*.

Cross-Platform Code 4: Coping with php.ini Differences

If you have made a lot of changes to your *php.ini* file, or indeed *any* changes from the default *php.ini* file, it is possible that scripts you write will not work elsewhere. There are three common culprits: extensions, register_globals, and safe mode.

If you have enabled an extension that isn't enabled in someone else's *php.ini* file, people deploying your script will get lots of errors about undefined functions. The best way around this, other than adding warnings about required extensions in your *readme* file, is to have a *checkconfig.php* file that runs checks on the current configuration to make sure it has the correct extensions available.

Register_globals is a setting that, when enabled, makes PHP put all user-submitted variables into the global scope automatically—not very secure, as you can imagine. The problem is that this setting was enabled by default in old versions of PHP 4, which means that a lot of people still have this setting enabled. If someone gives you a script that requires register_globals being enabled, it is probably best that you don't use it—it's just not worth the security risk. Similarly, you should avoid writing scripts that rely on register_globals, even if you choose to enable it locally—most people out there leave it disabled, as recommended.

The third problem you are likely to encounter when people use your scripts elsewhere is safe mode. With safe mode enabled, there is very little you can do to ensure your script will work without flaw, because administrators can disable whichever functions they deem unsafe—even very basic functions. If you think there might be problems with your script (reading files is the most common problem), your best bet is to provide a list of what your script requires with your documentation. That way, people stuck with safe mode enabled can at least see what the problem is, and maybe even ask their ISP to relax their restrictions a little.

Cross-Platform Code 5: Checking the PHP Version with phpversion( ) and version_compare( )

If you only want your script to work on certain versions of PHP, there are two functions just for you: phpversion( ) and version_compare( ). The first takes no parameters, and returns a string containing the version number of the current version of PHP. The second takes two parameters, which should be two version strings of the type returned by phpversion( ), and returns -1 if the first version is lower than the second, 0 if they are the same, and 1 if the first version is higher than the second.

```
$CurrentVer = phpversion( )
print "Current PHP version: $CurrentVer\n";

switch (version_compare($CurrentVer, '5.0.0') {
        case -1:
                print "You're running an old PHP: $CurrentVer\n";
                break;
        case 0:
                print "You are running PHP 5\n";
                break;
        case 1:
                print "You are running a version of PHP after 5.0.0:
$CurrentVer\n";
}
```

That should output "Current PHP version: <your version here>", then either "You are running PHP 5" or "You are running a version of PHP after 5.0.0: <your version here>". Internally, this is actually a very advanced function, as it automatically distinguishes between development code, alpha, beta, and release candidate versions, and it allows you to check an arbitrary amount of version numbers. For example: 5.0.0b1 < 5.0.0RC1-dev < 5.0.0RC1 < 5.0.0RC2 < 5.0.0 < 5.0.0.0.0.0.1 < 5.0.1, etc.

What's more, there's nothing to say you have to use the PHP version for your checks. For example, if you are distributing your PHP application and want to check that each file is the correct version, you can compare your own version strings using this function as long as they match the same format as PHP.

Instead of using the function phpversion( ), you can also use the constant PHP_VERSION. Many people still prefer to use the function, however, as its behavior is clearer—the choice is yours, as they both do exactly the same thing.

22

Debugging

> *Debugging is twice as hard as writing the code in the first place. Therefore, if you write the code as cleverly as possible, you are, by definition, not smart enough to debug it.*

> —Brian W. Kernighan

No matter how good a programmer you are, you will at some point find that there are at least one or two errors in your code—sometimes because you hit the wrong key while typing, other times because you misunderstood how a function worked, and sometimes even because you were coding at 5 a.m. It is important to understand the arsenal that PHP puts at your disposal.

The Most Basic Debugging Technique

If you are experiencing a problem with your script, the time-honored way to figure out what's going on is to sprinkle your code with lots of print statements. This is a technique that few people will admit they use, but I can assure you it is widespread—and not just in the PHP programming world! Consider this following script:

```
$foo = "bar";
$wombat = somefunc($foo);
print "After somefunc( )\n";
$wombat2 = somefun2($wombat);
print "After somefunc2( )\n";
```

If we found that somefunc2( ) was causing a problem that caused PHP to silently exit the script, we would see the output "After somefunc( )", but not "After somefunc2( )", which points to the problem function.

This method has benefits: it is easy to use, and will generally find the problem through trial and error. The downsides are clear, though: you need to edit your script quite heavily to make use of the print statements, then you need to re-edit it once you have found the problem to take the print statements back out. Furthermore, the technique is a relatively slow way of finding problems, as you literally need to keep placing more and more print statements until you find the problem.

Many people combine this with the use of var_dump( ) to inspect variable contents at various points in their script. If you do not have a good debugger (such as the one built into the Zend Studio IDE), this is the only way you will find out what your variables contain; however, you may find it easier to use the function debug_zval_dump( ), which takes one parameter (the variable to dump information about) and prints out even more detailed information than var_dump( ). The key advantage of debug_zval_dump( ) is that it prints out the refcount value of variables sent into it—that is, how many times each variable is being used. If you have trouble getting references to work, using debug_zval_dump( ) is a smart move.

For more advanced debug output, use the debug_backtrace( ) function discussed in the section "Backtracing Your Code" later in this chapter.

Making Assertions

The assert( ) function is a clever one that works along the same lines as our print statements, but it only works if a certain condition is not matched. Essentially, assert( ) is used to say "This statement must be true—if it isn't, please tell me." For example:

```
print "Stage 1\n";
assert(1 == 1);
print "Stage 2\n";
assert(1 == 2);
print "Stage 3\n";
```

Here we have two assert( )s, with the first call asserting that one must be equal to one, and the second call asserting that one must be equal to two. As it is impossible to redefine constants like 1 and 2, the first assert( ) will always evaluate to true, and the second will always evaluate to false. Here is the output from the script:

```
Stage 1
Stage 2
Warning: assert( ) [http://www.php.net/function.assert]: Assertion failed
        in /home/paul/sandbox/php/assert.php on line 5
Stage 3
```

The first assert( ) is not seen in the output at all because it evaluated to true, whereas the second assert( ) evaluated to false, so we get a warning about an assertion failure. However, script execution carries on so that we see "Stage 3" after the assertion failure warning. As long as assertions evaluate to true, they have no effect on the running of the script, which means you can insert them for debugging purposes and not have to worry about taking them out once you are finished debugging.

If you are worried about your assertions slowing execution down, which, although the speed hit will be minimal, is still a valid concern, you can disable execution of assert( ) by using the assert_options( ) function or by setting assert.active to Off in your *php.ini* file. If you want to use assert_options( ), it takes two parameters: the option to set and the value you wish to set it to.

Table 22-1 shows the list of options you can use for the first parameter of assert_options( ):

Table 22-1. First parameter of assert_options()

Parameter	Default	Description
ASSERT_ACTIVE	On	Enables evaluation of assert( ) calls
ASSERT_WARNING	On	Makes PHP output a warning for each failed assertion
ASSERT_BAIL	Off	Forces PHP to end script execution on a failed assertion
ASSERT_QUIET_EVAL	Off	Ignores errors in assert( ) calls
ASSERT_CALLBACK	Off	Names user function to call on a failed assertion

To disable assert( ) calls, use this line of code:

```
assert_options(ASSERT_ACTIVE, 0);
```

And to make PHP end script execution rather than just issue a warning, we can use this line of code:

```
assert_options(ASSERT_BAIL, 1);
```

Note that all of these options can be set in your *php.ini* file so that they are always in effect. The options to change there are assert.active, assert.warning, assert.bail, assert.quiet_eval, and assert_callback.

ASSERT_CALLBACK is a useful option, as it allows you to write an error handler for when your code fails an assertion. It takes the string name of a function to execute when assertions fail, and the function you define must take three parameters: one to hold the file where the assertion occurred, one to hold the line, and one to hold the expression. Using all three together in your callback function allows you to generate meaningful error messages that you can debug. For example:

```
function assert_failed($file, $line, $expr) {
        print "Assertion failed in $file on line $line: $expr\n";
}

assert_options(ASSERT_CALLBACK, 'assert_failed');
assert_options(ASSERT_WARNING, 0);

$foo = 10;
$bar = 11;
assert($foo > $bar);
```

That example shows a callback function defined that takes $file, $line, and $expr for the three variables passed in, and outputs them whenever an assertion fails. To make that result actually happen, assert_options( ) is called to let PHP know that assert_failed( ) is the correct function to use as a callback—note that there are no brackets after the string being passed into assert_options( ).

ASSERT_WARNING is also disabled, which stops PHP from outputting a warning as well as running the callback function. Finally, two variables are set, and are used as part of a call to assert( )—as you can see, $foo is quite clearly not greater than $bar, which means the assertion will fail and call our callback. So, the output from the script is: Assertion failed in /home/paul/tmp/blerg.php on line 9: $foo > $bar.

You can assert( ) any statement you like, as long as it will return either true or false. This makes the assert( ) function incredibly powerful—even more so when you think that you can just turn off assertion execution to make the code run at full speed.

Here are some more examples of assert( )able things:

```
assert($savings >= $salary / 10);
assert($myarray == array("apone", "burke", "hicks"));
assert(preg_match("/wild sheep chase/", $book));
```

Triggering Your Own Errors

It is a fairly common task to want to bring up an error message similar to PHP's when your code is being used incorrectly, and this is what trigger_error( ) does. While it is not often necessary to throw up error messages in your code when only you use it, it becomes much more important when your code is being distributed to other programmers—it is often important to make sure they are using your code in the correct way, and to force output of a certain type of error if they are doing something unexpected.

The trigger_error( ) function takes two parameters: the string output message to be printed out as the error and an optional second parameter of the type of error you want to issue. The first parameter can be whatever you wish, "Function X called with wrong parameter type" or "Objects of class MyElephant can only be gray"—it is just a string that is sent directly to users who find themselves on the receiving end of your error. The second parameter affects how the script should react to the error. If you do not provide the second parameter, the default is a user notice—a minor message that many people might not even see. However, you can select from any of the user error types as the second parameter, which can allow you to halt execution of the script if your error is triggered.

Using trigger_error( ) is better than just printing an error message and exiting the script, because trigger_error( ) takes the form of PHP's default errors—it will automatically print out the filename and line number where the error occurred. Furthermore, it will uses PHP's default settings, which allow people to ignore certain classes of errors if they wish. That said, most people tend to write their own error-handling code, as it allows them more control over the content and style—keep use of trigger_error( ) for errors that other programmers must fix when they use your code.

Testing with php_check_syntax( )

Because PHP is an interpreted language, you can run tests on individual scripts simply by executing them—any execution errors will be reported back immediately. If you would rather not execute your scripts again and again, use the "lint" mode of the PHP CLI SAPI by typing **php -l yourscript.php** from the command prompt. Users on Windows will need to change directory to where they placed *php.exe* (or have it in their PATH variable). Note that linting your script only returns syntax errors—execution errors, such as treating an integer variable as an array, are not reported.

You can also lint your script from within PHP by using the php_check_syntax( ) function, which takes a filename as its first parameter and an optional variable passed by reference as its second parameter. If the script has no problem, true will be returned and the variable will be empty. If the script does have problems, false will be returned and the variable will be filled with the first error message that was encountered. This is a lot slower than using the CLI directly, as you have to work through each error one at a time; however, it is the only option if you do not have the CLI on hand and don't want to execute the script.

As well as linting and running your scripts, you should also try going through entire scenarios as part of your tests. If you have the resources, a member of your team should spend some time creating test cases for each part of your system that involves complete, standalone transactions that can be performed, such as "Adding a user," "Editing a message," etc. For each major test build that is made, a team of testers (depending on the size of your project) can simply work through the tests, checking them off as they go.

Source Highlighting

An easy way to spot very basic errors is to use a text editor that has syntax highlighting capabilities. Editors like these will recognize that you are editing a PHP script and automatically highlight the text in such a way as to make each element stand out in the source code. We discussed syntax highlighting earlier, but what I want to mention here is that PHP has built-in support for syntax highlighting itself.

The two key functions here are highlight_file( ) and highlight_string( ), although there is also a function show_source( ) that is an alias to highlight_file( ). This takes a filename as its parameter and outputs that file to the screen, with all keywords, strings, numbers, and functions highlighted in various colors, as shown in Figure 22-1. The highlight_string( ) function is almost identical, except it takes a string as its parameter.

 Many people use these two functions to allow visitors to their site to view the source code for their pages. However, it is important to remember that doing so potentially reveals secret information, such as database passwords.

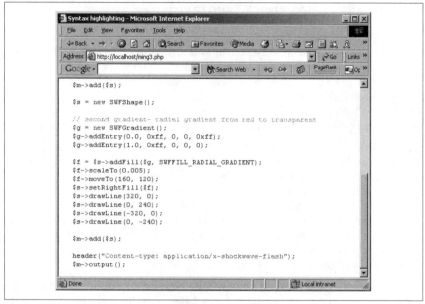

Figure 22-1. PHP has its own syntax highlighting system that provides a little help for debugging, but is still no replacement for full syntax highlighting

This example shows how to highlight a string of code and also a file:

```
$mystr = '<?php $foo = "bar"; $bar = array("baz", "wombat", "foo");
    var_dump($foo); ?>';

highlight_string($mystr);
file_put_contents("highlighter.php", $mystr);
highlight_file("highlighter.php");
```

As you can see, that passes the string into highlight_string( ), then saves it out as *highlighter.php* and passes that filename into highlight_file( ) to print out again. Both highlight_string( ) and highlight_file( ) can take a second parameter, which, if set to true, will make these functions return the highlighted HTML rather than just print it out directly, giving you more control over it.

Handling MySQL Errors

When it comes to handling SQL querying problems, these are often easier to fix than pure PHP problems because you can narrow down the position of the error very easily, then analyze the faulty SQL line to spot the problem.

Always check that your code is actually correct. Use the MySQL monitor to try your queries out to make sure they do what you think they should do, as it will show you your results in an easy-to-read manner and will also give you meaningful error messages if you have slipped up along the way.

Also, remember that mysql_query( ) will return false if the query failed to execute, which means you can test its return value to see whether your SQL statement is faulty. You should be wary of trying to wrap mysql_query( ) up inside another function call, because if it returns false due to a bad query, the chances are the parent function will error out. For example:

```
extract(mysql_fetch_assoc(mysql_query("SELECT Blah FROM Blah
    WHERE Blah = $Blah;")));
```

Yes, it is perfectly valid SQL and under ideal conditions should work, but what if $Blah is unset? Another possibility is that $Blah might end up being a string—there are no quotes around $Blah, which means that if $Blah is a string, MySQL will consider it to be a field name, and the query will likely fail.

If the query does fail for some reason, mysql_fetch_assoc( ) will fail and output errors, then extract( ) will fail and output errors, causing a mass of error messages that hinder more than help. This code is much better:

```
$result = mysql_query("SELECT Blah FROM Blah WHERE Blah = $Blah;");
if ($result) {
        extract(mysql_fetch_assoc($result));
}
```

That isn't to say that having all three functions on one line is incorrect. However, you should be very sure of any SQL statement you use in that manner, because any mistakes will be very visible to your users.

A helpful function for debugging MySQL queries is mysql_error( ), which returns any MySQL errors from the last function call. Each time you call a new MySQL function, the value mysql_error( ) is wiped, which means you need to call mysql_error( ) as soon as your suspect mysql_query( ) has been called; otherwise, it might be wiped over by subsequent queries from your connection.

Exception Handling

Although solving all the bugs and potential errors in your code sounds like a nice idea, it's not likely for anything beyond "Hello, world" scripts. The main reason for this is because it's hard to predict how your code will operate in all scenarios, so you can't write code to handle it all.

The solution here is to write exception handlers, which allow you to explicitly state what PHP should do if there's a problem in a block of code. Exceptions are interesting because they all come from the root class Exception, but you can extend that with your own custom exceptions to trap specific errors.

As exceptions are new in PHP 5, they are primarily for userland code (PHP code you write) as opposed to internal PHP functions. As new versions of PHP get released, more and more internal code should be switched over to use exceptions so that you have a chance to handle errors smoothly, but this is a gradual process.

The basic exception handler uses try/catch blocks to encase blocks of code in a virtual safety barrier that you can break out of by throwing exceptions. Here's a full try/catch statement to give you an idea of how it works:

```
try {
        $num = 10;
        if ($num < 20) {
```

```
            throw new Exception("D'oh!");
    }
    $foo = "bar";
} catch(Exception $exception) {
        print "Except!\n";
}
```

In that example, PHP enters the try block and starts executing code. When it hits the line "throw new Exception", it will stop executing the try block and jump to the catch block. Here it checks each exception option against the list in catch and executes the appropriate code. Once PHP has left the try block, it will not return to it, which means that the line $foo = "bar" will never be executed.

The Exception class in there is necessary because PHP decides which catch block to execute by looking for the same class type as was thrown. Well, that's the "easy" way of looking at it: what *actually* happens is that PHP searches each catch block, using what is essentially an instanceof check on it. This means that if the exception thrown is of the same class as the exception in the class block, or if it is a descendant of that class, PHP will execute that catch block.

The $exception variable after the Exception class is there because PHP actually hands you an instance of that Exception class, set up with information about the exception you've just experienced. As all exceptions extend from the base class Exception, you get a basic level of functionality no matter what you do. What's more, most of the functions in the Exception class are marked final, meaning they can't be overridden in inherited classes, again guaranteeing a set level of functionality. For example, you can call $exception->getMessage() to see why the exception was thrown (the "D'oh!" part in the throw() statement), you can call getFile() to see where the exception was called, etc.

This example demonstrates how PHP handles multiple catch blocks:

```
class ExceptFoo extends Exception { }
class ExceptBar extends ExceptFoo { }

try {
        $foo = "bar";
        throw new ExceptFoo("Baaaaad PHP!");
        $bar = "baz";
} catch (ExceptFoo $exception) {
        echo "Caught ExceptFoo\n";
        echo "Message: {$exception->getMessage()}\n";
} catch (ExceptBar $exception) {
        echo "Caught ExceptBar\n";
        echo "Message: {$exception->getMessage()}\n";
} catch (Exception $exception) {
        echo "Caught Exception\n";
        echo "Message: {$exception->getMessage()}\n";
}
```

That will output the following:

```
Caught ExceptFoo
Message: Baaaaad PHP!
```

So we throw an ExceptionFoo, and PHP jumps to the ExceptionFoo catch block. However, the output remains the same even if we change the throw( ) line to this:

```
throw new ExceptBar("Baaaaad PHP!");
```

Why? Because PHP matches the first catch block handling the exception's class or any parent class of it. Because ExceptionBar inherits from ExceptionFoo, and the ExceptionFoo catch block comes before the ExceptionBar catch block, the ExceptionFoo catch block gets called first.

You can rewrite the code to this:

```
class ExceptFoo extends Exception { }
class ExceptBar extends ExceptFoo { }

try {
        $foo = "bar";
        throw new ExceptBar("Baaaaad PHP!");
        $bar = "baz";
} catch (ExceptBar $exception) {
        echo "Caught ExceptBar\n";
        echo "Message: {$exception->getMessage( )}\n";
} catch (ExceptFoo $exception) {
        echo "Caught ExceptFoo\n";
        echo "Message: {$exception->getMessage( )}\n";
} catch (Exception $exception) {
        echo "Caught Exception\n";
        echo "Message: {$exception->getMessage( )}\n";
}
```

This time, we have the exception classes in descending order by their inheritance, so the script works as we would expect.

If you want to, you can throw an exception inside a catch block—either a new exception or just the old exception again. This is called rethrowing the exception, and is commonly used if you have ascertained that you cannot (or do not want to) handle the exception there.

Using this form of debugging allows you to have debugging code next to the code you think has a chance of breaking, which is much easier to understand than having one global error-handling function. Whenever you have code that you know might break and want to include code to handle the problem in a smooth manner, try/catch is the easiest and cleanest way of debugging.

Backtracing Your Code

Debugging complex scripts can sometimes be a nightmare because objects call functions, which call other objects and other functions, and so on—you end up with a nest of calls that make tracing the problem difficult. To make your life easier, you can use the function debug_backtrace( ) to tell you about the chain of events that led up to the call to debug_backtrace( ).

For example:

```
function A($param1, $param2) {
        B("bar", "baz");
}

function B($param1, $param2) {
        C("baz", "wom");
}

function C($param1, $param2) {
        var_dump(debug_backtrace());
}

A("foo", "bar");
```

That script calls function A( ), which calls B( ), which calls C( ), which var_dump( )s the output from debug_backtrace( ). Now, what debug_backtrace( ) will return is an array of the steps that occurred in getting to it, so that script should output the following:

```
array(3) {
        [0]=>
        array(4) {
                ["file"]=>
                string(20) "C:\php\backtrace.php"
                ["line"]=>
                int(6)
                ["function"]=>
                string(1) "C"
                ["args"]=>
                array(2) {
                        [0]=>
                        &string(3) "baz"
                        [1]=>
                        &string(3) "wom"
                }
        }
        [1]=>
        array(4) {
                ["file"]=>
                string(20) "C:\php\backtrace.php"
                ["line"]=>
                int(3)
                ["function"]=>
                string(1) "B"
                ["args"]=>
                array(2) {
                        [0]=>
                        &string(3) "bar"
                        [1]=>
                        &string(3) "baz"
                }
        }
        [2]=>
```

```
array(4) {
        ["file"]=>
        string(20) "C:\php\backtrace.php"
        ["line"]=>
        int(11)
        ["function"]=>
        string(1) "A"
        ["args"]=>
        array(2) {
                [0]=>
                &string(3) "foo"
                [1]=>
                &string(3) "bar"
        }
    }
}
```

Start from the first element, 0, and work your way down in order to visually back-trace the steps performed before debug_backtrace( ) was called. Each element in the return from debug_backtrace( ) is an array of values that together form a "step"—here is how it works:

1. The first element (step) has a "file" of *c:\php\backtrace.php*, which means this is where the code was at this step. "Line" is set to 6, and "function" is set to "C", which means that on line 6 of *c:\php\backtrace.php*, C( ) was called. There is also an "args" array containing "baz" and "wom"—the two parameters passed into C( ).

2. The second element tells us that B( ) was called on line three of the same script, with the parameters "bar" and "baz".

3. The third element tells us that A( ) was called on line 11 of the same script, with "foo" and "bar" passed in.

That is the complete contents of the array, but you can see it has told us exactly how PHP got to where it was, including all the parameters passed into functions. This is invaluable for tracking down bugs, particularly when bad parameters are being passed into functions. Having the "file" element in each step also means that it works very nicely across multiple files, so even the most complicated scripts are brought to heel with debug_backtrace( ).

Custom Error Handlers

While assert( ) is a good function to make extensive use of, it only catches errors you were expecting. While that might sound obvious, it is quite crucial—if an error you have not planned for occurs, how are you to find out about it? Never fear—there are two functions available to make your life much easier: set_error_handler( ) and error_log( ).

The set_error_handler( ) function takes the name of a user callback function as its only parameter, and it notifies PHP that any errors should use that function to handle them. The user function needs to accept a minimum of two parameters, but in practice you will likely want to accept four. These are, in order, the error number that occurred, the string version of the error, the file the error occurred in, and the line of the error. For example:

```
function on_error($num, $str, $file, $line) {
        print "Encountered error $num in $file, line $line: $str\n";
}

set_error_handler("on_error");
print $foo;
```

On line four, we define the general error handler to be the on_error( ) function, then call print $foo, which, as $foo does not exist, is an error and will result in on_error( ) being called. The definition of on_error( ) is as described: it takes four parameters, then prints them out to the screen in a nicely formatted manner.

There is a second parameter to set_error_handler( ) that lets you choose what errors should trigger the error handler, and it works like the error_reporting directive in *php.ini*. However, you can only have one active error handler at any time, not one for each level of error. This code should explain it:

```
function func_notice($num, $str, $file, $line) {
        print "Encountered notice $num in $file, line $line: $str\n";
}

function func_error($num, $str, $file, $line) {
        print "Encountered error $num in $file, line $line: $str\n";
}

set_error_handler("func_notice", E_NOTICE);
set_error_handler("func_error", E_ERROR);

echo $foo;
```

As before, the error is that $foo isn't set; that should output a notice. On the surface, that looks as though we're assigning func_notice( ) to handle E_NOTICE-level messages and also assigning func_error( ) to handle E_ERROR-level messages. However, because we can only have one error handler at any one time, the second call to set_error_handler( ) replaces the first with one that only listens to E_ERROR messages.

The restore_error_handler( ) takes no parameters and returns no meaningful value, but it restores the previous error handler. There is only really one potential slip-up here, and that's when you accidentally call set_error_handler( ) twice with the same function name. If you've done this, calling restore_error_handler( ) won't make any change on the surface. Internally, it will be using the previous error handler, but as that happens to be same as the other handler, it will appear the same.

It's important to note that set_error_handler( ) does stack up previous error handlers neatly, as this script demonstrates:

```
function func_notice($num, $str, $file, $line) {
        print "Encountered notice $num in $file, line $line: $str\n";
}
```

```
set_error_handler("func_notice", E_NOTICE);
set_error_handler("func_notice", E_NOTICE);
set_error_handler("func_notice", E_NOTICE);

echo $foo;
set_error_handler("func_notice", E_NOTICE);
echo $foo;
restore_error_handler( );
echo $foo;
restore_error_handler( );
echo $foo;
restore_error_handler( );
echo $foo;
restore_error_handler( );
echo $foo;
```

That will only really make sense once you've seen the output:

```
Encountered notice 8 in C:\home\error.php, line 14: Undefined variable:  foo
Encountered notice 8 in C:\home\error.php, line 18: Undefined variable:  foo
Encountered notice 8 in C:\home\error.php, line 22: Undefined variable:  foo
Encountered notice 8 in C:\home\error.php, line 26: Undefined variable:  foo
Encountered notice 8 in C:\home\error.php, line 30: Undefined variable:  foo
PHP Notice:  Undefined variable:  foo in C:\home\error.php on line 34
```

So you can see that we need to call restore_error_handler( ) enough times to fully unwind the stack of error handlers, until eventually the default PHP error handler has control and spits out the usual message.

The error_log( ) function is a great way to get error data saved to disk (or elsewhere) in just one call. At its simplest, you can pass error_log( ) just one parameter—an error message—and it will log it for you. To get that, edit your *php.ini* file and set the error_log directive to a location Apache/PHP can write to. For example, */var/log/php_error* would be good for Unix, and *c:/windows/php_error.log* is good for Windows.

With that done (don't forget to restart Apache, if necessary), we can go ahead and use error_log( ) in its most simple form:

```
if (!mysql_connect("localhost", "baduser", "badpass")) {
        error_log("Failed to connect to MySQL!");
}
```

That will output data to our error log. It should also output actual execution errors into the file—something like Warning: mysql_connect( ): Access denied for user: 'baduser@localhost' (Using password: YES) in C:\home\log.php on line 2. If not, enable log_errors in your *php.ini* file. PHP automatically inserts line breaks for you after each error.

The next two parameters really work in tandem, so I'll cover them together. The second parameter—oddly—takes an integer to determine where your error should be sent: 0 sends it to the error_log (the default), 1 sends it by email using the mail( ) function, 3 is unused, and 4 saves it to a file of your choice.

The third parameter qualifies the second in that if you set the second parameter to be 1 (send error by email), the third parameter should be the email address of the recipient. Similarly, if you set the second parameter to be 3, parameter three should be the filename to save the error to. There is a slight twist to saving to a custom file, because PHP will not do any of the nice formatting for you like it does in the default error log. For example, it won't insert line breaks for you, and neither will it insert timestamps automatically—you need to insert all that yourself. This works out for the best, as it means you have complete control over your custom error log.

Here's a Windows example:

```
if (!mysql_connect("localhost", "baduser", "badpass")) {
        error_log("Failed to connect to MySQL!\r\n", 3, "c:/myerror.txt");
}
```

Custom Exception Handlers

In the same way that set_error_handler( ) sets a handler for uncaught errors, set_exception_handler( ) sets a handler for uncaught exceptions. As exceptions are more powerful than errors, your exception-handling function need only take one parameter: an exception object. From that, you can glean the usual information such as message, line number, etc.

Apart from the parameters passed, these work the same as set_error_handler( ). Here's an example:

```
function handle_exception($exception) {
        echo "Caught exception: {$exception->getMessage( )}\n";
}

set_exception_handler("handle_exception");

throw(new Exception('The engines cannot take much more!'));
```

Having a custom exception handler is a smart move wherever you're using exceptions, because it essentially captures all exceptions that would otherwise have been uncaught, and gives you one last chance to take some action before the script potentially terminates.

Using @ to Disable Errors

If you find an error message particularly annoying and you are sure it definitely does not apply to you, PHP has a method for you to silence the message entirely. If you place an *at* symbol, @, before a function that generates an error, PHP will catch the error and silence it entirely. Consider the following two complete scripts:

```
$passwd = fopen("/etc/shadow", "r");
if (!$passwd) {
        echo "Failed to open /etc/shadow.\n";
}

$passwd = @fopen("/etc/passwd", "r");
```

In script one, fopen( ) is used to open the */etc/shadow* Unix password file, which is inaccessible to everyone but the superuser. If our user isn't running as root, this will fail, but fopen( ) will also output an error message. We already have code to handle the possibility that the file open failed, so we don't want that error message to be printed. So, the second script shows us using the @ symbol to ignore errors in that function call—if the open fails, nothing will happen. Even if the function doesn't exist for some reason, nothing will happen—it is all suppressed by @.

While there are legitimate uses for suppressing errors in this way, it is not advised, because it usually works in the same way that sweeping dust under a carpet does not make a house any cleaner. If you explicitly wish to have errors suppressed with @, it is strongly advised that you always write your own code to check return values of functions.

phpinfo( )

The phpinfo( ) function serves two very helpful purposes:

- It replaces the standard "Hello, world!" scripts that verify a PHP installation is working correctly.
- It outputs a massive amount of very helpful information about a PHP installation, including what is installed and how it is configured.

Not surprisingly, it is the second instance we're most interested in, because phpinfo( ) outputs information on all extensions enabled in your PHP installation, as well as how they are configured. As such, if you ever want to know a setting, you can read it from *php.ini*—all the way down to the current level of error reporting, the time that PHP was compiled, and whether or not you have a PHP accelerator installed.

Output Style

Owing to the fact that PHP generates its output dynamically, it is easy to generate messy output that is hard to read. While this is not a problem in itself, it does not look good on you and your web site, and also makes the outputted HTML source code hard to read if you have debugging to do. Help is at hand: the Tidy extension, amongst other things, can clean up and repair poorly written HTML.

Here's an example HTML document:

```
<TITLE>This is bad HTML</title>

<BODY>
This would get rejected as XHTML for a number of reasons.
First, the <FOO> tag doesn't exist.<BR>Second, the tags aren't the same
case.
Third, tags that don't end, like <HR>, aren't allowed.<BR>
Tidy should fix all this for us!
```

As you can see, it's quite messy. Let's put it through Tidy with no particular options set:

```php
<?php $tidy = new tidy("lame.html");
    $tidy->cleanRepair();
    echo $tidy;
?>
```

That will output the following:

```
<!DOCTYPE html PUBLIC "-//W3C//DTD HTML 3.2//EN">
<html>
<head>
<title>This is bad HTML</title>
</head>
<body>
This would get rejected as XHTML for a number of reasons. First,
the tag doesn't exist.<br>
Second, the tags aren't the same case. Third, tags that don't end,
like
<hr>
, aren't allowed.<br>
Tidy should fix all this for us!
</body>
</html>
```

Tidy has added all the right header and footer tags to make the overall content compliant, and normalized the case of the elements. Second, it has taken away the FOO tag because it is invalid. Third, it has wrapped the lines so they aren't too long. Finally, it added a new line after each tag.

If you would rather do without line wrapping, you can turn it off. Tidy accepts a variety of options, and we'll go over some of the popular ones in a moment. First things first, though: blast line wrapping and make the output actually look tidy!

```php
$tidyoptions = array("indent" => true,
                              "wrap" => 1000);
$tidy = new tidy("lame.html", $tidyoptions);
$tidy->cleanRepair();
echo $tidy;
```

This time, we use an array to store the options, enabling indent mode and setting the character-wrap limit to 1000 characters. The output now looks like this:

```
<!DOCTYPE html PUBLIC "-//W3C//DTD HTML 3.2//EN">
<html>
  <head>
    <title>
      This is bad HTML
    </title>
  </head>
  <body>
    This would get rejected as XHTML for a number of reasons.
        First, the tag doesn't exist.<br>
    Second, the tags aren't the same case. Third, tags that don't end, like
    <hr>
    , aren't allowed.<br>
```

```
        Tidy should fix all this for us!
    </body>
</html>
```

Much better, but not yet perfect: it's valid HTML 3.2 now, but XHTML is the
future, so it is recommended that you try to write conforming code—or let Tidy
do it for you, like this:

```
$tidyoptions = array("indent" => true,
                     "wrap" => 1000,
                     "output-xhtml" => true);
$tidy = new tidy("lame.html", $tidyoptions);
$tidy->cleanRepair();
echo $tidy;
```

That extra option makes the world of difference to the output:

```
<!DOCTYPE html PUBLIC "-//W3C//DTD XHTML 1.0 Transitional//EN"
    "http://www.w3.org/TR/xhtml1/DTD/xhtml1-transitional.dtd">
<html xmlns="http://www.w3.org/1999/xhtml">
  <head>
    <title>
      This is bad HTML
    </title>
  </head>
  <body>
    This would get rejected as XHTML for a number of reasons.
        First, the tag doesn't exist.<br />
    Second, the tags aren't the same case. Third, tags that don't end, like
    <hr />
    , aren't allowed.<br />
    Tidy should fix all this for us!
  </body>
</html>
```

Debugging

Now we get the works: a full XHTML doctype, all our tags are indented, and all
our tags are closed. This is what we should be aiming for as standard.

To let you customize various aspects of how your tidied output should look, there
is a wide variety of options that can be passed in. As you saw in the previous
script, the way to do this is to create an array where the keys are the option names
and the values are the settings for those options, then pass that in as the second
parameter when creating a Tidy object.

The official list of Tidy options is available online in the Tidy manual (see *http://
tidy.sourceforge.net/docs/quickref.html*), but here are a few to get you started:

`logical-emphasis`
> Set to true to have Tidy change <i> tags to <em>, and <b> to <strong>.

`replace-color`
> Set to true to have Tidy change numeric HTML color values to their named
> equivalents, wherever possible. That is, #FFFFFF becomes "white".

show-body-only

> Set to `true` to have Tidy only output the contents of the `<body>` tag—no headers, no titles, not even the body tag itself. This is used to grab the content (and only the content!) of a web page.

word-2000

> My favorite. Set to `true` to have Tidy turn Word 2000's mangled attempt at HTML into proper HTML.

vertical-space

> Set to `true` to have Tidy insert blank lines in the output to make it more readable.

fix-backslash

> Set to `true` if someone in your company likes writing URLs with a \ rather than a /—this corrects it.

Installing Tidy

If you're using Windows, you can enable Tidy support by enabling the extension in your *php.ini* file. Look for the line `";extension=php_tidy.dll"` and take the semicolon off from the beginning.

If you're using Unix, you either have to install Tidy support through your package manager, or you need to compile it from source. Compiling Tidy support into your PHP takes two steps: installing the Tidy development libraries on your machine (do this through your package manager), then recompiling PHP with the `--with-tidy` switch in your configure line. As long as you have the *development* version of Tidy installed, this should work fine.

23

Performance

Many people see performance and security as mutually exclusive, particularly in the cost-restricting IT environment in which we currently live. Faced with that choice, it's not surprising that many choose to write very secure—but very slow—PHP scripts. "Fast, cheap, good—pick two" is a compromise we all have to live with to some degree, but you may be surprised to learn that you can speed up your code and add security if you take the time to plan.

Write Your Code Sensibly

"The fastest code is the code that is never executed."

If you are working on something you originally thought would be easy but has ended up being many more lines of code than you originally intended, it is quite possible that your code is getting a little bloated, and more than a little slow. Hoare's law tells us, "Inside every large program is a small program struggling to get out," so you should consider chopping out blocks of code that are outdated, outmoded, replaced, or irrelevant.

In his book *The Art of Unix Programming* (Addison-Wesley), Eric Raymond says, "The most powerful optimization tool in existence may be the delete key." He also quotes Ken Thompson (one of the most highly respected Unix hackers in the world) as saying, "One of my most productive days was throwing away 1000 lines of code." Very true.

Optimization is down to personal intuition, and is hard to do at first. However, try this out to give you an idea of script performance:

```
print "Start: ", microtime(true);
// ...[snip]...
print "End: ", microtime(true);
```

This allows you to time the execution of your script, or at least certain parts of your script. If you see something running particularly slowly, it may be because your implementation is bad, or because your actual algorithm is faulty.

There are many optimizations that can be implemented to make your code run faster/smoother; however, most of them also make the code harder to read and/or edit.

Use the Zend Optimizer

The Zend Optimizer is a free product that helps your PHP code go faster by changing your compiled code around (but leaving the "meaning" of the code the same) to increase execution speed.

Even though it runs every time your page is executed, it has little to no noticeable overhead and can drastically improve performance. Note that there are some cases where using the Optimizer will actually slow things down—usually when scripts are short or exit early. Even these situations become irrelevant if you install a PHP code cache (see next section).

Use a PHP Code Cache

There is one simple way you can double the speed of your server, and that is to install a PHP code cache. There are a few to choose from, but several of them don't keep up-to-date with new releases. IonCube's PHP Accelerator (*http://www.ioncube.co.uk*) used to be good, but hasn't seen an update for a while at the time of writing.

The finest code cache available is now unequivocally Zend Platform, which combines an advanced code acceleration system with numerous management features. The downside is that it's expensive, but if you're a small business, you can sign up for their Small Business program, which gives you a cutdown version of their code cache for a much lower price.

If you're watching your pennies, the Alternative PHP Cache (*http://pecl.php.net/package/APC*) will get you almost as much performance as Zend Performance Suite, at no cost.

Compress Your Output

HTML is a very wordy format, which means there's a lot of duplication in the form of HTML tags, and in the main body text. Furthermore, by default, PHP will send text to Apache as soon as it is ready, which results in less efficient transfer of data.

The solution is to enable output buffering, and to use gzip compression for the buffers. Not all clients support receiving compressed content (every browser made in the last five years will), and to handle that, PHP will only compress data if the client can support it—this means you can enable compression and not have to worry about old clients, because PHP will not send them compressed data.

The best way to use output buffering is to use the commands shown in Chapter 11. However, if you don't want to change your scripts, open up your *php.ini* file and set output_buffering to 1 and output_handler to ob_gzhandler (without the quotes). You'll find those values already set in your *php.ini* already, so just change the existing values. You should check your phpinfo( ) output to make sure output buffering is enabled correctly.

Don't Use CGI

You have two options when installing PHP: use it as a CGI executable, or use it as an Apache/ISAPI module. Although there are advantages to both options, running PHP as a module is overwhelmingly favorable when it comes to performance, as all of PHP and its extension modules reside in memory as opposed to being loaded with every request.

From a purely performance-motivated point of view, you would be crazy to run PHP as a CGI executable.

Debug Your Code

One problem with PHP is that it's very easy to miss some error messages because it outputs them along with the rest of your content, if they are minor. To avoid this, check the output your pages produce in order to make sure PHP is not emitting errors behind your back. Alternatively, make sure error logging is turned on in your *php.ini* file, then check the error log regularly.

Use Persistent Connections

If you connect to a database with each script, consider using a persistent connection rather than a normal connection. For MySQL users, that is the difference between using mysql_pconnect( ) rather than mysql_connect( ). Persistent connections remain connected even after your script has ended, which means that the next time a script asks for a connection, it uses the one that is already open—this saves a lot of time negotiating passwords and such that can otherwise be used to execute important code.

Switching to persistent connections does not require any other change than adding a "p" in the function name—the parameters are still the same. If your database server is not on the same machine as your web server, consider using CLIENT_COMPRESS as the fifth parameter to your mysql_connect( )/mysql_pconnect( ) call, as it allows MySQL to compress data to save space, and can drastically lower network bandwidth and transfer speed, particularly when reading in lots of data.

Compile Right

One of the biggest advantages to using a Unix box is that you get to compile your software yourself, and it does make a difference to the speed of your software. If you are able to, I suggest you compile Apache, PHP, and MySQL yourself, using GCC 4.x and as many optimizations turned on as you have time to wait for.

Particularly important here is the PHP compilation, as you are not likely to get much improvement in your MySQL compilation over the stock binaries you can grab directly from MySQL.

Index

We'd like to hear your suggestions for improving our indexes. Send email to *index@oreilly.com*.

opendir( ) function, 210
operators
  arithmetic, 79–80
  array operator, 63
  assignment, 80
  associativity, 87
  bitwise, 81
  comparison, 82
  decrementing, 83
  examples, 85
  execution, 86
  incrementing, 83
  logical, 84
  precedence, 87
  scope resolution operator, OOP, 131
  string, 81
  ternary, 86
ord( ) function, 107
output, 3
  compressed, performance and, 336
  compression, 187
  debugging and, 331
  flushing, 185–187
  XML, 289
output buffering, 3
  buffer creation, 182
  buffer reuse, 182
  buffer stacking, 182
  functions, 185
  introduction, 181
  nest count, 185
  reading buffers, 184
  stackability, 181
  stacking buffers, flushing, 183
  web server speed and, 181
outputting text, 251–254
overriding methods, OOP classes, 131
overriding scope, GLOBALS array, 45
ownership, files, 209

P

parameters
  counts, variable, 43
  functions, 41
    default parameters, 42
parent constructors, OOP, 143
parse_ini_file( ) function, 213
parse_str( ) function, 107
parsing configuration files, 213

passing
  by reference, 41
  by value, 89
passthru( ) function, 108
path separators, code distribution
      and, 314
pathinfo( ) function, 204
PCRE (Perl-Compatible Regular
      Expressions), 234
pdf_begin_page( ) function, 272, 273
pdf_end_page( ) function, 273
pdf_findfont( ) function, 272
pdf_open_file( ) function, 272
pdf_open_image_file( ) function, 274
pdf_place_image( ) function, 274
pdf_rotate( ) function, 275
PDFs
  adding pages, 273
  creating, 271–273
  document data, adding, 275
  images
    rotating, 275
    skewing, 275
  images, adding, 274
  styles, 273
pdf_setfont( ) function, 272
pdf_show_xy( ) function, 272
pdf_skew( ) function, 275
PDO (PHP Data Objects), 223
PEAR (PHP Extension and Application
      Repository), 21
PEAR::DB
  introduction, 223
  prepared statements, 227
  queries, 225
  quick calls, 225
PEAR::Mail, 303
PEAR::Mail_Mime, 303
  email attachments, 305
PECL code, 21
performance
  CGI and, 337
  code caches and, 336
  compiling and, 337
  compressed output, 336
  debugging and, 337
  introduction, 4
  persistence connections and, 337
  writing code and, 335
  Zend Optimizer and, 336

W

X

Z

About the Author

Paul Hudson, an avid PHP programmer, is Deputy Editor of the popular European Linux journal *Linux Format* and author of the publication's PHP tutorial section. He is the author of *Red Hat Fedora 4 Unleashed* (Sams) and the online book *Practical PHP Programming*, available at *www.hudzilla.org*.

Colophon

Our look is the result of reader comments, our own experimentation, and feedback from distribution channels. Distinctive covers complement our distinctive approach to technical topics, breathing personality and life into potentially dry subjects.

The animal on the cover of *PHP in a Nutshell* is a cuckoo (*Cuculus canorus*). Cuckoos epitomize minimal effort. The common cuckoo doesn't build a nest—instead, the female cuckoo finds another bird's nest that already contains eggs and lays an egg in it (a process she may repeat up to 25 times, leaving 1 egg per nest). The nest mother, who is usually of a different bird species, rarely notices the addition, and usually incubates the egg and then feeds the hatchling as if it were her own. Why don't nest mothers notice that the cuckoo's eggs are different from their own eggs? Recent research suggests that it's because the eggs look the same in the ultraviolet spectrum, which birds can see.

When they hatch, the baby cuckoos push all the other (non-cuckoo) eggs out of the nest. If the other eggs hatched first, the babies are pushed out too. The host parents often continue to feed the cuckoo even after it grows to be much larger than they are, and cuckoo chicks sometimes use their call to lure other birds to feed them as well. Interestingly, only Old World (European) cuckoos colonize other nests. The New World (American) cuckoos build their own (untidy) nests. Like many Americans, these cuckoos migrate to the tropics for winter.

Cuckoos have a long and glorious history in literature and the arts. The Bible mentions them, as do Pliny and Aristotle. Beethoven used the cuckoo's distinctive call in his Pastoral Symphony. And here's a bit of etymology: the word "cuckold" (a husband whose wife is cheating on him) comes from "cuckoo." Presumably, the practice of laying one's eggs in another's nest seemed an appropriate metaphor.

Adam Witwer was the production editor and Chris Downey was the copyeditor for *PHP in a Nutshell*. Carol Marti proofread the text. Sanders Kleinfeld and Claire Cloutier provided quality control. Johnna VanHoose Dinse wrote the index.

Karen Montgomery designed the cover of this book, based on a series design by Edie Freedman, and produced the cover layout with Adobe InDesign CS using Adobe's ITC Garamond font. The cover image is a 19th-century engraving from the Dover Pictorial Archive.

David Futato designed the interior layout. This book was converted by Judy Hoer to FrameMaker 5.5.6 with a format conversion tool created by Erik Ray, Jason McIntosh, Neil Walls, and Mike Sierra that uses Perl and XML technologies. The text font is Linotype Birka; the heading font is Adobe Myriad Condensed; and the code font is LucasFont's TheSans Mono Condensed. The illustrations that appear in the book were produced by Robert Romano, Jessamyn Read, and Lesley Borash using Macromedia Free-Hand MX and Adobe Photoshop CS. The tip and warning icons were drawn by Christopher Bing. This colophon was written by Nathan Torkington and Rachel Wheeler.

Better than e-books

Buy *PHP in a Nutshell* and access the
digital edition FREE on Safari for 45 days.

Go to www.oreilly.com/go/safarienabled
and type in coupon code UPQX-HRGP-CBY9-N6PP-438Y

Search
thousands of
top tech books

Download
whole chapters

Cut and Paste
code examples

Find
answers fast

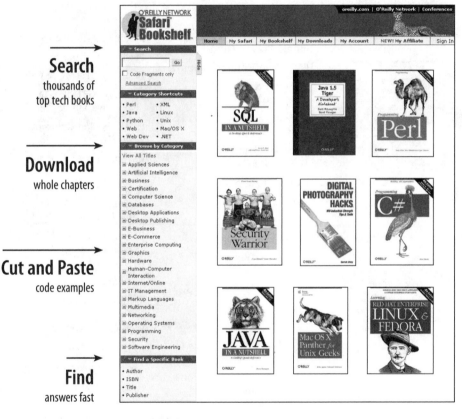

Search Safari! The premier electronic reference
library for programmers and IT professionals.

Related Titles from O'Reilly

Web Programming

ActionScript Cookbook

ActionScript for Flash MX: The Definitive Guide, *2nd Edition*

Dynamic HTML: The Definitive Reference, *2nd Edition*

Flash Hacks

Essential PHP Security

Google Hacks, *2nd Edition*

Google Pocket Guide

HTTP: The Definitive Guide

JavaScript & DHTML Cookbook

JavaScript Pocket Reference, *2nd Edition*

JavaScript: The Definitive Guide, *4th Edition*

Learning PHP 5

PayPal Hacks

PHP Cookbook

PHP in a Nutshell

PHP Pocket Reference, *2nd Edition*

PHPUnit Pocket Guide

Programming ColdFusion MX, *2nd Edition*

Programming PHP

Upgrading to PHP 5

Web Database Applications with PHP and MySQL, *2nd Edition*

Webmaster in a Nutshell, *3rd Edition*

Web Authoring and Design

Cascading Style Sheets: The Definitive Guide, *2nd Edition*

CSS Cookbook

CSS Pocket Reference, *2nd Edition*

Dreamweaver MX 2004: The Missing Manual, *2nd Edition*

Essential ActionScript 2.0

Flash Out of the Box

Head First HTML & CSS

HTML & XHTML: The Definitive Guide, *5th Edition*

HTML Pocket Reference, *2nd Edition*

Information Architecture for the World Wide Web, *2nd Edition*

Learning Web Design, *2nd Edition*

Programming Flash Communication Server

Web Design in a Nutshell, *3rd Edition*

Web Site Measurement Hacks

Web Administration

Apache Cookbook

Apache Pocket Reference

Apache: The Definitive Guide, *3rd Edition*

Perl for Web Site Management

Squid: The Definitive Guide

Web Performance Tuning, *2nd Edition*

Keep in touch with O'Reilly

Download examples from our books

To find example files from a book, go to: *www.oreilly.com/catalog* select the book, and follow the "Examples" link.

Register your O'Reilly books

Register your book at *register.oreilly.com* Why register your books? Once you've registered your O'Reilly books you can:

- Win O'Reilly books, T-shirts or discount coupons in our monthly drawing.
- Get special offers available only to registered O'Reilly customers.
- Get catalogs announcing new books (US and UK only).
- Get email notification of new editions of the O'Reilly books you own.

Join our email lists

Sign up to get topic-specific email announcements of new books and conferences, special offers, and O'Reilly Network technology newsletters at:

elists.oreilly.com

It's easy to customize your free elists subscription so you'll get exactly the O'Reilly news you want.

Get the latest news, tips, and tools

www.oreilly.com

- "Top 100 Sites on the Web"—PC Magazine
- CIO Magazine's Web Business 50 Awards

Our web site contains a library of comprehensive product information (including book excerpts and tables of contents), downloadable software, background articles, interviews with technology leaders, links to relevant sites, book cover art, and more.

Work for O'Reilly

Check out our web site for current employment opportunities:

jobs.oreilly.com

Contact us

O'Reilly Media, Inc.
1005 Gravenstein Hwy North
Sebastopol, CA 95472 USA
Tel: 707-827-7000 or 800-998-9938
    (6am to 5pm PST)
Fax: 707-829-0104

Contact us by email

For answers to problems regarding your order or our products:
order@oreilly.com

To request a copy of our latest catalog:
catalog@oreilly.com

For book content technical questions or corrections: **booktech@oreilly.com**

For educational, library, government, and corporate sales: **corporate@oreilly.com**

To submit new book proposals to our editors and product managers:
proposals@oreilly.com

For information about our international distributors or translation queries:
international@oreilly.com

For information about academic use of O'Reilly books:
adoption@oreilly.com
or visit:
academic.oreilly.com

For a list of our distributors outside of North America check out:
international.oreilly.com/distributors.html

Order a book online

www.oreilly.com/order_new

Our books are available at most retail and online bookstores.
To order direct: 1-800-998-9938 • *order@oreilly.com* • *www.oreilly.com*
Online editions of most O'Reilly titles are available by subscription at *safari.oreilly.com*